THE NATIVE AMERICAN WORLD

DONNA HIGHTOWER LANGSTON

A Wiley Desk Reference

John Wiley & Sons, Inc.

Published by John Wiley & Sons, Inc., Hoboken, New Jersey

For general information about our other products and services, please contact our Customer Care Department within the United States at (800) 762-2974, outside the United States at (317) 572-4002.

Wiley also publishes its books in a variety of electronic formats. Some content that appears in print may not be available in electronic books. For more information about Wiley products, visit our web site at www.wiley.com.

Produced by New England Publishing Associates, Inc.
President: Elizabeth Frost-Knappman
Vice President: Edward W. Knappman
Staff: Ron Formica, Kristine Schiavi, Victoria Harlow

Design and Production: Ron Formica
Photo Researcher: Victoria Harlow
Copy Editor: Phil Saltz
Proofreading: Elizabeth D. Crawford of Miccinello Associates

Library of Congress Cataloging-in-Publication Data
Hightower-Langston, Donna, date.
  The Native American world / by Donna Hightower-Langston.
    p.   cm.
  Includes bibliographical references.
  ISBN: 0-471-40322-9 (cloth)
    1. Indians of North America—History—Handbooks, manuals, etc. 2. Indians of North
  America—Social life and customs—Handbooks, manuals, etc. I. Title.
E77 .H54 2002
973.04'97—dc21   2002033115

Printed in the United States of America

10 9 8 7 6 5 4 3 2 1

Contents

PART III Nations **103**

PART IV   Politics and Post-Contact History   313

Bibliography 435

Acknowledgments

I was fortunate to have the chance to work with Chip Rossetti, my editor at John Wiley & Sons. He was supportive and had many useful ideas that greatly improved this volume. It was a pleasure to have the chance to work under his guidance. My friend Marge Freking proofed the entire manuscript for me. She performed this tedious and detailed task with good spirits and formed the base of my support throughout. My literary agent, Elizabeth Frost-Knappman, assisted in the initial drafts of the book proposal and was there for me at every turn of events. Victoria Harlow located all the visual images in the text. The final project was made stronger by her diligent contributions. A few students assisted with research questions: Maureen McDowell, Lydia Graecyn, Laura Fulton, Ellen Monroe, and Adrienne Baker.

Finally, I dedicate the book to my grandparents, Cornell Watts Freeman Langston and Christine Redman Hightower Downing Langston. Their families survived removal; they survived the period of self-hatred inflicted by John Wayne movies by repressing a great deal. But the role model of their survival, our tribal enrollment as a family, and parts of their story that were not repressed inspired our love, devotion to family, and pride in history and community.

Adadoligi, Donna Langston

Introduction

American Indian studies are in a state of constant change. The current status of American Indians is under debate, but their past is even murkier. Many of the records on which we base our knowledge of American Indians are documents that white observers produced. It is a truism that conquerors write history, and non-Indians have written more than 90 percent of all works about Indians. Limited access to education and high dropout rates continue to affect the number of works on Indian history that are produced by American Indians themselves. There are pressing questions that we need to ask ourselves in approaching American Indian history and cultures. Should European scholars, sources, norms, and ideas be used to explain Indian worlds? What code of ethics and responsibilities must be used to avoid exploiting American Indians? The exploitation, beginning with enslavement under Christopher Columbus, has never stopped. Is Indian history confined to the history within a tribe, in relation to other tribal histories, or in relation to European history? We rarely know Indians alone; we know them in their encounters with whites.

Even the labels given to the members of Indian nations—"American Indians," "Native Americans," "First Nations"—need to be questioned. I even debated about the title of this volume: you will notice throughout that I use the term "American Indian," since it is more commonly used in Indian communities in the United States. The publisher, however, insisted on using "Native American" in the title, since consumers in the United States are more familiar with that phrase.

Indians were living in the Americas tens of thousands of years before Columbus. Indians near the Mississippi River lived in agricultural societies and built huge earthen mounds. They also built great Mississippian cities like Cahokia, near the modern city of St. Louis. By the 12th century, Cahokia numbered about 20,000 people and contained more than 120 mounds. Indians also built the great mound center Etowah in northwestern Georgia, which existed from the 10th to the 13th centuries. In the 14th century, the Iroquois and Huron formed confederacies. In the Southwest, ancestors of today's Pueblo Indians built impressive stone and adobe towns that still exist, and they practiced advanced horticulture. The pre-contact Indian population north of Mexico has been estimated at anywhere from 7 to 18 million. During the 12th century, at Anasazi settlements at Chaco Canyon in New Mexico the total population approximated 15,000. Throughout the continent, important Indian events were documented with petroglyphs, drawings, and oral histories. At one time, hundreds of different tribes and languages existed. After contact with whites, some disappeared entirely.

Columbus discovered the Americas quite by accident while looking for a shortcut to the riches of Asia. He believed he had found the East Indies off the coast of Asia, hence the name *Indios* for the inhabitants. Within decades of European contact, the indigenous people of the Americas experienced as much as a 90 percent reduction in population through smallpox, measles, bubonic plague, and other Old World diseases to which they had no immunity. Columbus believed that the Carib people he encountered on San Salvador Island would make good servants. He also hoped to convert Indians to Christianity, but conversion was not always voluntary. The *Requerimiento* (requirement) mandated that Indians surrender their religion and submit to Spanish authority. Indians faced death if they refused.

In the 16th century, the Spanish attempted to colonize the Southeast and established the first permanent European American settlement on the North American mainland at St. Augustine on the Florida peninsula. Severe epidemics eliminated whole village populations following European contact. Spanish rule in the Southwest included forced labor, suppression of indigenous religions, and the sale of Indians into slavery. The Pueblo Revolt of 1680 drove the Spanish from the region for a decade, but the Spanish were able to reimpose their rule by the 1690s.

Both Spain and France sent Catholic missionaries among the Indians, hoping to speed their conversion to Christianity and eventual integration. The Spanish focused their contact efforts in the South, beginning in the 16th century; in the 18th century, France extended its influence to the region of Louisiana. The Indians' religious world, however, was not monotheist, as the Europeans' was. Many Indian nations found spiritual power in all living creatures and in inanimate objects; their religion was often connected to sacred places and to land. California began as one of the most populous Indian areas in North America. Today, California has one of the smallest indigenous populations, the result of missions and missionary work by the Spanish and the vigilante hunting of Indians by whites that followed the gold rush of 1848.

In the mid-Atlantic region, the English and French were the primary colonialists. Fur trade was important in early interactions, since the settlers relied on Indian hunters and guides. A fair number of interracial marriage between European men and some Indian women occurred at this time.

In the 1760s, the English government tried to limit the expansion of whites into Indian territory in order to avoid the expense that war and conflict caused. With a proclamation in 1763, it established a boundary between white settlements and Indian country. All lands west of the Appalachian Mountains were to be Indian lands forever. The American Revolution had significant impact on various Indian nations. Indian nations sided with either the British or Americans, or attempted to remain neutral. Regardless of which position they chose, all groups were harshly punished after the revolution.

In the new republic, Indian nations pressed their rights through the legal system. The Cherokee in Georgia made every effort to assimilate white values, but when gold was discovered on their lands, white Georgians demanded the Indians' removal. The Supreme Court decision in *Cherokee Nation v. Georgia*, in 1831, sided with the Cherokee, but President Andrew Jackson ignored the ruling and ordered their removal anyway. The Cherokee and other tribes living in the East were force marched to the state of Oklahoma, into what was supposed to be Indian land forever. Many

Native Americans died on the journey that was later to be known as the "Trail of Tears."

During the American Civil War, many nations were once again divided in their loyalties, as during the American Revolution. Many tribes believed the Union was more likely to protect their freedom. Other Indian tribes assumed their freedom would be more secure under the Confederacy. The Confederacy even promised to grant some Indian nations the status of statehood. Indians enlisted in both Union and Confederate armies. After the Civil War, once again, regardless of where their loyalties had remained, Indian nations were punished and their lands confiscated.

After the Civil War, national attention focused on westward expansion. The Homestead Act was passed in 1862. The first transcontinental railroad was completed in 1869. Leaders in the Plains and Southwest led campaigns of resistance to trespassing settlers on their lands.

By the 1880s, most tribes were confined to reservations. Liberals sought to assimilate Indians into the white man's world by stressing Christianity, English language, private property, and education that would teach a useful trade. The General Allotment Act of 1887, popularly called the Dawes Act, broke up communally held reservation lands and allotted surplus lands to whites. The Five Tribes (Cherokee, Chickasaw, Choctaw, Creek, and Seminole) struggled against allotment until 1907, when dispersion of their lands cleared the way for the emergence of the new state of Oklahoma.

The Allotment Act caused Indian nations to lose two of every three acres they held before its passage in 1887. The early 20th century found nations embroiled in struggles for water rights. Indians won an important legal victory in 1908 when the United States Supreme Court decided that the Gros Ventre and Assiniboine of the Fort Belknap Reservation in northern Montana were entitled to water. That decision became known as the Winters Doctrine. Indians also participated in the First World War, even though many native people had not yet been accorded full citizenship by the government of the United States.

The 1920s saw the emergence of Indian reformers who understood the ways that federal policy had failed. The majority of Indian land holdings had been lost; disease continued to plague reservations; and distant boarding schools removed young children from their families. Also, Indian religious practices continued to be suppressed. The 1933 Indian New

Deal during Franklin Roosevelt's administration and Commissioner of Indian Affairs John Collier turned away from many earlier assimilationist policies. Collier called for Indian religious freedom, bilingual and bicultural education, and the retention of Indian land. Collier's support for cultural revitalization may have led to an early foundation for other modern American social movements toward self-determination.

During World War II, Navajo code talkers played a crucial role in military campaigns by communicating in a code that was never broken. During that time there was a renewed push for assimilation. In 1946, the Indian Claims Commission Act was passed to handle settlements of tribal claims over land and resource loss. Postwar relocation policy pushed reservation residents to move into urban areas, offering them a one-way bus ticket and one month's rent. The termination policy, as enacted by Congress in 1953, was intended to end the federal status of all tribes. Dozens of tribes were terminated, including the Menominee in Wisconsin and the Klamath in Oregon. New groups like the Congress of American Indians lobbied against these termination policies.

During the 1960s and 1970s, the American Indian population became largely urban. With this shift came increased visibility. Many younger generation Indians joined protest movements such as the occupation of Alcatraz Island in 1969 and the 1973 occupation of Wounded Knee. Indian nations continued to struggle for custody of sacred sites and the enforcement of the treaty rights they had been guaranteed, including fishing rights. The Navajo Community College—the first tribally controlled college in America—was founded in 1968. Around two dozen similar colleges were established by other tribes in subsequent decades. Beginning in the 1970s, several tribes, such as the Menominee, were successful in overturning their terminated status; many continue to struggle for this recognition today.

Struggles in Indian communities continue over education and high dropout rates, health care and lower life expectancies rates, unemployment, shelter, Indian mascot names, resources, gaming, and burial sites. A cultural revitalization in language and spiritual gatherings has taken place.

This book has been organized into four sections: Culture, Individuals, Nations, and Politics and Post-Contact History. This volume is not all-inclusive, since many volumes would be needed to cover all the nations and all the individuals worthy of consideration. Instead, this is meant to be an introductory volume for the general reader of American Indian studies. For the reader's convenience, cross-referenced entries will appear in bold italics the first time they appear in the text of an entry. If the bolded italicized cross-reference refers to an entry from a different section of the book, its location will be identified with the section number in brackets; otherwise, the cross-reference will simply appear in bold italics.

PART I

Culture

It is undeniable that many Indian nations continue vibrant cultural traditions that are centuries old. The survival of these cultures over the past 500 years is a testimony to the persistence, dedication, and true belief held by generations of American Indians, as well as the endurance and power of their teachings.

But the history of indigenous peoples following the arrival of Columbus is just the tip of the iceberg. No one knows exactly how indigenous peoples came to reside in the Americas. Anthropologists have theorized that they originally crossed the Bering Strait on a land bridge from northern Siberia. The creation stories of many nations teach that they originated on their holy lands, with some emerging from the earth or caves. More recent scientific evidence suggests that there were probably several waves of migration from many areas of Asia, Polynesia, and possibly southern Europe, with the wave that might have come over on a land bridge from Siberia being the latest group. Scientists estimate that humans have populated the Americas since at least 30000 B.C.

The Paleo-Indian period, a broad label applied to the earliest nomadic inhabitants in North America, can be considered to cover the time of their arrival in North America up to 5000 B.C. Around 12,000 to 15,000 years ago, Paleo-Indians began hunting animals, giving rise to various spear-point cultures, such as the Clovis, Sandia, Folsom and Plano cultures. (Plano, which was prominent in the Great Plains area, was the most recent, lasting from 8000 to 4500 B.C.)

Around 5000 B.C., the Paleo-Indian period began to give way to the Archaic period. Archaic cultures relied on plant foods and agriculture for a greater share of their diet, and people began to live in permanent villages. Archaic cultures were divided by region, such as the Old Cordilleran culture (Columbia River valley, 9000–5000 B.C.), Desert-Cochise cultures (the Southwest, 9000–500 B.C.), Old Copper culture (Great Lakes area, 4000–1500 B.C.) and the Red Paint People (New England, 3000–500 B.C.).

The Formative period (1000 B.C.–A.D. 1500) followed the Archaic and takes American Indian history up to their contact with European explorers. By 2000 B.C., Woodland cultures had developed pottery, basketry, elaborate tools, art, and burial rituals. The Adena and Hopewell cultures in the Ohio valley constructed temple mounds and observatories. The Hohokam culture (circa A.D. 400–1500) built extensive irrigation systems in the Southwest. To the northeast of the Hohokam, the Anasazi built elaborate pueblos that still exist. By A.D. 800, the Mississippian culture had developed in the mid-South. Elaborate political systems were evident before the arrival of Europeans, such as that of the Iroquois League, a confederacy of five initial nations formed around the 1300s that became a role model of democracy for the later founding of the U.S. government. The cultural contributions of indigenous peoples to the Americas have been extensive, pervasive, and often underacknowledged in dominant culture.

Beyond the physical artifacts uncovered by archaeologists, indigenous cultures in the Americas trace their link to the past through the spiritual practices that endure. Until the 1978 American Indian Religious Freedom Act guaranteed the right of Indians to practice their traditional forms of spirituality and worship, Indian religions were outlawed, suppressed, and, at best, openly discouraged by non-Indians. Some continued to practice their spirituality in private as best they could but there were harsh punishments from colonizers, including, for example, the Spanish practice of slowly roasting or strangling those who were caught. Despite colonial prosecution, medicine people continued to foretell the future, cure, or practice herbology. Some received their gift through inheritance or training, others through quests or dreams.

Vision quests, in particular, were an important part of many Indian cultures. Vision quests typically involved a period of seclusion and fasting, during which an Indian could obtain animal guides, special songs, or power objects. In some cultures, both men and women undertook vision quests; in others it was more commonly practiced by men since women were thought to have inherent power through their ability to give birth, while men had to seek, or go begging, for spiritual power.

Many nations also believed in the spirits of the dead, particularly of ancestors; in many cultures the possessions of the dead were destroyed or discarded so that they might be released into another world. Many nations find that spiritual power resides in land, animals, rocks, plants, and most natural phenomena. Some nations find that certain areas of land or kinds of animals, such as the salmon or buffalo, for example, hold special spiritual significance for them.

A debate in Indian communities continues over who has the right to practice spiritual traditions. Whites have long been fascinated with this aspect of American Indian history. At the same time that the spiritual practices of the "heathens" were outlawed, train loads of tourists were headed to areas of the United States like the Southwest to try and catch a glimpse of, and photograph, these very ceremonies.

Spiritual practices in many Indian communities are precious, private, and vulnerable resources that are to be protected. Despite the American Indian Religious Freedom Act of 1978, there are continued court battles for the right to practice traditional beliefs.

CHRONOLOGY   Culture

30000 B.C. *Evidence of groups in the Americas.*

28000 *California is settled.*

25000 *Clovis stone points indicate settlement in New Mexico.*

25000–10000 *Paleo-Indians settle throughout North and South America.*

10000–3000 *During the Archaic Period, many Native Americans live in permanent villages; there is some mound burial.*

5000 *Homes are built in cliffs in Arizona and New Mexico, surrounded by extensive agricultural development.*

4500 *Some of the first mounds are built along the lower Mississippi.*

2000 *Copper is mined in the Great Lakes region for tools, trade, and decoration.*

2000–1200 *Woodland period; mound burials, horticulture, pottery, and basketry are widely evident.*

1500 *First of the large Mississipian sites at Poverty Point, Louisiana.*

750 *The Adena Hopewell civilization in the Ohio valley builds temple mounds, ceremonial centers, observatories, and farms.*

300 *Hohokam culture appears in the Arizona area.*

100 *Serpent Mound built by the Adena Hopewell Indians in Ohio.*

A.D. 1 *The Hohokam civilization develops an irrigation-farming system in Arizona. The canal system is still being used today, although it is now lined with concrete.*

Culture (continued)

400 *The Anasazi civilization in northern Arizona acquires pueblos, wells, and canals.*

600 *The Caddo Indians, believed to be ancestors of the Mississippian civilization, settle on the Red River near Spiro, Oklahoma.*

825–1000 *The Southern Athapascans separate from northern groups and migrate to the Southwest. The Southern Athapascans are thought to be ancestors of the Apache and Navajo.*

900–1250 *The Mississippian culture peaks. Other large Mississippian sites, located in Arkansas and Oklahoma, include Ocmuigee, Spiro, Etowah, and Moundville.*

1100–1300 *The Mesa Verde settlement in southern Colorado is at its peak. The Cliff Palace, one of its largest dwellings, is composed of 220 rooms and 23 kivas that housed as many as 350 people. By 1300, the site is abandoned.*

1119–1180 *The Chaco Canyon people build more than 500 miles of road, which are 50 feet wide, perfectly straight, and connect more than 70 settlements.*

1300 *The population of the Americas is estimated at 30 million in Mexico, 20 million in South America, and 15 million in North America.*

1390 *Probable founding date of the Iroquois League which united the Seneca, Oneida, Onondaga, Mohawk, and Cayuga tribes.*

Adena (mound building) culture

Thousands of human-made earthen mounds, some in the shape of animals, exist throughout the eastern part of North America. Mound builders were prehistoric Indians. They have been categorized in four different cultural groups in chronological order: *Poverty Point culture* of the Southeast; Adena; *Hopewell culture* in the Northeast and Midwest; and *Mississippian culture* in the Southeast. Most of the mounds were built in the *Formative period* (circa 1000 B.C.–A.D. 1500).

Formative villages were composed of farming communities whose members had highly developed pottery and weaving skills. Some of these villages expanded into cities. Mound builders, as well as the Southwest Indians, were the most highly developed civilizations north of Mexico. Although early European Americans, including Thomas Jefferson, wrote about mound builders, most whites believed that American Indians were too primitive and lacked the necessary engineering knowledge to have undertaken such projects.

Evidence of the Adena (pronounced uh-DEE-nuh) culture, circa 1000 B.C. to A.D. 200, was first found at a large mound near Chillicothe, Ohio. Adena mounds have also been found in Kentucky, West Virginia, Indiana, Pennsylvania, and New York along the Ohio Valley. Most Adena sites are burial mounds; there are an estimated 300 to 500 of them. In the early and middle Adena periods, mounds began with the burial of a single person; later, more burials were added to the mound, which grew in size. The dead were buried with their personal possessions. The late Adena period reflects more elaborate mound burial chambers, as well as log tombs and sacred sites, circular in design. Some of the largest and most elaborate mounds are found in the central Ohio Valley. The Moundville, West Virginia, site is more than 67 feet high.

Unlike the earlier Poverty Point mounds, which were built in the shape of sacred objects such as birds, the Adena built their mounds for burial, usually a burial pit or log-lined tomb. The earth was excavated with sticks, bones, and shells, then transported to the burial site in woven baskets or animal skin bags. Additional layers of dirt covered each new burial. Like ancient Egyptian pharaohs, Adena leaders were buried with objects, which included ceremonial items, copper tools, pottery, woven cloth, masks, stone pipes, stone tablets, mica ornaments, and pearl *beads*.

In addition to the construction of burial mounds, the Adena built mounds with symbolic shapes such as the Serpent Mound near Peebles,

Ohio. The Serpent Mound rises up to 6 feet high, stretches up to 20 feet across, and extends 1,348 feet in length. Some Adena mounds also had geometric shapes, with circular earthen walls surrounding the burial mounds.

The Adena lived in permanent villages of pole-framed houses covered with mud and thatch. Among the crops they grew were sunflowers, pumpkins, and tobacco. Some researchers believe that the Adena may have been ancestors of the Hopewell Indians. Adena sites have been found along every major tributary stream of the Ohio River from southeastern Indiana to central Pennsylvania and so may have been related to peoples in these areas, but no definite connections have been made to date.

Agricultural period

Evidence of cultivated crops dating as far back as 7000 B.C.—beans, peppers, and pumpkins—has been found around the Gulf of Mexico. Some of the earliest domesticated corn crops in southern Mexico date back to 4000 B.C. Evidence of agriculture from 2500 B.C has been found near Bat Cave in New Mexico, where cultivated corn was discovered among the artifacts of the *Desert-Cochise culture.*

American Indian women were the primary agriculturists, except among groups in the Southwest. Corn (maize), beans, and squash were

An engraving of Florida Indians planting, by 16th-century artist Theodore DeBry. *Library of Congress.*

the most important cultivated crops. Other crops were important regionally, such as cotton in the South and wild rice in the Great Lakes region. Indian farmers developed many varieties of corn, beans, and squash to match the climatic conditions in their specific areas. They also cultivated cotton, dye plants, herbs, medicines, and stimulants.

More than 150 Indian plants cultivated in North and Middle America were not found in the rest of the world. These plants included: corn, beans, squash, pumpkins, tomatoes, potatoes, sweet potatoes, peanuts, cashews, pineapples, papayas, avocados, sunflowers, chili peppers, cacao (chocolate), vanilla, tobacco, indigo, and cotton.

The Indians used hoes made of wood, bone, or stone. They also used fire to remove brush. The ashes from burned weeds fertilized the soil. Women used baskets, sticks, pestles, and mortars to gather and process the crops. In the North, baskets were used to store corn in houses; in the South, corn was stored in roofed granaries; and in the Midwest and West, storage pits were used to store corn.

Most nations recognized individual rights as well as group rights for cultivating land. They did not commonly practice the European concept of land sale and absolute ownership. If a woman stopped farming a particular area, someone else could use the plot or the village could use it. Land was inherited matrilineally in many nations in the East and Great Plains, though land ultimately belonged to the village. In the

---

IN THEIR OWN Words

It was you who sent out the first soldier, and it was we who sent out the second. Two years ago, I came up upon this road, following the buffalo, that my wives and children might have their cheeks plump, and their bodies warm. But the soldiers fired on us, and since that time there has been a noise, like that of a thunderstorm, and we have not known which way to go.

But there are things which you have said to me which I do not like. They were not sweet like sugar but bitter like gourds. You said that you wanted to put us upon a reservation, to build us houses and to make us Medicine lodges. I do not want them.

I was born upon the prairie, where the wind blew free, and there was nothing to break the light of the sun. I was born where there were no enclosures, and where everything drew a free breath. I want to die there, and not within walls. I know every stream and every wood between the Rio Grande and the Arkansas. I have hunted and lived over that country. I lived like my fathers before me, and like them, I lived happily.

—CHIEF TEN BEARS, COMANCHE, SPEECH AT MEDICINE LODGE COUNCIL ON OCTOBER 20, 1867.

Southwest individual males could own land. Land was also inherited patrilineally among other nations, including the *Pima [III]*, Papago, and *Yuma [III]*. Most *Pueblo [III]* Indians practiced matrilineal inheritance, and the *Navajo [III]* practiced shared inheritance.

European settlers learned from the Indians how to raise corn and other crops. The United States government used a system of *reservations [IV]* to limit American Indian land claims so white agriculture might expand. Large tracts of land were ceded to whites in numerous treaties. The General Allotment Act in 1887 (see *Dawes Act [IV]*) divided tribal lands into individual plots of land with the "surplus" being sold to whites. The Allotment Act allowed whites to take over individual Indian plots, further reducing tribal land holdings by two-thirds by 1934. American Indians did not have access to the capital or the technology needed to farm on their marginal relocated lands and therefore, American Indians could not compete with white landowners on a commercial scale.

Anasazi

With its limited game resources, the harsh environment of the Southwest led to the development of four agrarian cultures. In chronological order, they are: the *Archaic period, Mogollon culture, Hohokam culture*, and Anasazi. These people lived in areas that included southern Utah, Colorado, Arizona, New Mexico, and a corner of Texas.

Anasazi means "the ancient ones who are not among us" or "enemy ancestors" in the Athapascan language of the *Navajo [III]*. Their culture became distinct by 100 B.C. The first stage in Anasazi development was the basket-making period in which weaving food containers and other goods from straw, vines, and yucca was developed. The Anasazi lived in semi-permanent rounded and domed houses. The architecture was influenced by Mogollon and Hohokam style pit houses. After A.D. 750, the *Pueblo [III]* period developed. ("Pueblo" comes from the Spanish word for town or community.)

The Pueblo period was the high point of Anasazi culture. Modern Pueblo Indians inherited many Anasazi traits. The above-ground pueblos had beamed roofs and were constructed either of stone and adobe mortar or of adobe bricks. They were originally developed as single storage rooms, but later evolved into single-family houses. Eventually, the rooms were grouped together with shared walls and built on top of each other as elaborate apartment buildings with rooms connected by ladders. The roof of one pueblo served as the front yard and terrace of another.

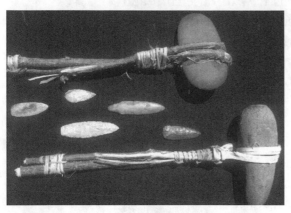

Hafted stone axes and stone bi-faces from Anasazi sites. *BLM/Anasazi Heritage Center, Dolores, Colorado.*

Anasazi usually built pueblos on top of mesas or canyons for protection against invaders. An extensive network of stone roads connected Pueblo communities. Chaco Canyon in New Mexico, for example, was first occupied around A.D. 900. Pueblo Bonito is one of the largest of the Chaco ruins, having 5 stories and 800 rooms, which housed a population of at least 1,000. Thirty-seven kivas, underground ceremonial chambers bordering the central plaza, have been identified, and the largest was 45 feet in diameter.

Around A.D. 1300, the Anasazi abandoned their villages and moved south. Scholars have various theories to explain this removal, including the possibilities of drought, invaders, depletion of food supplies, and disease. After leaving their settlements, they established smaller pueblos. Their descendants include Pueblo Indians, the Keres, Tewa, Tiwa, Towa, *Hopi [III]*, and *Zuni [III]*.

ancient peoples

Archaeological evidence indicates that both North and South America were settled more than 35,000 years ago. Computer projections of the 143 language-family groups in the Americas also estimate the beginning of settlement at 35,000 years ago.

Scholars have long debated how people came to occupy the Americas. Many believe there was a migration from Siberia over a Bering Strait land bridge, or *Beringa*. Some theorize that where the water is now 180 feet deep in the Bering Strait there may have been a stretch of frozen tundra during the Ice Age at least 1,000 miles wide to bridge the two continents. DNA evidence finds three distinct mutations among American Indians that are also found among people in Mongolia and Siberia. If this theory of a land bridge proves valid, it can still be difficult to say which direction the migration might have followed. Geneticists have found at least four different blood types and DNA strains among American Indians that might indicate multiple migrations from multiple areas. Many Indian communities believe that they were created in their traditional lands, as their oral histories indicate.

Some American Indians migrated to North America by boat. After the period in which a land bridge may have existed, *Inuit [III]* and *Aleut [III]* used wooden dugouts and skin boats to cross the Bering Sea. Other coastal cultures may also have arrived by boat. The finding that three percent of American Indians share a genetic trait that occurs only in parts of Europe may indicate that some ancient Indians traveled via North Atlantic ice sheets, though assuming migration in only one direction may again be premature.

Archaic period

The Archaic period was characterized by foraging of game and plants in the West and agricultural settlements in the East from about 5000 to 1000 B.C. *Plano Spear-Point culture* hunters from the earlier Paleolithic period remained active on the Great Plains until approximately 4500 B.C. Archaeologists believe that Archaic Indians descended from *Paleo-Indian period* ancestors. Archaic Indians remained more localized in their foraging than earlier groups.

The Archaic Indians had a more varied diet than the Paleo-Indians and a wider variety of tools. Stone, wood, bone, antler, shell, and ivory were used to make mortars and pestles, spears, bolas, harpoons, knives, axes, wedges, chisels, scrapers, hammers, anvils, awls, drills, traps, fishhooks, and lines. They constructed boats and domesticated dogs.

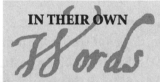

IN THEIR OWN *Words*

This history of humankind in North and South America can be divided into two parts: the history of the aboriginal peoples of the Western Hemisphere prior to the landfall of Western man, and the history of North and South America after the voyages of Columbus. These histories can be likened to an iceberg . . . Seven-eighths lie beneath the surface of the water. We can see Western Occupation above the surface and visible. The aboriginal peoples' time is below the surface and invisible.

—OREN LYONS (JOAGQUISHO), ONONDAGA (1930–).
IN *EXILED IN THE LAND OF THE FREE*,
CLEAR LIGHT PUBLISHERS, 1992.

Pipes, cooking pots, and storage pots were made of stone. Some of the first woven cloths and baskets appeared. Heated stones were used for boiling water and roasting meat in pits. Baskets and skin containers were used to store food. Ornaments and rituals were incorporated into customs to bury the dead.

Archaic period spear points. *National Park Service.*

The Archaic period was divided into Eastern Archaic and Western Archaic, with the Mississippi River serving as the dividing line between the two. The wooded landscape of the East supported a denser population than the barren area of the West. There were five primary Archaic cultures, with geographical differences in adaptation to environments. The five cultures included: the *Old Cordilleran culture* of the Columbia River Valley, circa 9000 to 5000 B.C.; the Desert culture of the Great Basin area, circa 9000 to 1000 B.C.; the Cochise culture of the Great Basin, circa 7000 to 500 B.C.; the *Old Copper culture* of the Great Lakes region, circa 4000 to 1500 B.C.; and the *Red Paint people* of New England, circa 3000 to 500 B.C.

Evidence of the Eastern Archaic period has been excavated at mounds at Poverty Point Louisiana (see *Poverty Point culture*). There is also archaeological evidence of agricultural settlements in Eastern Archaic sites.

atlatl or spear thrower

The atlatl was developed during the *Folsom Spear-Point culture* period, 9100 to 8000 B.C. Atlatls were two-foot-long wooden sticks with animal hide hoops that allowed for a firm grip. They also had a stone weight and hook. The atlatl propelled spears harder and faster than people could throw them. Folsom Indians began using atlatls to pursue smaller animals once big game was gone. Folsom projectile points have been found throughout the Plains, Southwest, and West.

The spear required added force by the hunter to penetrate the hides of large animals and could only be used at a close distance when the animal was trapped. The atlatl increased velocity, allowed the use of lighter shafts, and had a longer range than the handheld spear.

basket makers

The first stage in *Anasazi* cultural development is called the basket maker period. The Anasazi culture existed from 100 B.C. to A.D. 1300. The Anasazi developed techniques to weave food containers and other items from straw, vines, and yucca. Basketry was usually women's art, but among the *Pomo [III]* and Yupik Indians, men also wove. Other skills were refined during this period as well, including ceramics and agricultural techniques. During this period, the Anasazi also began living in semi-permanent rounded and domed housing erected over shallow pits.

Basketry is one of the oldest and most widespread of American Indian arts. After gathering materials at specific times of year, the Anasazi then cleaned and prepared them. Materials had to be sized to uniform widths and diameters. Three basic techniques were used in basket production: plaiting, twining, and coiling. Baskets were used to gather, prepare, store, cook, and serve food.

IN THEIR OWN *Words*

M y heart is filled with joy
When I see you here,
As the brooks fill with water
When the snow melts
In the spring;

And I feel glad as the ponies do
When the fresh grass starts
In the beginning of the year . . .

I was born upon the prairie
Where the wind blew free
And there was nothing to break the light of the sun . . .

Do not ask us
To give up the buffalo
For the sheep.

—TEN BEARS (PARIA SEMEN), COMANCHE (1792–1873), SPOKEN TO U.S. COMMISSIONER AT 1867 COUNCIL OF MEDICINE LODGE CREEK.

beads

Some of the oldest known beads in America, found at the *Folsom Spear-Point culture* site near Midland, Texas, are more than 11,000 years old and are made of bone. The second oldest bead, found in Colorado, is made of oil shale and is about 10,000 years old. Other materials that were used to make beads by American Indians included clay, fruit pits, copper, gemstones, gold, horn, ivory, pearls, porcupine quills, seeds, shells, silver, stones, and wood.

Decorative beadwork and the possession of large amounts of beads were a mark of high status in various tribes. The *Iroquois [III]* and Algonquin tribes recorded their histories on wampum made from shell beads. A *Mississippian culture* mound site at Cahokia, near St. Louis, Missouri, found beads in the graves of high-ranking individuals. Beads replaced quillwork in some areas after Europeans brought glass beads to the Americas.

Europeans traded their manufactured glass beads in Africa and the Far East before using them in the Americas. Columbus carried beads on his first voyage. As contact with Europeans spread from east to west, some tribes developed preferences for particular colors. Sixteenth-century European beads were too large for embroidery purposes, but they were used in necklaces. Beads were strung, sewn, woven, netted, and used as inlay. Bead embroidery replaced porcupine quillwork in some areas by the mid-19th century.

Shell and turquoise beads continue to be made in the Southwest and steatite beads are made in California by traditional methods. Most bead artists have been women, although men also beaded in the Southwest. The work is very labor-intensive. Beadwork continues as an artistic tradition in Indian communities, but the income earned from beadwork today is probably equivalent to minimum wage.

IN THEIR OWN

Words

*We live, we die, and like the grass and trees,
Renew ourselves from the soft clods of the grave.*

*Stones crumble and decay, faiths grow old
And they are forgotten, but new beliefs are born.*

*The faith of the villages is dust now,
But it will grow again like the trees.*

—ANONYMOUS, WANAPUM.

Beringa

Many American Indians believe they were created in the Americas on their traditional and sacred lands. The Bering Strait theory proposes that a land bridge called Beringa created a surface of frozen tundra from eastern Asia to the Americas during the Ice Age. The period in which humans came into existence, the Pleistocene epoch, lasted at least a million years and was marked by a series of four ice ages. Scholars believe that humans arrived in the Americas during the last of the four ice ages, known as the Wisconsin glaciation in North America, which began around 90000–75000 B.C. and ended around 10000–8000 B.C. According to this theory, a frozen tundra of 1,000 miles bridged the two continents, now covered by water. The Monte Verde archaeological site in Chile suggests that humans existed in the Americas more than 33,000 years ago. DNA studies comparing American Indians to people in Mongolia and Siberia also suggest a separation in the two groups more than 30,000 years ago, although it is possible that migration could have occurred in either direction. Linguistic studies of the 150 language groupings indicate that humans existed more than 40,000 years ago in the Americas. These recent studies suggest a much earlier presence than scientists had previously thought.

Some American Indians migrated to North America by boat after the submersion of Beringa. The *Inuit [III]* and *Aleut [III]* used wooden dugouts and skin boats to cross the Bering Sea around 2500 to 1000 B.C., a much later date than Paleo-Indians. Geneticists have also found that 3 percent of American Indians share a genetic trait with people in Europe, which suggests that some American Indians may have crossed the North Atlantic on ice sheets or by boat.

Blood group and DNA studies indicate that modern American Indians have at least four different lineages. Other researchers have found as much genetic variation among American Indian populations as among any other group, which suggests that the peopling of the Americas was not the result of a few migrations of genetically homogeneous people. As a result, the debate regarding the origins of humankind and of the American Indians continues.

buffalo

The American bison, commonly known as the buffalo, was central to the Plains Indian economy. Buffalo could be more than six feet tall and weigh up to a ton. Before European contact, buffalo were often hunted by groups who drove them over cliffs, herded them into corrals, or surrounded them with fire. Contact with Europeans introduced the *horse* to Indian cultures and the horse was then used to hunt buffalo. Plains Indians used every part of the buffalo: what they did not eat they used to make tipi coverings, shields, bedding, and clothing. Thread was made from the buffalo's hair, glue from the hooves, and fuel from the buffalo chips. The buffalo herd in North America was estimated at 75 million in the mid-1800s. While Indians had hunted buffalo for generations, whites caused the near extinction of the buffalo within a short period of time. By the 1840s, wealthy whites were going on buffalo hunts for adventure. In the 1860s, the railroads hunted buffalo to feed crews. With the completion of the Union Pacific transcontinental railroad in 1869, buffalo hides could be transported easily to distant markets. However, the large-scale slaughter of thousands of buffalo really began in earnest in the 1870s. By killing buffalo, whites could remove food sources from Indians and thereby subdue them. The buffalo were killed, not for subsistence, but as a systematic enterprise. Americans used high-powered telescopic rifles that were accurate at 600 yards and often shot the buffalo from traveling railroad cars. Destruction of the buffalo forced the Indians onto reservations and ensured their dependency on government rations. With the Indians on reservations, vast areas of land opened to white ranchers and farmers. By 1900, whites had destroyed the great buffalo herds and confined Plains Indians to reservations after taking most of their land. Some tribes have begun to breed new buffalo herds in the last decade.

> ## IN THEIR OWN Words
>
> *The buffalo is our money. It is our only resource with which to buy what we need and do not receive from the government. We love them just as the white man does his money. Just as it makes a white man feel to have his money carried away, so it makes us feel to see others killing and stealing our buffaloes, which are our cattle given to us by the Great Father above to provide us meat to eat and means to get things to wear.*
>
> —Bull Bear, Southern Cheyenne war chief (fl. 1860s–1870s). Quoted in *The Buffalo War: The History of the Red River Uprising of 1874*, by James Haley, Doubleday, 1976.

Clovis Spear-Point culture

The Clovis culture began as early as 13,500 years ago over a wide area of North America, and is the earliest known culture in North America. These foragers camped along rivers and streams where big game tended to feed. Hunters appear to have worked in pairs, with one attracting the animal's attention while the other attacked with a spear.

The Clovis culture, sometimes referred to as Llano, is named after the Clovis site in New Mexico where particular, shaped spear points were found, usually among mammoth bones. Four spear-point cultures have been identified from the Pleistocene period: the Clovis, *Sandia*, *Folsom*, and *Plano* or Plainview.

Clovis points were one and one-half to five inches long with lengthwise channels on both sides of the base that allowed attachment to wooden shafts. Clovis points have been dated from 9200 to 8000 B.C. Clovis points have been found in every state, indicating a widespread culture.

Desert-Cochise culture

The *Archaic period* in North America was divided into eastern and western Archaic regions, with the Mis-

Typical Clovis spear points. *Blackwater Locality #1 Archives, ENMU, Portales, New Mexico.*

A re-creation of a Clovis Spear-Point culture buffalo hunt. *Blackwater Draw Museum/Site Archives, ENMU, Portales, New Mexico.*

sissippi River serving as the division between the two. The wooded landscape of the East supported a denser population than the barren West. There were five primary Archaic cultures: the *Old Cordilleran culture* of the Columbia River Valley (9000–5000 B.C.), the Desert culture of the Great Basin area (9000–1000 B.C.), the Cochise culture of the Great Basin (7000–500 B.C.), the *Old Copper culture* of the Great Lakes region (4000–1500 B.C.), and the *Red Paint people* of New England (3000–500 B.C.).

The harsh environment of the Southwest, with its limited game resources, led to the development of four agrarian cultures—the *Desert-Cochise*, *Mogollon*, *Hohokam*, and *Anasazi*—in an area that included southern Utah, Colorado, Arizona, New Mexico, and a corner of Texas.

The Desert culture (9000–1000 B.C.), a foraging society, was based in the Great Basin area of Utah, Nevada, and Arizona. Grinding stones and woven containers have been found at Danger Cave in Utah, as well as some of the earliest samples of basketry in North America (see *basket makers*).

The Cochise culture in New Mexico and Arizona (7000–500 B.C.) was an offshoot of the Desert culture. Cochise Indians foraged around Lake Cochise. They milled seeds, grains, and nuts. At Bat Cave in New Mexico, cultivated corn was found, establishing the earliest known evidence of agriculture north of Mexico at around 3500 B.C. Cochise Indians made houses of brush over dug holes. They also shaped pottery figurines. Later, Hohokam and Mogollon cultures were derived from this Desert-Cochise culture.

Folsom Spear-Point culture (Spear Throwing)

The Folsom culture is named after the Folsom site in New Mexico. Most evidence for this culture has been found in the Southwest and West, but some has been found on the Great Plains as well. Folsom culture followed the *Clovis Spear-Point culture* of 11,000 years ago and has been dated from 9100 to 8000 B.C.

The Folsom culture produced distinctive spear points that were three-quarters of an inch to three inches long. The points were made by flaking and striking off particles until a thin, sharp edge was achieved. Fluting channels ran along both sides of the point almost the entire length. Those long channels facilitated attachment to spear shafts and increased the flow of blood from an animal pierced by the spear. They also increased the speed at which a spear could be thrown.

Folsom Indians began using a spear-throwing tool called an *atlatl*. Atlatls were two-foot-long wooden sticks with animal hide hoops that allowed for a firm grip. They also used stone weights and hooks.

Formative period

The Formative period (1000 B.C.–A.D. 1500), the time of contact with Europeans, followed the *Archaic period*. Cultural traits included agricultural villages, houses, domesticated animals, pottery, weaving, basketry, trade, use of the bow and arrow, and ceremonies. Within the Formative period, regional cultural differences existed. The Formative period was distinct in its development of farming, taming animals, building villages and houses, trading, *pottery making* and basketry, weaving, and using the bow and arrow.

Advanced cultures of this time period in the Southwest included the *Hohokam culture, Mogollon culture,* and the *Anasazi.* In the East, mound builders' cultures overlap in this time period, specifically the *Adena* and *Hopewell* cultures.

Spear points from the Folsom and Yuma periods. *Wyatt Davis, Museum of New Mexico.*

Ghost Dance

The Ghost Dance was the name given to religious dances created by various groups in the late 19th century. Widely practiced in the 1870s and revived in the 1890s, Indians in western states adopted circular dancing in ceremonies with the hope that human and animal ancestors would return to earth.

In the late 1860s, a *Paiute [III]* named Wodziwob had a vision that led him to preach that Indians could bring the old times back by practicing a particular style of dancing. His teachings spread among Indians in

California and Oregon including the *Klamath [III]*, Miwoks, *Modoc [III]*, and Yurok. The dance consisted of people joining hands and sidestepping leftward in a circle.

The Ghost Dance movement returned with new fervor in the 1890s. In 1889, another Paiute named Wovoka had a vision and began to preach that by practicing the circular dance and living a virtuous and peaceful life, not only could Indians regain their lands and dead ancestors, but whites would die. Modern communication spread his teachings across tribes in the western United States, including the *Arapaho [III]*, *Cheyenne [III]*, *Caddo [III]*, *Kiowa [III]*, *Lakota [III]*, and *Paiute [III]*. Wovoka's followers, performing the dance for several days in a row, sought to see visions themselves.

Arapaho Ghost Dance. *National Archives.*

Whites felt threatened by any traditional spiritual practices. They moved quickly to repress the Ghost Dance. Their actions resulted in the massacre of *Lakota [III]* at Wounded Knee in 1890 (see *Wounded Knee Massacre [IV]*). Wovoka remained a prophet until his death in 1932. Some tribes continued to practice the Ghost Dance into the 1960s.

IN THEIR OWN *Words*

M y father, you see us as we are. We are poor. We have but few blankets and little clothing. The great Father of Life who made us and gave us this land to live upon, made the buffalo and other game to afford us sustenance; their meat is our only food; with their skins we clothe ourselves and build our lodges. They are our only means of life—food, fuel, and clothing . . . We soon will be deprived of these; starvation and cold will destroy us. The buffalo are fast disappearing . . . As the white man advances, our means of life grows less . . .

We hear a great trail is to be made though our country. We do not know what this is for; we do not understand it, but we think it will scare away the buffalo.

—OLD BRAVE, ASSINIBOINE (1853– ?). OLD BRAVE SPOKE ON AUGUST 1, 1853, WHEN GOVERNOR ISAAC STEVENS VISITED THE CAMP ALONG THE RIVER OF LAKES.

Hohokam culture

Hohokam culture, along with *Mogollon culture*, was derived from the earlier *Desert-Cochise culture* of the *Archaic period*. Hohokam translates as "the vanished ones" in the Akimel O'odham language. The Hohokam lived to the west of the Mogollon culture in the desert of the Gila and Salt River valleys in Arizona. They were successful agriculturists who used irrigation systems that included diversion dams made of woven mat valves. Their primary crops were corn, beans, squash, tobacco, and cotton. Their advances in agriculture supported large settlements. The principal village of Snaketown, occupied 1,500 years ago near present-day Phoenix, covered 300 acres and had 100 pit houses.

They produced red-on-buff pottery, copper bells, ball courts, and rubber balls. They were also the first people in the world to develop etching, around A.D. 1000.

The Hohokam abandoned Snaketown and other settlements around A.D. 1500 and scattered in small groups. Scholars are not certain if the reasons for abandonment were drought, invasions, or other factors. The

IN THEIR OWN *Words*

My brothers, I bring to you the promise of a day in which there will be no white man to lay his hand on the bridle of the Indian's horse; when the red men of the prairie will rule the world and not be turned from the hunting grounds by any man. I bring you word from your fathers the ghosts, that they are now marching to join you, led by the Messiah who came once to live on earth with the white men but was cast out and killed by them. I have seen the wonders of the spirit-land and have talked with the ghosts. I traveled far and am sent back with a message to tell you to make ready for the coming of the Messiah and return of the ghosts in the spring . . . then he whom we had followed showed us his hands and feet, and there were wounds in them which had been made by the whites when he went to them and they crucified him. And he told us that he was going to come again on earth, and this time he would remain and live with the Indians, who were his chosen people.

—KICKING BEAR (MATO ANAHTAKA), OGLALA LAKOTA SHAMAN (C. 1846–1904).
STATED AT MEDICINE LODGE CREEK MEETING, 1867.

Hohokam groups were ancestors of the Akimel O'odham (*Pima [III]*) and *Tohono O'odham [III]* (Papago).

Hopewell culture

Like the earlier *Adena culture*, the Hopewell culture (or Hopewellian) (200 B.C.–A.D. 700) was centered along the Ohio Valley but also ranged over the Illinois, Mississippi, and other river valleys of the Midwest and East. Artifacts suggest that their trading network was far ranging and included the Rocky Mountains, Atlantic Ocean, Great Lakes, Appalachian Mountains, and Florida. They manufactured complex objects, including mica mirrors, pearl jewelry, copper headdresses and ornaments, pottery with designs, and obsidian blades. The Hopewell placed objects in tombs with their deceased, just as the Adena did.

Hopewell Culture burial mounds near Newark, Ohio. *National Park Service.*

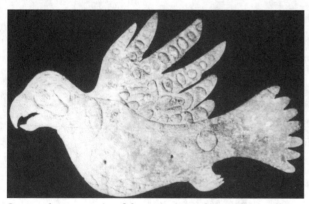

Copperplate peregrine falcon excavated at a Hopewell site. *National Park Service.*

Also like the Adena, the Hopewell left behind numerous earthen burial mounds. Up to 40 feet in height, they were in fact larger than the Adena mounds. Some mounds portrayed animals; others served as walls up to 200 feet in length and were laid out in geometric patterns. Hopewell sites near Newark, Ohio, included octagonal, square, and circular designs over an area of four square miles. The scale and complexity of construction indicate an organized, hierarchical society.

Most often, circular mounds cluster in groups up to 40 in number. Some linear earthworks are hundreds of feet long. Most mounds were roofed with poles or logs, although in later periods more elaborate dry masonry, chambered mounds were constructed.

Among the crops the Hopewell farmed were corn, beans, and squash. They lived in domed structures framed with poles and covered with bark,

woven mats, or animal skins. Their shelters were similar to the wigwams
of the later Algonquians. Scholars believe that the Hopewell may have been
ancestors of later eastern Indian tribes, such as the *Assiniboine [III]*, *Cheyenne [III]*, and *Dakota [III]*.

horse

The first tribes to own horses were those who encountered the Spanish.
Those tribes that did acquire horses first used them as pack animals just as
they had used dogs. Only later did they begin to ride them. Wide-scale
use of horses did not occur until after 1640; it had spread to the northern
Great Plains by 1750, and thereafter it continued moving north over the
plains. Some tribes referred to the horse as an elk dog or a big dog. Nomadic tribes were able to travel farther by using the strength of the horses
to carry large loads. Hunting *buffalo* on horseback spread among Plains
tribes and their neighbors. The range of raiding parties also increased.
Agricultural tribes, however, had a limited interest in acquiring horses.
Indian horsemanship differed from the European style in some ways. For
example, they didn't use spurs. Horses were not branded or marked, since
their owners could identify horses by sight. Tribes that owned large herds
of horses lost most of their stock when they moved to reservations. They
grieved for that loss as well as the loss of their lands.

medicine

There are so many different medicinal practices among tribes that a
complete discussion of them is all but impossible. Some commonali-
ties in practices, however, have been observed. Many tribes, for example,
believed that individuals who practiced medicine had special power.
This power was sometimes inherited through family lines or found
through visions. Leaders such as *Geronimo [II]* were often born into a
family that included generations of medicine people. Many tribes had
both medicine men and women; among some tribes, only men could
practice medicine, while others, such as the *Yurok [III]*, had only female practitioners. Medicine people often had a specialty such as an
herbalist, midwife, counselor, visionary, or someone who worked with

energy fields. Medicine people often occupied places of respect in their communities.

While whites referred to medicinal practitioners in various tribes as medicine men, each tribe had different titles for their healers. A long apprenticeship was usually required. Traditional Indian medicine usually involved an active relationship between the healer and patient rather than the passive relationship encouraged in western cultures. Some ceremonies were meant for restoring harmony but not for healing, such as talking circles, in which all involved parties stated their thoughts in a group discussion session, or smudging, in which sage was burned and the smoke waved over the body for cleansing.

Even today, many healers do not charge for their services, although gifts are usually offered. Maintaining harmony, including stress control, is central to maintaining healthy living according to numerous Indian medicinal traditions. Herbs, fasting, and prayer may help to maintain this harmony. Illnesses are often viewed as being directly or indirectly tied to a spiritual cause.

Some nations also recognize the use of bad power, which can harm an individual only when that person's spiritual energy is low. The best defense against bad power is to keep your spirit strong and pure.

Many tribes also believe in a Supreme Creator. Some tribes have female deity figures such as the *Navajo [III]* Changing Woman, *Yaqui [III]* Maala Mecha, or the *Lakota [III]* White Buffalo Calf Woman. Other groups have mediators between the spirit world and the earth such as Hopi Kachinas who dance to bring blessings from the creator.

Today, *Indian Health Service [IV]* hospitals and clinics are often staffed with non-Indian physicians and offer modern medicines. Western medicine is sometimes seen as good for "white man's diseases" such as tuberculosis, measles, and whooping cough; however, traditions such as sweat baths and wearing medicine bags and charms continue to be practiced. Training healers today is a private matter that involves years of apprenticeship, and transfer of knowledge is usually based on memory. Many fear that ancient arts of healing will disappear in future generations.

Mississippian culture

The Mississippian culture, also known as the temple mound builders, followed the *Hopewell culture.* Lasting from A.D. 1000 to 1500, it is distinguished by institutionalized religion. Art emerged in the building of mounds, with many in the shape of birds. The mounds consisted of earthen platforms constructed of layered earth over many burials. There is evidence of ancestor worship supervised by priests who were responsible for maintaining temples, burial houses, and sacred fires. The Mississippian culture has been found throughout the South and Southeast.

It was centered along the Mississippi River, with sites located as far south as Florida and as far north as Wisconsin. Mississippians constructed mounds for a different purpose from their predecessors, who had used them for burial. They placed temples for spiritual purposes on top of their mounds, a practice similar to the Mesoamerican tradition of placing temples on top of stone pyramids.

Mississippian mounds had sloping sides and flat tops where the temples were constructed. Log steps on terraced sides led to the top. Some mounds had the homes of priests and leaders built into the structures. The higher the rank of an individual, the higher the home was built on the mound. Other community members lived in pole-and-thatch huts surrounding the mounds. Business was conducted in a central open village plaza.

Triangular points from the Mississippi Woodland period. *National Park Service.*

Temple mounds were impressive in size. For example, Monk's Mound, at the Cahokia site near East St. Louis, Illinois, covered 16 acres and stood 100 feet high. Archaeologists believe this site was built in 14 stages from about A.D. 900 to 1500. At its height, Cahokia was a city with a population of more than 30,000, covering about 4,000 acres and including 85 temple and burial mounds. Other sites with large populations existed at Moundville in Alabama; Etowah and Ocmulgee in Georgia; Hiwassee Island in Tennessee; Spiro in Oklahoma; Belcher in Louisiana; Aztalan in Wisconsin; and Mount Royal in Florida. With big populations, farming was conducted on a large scale, and crops included corn, beans, squash, pumpkins, and tobacco. By 1550, mound building had ended; scholars surmise that European *diseases [IV]* spread inland and decimated many population centers. Many Eastern Indians, especially in the Southeast, continued to use the mounds. Some tribes, including the Nachez, continued many of the practices of the mound builders. Scholars believe that many tribes may have descended from the Mississippian mound builders, including the *Choctaw [III]* and *Creek [III]*.

Mogollon culture

The Mogollon Indians were named for the mountain range on the southern Arizona and New Mexico border where they lived in high valleys. They were established by A.D. 300. Descendants of the *Desert-Cochise culture*, they are thought to be the first Southwest people to develop agriculture, house building, and *pottery making*.

Farming was conducted with simple digging sticks. They adopted the bow and arrow about A.D. 500. Their pit houses were built three to four feet in the ground, and they had log frames with roofs made of branches, reeds, bark, and mud. Those dwellings were very effective in the region's extreme temperature ranges. After A.D. 1100, they began building above-ground pueblos, influenced by their *Anasazi* neighbors to the north.

The earliest Mogollon pottery was brown and was built from coils and covered with a thin film of clay before firing. Again influenced by the Anasazi, they began painting their pottery with geometric designs. They wove clothing and blankets from cotton, feathers, and animal fur yarn. Between A.D. 1200 and 1400, the Mogollon culture blended into the Anasazi. They became the ancestors of the *Zuni [III]*.

Native American Church

The Native American Church (NAC) has approximately 250,000 members across dozens of Indian tribes in North America. The NAC had its origins in the fight over one traditional practice, the Indian use of peyote in curing ceremonies. It was officially chartered in 1918 in the wake of Congressional hearings on peyote use. Peyote is a light green, two-inch cactus that possesses psychedelic properties. The tops of the peyote are cut off and dried before it is consumed, often in the form of a tea. Peyote tastes bitter and can produce vomiting, but it is not addictive. It is usually consumed during all-night ceremonies in the NAC. It grows principally in northern Mexico and southern Texas.

The *Apache [III]*, *Caddo [III]*, and other southwestern tribes began the peyote movement in the 1870s and 1880s. Peyote spread quickly among many western Oklahoma tribes. Those tribes include the *Comanche [III]*, *Kiowa [III]*, Delaware, *Wichita [III]*, Southern *Cheyenne [III]* and *Arapaho [III]*, *Osage [III]*, *Quapaw [III]*, *Seneca [III]*, *Ponca [III]*, *Kaw [III]*, *Otoe [III]*, *Pawnee [III]*, *Kickapoo [III]*, *Shawnee [III]*, Sac, and Fox. Ceremonial use of peyote also spread to tribes beyond Oklahoma, such as the Hochunk, *Omaha [III]*, *Menominee [III]*, *Lakota [III]*, Northern Cheyenne, *Arapaho [III]*, *Crow [III]*, Wind River *Shoshone [III]*, Bannock, *Cree [III]*, *Blackfeet [III]*, *Assiniboine [III]*, *Paiute [III]*, *Navajo [III]*, and *Ute [III]*. One of the early leaders was Comanche Chief Quanah Parker.

By 1912, organized resistance to the peyote movement, based in the *Bureau of Indian Affairs [IV]* and Christian churches, attempted to get federal laws passed to ban peyote. The House of Representatives considered such legislation in 1918. The bill was defeated, but to make their religious practices more acceptable to the general population, peyote groups organized the NAC. Attempts to pass federal antipeyote legislation continued unsuccessfully, but several states with questionable jurisdiction over *reservations [IV]* did pass such laws. Many states later rescinded their antipeyote laws. The Navajo and Taos Pueblo tribal councils forbade the use of peyote on their reservations and pursued peyotists with arrests, fines, and jail terms. In 1944, the NAC of Oklahoma incorporated as the NAC of the United States. By the 1950s, members of more than 80 American Indian nations participated in the peyote movement. In 1955, the NAC of the United States incorporated as the NAC of North America, and several Canadian churches joined the group.

Since the American Indian Religious Freedom Act was passed in 1978, some protection for members of the NAC who use peyote has been in place. In a controversial case, *Employment Division vs. Smith* (in which two Indian drug counselors had been fired from their jobs after it was discovered that they had taken peyote as part of an NAC ceremony), the Supreme Court restricted the use of peyote in American Indian and Native American Church religious practices. In 1993, Congress passed the

IN THEIR OWN *Words*

I never kill a bird or other animal without feeling bad inside. All true hunters must have that feeling that prevents them from killing just for killing's sake. There's no fun in just destroying life, and the Great Spirit puts that shadow in your heart when you destroy his creatures.

—JOE FRIDAY, WOODS CREE, STATEMENT IN 1940.

Religious Freedom Restoration Act to counterbalance the restrictions of the Supreme Court ruling. The act has been somewhat effective in allowing NAC members to practice their peyote ceremonies.

Norse

The Norse arrived in the Americas at the beginning of the eleventh century. Archaeological sites have been found at a number of locations, including L'Anse aux Meadows, Newfoundland. These sites seem to confirm Norse documents that recount Atlantic transoceanic crossings. Archaeologists believe that the Vikings had contact with the *Beothuk [III]* or *Micmac [III]* around A.D. 1000. The *Inuit [III]* of Greenland also had contact with the Norseman Eric the Red circa A.D. 984. Norse settlers from Iceland established several settlements among the Inuit in Greenland and for a brief time they had a settlement among the Beothuk in Newfoundland.

The Norse withdrew from the Americas by the 1500s just as other Europeans were beginning to arrive. Even before large seafaring vessels, small wooden or reed crafts were able to cross oceans so that unintentional drift voyages may have occurred. It is also possible that other pre-Renaissance sailors besides the Vikings have attempted crossings. Indians

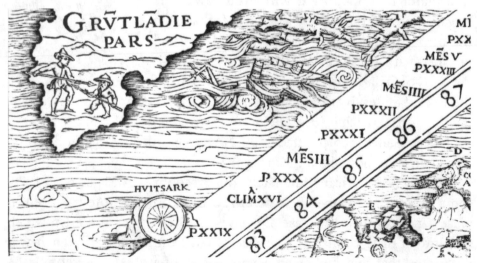

Detail of a 1537 map (Carta Marina) of Greenland and Scandinavia showing the first known European depictions of Inuit. *Uppsala University Library, Uppsala, Sweden.*

most likely voyaged to other continents, as well. Geneticists argue that American Indians showed A, B, and O blood groups, and in historic times, they had developed no immunity to European *diseases*, which indicates that early contact might not have been extensive between American Indians and Europeans.

Old Copper culture

The Old Copper culture covered the Great Lakes region from around 4000 to 1500 B.C. It was a foraging culture typical of eastern *Archaic period* traditions. Unlike other Archaic Indians, however, they made tools out of copper, which have been found at Indian sites. The Indians used natural deposits of copper sheets in rocks or nuggets in the soil to make tools and ornaments. Heating the material allowed the Indians to shape the copper by hammering it into the forms needed. Some of the sites with outcrops of pure copper included regions near the Lake Superior Basin and Wisconsin. Like most societies of the time, they appear to have been hunter-gatherers.

Old Cordilleran culture

The Old Cordilleran, or Cascade, culture of the Columbia River Valley dated from 9000 to 5000 B.C. Their descendants comprised the Indians of the Columbia Plateau and the Pacific Northwest. The Cascade spear point, unique for its willow-leaf shape and lack of fluting, was used mainly for hunting small animals. Other artifacts include fishhooks and gathering tools. (See *Archaic period*.)

Paleo-Indian period

The earliest Indians in the Americas are called Paleo-Indians, or Lithic Indians. Recent archaeological, genetic, and linguistic evidence suggests that Indians were in this hemisphere since at least 40000 B.C. (see *Beringa*).

Paleo-Indians lived in caves and lean-tos. They wore hide and fur clothing and used fire. Fires were started by striking a spark with flint or by rubbing pieces of wood together. Two sticks and a strip of rawhide were used to create the rapid spinning of wood needed to generate enough friction to ignite a fire.

The first Indians gathered plant foods and hunted a variety of animals, including woolly mammoths, mastodons, bighorn bison, and saber-toothed tigers. Early Indians sharpened the wooden points of spears by using fire. They also had tools made of stone and bone. Later, Paleo-Indians shaped flint and obsidian into sharp points by striking those objects with a stone to remove flakes, a process called percussion flaking. Another technique, pressure flaking, pressed bone tools in order to shape and sharpen them. The Paleo-Indian period was followed by the *Archaic period*.

Transitional Paleo-Indian and Archaic period spear points. *National Park Service.*

Plano (Plainview) Spear-Point culture

Plano or Plainview cultures are named after the Plainview site in Texas. This culture ranged on the Great Plains from 8000 to 4500 B.C. in the same regional area as the earlier *Folsom Spear-Point culture*. People in the Plano culture did not flute their spear points, unlike the earlier *Clovis* and Folsom cultures. Plano Indians built corrals to trap animals and sometimes drove herds over cliffs. They also developed meat-preserving methods that mixed meat with animal fat and berries. The mixture could be packed in hides or gut containers for long-term storage or travel.

potlatch

In the Pacific Northwest region, traditional gift giving was known as the potlatch. Tribal groups in this region hosted feasts that gave away most, if not all, of their wealth. This redistribution of wealth had the effect of maintaining social status. Gifts included blankets and jewelry and, by the twentieth century, money and appliances. Tribes that practiced the potlatch included the *Haida [III]*, *Kwakiutl [III]*, *Makah [III]*, *Nootka [III]*, *Tlingit [III]*, and *Tsimshian [III]*.

Canada outlawed the potlatch in 1884; the United States outlawed the practice in the early 20th century. The potlatch was allowed to resume legally in 1934 in the United States and in 1951 in Canada. It is a tradition actively practiced today throughout the Pacific Northwest.

pottery making

Pottery dating to 2400 B.C. has been found at sites in the Southeast near Stallings Island, Georgia. The earliest known pottery in the Northeast dates to 1400 B.C. Pottery was developed as groups made the transition from hunter-gatherer societies to farming societies. Pottery was used for domestic purposes, trade, ceremonies, and burial. The pottery of the *Anasazi*, *Mogollon*, and *Hohokam* cultures in the Southwest reached its peak in technology and design centuries prior to the arrival of the Spanish in 1540. Stamped pottery in the Southeast also reached its peak before contact with Europeans. European contact and the copper, cast iron, and enamel containers the Europeans introduced replaced the use of pottery for domestic purposes.

Poverty Point culture

The earliest evidence of mound building in North America was found at the Poverty Point site near Floyd in northern Louisiana. More than one hundred Poverty Point sites built between 1800 and 500 B.C. have been found in Louisiana, Arkansas, Mississippi, Tennessee, Missouri, and Florida. Poverty Point was a transitional culture between the *Archaic period* and the *Formative period.*

The largest mound at Poverty Point is 70 feet high, 710 feet long, and 640 feet wide. It resembles a bird in flight when viewed from the air and was used for ceremonial purposes. Poverty Point also has 5 smaller conical mounds, 4 to 21 feet high, and 6 concentric ridges with a diameter of two-thirds of a mile. Poverty Point Indians did not use their mounds for burials as later mound builders did.

Poverty Point artifacts include stone *beads*, pendants, clay figurines, and flint tools. Artifacts of copper, lead, and soapstone from trading networks are also present. Some scholars believe that Poverty Point people migrated northward and formed the *Adena* culture.

Pueblo

"Pueblo" is a Spanish word meaning village or town, and refers to a particular type of American Indian village with a particular type of architecture. There are many different groups of *Pueblo [III]* Indians. The *Hopi [III]* and *Zuni [III]* live on the Colorado Plateau, the Hopi in northeastern Arizona, and the Zuni in western New Mexico. Other Pueblo Indians live along the Rio Grande, including the Tewa, Tiwa, Towa or Jemez, and Keres. The first three of these groups speak Kiowa-Tanoan language, and the Kereses speak Keresan. Pueblo Indians are believed to be the descendants of earlier *Anasazi* and *Mogollon* cultures, and their settlements are often located on the tops of mesas.

Pueblo apartment buildings were unique among American Indian dwellings. The roof of one dwelling served as the floor and yard of the level above it. Ladders connected the stories. For defense purposes, the walls on the ground level had no doors or windows. Homes were entered through holes in the roofs.

Depending on geographic location, different building materials were used for construction. The Hopi and Zuni used mortared stones that were covered with plaster, while Rio Grande Indians used adobe bricks shaped from sun-dried earth and straw. Ceremonial pit houses were generally located in the central plaza of the village. The Hopi word "kiva" was applied to all these Pueblo pit houses.

Pueblo men wore cotton kilts and sandals; the women wore cotton dresses and either sandals or moccasins. The women produced coiled pottery and coiled wicker baskets. Farming crops included corn, squash, beans, sunflowers, cotton, and tobacco crops.

Red Paint people

The Red Paint people of New England and eastern Canada were eastern *Archaic period* people. Their name is derived from the ground red iron ore used to line graves. This symbolic use of red, the color of blood, lasted from 3000 to 500 B.C. At Port au Choix, Newfoundland, the northern end of Red Paint culture, 100 burials have been located. In some of the graves, firemaking kits of flint have been found, as well as tools and ornaments made of slate, bone, and antler.

Sandia Spear-Point culture

The Sandia culture was located in the Southwest. The name was derived from a cave site in the Sandia Mountains of New Mexico. Sandia stone points were two to four inches long with rounded bases and a bulge on one side where they were attached to wooden shafts. Sandia points have been dated from 9100 to 8000 B.C.

totem poles

In the Pacific Northwest, sacred objects known as totem poles were carved from red cedar trees with symbols that contained family and clan crests along with important mythical and historical figures. Tribes that carve totem poles range from Alaska to Vancouver Island and include the *Haida [III]*, *Kwakiutl [III]*, *Tsimshian [III]*, *Tlingit [III]*, Coast *Salish [III]*, and *Bella Coola [III]*.

A ceremony is involved in the creation of a totem pole, from the selection of the tree to its finished carving. Types of totem poles include house posts, memorial poles, welcome figures, and mourning posts. Between 1920 and 1950, many white scholars moved totem poles into museums without permission from tribes because of their concern that the tribes and poles were remnants of a vanishing people. Carving of totem poles emerged as a commercial art form again in the 1950s and continues today.

vision quest

In the traditions of a number of Indian nations, individuals undergo vision quests to seek visions or dreams that can help them gain understanding of their life, or even reveal the future. In some nations, men and women undergo vision quests as adolescents, although people can pursue quests at any point in life. Some nations see vision quests as more important for males to undertake since they must go begging for spiritual power, whereas women are seen as inherently possessing it through the ability to give birth to children.

A vision quest is usually undertaken in an isolated area without water or food for three or four days. A successful quest produces a vision of a spirit helper or guide, sometimes an animal spirit, whose character will manifest itself in the individual or teach important life lessons. Sometimes visions may also point out possible life vocations or predict future events.

Woodland cultures

Eastern Woodland plant-collecting economies developed by 1000 B.C. The Woodland Indians domesticated plants and animals and lived in settled villages. Pottery was used to store grain. Besides agriculture and pottery, Woodland cultures were characterized by the practice of using burial mounds. *Adena*, *Hopewell*, and *Mississippian* were the best-known cultures of this period.

The Adena culture was spread across the American midlands and along the Atlantic Coast. Five hundred Adena sites, most dating after 500 B.C., have been found. The Hopewell culture, circa 200 B.C.–A.D. 500, was discovered near Chillicothe, Ohio. Thirty-eight conical mounds surrounded by geometric walls have been uncovered. The Hopewell culture dominated eastern North America for centuries.

By A.D. 800, the Mississippian culture became dominant. It continued until the period of European contact in the 16th century. The *Iroquois [III]* developed from the Woodland tradition. The *Cherokee [III]* of the Southeast were also part of the Iroquoian language family and may have separated from the Iroquois and migrated south.

PART II

Individuals

Because of the brevity of this volume, a section on individual American Indians could never begin to do justice to all of those who should be included. In this section, I have attempted to include a cross-section of leaders who have offered role models in various endeavors, such as tribal leadership and culture. Included here are a number of chiefs and leaders who were notable in the defense of their nations and people in the face of white encroachment or military invasions, such as Cochise, Chief Crazy Horse, Chief Joseph, Geronimo, Chief Red Cloud, Chief Sitting Bull, and Tecumseh. Other leaders found different ways to resist the onslaught against Indian territory and cultures. Paiute activist Sarah Winnemucca, for example, lectured throughout the country in an attempt to educate the white public about the plight of her people. In 1883, she published *Life Among the Paiutes*, the first book written in English by an American Indian woman.

A number of individuals are included here for their significant cultural contributions. Sequoyah, for example, invented the Cherokee syllabary, an accomplishment that makes him the only known individual to have invented an entire written language by himself. N. Scott Momaday was the first American Indian author to win a Pulitzer Prize. Jim Thorpe was a renowned athlete who won gold medals in the decathlon and pentathlon in the 1912 Olympics in Stockholm, Sweden. Ella Deloria was an anthropologist and linguist who taught at Columbia University beginning in 1929. Her work saved the Dakota language for future generations. Her nephew Vine Deloria became the preeminent American Indian intellectual of the twentieth century, beginning with his 1969 publication of *Custer Died for Your Sins*.

In addition to historical figures, I also wanted to offer a selection of leaders from the present day. Leaders in recent decades have included Chief Wilma Mankiller, chief of the largest American Indian nation (the Cherokee) from 1985 to 1995. Also included here are Dennis Banks and Russell Means, leaders in the American Indian Movement, an organization that changed the face of tribal politics as well America's policies and attitudes toward Indian tribes. Modern leaders encompass activists like Winona LaDuke, who has battled environmental abuses that harm Indian lands and endanger the health and lives of Indians themselves. In all these stories of individuals' lives one can trace a common heritage among Indian peoples on which each generation builds.

1492 *The Christopher Columbus voyage, financed by Spain, lands in San Salvador, territory of the Arawak and Taino.*

1511 *Clerics in Spain formally debate the question of whether Indians are humans with souls or whether they are animals.*

1512 *The Encomienda System gives Spanish landholders the legal right to enslave the Indians.*

1519–1521 *Hernando Cortez and 400 soldiers conquer the more than 200,000-member Aztec Empire.*

1539 *The Natchez, Coosa, Tincua, Appalachia, Mobile, and Tonkawa successfully resist invasion by Hernando DeSoto and his troops in the southeastern United States but succumb to European diseases within three decades.*

1540 *DeSoto encounters the Creek town of Cofitachequi, which is ruled by a female chief, and loots the great temple mound.*

1540 *Francisco Vásquez de Coronado invades the American Southwest in search of gold.*

1545 *The first permanent European settlement in North America is established by the Spanish at St. Augustine, Florida.*

1560 *Epidemics wipe out several southeastern tribes. Europeans report finding deserted settlements.*

1585 *An English colony is founded on Roanoke Island but disappears by 1591.*

1598 *The first Spanish colony is established in New Mexico. Apache and Pueblo people had resisted invasion for more than a decade.*

1598–1599 *Rebellion against the Spanish takes place by the Acoma Pueblo in New Mexico.*

1600 *The Spanish kidnap Apache, Navajo, and Ute Indians for slave labor in their mines, fields, and homes. The kidnapping of Native Americans continues until the early 1900s.*

1607–1609 *The first permanent English settlement is established at Jamestown, Virginia, in the territory of the Powhatan Confederacy, in 1607. The Indians feed the starving English immigrants and show them how to raise tobacco. In 1609, the English burn the Indian villages to obtain land already cleared, then enslave the Indians.*

1613 *Pocahontas is kidnapped by the English. Already married to a Powhatan man, she marries one of her English captors, widower John Rolfe. She gives birth to a son in 1615 and dies in 1617 of a European disease at age 22 while visiting England.*

Individuals (continued)

1613 *The Beothuk defend themselves against the French. The French arm the Micmac and offer bounties for Beothuk scalps, which results in the extermination of the Beothuk.*

1614 *Patuxet tribal member Squanto is kidnapped with 24 others by the English and sold in a slave market in Spain. He returns in 1619 to discover his entire village had succumbed to smallpox.*

1616–1620 *A smallpox epidemic decimates New England tribes, making some tribes extinct.*

1620 *Pilgrims from England arrive in Plymouth.*

1621 *Wampanoag invite the Pilgrims to their annual harvest ceremony, which becomes the holiday of Thanksgiving.*

1623 *The English-Powhatan Peace Conference occurs, where the English serve glasses of poisoned wine to toast eternal friendship with the Indians. Survivors of the poisoning are shot to death.*

1624 *The Dutch establish Fort Orange in New Netherlands (Albany, NY).*

1626 *The governor of New Netherlands trades $24 in goods to the Shinnecock tribe for Manhattan Island.*

1633–1635 *Smallpox decimates Indian tribes in New England, New Netherlands, and New France.*

1636 *Minister Roger Williams of Salem flees the Massachusetts Bay Colony because of white land stealing policies. He founds Rhode Island and insists that land be purchased from the Indians instead of taken by force.*

1636–1637 *The Pequot War occurs in New England.*

1642 *Minister Roger Williams publishes the first dictionary of an American Indian language, the Algonquian-English dictionary.*

1644 *The Powhatan Confederacy uprising takes place in Virginia.*

1659 *More than 10,000 Florida Indians die of measles.*

1661 *The Spanish in the Southwest raid kivas, destroying masks and spiritual items as part of an organized effort to suppress traditional religious practices of the Indians.*

1675–1676 *King Philip's War is fought between New England colonists and the Wampanoag, Narragansett, and Nipmuc led by Metaco (called King Philip by white colonists). At the conclusion of the war, his head is severed from his body and mounted on a pole in Plymouth. His wife, son, and 500 survivors are sold as slaves and sent to the West Indies.*

1675 Bacon's Rebellion. Former indentured servants, who had been promised land at the end of their seven-year period of servitude, attack Nanticoke and Susquehannock villages.

1680 The Pueblo Rebellion against the Spanish, led by religious leader Popé. The revolt successfully removes the Spanish from Pueblo lands until 1689.

1689–1697 King William's War is fought between the French and their allied Algonquian tribes and the English and their Iroquois League allies.

1691 Virginia banishes white colonists who marry people of different races.

1695 The first Pima uprising against the Spanish in the Southwest.

1711–1713 The Tuscarora War is fought in North Carolina between English colonists and the Tuscarora tribe. Tuscarora survivors of the war move north and in 1722 become the sixth tribe to join the Iroquois Confederacy.

1712–1734 The Fox uprising against the French in the Great Lakes region.

1715 Powhatan tribal leader, called Queen Anne by the English, speaks to the Virginia legislature.

1715 The Yamasee War in Georgia against English slave traders.

1736–1739 The Chickasaw resist the French on the lower Mississippi.

1738 A smallpox outbreak in the Southeast kills half the Cherokee population and extends into western Canada.

1746 Typhoid fever epidemic decimates the Micmac.

1750 Moor's Indian Charity School is founded and evolves into Dartmouth College.

1751 The second Pima uprising.

1754–1763 The French and Indian War. The defeat of France and its Indian allies results in the French ceding their land claims to New France territory to England and ceding Louisiana to Spain.

1760–1761 The Cherokee uprising in the Carolinas (Cherokee War).

1761–1766 The Aleut uprising against the Russians in Alaska.

1763 An English proclamation bans settlement west of the Appalachians, but white colonists ignore the ban.

1763–1766 Pontiac's Rebellion unites tribes against the English invasion of their lands in the Old Northwest.

1765 Paxton riots. White colonists massacre peaceful, Christianized Susquehannock Indians.

1765 The Reserve system is established in Canada, starting with the land set aside for the Maliseet.

1769 *Spain claims California lands and establishes a mission system. More than 300 Indian bands become extinct. The coastal Indian population declines from more than 70,000 to less than 1,500 in 30 years.*

1769 *White colonists defy the Appalachian boundary line set by the Proclamation of 1763 and invade the lands of the Shawnee and Cherokee in western Virginia, Tennessee, and Kentucky.*

1774 *Lord Dunmore's War is fought in Virginia between the Shawnee and the white colonists who are invading their lands.*

1777 *The Six Nations of the Iroquois League permanently separate over their divided loyalties in the American Revolution.*

1778 *The first treaty between the United States and an Indian tribe. The Delaware are promised representation in Congress, which is never implemented.*

1780–1800 *Smallpox and measles epidemics decimate tribes in Texas and New Mexico. Smallpox spreads north to Washington State.*

1781–1789 *The Articles of Confederation establish federal control of Indian affairs, thus superceding the control of individual states.*

1782 *Christian Delaware Indians are massacred by whites.*

1783 *A proclamation by the Continental Congress bans white squatters from Indian lands; the ban is ignored.*

1783 *The Iroquois Confederacy formally disbands.*

1787 *The Northwest Ordinance outlines plans to develop the Old Northwest with an increased white presence in the area and also calls for the establishment of reservations.*

1787–1789 *The United States Constitution grants the federal government power to regulate Indian affairs.*

1789 *The department of Indian affairs is moved to the War Department. Sale of appropriated Indian land accounts for 80 percent of the federal government's annual budget until 1850.*

1790 *Spain cedes its claims to the Pacific Northwest to England and the United States during the Nootka Convention.*

1790–1791 *Little Turtle's War is fought in the Ohio valley between the Shawnee, Miami, and other tribes against white invaders of their lands.*

1794 *Jay's Treaty establishes trade relations between the United States and English-controlled Canada. Indians are guaranteed free travel across the border.*

Individuals (continued)

1799 *Seneca Chief Handsome Lake founds the Longhouse religion, encouraging a policy of peace toward whites and the vigilant maintenance of Iroquois cultural practices.*

1802 *The Federal Trade and Intercourse Act prohibits the sale of alcohol to Indians. Trading posts ignore the law.*

Aquash, Anna Mae

Anna Mae Aquash was a *Micmac [III]* activist in the *American Indian Movement [IV]* (AIM).

Born in 1945, Aquash was raised in Nova Scotia, Canada. She served as a teacher at an Indian survival school in Boston in the early 1970s before joining AIM as an organizer. She turned down a college scholarship to Brandeis in order to continue her work with AIM, serving in their St. Paul and Pine Ridge offices. She was present at the major American Indian protests of the early 1970s, including AIM's 1973 *Wounded Knee Occupation [IV]*.

A common tactic of the FBI and other United States counterintelligence agencies during the 1970s was to spread false rumors that certain activists were actually government infiltrators. This was done to Aquash and others to cause dissent within the movement.

Aquash was arrested by the FBI as a possible material witness to the June 1975 shootout on the Pine Ridge Reservation, in which two FBI agents and one Indian activist were killed. Leonard Peltier, eventually sentenced for the murders of the FBI agents, remains imprisoned. No arrest was ever made for the death of the Indian activist during the shootout.

Aquash was found murdered on the Pine Ridge Reservation in 1976. Her body, discovered in February, remained unidentified for several days. The *Bureau of Indian Affairs [IV]* claimed that Aquash died of exposure. Her hands were severed and sent to the FBI's crime laboratory in Washington, D.C., reportedly for identification purposes. Aquash was buried at Holy Rosary Cemetery at Pine Ridge before the FBI announced her identity and notified her family.

Her family hired an independent pathologist from St. Paul, Minnesota, who revealed that a .32 caliber bullet, fired from a gun placed against the base of her skull, was the cause of her death.

Many AIM activists suspected that the FBI was directly implicated in the death of Aquash. Other activists were suspicious that some AIM members, believing rumors that Aquash was an FBI infiltrator, might have had a connection to her death. In 2000, AIM activist *Russell Means* gave testimony to a federal grand jury about her death. He named AIM activist Vernon Bellecourt as the person who ordered the murder and identified three other individuals as the perpetrators. To date, no one has been arrested or prosecuted for her murder, which remains unsolved.

Banks, Dennis

Dennis Banks, a Chippewa, was one of the original founders of the *American Indian Movement [IV]* (AIM). He was born in 1932 on the Leech Lake Reservation in northern Minnesota. Banks, with Oglala *Lakota [III]* Russell *Means*, became one of the most visible leaders of AIM. Following the 1973 *Wounded Knee Occupation [IV]*, Banks, Means, and other AIM activists were charged with assault, conspiracy, and larceny. Banks himself faced the possibility of 85 years in prison. The federal prosecution of Banks and Means in St. Paul, Minnesota, in 1974 ultimately resulted in the dismissal of all charges. The federal judge cited the false testimony and altered documents of the FBI as a central factor in his decision.

After the 1975 shootout at the Pine Ridge Reservation, which resulted in the deaths of two FBI agents and an Indian activist, Banks went into hiding. After receiving amnesty from California Governor Jerry Brown, Banks decided to remain in California for several years. During his stay in California, he earned an associate of arts degree from the University of California, Davis. Banks then helped found and also served as director of the Deganawidah-Quetzalcoatl University, the first Indian-Chicano University in the United States.

In 1984, Brown's term as governor ended and Banks was then harbored on the *Onondaga [III]* Reservation near Nedrow, New York. Banks surrendered in 1984 and served 18 months in prison for charges resulting from his 1970s activism in South Dakota. After serving his sentence, Banks worked as a drug and alcohol counselor on the Pine Ridge Reservation.

Today, Banks continues his work as an activist to prevent the desecration of Native Indian graves (see *burial grounds [IV]*) and to fight for the return of tribal sacred objects to their rightful owners.

IN THEIR OWN Words

There has been . . . a new way to express our manhood, and that's been the American Indian Movement to express our Indianness. . . . I was an accountant by trade in Cleveland, Ohio, and in the Dakota way, if you cut your hair, that means you're in mourning. And it is our contention that a lot of Dakotas now, who are misguided, cut their hair because they're mourning, because they lost their Indianness.

—DENNIS BANKS (NOWACUMIG), CHIPPEWA (1932–); TESTIMONY AT WOUNDED KNEE OCCUPATION TRIALS, 1974.

Banks has also acted in several films, including *War Party, The Last of the Mohicans,* and *Thunderheart.* In 1994, he organized a five-month cross-country walk in support of Leonard Peltier, who had been sentenced for the deaths of the two FBI agents at Pine Ridge Reservation in 1976. He remains one of the most respected American Indian activists today.

Big Foot (Spotted Elk)

Big Foot (c.1825–1890) was a leader of the band of *Lakota [III]* who suffered the majority of deaths at the *Wounded Knee Massacre [IV]* in December 1890. Big Foot became leader of his band following the death of his father in 1874. He was known among the Lakota as Spotted Elk and as someone who sought peace. After the War for the Black Hills in 1876–1877, his people surrendered and settled on the Cheyenne River Reservation in South Dakota.

By 1890, most Lakota were incarcerated on reservations in prison camp–like conditions. In this atmosphere the *Ghost Dance [I]* religion, begun by the *Paiute [III]* prophet *Wovoka,* flourished, particularly among groups now composed mostly of widows who danced in the hope of bringing their dead husbands back to life. The Ghost Dance religion taught that the buffalo and the dead relations would return if certain religious practices were maintained. The Indian Bureau outlawed the practice of the religion, as whites in the area felt threatened by its revolutionary message. In 1890, a Lakota named Kicking Bear brought the Ghost Dance to the band on the Cheyenne River. Following *Sitting Bull*'s assassination on December 15, many of his followers left the Standing Rock Reservation in North Dakota; some joined Big Foot at Cheyenne River in South Dakota. Big Foot then led the group toward the Pine Ridge Reservation in South Dakota to seek the protection of *Red Cloud*. On the journey Big Foot contracted pneumonia.

Intercepted by 500 soldiers of the Seventh Cavalry at Wounded Knee Creek, Big Foot's band of around 350 surrendered there under a white flag three days after Christmas in 1890. Big Foot had renounced the Ghost Dance. On December 29, 1890, the troops searched all the groups , confiscating anything they thought might serve as a weapon, including tent stakes and sacred bundles. When one deaf Lakota man accidentally discharged his weapon in the air, the troops opened fire with their machine guns. More than 200 Lakota, including Big Foot, were killed. Thirty-one soldiers were killed, several by friendly fire.

The soldiers chased several dozens of survivors as far as two miles from the scene of the massacre and killed them. Twenty-eight soldiers were awarded the Medal of Honor for their actions at Wounded Knee. One hundred and forty-six Lakota were buried in a mass grave.

Groups travel by horseback in remembrance of the massacre every December. They usually start at Sitting Bull's residence near the North Dakota border and ride through the Badlands to the site of the Wounded Knee massacre in South Dakota on the Pine Ridge Reservation.

Brandt, Joseph

Thayendanegea, meaning "he places together two bets," was an ally of the British during the *American Revolution [IV]*. Also known as Joseph Brandt, he was born in the Ohio Valley in 1742, the son of Tehonwagh-kwangeraghkwa and Margaret. He was educated at the Anglican Mohawk Mission School and Moor's Charity School, which later became Dartmouth College. At age 13, he fought with the British in the French and Indian War. In 1763, Brandt fought for the British again against united Algonquin tribes in *Pontiac's Rebellion [IV]*. His wife, Catherine, was the daughter of a Mohawk sachem.

When choosing between the British or the American rebels in the American Revolution, many tribes allied themselves with the British, because they recognized the Indians' land rights. Joseph Brandt allied himself with the British and was instrumental in gaining the support of other Iroquois groups for the British cause. The British had told Brandt that Mohawk lands would be returned to them as a reward for their alliance. Commissioned as a colonel by the British, he succeeded in winning over the Mohawk, *Seneca [III]*, *Onondaga [III]*, and *Cayuga [III]*, while the *Oneida*

Joseph Brandt, also known as Thayendanegea, circa 1776. *Library of Congress.*

51

[III] and *Tuscarora [III]*, on the other hand, supported the American rebels. This caused a division in the *Iroquois League [IV]* that was never repaired.

In the course of the war, Americans torched Iroquois settlements and many Indians fled with Joseph Brandt to Canada. Both the British and Americans deserted the tribes who had fought with them. Afterwards, the border between the United States and Canada was drawn through the middle of Iroquois country without their consent, although Brandt was able to secure lands in Canada for his people. He later promoted the concept of a pan-tribal Confederacy to defend lands after the war. He died on November 24, 1807.

IN THEIR OWN

Words

Among us we have no prisons, we have no pompous parade of courts; we have no written laws, and yet judges are as highly revered among us as they are among you, and their decisions are as highly regarded.

Property, to say the least, is well guarded, and crimes are as impartially punished. We have among us no splendid villains above the control of our laws. Daring wickedness is never suffered to triumph over helpless innocence. The estates of widows and orphans are never devoured by enterprising sharpers. In a word, we have no robbery under color of the law.

—JOSEPH BRANT (JOSEPH BRANDT; THAYANDANEGA, THAYENDANEGEA), MOHAWK SACHEM AND WAR CHIEF (1742–1807). FROM A LETTER ON THE TOPIC OF LAW WRITTEN IN 1807 TO AN UNKNOWN CORRESPONDENT.

Captain Jack

Captain Jack, or Kintpuash, meaning "having indigestion," was a leader in the *Modoc Conflict [IV]*. He was born around 1840 at Wa'chamshwash Village in California near the Oregon border. In the Ben Wright massacre of 1846, whites killed his father, a chief. As a result, he became leader of his band while still a youth.

California Indians carried out few rebellions, so the Modoc "War" was one of the few conflicts to occur within the state of California. In 1864, a *Modoc [III]* chief signed away most of the Modoc lands and moved to the *Klamath [III]* Reservation in Oregon. Food was scarce, disease rampant, and conflict between the Modoc and Klamath grew. The Modoc requested their own reservation in California, north of Tule Lake. The state and federal government rejected their request.

Kintpuash, nicknamed Captain Jack by whites because he wore a uniform with brass buttons, left the reservation with about 200 followers in 1865 to return to California. The federal government sent troops to round up the Modoc in California in 1872. Gunfire was exchanged in the Battle of Lost River in November 1872. Two soldiers died and one Modoc lost his life.

Captain Jack, or Kintpuash, leader of the 1872–1873 Modoc Conflict. *National Archives.*

Government reinforcements arrived in the form of 309 California and Oregon troops and volunteers, who joined in attacking the Modoc. In the Battle of the Stronghold in January 1873, the troops suffered 11 dead. No Modoc were wounded.

A massive force of 1,000 troops was brought into the conflict and peace negotiations began. About 50 Modoc men fought the thousand-member forces in a series of battles. The white loss of life totaled 64, the Modoc, 18.

During the negotiations in April 1873, Captain Jack drew a gun and killed General Edward Sprigg Canby. Outraged whites called for the extermination of the tribe. Another Modoc leader, Hooker Jim, was caught, and he bargained for his life by offering to lead the troops to Captain Jack's hideout, where he was captured.

Captain Jack and three of his warriors were sentenced to hang in October 1873. Two other Modoc men

IN THEIR OWN *Words*

I am very sad. I want peace quick, or else let the soldiers come and make haste to fight . . . Let everything be wiped out, washed out, and let there be no more blood. I have got a bad heart about those murderers. I have got but a few men and I don't see how I can give them up. Will they give up their people who murdered my people while they were asleep? I never asked for the people who murdered my people . . . I have given up now and want no more fuss. I have said yes and thrown away my country.

—CAPTAIN JACK (VARIANTS OF HIS NAME INCLUDED KEINTPOEES, KEINTPOOS, KINTPOOS, KINTPUAS, KINTPUASH), MODOC CHIEF (C.1837–1873). FROM A LETTER WRITTEN MARCH 6, 1873, DURING THE MODOC CONFLICT.

were imprisoned for life. The day after the hanging, grave robbers dug up Captain Jack's body and embalmed it in order to display it in a carnival tour. The 155 Modoc survivors were exiled to *Indian Territory [IV]* (Oklahoma). That same year, a play called *Captain Jack* toured the United States. In 1909, 51 Modoc were allowed to return to the Klamath Reservation.

Chief Joseph (Joseph Younger, Hinmaton Yalatik, Hin-Mah-Too-Yah-Laht-Ket)

Nez Perce [III] leader Chief Joseph was born in 1841 in the Wallowa Valley of eastern Oregon and followed his father of the same name in assuming leadership of his tribe. His father had converted to Christianity, and Joseph was educated in a mission school. As chief, Joseph encouraged education, abstinence from drinking and gambling, and nonviolence in general. A gold rush in 1861 led to an 1863 proposed treaty that further reduced the land holdings of the Nez Perce Reservation. Joseph refused to sign the treaty. When white homesteaders continued to move onto Nez Perce lands, Joseph protested the intrusions, which led to an investigation by the *Bureau of Indian Affairs [IV]*. President Ulysses Grant in 1873 decided to formally establish the Wallowa Valley as a reservation. White intruders ignored the order and the administration eventually reversed its decision in 1875 due to political pressure. The valley was opened to whites and in 1877, General Howard gave the Nez Perce 30 days to relocate. Chief Joseph refused to surrender to reservation life and led a three-month, 1,500-mile march in an attempt to reach Canada with his people. He hoped to join *Sitting Bull*, who had escaped to Canada with his *Lakota [III]* band the same year. Two hundred warriors fought over a dozen battles with four army columns. Despite the armed conflicts between Nez Perce and U.S. troops, both General William Tecumseh Sherman and General Nelson A. Miles noted the generally nonviolent nature of the resistance. General Sherman commented that Chief Joseph had "spared hundreds of lives and thousands of dollars worth of property that they might have destroyed." The tribe fled through the Bitterroot Mountains, Yellowstone National Park, and the Bear Paw Mountains—a total of four states (Washington, Oregon, Idaho, and Montana).

The group surrendered on October 5, 1877, just 30 miles south of the Canadian border. Many were sick, starving, and freezing. About 275 warriors had died as they fought off 2,000 soldiers who sustained 266 casualties. Chief Joseph pleaded for a return to their homelands but the War Department refused. The 400 Nez Perce, remainder of the 650 who began the march, were imprisoned at Fort Leavenworth, Kansas, where many died of malaria. In 1885, 268 survivors were moved to Oklahoma, where more died. One hundred forty survivors were finally allowed to return to the Northwest, most to the Colville Reservation in eastern Washington. Chief Joseph died at Colville in 1904.

At his October 5, 1877, surrender, Chief Joseph offered one of the most quoted speeches by an Indian leader: "My people ask me for food, and I have none to give. It is cold, and we have no blankets, no wood. My people are starving to death. Where is my little daughter? I do not know. Perhaps, even now, she is freezing to death. Hear me, my chiefs. I have fought, but from where the sun now stands, Joseph will fight no more forever."

Chisholm, Jesse

Jesse Chisholm was a mixed blood *Cherokee [III]* who was born in Tennessee around 1805. His father was a Scottish trader and his mother was a Cherokee. Chisholm immigrated to Arkansas around 1816 and settled near Fort Smith, Arkansas, with a band of Cherokee. He became involved in the fur trade. Chisholm, who spoke 14 Indian languages, served as an interpreter for U.S. military expeditions and as a government interpreter to many Southern Plains tribes.

Chisholm ran three trading posts in *Indian Territory [IV],* at Oklahoma City, Camp Holmes, and Lexington. During the *Civil War [IV]*, he served as an interpreter for the Confederacy but moved to Wichita, Kansas, in order to maintain his neutrality. He married the daughter of a white trader and had 13 children. At the end of the Civil War in 1865, he blazed the Chisholm Trail from Kansas to Texas.

He continued his work as an interpreter and negotiator at Indian treaties, facilitating both the Little Arkansas Treaty in 1865 and the *Treaty of*

Medicine Lodge [IV] in 1867. He died at Left Hand Spring near Oklahoma City in 1868.

Cochise

Cochise, a chief of the Chiricahua *Apache [III]* for part of their decades-long conflict with the United States, was born in Arizona around 1815. Because of their disputes with Mexico, the Apache had been U.S. allies during the Mexican-American War; it was only after valuable resources such as *gold [IV]*, copper, silver, and coal were discovered on Apache land that white Americans began encroaching on their territory. Open conflict began in 1860, when American miners bullwhipped Mimbreno Apache chief (and Cochise's father-in-law) *Mangas Coloradas*, an insult that launched a general Apache uprising. The following year, Cochise was drawn into the conflict when a white rancher wrongfully accused him of theft and kidnapping. Lieutenant George Bascom took a force of 54 soldiers to Apache Pass and called Cochise to a meeting. When Cochise arrived with his brother and two nephews, Bascom attempted to arrest him. Cochise escaped, but Bascom held his family members as hostages. As a bargaining chip, Cochise took white hostages. When peace talks broke down, both sides killed their hostages. (See *Bascom Affair [IV]*). Now joined to the wider Apache resistance campaign, Cochise soon became its leader after Mangas Coloradas's capture and murder in 1863. Cochise fought a relentless guerrilla war against the U.S. Army for several years, retreating to a remote mountainous area. In 1871, he was captured, but managed to escape, and renewed his campaign of resistance.

In 1872, General Oliver Otis Howard, the Indian commissioner, negotiated a new treaty with Cochise, in which the Apache would agree to live on a reservation that Howard promised would be created from the chief's native territory. Cochise died on the new reservation in 1874.

Columbus, Christopher

Christopher Columbus is credited by Europeans with discovering America. He was born in 1451 in Genoa, Italy, and became a seaman in the 1470s. The overland route from Europe to Asia was costly and time consuming, so there was great interest in the possibility of reaching Asia by ship. Columbus devised a plan for reaching the coast of Asia by sailing westward across the Atlantic Ocean. In 1492, King Ferdinand and Queen Isabella of Spain funded his first expedition.

With three ships and a crew of 90, Columbus reached the Bahama Islands in a few months. He believed he had reached Asia—specifically, the islands off Japan and China. Columbus first used the term Indians to refer to the people of the Americas, since he thought he must be near India. Scholars today still debate where his exact landing location was.

The first people he encountered were the Arawak (Taino). Columbus remained on the island for a few weeks while exploring other islands in the area. The Arawak were enslaved and treated brutally by the men that Columbus left in charge. Their limbs were cut off if they did not mine a certain quota of coal. *Diseases [IV]* also decimated the population. Columbus next sailed to Cuba and Hispaniola (now Haiti and the Dominican Republic). He left some of his men there to start a colony. The Arawak shared their food and helped Columbus when one of his ships on the first voyage was wrecked off the coast of Hispaniola.

Columbus led three more voyages to America, but after the second of these voyages, the Spanish arrested him for mismanagement and cruelty to the Indians. He was returned to Spain in chains, and subsequently exonerated. He died relatively unknown in 1506. What he had "discovered" was called the New World by Europeans. Within 300 years of Columbus's

An 1860 painting depicting Columbus's first encounter with Indians. *Library of Congress.*

first voyage, more than 90 percent of the indigenous population of the Americas would die. In recent years, American Indian activists have protested Columbus Day celebrations and asked for Indigenous Peoples events instead.

Crazy Horse (Tashunka Witco)

Crazy Horse (Tashunka Witco) was a major Oglala-Brule *Lakota [III]* leader during the conflicts that erupted on the plains in the years following the *Civil War [IV]*. He was born around 1842 near Rapid City, South Dakota. Records of his family and tribal history were recorded on buckskin. His father was a Lakota spiritual leader and his mother was Brule Lakota. He was also the nephew of Lakota leader Spotted Tail. As a child he was called the "light-haired one, or curly," in reference to his appearance. His complexion was lighter than that of most other Lakota.

He inherited the name Crazy Horse from his father when he was about 16 years old. Following a vision he had around that time, which was interpreted as a sign of his future greatness as a warrior, he began wearing his hair free and wore a stone earring and a headdress with a red hawk feather in it. His face was painted with a red lightning bolt down one cheek and

Crazy Horse and his followers on their way to surrender at the Red Cloud agency in May 1877. *Library of Congress.*

his body was decorated with hailstones. One of his marriages was to a *Cheyenne [III]*; he later became a son-in-law to *Red Cloud*. (Intertribal marriages were somewhat common.) He became the war chief of the Oglala. He was never seriously injured in battle, never wore European-style clothing, and never accepted reservation life. He was very introverted, was thought to be eccentric, and never let himself be photographed.

In 1876, General George Armstrong Custer made an arrogant and fatal mistake at Little Big Horn when he decided to attack more than 2,000 warriors under the command of Crazy Horse and Hunkpapa chief Gall. Custer only had a force of 225 soldiers. After the Battle of Little Big Horn, Indians who were not confined to reservations were hunted relentlessly by U.S. Army troops. Crazy Horse and 800 of his followers were among the last to surrender. Alone among the leaders of the Plains wars, he never signed a treaty with the United States.

In May 1877, Crazy Horse and his group surrendered their horses and guns at the Red Cloud Agency. Shortly after, his wife, Black Shawl, became ill with tuberculosis. Crazy Horse escaped from the reservation to seek treatment for his wife but was recaptured. While in custody at Fort Robinson in September 1877, Crazy Horse was held by Little Big Man and other Indian scouts while U.S. Army Private William Gentles ran his bayonet through him. His last words were recorded: "We preferred our own way of living. We were no expense to the government then. All we wanted was peace, to be left alone . . . they tried to confine me, I tried to escape, and a soldier ran his bayonet through me. I have spoken."

IN THEIR OWN *Words*

We preferred hunting to a life of idleness on our reservations. . . . At times we did not get enough to eat and we were not allowed to hunt. All we wanted was peace and to be let alone. Soldiers came . . . in the winter . . . and destroyed our villages. Then Long Hair (Custer) came . . . they said we massacred him, but he would have done the same to us. . . . Our first impulse was to escape . . . but we were so hemmed in we had to fight. After that I . . . lived in peace; but the government would not let me alone. . . . I came back to the Red Cloud Agency. Yet I was not allowed to remain quiet, I was tired of fighting . . . they tried to confine me . . . and a soldier ran his bayonet through me. I have spoken.
—CRAZY HORSE, OGLALA LAKOTA (C. 1842–1877). HIS LAST WORDS BEFORE DYING.

According to legend, Crazy Horse was buried somewhere near Wounded Knee near Pine Ridge Reservation in South Dakota. After Crazy Horse's assassination, his followers migrated to Canada, where they joined *Sitting Bull*. An 883-foot monument, as big as Mount Rushmore, is being sculpted in the Black Hills of South Dakota to commemorate Crazy Horse, though some Indians object to carving into natural landscapes. He remains an important cultural figure to all American Indians as a leader who resisted reservation life, upheld tradition, and protected his people.

Curtis, Charles

Republican Charles Curtis (1860–1936) served as vice president in the Herbert Hoover administration from 1929 to 1933. He was a career politician who also served in the United States House of Representatives and as a United States senator.

Charles Curtis, left, with a Pawnee Indian in 1928. Curtis, one-eighth Kaw-Osage Indian, was Herbert Hoover's vice president. *Library of Congress.*

Curtis was born on Indian land that was ceded to form North Topeka, Kansas. His father, Oren Curtis, was a white abolitionist and *Civil War [IV]* Union cavalry officer; his mother, Helen Pappan, was one-quarter Kaw-Osage. She was a descendant of White Plume, an *Osage [III]* who had been adopted into the *Kaw [III]* tribe. Curtis was raised on the Kaw Reservation by his maternal grandmother after his mother died when he was three years old. He left the Indian mission school on the Kaw Reservation in 1868 and moved to Topeka, where he finished high school. He studied law, worked as a law clerk, and gained admittance to the Kansas Bar in 1881.

Curtis served eight terms in the United States House of Representative, from 1892 to 1906. Political opponents called him "the Injun." He was the author of the *Curtis Act [IV]* of 1898, which focused on the goal of assimilation by permitting civil government within *Indian Territory [IV]*, but also abolishing tribal governments. The policy allotted the lands of the *Five Civilized Tribes [IV]* of Oklahoma, who had been successful in gaining exemption from the earlier *Dawes Act [IV]* of 1887, which had enacted allotment of other Indian lands. The Curtis Act was unsuccessfully opposed by Oklahoma tribes. Curtis then served, from 1907 to 1929, as the first American Indian United States senator. He served as Republican Party whip from 1915 to 1924 and then as majority leader from 1924 to 1929. In 1924, Curtis sponsored the Indian *Citizenship Act [IV]*, which made American Indians United States citizens, allowing them the right to vote. Curtis supported women's suffrage and national prohibition.

Curtis ran unsuccessfully for the presidential nomination but ran as his party's vice-presidential nominee with Herbert Hoover in 1928. He served as vice president from 1929 to 1933 until Democrat Franklin Delano Roosevelt defeated the Hoover-Curtis bid for a second term. He retired from politics in 1933 and practiced law in Washington, D.C., having served longer in national office than any other politician of the day. He died in 1936.

Deer, Ada

Ada Deer led the *Menominee [III]* Nation in its struggle to regain federal recognition and was later the first American Indian woman to serve as director of the *Bureau of Indian Affairs [IV]*.

Ada Elizabeth Deer was born on the Menominee reservation in rural northern Keshena, Wisconsin, on August 7, 1935, in a one-room log cabin that lacked heat and running water. She was the oldest of nine children, though only five survived childhood. Her father, Joseph, was a Menominee who had been sent to Indian boarding schools for his education and worked in the tribe's lumber mill. Her mother, Constance Wood, was of Scottish-English ancestry, growing up in a wealthy family in Philadelphia that employed servants. She became a nurse against her family's wishes and took a job with the Bureau of Indian Affairs on the Menominee reservation, where she met her husband.

Ada Deer graduated from high school in 1954, the same year Congress passed the Menominee Termination Act, which was to end the federal status of her tribe. Ada Deer won scholarships from the University of Wisconsin, Madison, and from her tribe to attend college. She became the first Menominee student to graduate from the University of Wisconsin, receiving a B.A. in Social Work in 1957. Deer next received an M.S.W. from the School of Social Work at Columbia University in 1961, making her the first member of her tribe to receive a graduate degree.

In 1964, Deer began a three-year job as the community services coordinator for the Bureau of Indian Affairs in Minneapolis. The federal government's *relocation program [IV]* sought to relocate reservation Indians to cities as part of their *termination [IV]* policy. Many cities like Minneapolis experienced a large increase in their population of urban Indians because of these policies.

In the 1970s, Deer led a successful campaign to regain federal recognition for her tribe. The termination of the Menominee's federal status had devastated the tribe economically, socially, and culturally. Because tribal members were unable to pay property taxes, most of its former holdings were sold and the hospital and schools were closed. But in 1970 Deer led a grassroots movement to stop the land sale. She was the co-founder of the Determination of the Rights and Unity for Menominee Shareholders (DRUMS). In this position, Deer led two years of intensive lobbying, which resulted in the Menominee Restoration Act, signed by President Nixon in December 1972. The tribe elected Deer as its chair and she served in this position for two years.

In 1978 and 1982, she ran unsuccessfully for the Wisconsin secretary of state position. She served as a board member of the Native American Rights Fund from 1984 to 1990, and as its chair from 1989 to 1990. In 1991 Deer joined the women's studies program at the University of Wisconsin, Madison. In 1992, she ran as the Democratic candidate for the House seat from Wisconsin's second congressional district but lost to the Republican incumbent.

In 1993, she became the first American Indian woman appointed as the assistant interior secretary for Indian affairs. The Bureau of Indian Affairs has had a long and sometimes troubled relationship with American Indian tribes. Deer approached the task hoping to "make a dent every day." In 1997, Deer left Washington to return to teaching; she is currently the director of the American Indian studies program at the University of Wisconsin, Madison.

Deganawida

Deganawida, called the Peacemaker, was the founder of the *Iroquois League [IV]*. Historians believe he was born around A.D. 1100 near Kingston, Ontario, though some research has indicated it might have been as early as

A.D. 900. Many believe he was a Huron who was adopted by the Iroquois. Some accounts also told of his living among the *Onondaga [III]* and then being adopted by the *Mohawk [III]*. In any case, as an adult, he met the Mohawk *Hiawatha* (Aionwantha). Together they founded the confederacy of Iroquois (Haundenosaunee) tribes. Haundenosaunee meant "people of the longhouse." Deganawida, who had a speech impediment, was believed to have originated the concept, but he used Hiawatha as his spokesperson. The message of alliance was spread among the Mohawk, *Oneida [III]*, Onondaga, *Cayuga [III]*, and *Seneca [III]*. The sixth nation, the *Tuscarora [III]*, joined in the eighteenth century.

Deganawida drafted the Great Law of Peace (Kaianerekowa) that ruled the alliance. It was recorded on wampum, a beaded form of written communication. An oral recitation of the Great Law could take several days. Excerpts of it were translated into English more than 100 years ago.

Many who participated in the *American Revolution [IV]* cited this law as their model. Benjamin *Franklin* followed the Great Law in his 1754 draft of the Albany Plan of Union. The Great Law called for a complex system of checks and balances. Deganawida had experienced a vision in which a giant white pine gained strength from three branches. The federal system of the Iroquois was similar to that of the United States system that followed. Each of the Iroquois nations in the confederacy maintained its own council, whose representatives were nominated by the clan mothers. The Grand Council of 50 members of the league held at Onondaga was drawn from representatives of the individual national councils. Clan mothers could impeach a representative for any abuse of office. Theirs was a power similar to judicial review in the United States federal system. Objections could be raised about proposed measures if they were inconsistent with the Great Law. The league emphasized debate and parliamentary procedure. The United States also borrowed the Iroquois symbol of the eagle with a bundle of arrows in its talons. The bundle of arrows represented that a group of arrows was more difficult to break than a single arrow, symbolizing strength that could be found by uniting with other groups.

The alliance was founded to prevent intertribal warfare and to strengthen the members through mutual support. Deganawida served as the first Pine Tree Sachem in the confederacy, a position chosen by merit.

The Iroquois Confederacy was finally torn apart by the American Revolution because its members were divided in their support. Four of the six Iroquois nations supported the British: the Mohawk, Cayuga, Onondaga, and Seneca. The Oneida and Tuscarora lent their support to the American rebels. The Great Law of Peace endures to this day as one of the oldest forms of participatory democracy.

Deloria, Ella Cara

Ella Deloria (1889–1971) was a renowned anthropologist and linguist who taught at Columbia University for a number of years and became a leading authority of her own *Dakota [III]* culture, heritage, and language. She was born in Wakpala, South Dakota, the daughter of an Episcopalian minister. Deloria attended Oberlin College in Ohio and completed a bachelor's degree from New York's Columbia University in 1915. She worked as a schoolteacher and then for the Young Men's Christian Association (YMCA) before becoming a professor at Columbia in 1929.

While at Columbia, Deloria worked on major studies of the Dakota language, publishing the bilingual *Dakota Texts* in 1932. Her work was instrumental in preserving the Dakota language for future generations. She published a pre-contact history of America in 1944, *Speaking of Indians.* Her novel *Waterlily* was written during the 1940s but not published until 1988, 17 years after her death. She died in 1971 in Vermilion, South Dakota.

Deloria, Vine, Jr.

Vine Deloria, Jr., a Standing Rock *Lakota [III]*, is one of the founders of and most prominent authors of American Indian studies. Born in 1933 in Martin, South Dakota, he served in the Marine Corps for two years before obtaining a bachelor's degree in 1958 from Iowa State University and a theology degree from the Lutheran School of Theology in 1963. He then served as director of the *National Congress of American Indians [IV]*.

He taught in some of the earliest American Indian studies programs and published numerous landmark volumes. One of his earliest and most influential works was *Custer Died for Your Sins: An Indian Manifesto,* published in 1960. His other frequently cited works include *Behind the Trail of*

Broken Treaties, published in 1974; *American Indians: American Justice,* published in 1984; *The Nations Within,* published in 1984; *American Indian Policy in the Twentieth Century,* published in 1985; and *God Is Red: A Native View of Religion,* published in 1992.

Deskaheh (Levi General)

Deskaheh (1873–1925) was an *Iroquois [III]* nationalist who drew attention to issues of his nation's sovereignty in the 1920s. He was a speaker of the Iroquois Grand Council in Ontario in the early 1920s. When the nation vocally asserted its independence from Canadian jurisdiction, the royal government closed the traditional longhouse where representatives met. Facing the possibility of arrest by Canadian police, Deskaheh traveled to the League of Nations in Geneva, Switzerland, to seek redress for his nation. Canada and Great Britain worked to suppress the issue, so Deskaheh never gained the hearing he sought before the international body. Despite the nonresponse from the League of Nations, Deskaheh and his supporters organized a meeting that drew several thousand people in support of Iroquois sovereignty. His last speech, in 1925, offered a poignant summation of his nation's difficulties: "Over in Ottawa, they call that policy 'Indian Advancement.' Over in Washington they call it 'Assimilation.' We who would be the helpless victims say it is tyranny. . . . If this must go on to the bitter end, we would rather that you come with your guns and poison gas and get rid of us that way. Do it openly and above board."

Deskaheh died in the spring of 1925. His U.S. relatives were refused entry into Canada to be by his bedside.

Dull Knife

Dull Knife was a Northern *Cheyenne [III]* war chief and a leader in the desperate flight of the Northern Cheyenne to return to their homelands in Montana from a reservation in Oklahoma. Dull Knife was his *Lakota [III]* name; Tahmelapashme, meaning "morning star," was his Cheyenne name. Born about 1810, he was a participant in the Cheyenne-Arapaho War in Colorado in 1864 and in Lakota *Red Cloud's [III]* war for the Bozeman

Trail in 1866. He was one of the signers of the 1868 Fort Laramie Treaty. He also joined Lakotas *Sitting Bull* and *Crazy Horse* in the battle for the Black Hills in 1876.

A year after the Lakota and their allies defeated General George Armstrong Custer at Little Big Horn, troops chased bands of Lakota and Cheyenne across the plains in order to incarcerate them on reservations. In November 1876, the army, under General George Crook, attacked Dull Knife's camp in the Battle of Dull Knife. Dull Knife and his followers surrendered in May 1877 at Fort Robinson in Nebraska. The Northern Cheyenne expected to be moved to the Lakota Reservation in the Black Hills, but instead they were sent to *Indian Territory [IV]* (Oklahoma) to join the Southern Cheyenne on the Cheyenne-Arapaho Reservation.

Once in Indian Territory, they found little food and rampant malaria. The promises of abundant game were a lie. The government did not deliver promised rations, either. Half the Cheyenne died of malaria and starvation during their first year in Indian Territory.

Dull Knife and 300 survivors escaped from the reservation in September 1877 and undertook a six-week, 1,500-mile flight to their homelands in northern Wyoming and southern Montana. Ten thousand soldiers and 3,000 civilians pursued them. They reached Nebraska before splitting into two groups. Dull Knife led a group of 150 followers, who were too ill and too exhausted to continue, to surrender at Fort Robinson.

When the group learned they would be sent back to Indian Territory, they refused to go. The army locked them in freezing barracks with no food or water until they changed their minds. Three days

IN THEIR OWN

Words

We bowed to the will of the Great Father and went far into the south where he told us to go. There we found a Cheyenne cannot live. Sickness came among us that made mourning in every lodge. Then the treaty promises were broken, and our rations were short. Those not worn by diseases were wasted by hunger. To stay there meant that all of us would die. Our petitions to the Great Father were unheeded. We thought it better to die fighting to regain our old homes than to perish of sickness. Tell the Great Father . . . if he lets us stay here, Dull Knife's people will hurt no one. Tell him if he tries to send us back we will butcher each other with our own knives.

—DULL KNIFE (MORNING STAR; TAHMELAPASHME; WOHEHIV), NORTHERN CHEYENNE WAR CHIEF (C. 1810–1883). STATEMENT TO U.S. ARMY CAPTAIN, 1878.

later, in January 1879, they escaped from the barracks and reservation to seek food and shelter. Troops managed to kill about half the escapees, including Dull Knife's daughter. Dull Knife and his family walked for 18 nights before reaching Pine Ridge Reservation. They ate bark and their own moccasins to survive.

The Northern Cheyenne eventually gained a reservation in Montana in 1884. Dull Knife, however, had died the year before and was buried near the Rosebud River.

Dull Knife, chief of the Northern Cheyenne. *National Archives.*

Franklin, Benjamin

Benjamin Franklin, a framer of the *Constitution [IV]*, acknowledged the influence of the *Iroquois League [IV]* in his work. Franklin was born in Boston in 1706, and worked as a printer. In 1723, he moved to Philadelphia, where his printing company published Indian treaties in small booklet forms that sold well. He was a delegate to the 1753 treaty with the Ohio Indians at Carlisle, Pennsylvania.

The *Iroquois [III]*, as early as 1744, were urging colonies to unite in a manner similar to their six-nation confederacy. At the Albany Congress in 1754, Franklin devised the first model of American government. Franklin acknowledged his debt to the Constitution of the Iroquois Confederacy. The Albany Congress was held in Albany, New York, devised by the British Board of Trade to formalize alliances with the Iroquois League during the French and Indian War. Franklin used the event to call for a union of British colonies in North America. His proposal to establish a colonial union was not adopted but became the germ of an idea in United States colonial history. His revised Albany Plan of Union formed the basis for the *Articles of Confederation [IV]*. He borrowed many details from the Iroquois system, including the tripartite system, a body of 50 representatives, and even the symbol of an eagle with a bundle of arrows in its talons. The arrows represented the difficulty of breaking a bundle of arrows compared to the ease of breaking a single arrow, denoting the safety and strength that unity could bring.

Franklin was judgmental of many Indian ways and supported westward expansion, but he called for moral behavior in European dealings with tribes. Franklin believed in material acquisition in life, and he thought the Indians lacked this value. He also felt that colonial domination was the realization of divine Providence. He believed that the alcohol and disease accompanying white contact would lead to the extinction of the Indians.

He publicly condemned the massacre of Christianized Conestoga Indians by a mob from Paxton, Pennsylvania, in his 1763 publication "Narrative of the Late Massacre in Lancaster County." He called the white mob "Christian white savages." In 1764, the same "Paxton Boys" marched on Philadelphia to exterminate the city's Indians. Franklin led a delegation to the Indian camp to talk peace.

IN THEIR OWN Words

It would be a strange thing if Six Nations of ignorant savages should be capable of forming a scheme for such a union, and be able to execute it in such a manner as that it has subsisted for ages and appears indissoluble; and yet that a like union should be impracticable for ten or a dozen English colonies, to whom it is more necessary and must be more advantageous and who cannot be supposed to want an equal understanding of their interests.

—BENJAMIN FRANKLIN, AT ALBANY CONGRESS, 1754.

While he served in the Pennsylvania assembly, Franklin supported payment for Indian lands rather than forced removals. He supported regulating traders in order to protect Indians from abuses.

In the 1760s, his defense of Indians cost him his seat in the Pennsylvania assembly. Afterwards he served as a colonial representative to England and France. In his 1784 publication, "Remarks Concerning the Savages of North America," Franklin spoke out against the use of the term savages to refer to Indians and referred to positive values in Indian societies.

Franklin died in 1790 just after the United States Constitution, which he had shaped with Iroquois influences, was adopted.

Geronimo

Geronimo was a Chiricahua *Apache [III]* leader in the Apache wars. The Mexicans referred to him as Geronimo, possibly because they appealed to

St. Jerome to assist in defeating him. His Chiricahua name was Goyathlay, meaning "one who yawns." He was born about 1829 near the Arizona and New Mexico border. His mother was a captive among the Mexicans during his childhood. In 1858, the Mexicans killed his mother, his wife, and three of his children in an unprovoked attack.

Geronimo became a chief through merit and fought with the Chiricahua *Cochise* and with the Mimbreno leaders, *Victorio* and *Mangas Coloradas*. His followers viewed him as a medicine man.

The Apache allowed whites to pass through their territory on their way to the California gold rush of 1848, but peaceful relations ended when the Apache were rounded up and placed on reservations. Miners and settlers wanted the Apache imprisoned in camps so they would have freer access to lands in the West. Two incidents of religious persecution sparked the Apache "wars." One involved the killing

Chief Geronimo. *Library of Congress.*

of a medicine man and the other concerned the banning of an Indian ceremonial beverage. In the first incident, in 1881, the army killed a White Mountain Apache prophet, Nakaidoklini. He had been accused of preaching a vision of the resurrection of dead warriors who would overwhelm

IN THEIR OWN *Words*

That night I did not give my vote for or against any measure—without arms we could do nothing. . . . Our chief, Mangas Coloradas, gave the order to start at once in perfect silence for our homes in Arizona, leaving the dead . . . .

I stood still until all had passed; hardly knowing what I would do—I had no weapon, nor did I hardly wish to fight, nor did I contemplate recovering the bodies of my loved ones, for that was forbidden. I did not pray, nor did I resolve to do anything in particular, for I had no purpose left. I finally followed the tribe in silence, keeping just within hearing distance of the soft noise of their feet.

—GERONIMO (GOKHLAYEH, GOYATHLAY [ONE WHO YAWNS]; JERONIMO), CHIRICAHUA APACHE SHAMAN (C. 1825–1909). HE LATER DESCRIBED HIS EMOTIONS ABOUT THE SLAUGHTER OF HIS FAMILY.

the whites. Geronimo and some followers escaped from the reservation and eluded capture for a few years; more than 5,000 troops were needed to chase a few dozen escaped Apache under Geronimo's leadership. In September 1886, however, Geronimo made a final surrender.

The Apache were sent in chains in railroad cars to Fort Marion in Florida. They were forced to cut their hair and wear European clothing. After a year, Geronimo and others were relocated to Mount Vernon Barracks in Alabama. Many died from tuberculosis at both locations.

The state of Arizona refused to allow Geronimo to return. The *Comanche [III]* and *Kiowa [III]* received him on their reservation in *Indian Territory [IV]* (Oklahoma) in 1892, and the remaining Apache were shipped to Fort Sill, Oklahoma. While in Oklahoma, Geronimo joined the Dutch Reformed Church and, in 1907, he dictated his memoirs, *Geronimo's Story of His Life*. He made money selling his photographs at national expositions in St. Louis and Omaha, and he rode in Theodore Roosevelt's inaugural procession in 1905. He died of pneumonia in Oklahoma in 1909 while still a prisoner of war. Three of his children survived him. Geronimo remains a powerful symbol of resistance to European domination.

Handsome Lake (Ganeodiyo)

Handsome Lake was born in 1733 at a *Seneca [III]* village near Avon, New York. He was the half brother of the Seneca chief Cornplanter and an uncle of Red Jacket. In 1799, he had a series of visions that led him to found a new religion that combined Quaker teachings with *Iroquois [III]* traditions. His teachings, known as the Code of Handsome Lake, or Longhouse religion, are still practiced today. Before he began having visions, he was bedridden for four years in a cabin, partially due to the effects alcohol had on his health. After the visions he stopped drinking completely. He became a prophet who urged Iroquois to abstain from the use of alcohol, to practice traditional ceremonies, and to maintain their land in order to retain their culture. He popularized spiritual and ethical concepts such as considering the effects of one's actions on seven future generations and regarding the earth as one's mother. These ideas may have been influenced by the ancient Iroquois Great Law of Peace. Quaker influence may have been reflected in the idea of one God, or the Great Spirit. The Code of

Handsome Lake was published in 1850, after his death, by his son and nephew. He attained more followers after his death in 1815, and today about one-third of all Iroquois attend Longhouse rites.

Hiawatha

The name Hiawatha became known as the fictional character in the writings of Henry Wadsworth Longfellow. The real Hiawatha was a *Mohawk [III]* who helped establish the *Iroquois League [IV]* in the 1100s. Although *Deganawida* conceived of the idea for the League, Hiawatha became his principal spokesperson.

Their idea for a confederacy was based on democratic and representative principles recorded in the Great Laws. The Great Laws were written on wampum, a beaded system of written language. The Great Laws included the formation of a tripartite system of government and a representative body of 50 *Iroquois [III]* representatives from various villages.

LaDuke, Winona

Harvard-educated Winona LaDuke is a nationally prominent American Indian activist fighting environmental racism, which targets Indian lands with uranium mining, strip mining, mercury contamination, toxic waste dumping, and nuclear bomb testing. She lives on the *Anishinabe [III]* White Earth Reservation in northern Minnesota, where she founded and now runs a land recovery project. As Ralph Nader's running mate, she also ran as the vice-presidential candidate for the Green Party in 1996 and 2000.

LaDuke is the daughter of Vincent LaDuke, a Mississippi band member of the Anishinabe from the White Earth Reservation, and Betty Bernstein, a Russian Jewish painter. In 1958, LaDuke's parents married on the White Earth Reservation, 220 miles northwest of Minneapolis. The couple moved to California, where Vincent LaDuke worked as an extra in Hollywood movies. Winona LaDuke was born in 1959. The family lived in an American Indian neighborhood in east Los Angeles. Later, after her parents' divorce in 1964, LaDuke lived with her mother in Ashland, Oregon.

After completing high school in 1976, LaDuke attended Harvard University. A speech she heard by Cherokee activist Jimmy Durham had a great impact on her. She soon began working for Durham, researching the health implications of uranium mining. She spent a summer in Arizona working with *Navajo [III]* who were organizing protests against uranium mining on their reservation. She worked with the International Indian Treaty Council (IITC), a nongovernmental organization of the United Nations. She was just 18 when she testified before the United Nations for the IITC on the issues of mining and multinationals on reservations.

LaDuke completed a degree in native economic development at Harvard in 1982, then attended the Massachusetts Institute of Technology (MIT). She earned a master's degree in rural development from Antioch College in Yellow Springs, Ohio in 1989.

LaDuke returned to live on the White Earth Reservation, working as a high school principal. While serving as principal she began a language immersion program in Anishinabe for preschoolers during the day, and for adults who attended night classes. She also initiated the use of Anishinabe words on reservation road signs.

In 1989, she was a recipient of one of Reebok's first International Human Rights Awards. She took the $20,000 in award monies and founded the White Earth Land Recovery Project (WELRP), which initially had the objective of repurchasing tribal lands that were under white ownership. An 1867 treaty formally acknowledged an 837,000-acre reservation for White Earth, one of seven Anishinabe tribes in northern Minnesota. Questionable sales and foreclosures due to unpaid land taxes reduced the reservation to less than one-tenth its original size. The majority of the reservation fell into white control during the 1880s, when the General Allotment Act led to a further loss of tribal lands. By 1934, only 7,890 acres remained under Anishinabe ownership. Loss of land forced many Anishinabes into even deeper poverty so that by the 1930s more than half the tribal members had fled to urban areas.

Today, only 5,000 of 20,000 tribal members reside on the reservation. Lack of jobs on the reservation is a continuing crisis, and median annual income for tribal members who reside on White Earth is just $3,500 per year. WELRP has repurchased 1,200 acres thus far. A priority exists to recover burial grounds and lands containing endangered species and/or medicinal plants. LaDuke hopes to meet the goal of reacquiring 750 acres a year. WELRP also helps develop projects on the reservation such as a wild rice cooperative and a 200-acre maple syrup project. WELRP operates as a nonprofit organization outside the traditionally male-dominated tribal council.

In 1994, *Time* magazine named LaDuke as one of its "50 Leaders for the Future." LaDuke was named "Woman of the Year" by *Ms.* magazine in 1997. She serves as co-chair of the Indigenous Women's Network (IWN).

LaDuke serves on the board of directors for Greenpeace. She remains committed to encouraging a better society for all Americans, including the first inhabitants. She remains committed to using her educational privileges to benefit her nation.

LaFlesche Picotte, Susan

Susan LaFlesche was the first American Indian woman trained in medical schools as a doctor. She returned to her tribe to work as a physician for the *Omaha [III]* and spent her life working on behalf of her nation.

Susan LaFlesche was born on the Omaha Reservation near Macy, Nebraska, on June 17, 1865. She was the youngest of four daughters. Her father, Joseph LaFlesche (Insta Maza, or Iron Eye), was the son of a French fur trader. Her mother, Mary Gale (Hinnuagnun, or the One Word), was the daughter of an army physician. Joseph LaFlesche was half white and half *Ponca [III]*, while Mary LaFlesche was half white and half Omaha. Her father supported a policy of assimilation for his tribe. A farmer, he encouraged conversion to Christianity and lived in a frame house instead of the traditional Omaha earth lodge. He also sent all his children to white schools.

After completing school on the reservation with Presbyterian and Quaker *missionaries [IV]*, Susan LaFlesche attended the Elizabeth Institute for Young Ladies in New Jersey. In 1882, she returned home to teach. She left again in 1884 to study at the Hampton Normal Agricultural Institute in Virginia, a school for African Americans and American Indians. The institute had been founded in 1868 to educate former slaves; the first Indian students were accepted 10 years later, in 1878. LaFlesche graduated from the institute with honors in the spring of 1886. She was awarded a gold medal for achieving the highest examination score in her class.

The following fall, LaFlesche entered the Woman's Medical College in Philadelphia, Pennsylvania. The Women's National Indian Association

(WNIA), founded by white liberals in 1879, funded all her education expenses. LaFlesche graduated at the head of her medical class of 36 students in the spring of 1889, becoming the first American Indian woman to receive training as a doctor of medicine from white society. (Of course, many tribes had a long tradition of recognizing American Indian women as trained medical practitioners, namely, as medicine women.)

LaFlesche was selected through a competitive examination to serve as a resident physician at the Woman's Hospital in Philadelphia. After a four-month internship in Philadelphia, LaFlesche returned to the Omaha Reservation. She had written the commissioner of Indian Affairs in the spring of 1889, requesting an appointment as physician for the Omaha. She served as a physician for the Omaha Agency from 1889 to 1891, providing medical care as the only doctor for the 1,300 Omaha tribal members. During her first winter, two epidemics of influenza among the Omaha claimed many lives. She also nursed the Omaha through a serious measles epidemic.

In addition to providing medical services, LaFlesche also served as interpreter, advisor, and teacher to the tribe. She implemented public health campaigns against the use of public drinking cups and against the distribution of alcohol among the Omaha.

LaFlesche married Henry Picotte, of Yankton *Lakota [III]* and French ancestry, in 1894. Of the four LaFlesche sisters, Susan LaFlesche was the only one to marry another American Indian, while the others married white men. The couple resided in Bancroft, Nebraska, where she treated both white and Indian patients. They had two sons.

After her husband's death in 1905 from alcohol poisoning, LaFlesche was appointed as a missionary to the Omaha by the Presbyterian Board of Home Missions. She was the sole support for her mother and children. In 1906, her work resulted in a congressional stipulation that every property deed on the Omaha reservation would prohibit the sale of alcohol.

LaFlesche worked to establish a hospital in Walthill, which was opened in 1913. She suffered from a chronic ear infection, which in 1914 was diagnosed as cancer. She had a series of operations, but her health declined drastically, and she died at age 50 on September 18, 1915.

The hospital she helped establish served as a care center for the elderly before being restored in 1989 and renamed the Susan LaFlesche Picotte Center. The hospital displays photos and artifacts from her life. Her medical skills and determination to serve the Omaha nation left a legacy that continues to benefit future generations.

Mangas Coloradas

Mangas Coloradas was a Mimbreno *Apache [III]* leader in the early Apache wars. He was born around 1792 in New Mexico. His name was Spanish for "red sleeves." He was the father-in-law of a later Apache leader, *Cochise.*

In the 1830s, Mexican authorities placed a bounty on all Apache scalps because of raids. In 1837, a group of trappers invited a group of Mimbreno to a feast, then murdered them for their scalps. In 1849, the California gold rush brought more whites to the area, and that year Mangas was publicly whipped by a group of miners. After this event, he and his son-in-law, Cochise, began leading attacks on settlers in his homeland.

In an 1862 battle, Mangas was wounded but recovered in Mexico. In 1863, under a flag of truce, a messenger from the U.S. Army was sent to offer Mangas, then in his 70s, safe conduct to a meeting. When Mangas arrived, he was imprisoned. General Joseph West at Fort McLane let it be known that he wanted the chief dead. Two guards heated bayonets in a fire and pressed them against the feet and arms of a sleeping Mangas. When he jumped up in pain, the soldiers shot him, claiming he had attempted to escape. General West conducted the follow-up investigation in which all the soldiers involved in the incident were cleared. The Mimbreno leader *Victorio* and the Chiricahua *Geronimo*, who had fought under Mangas Coloradas, assumed leadership in the later Apache "wars."

Mankiller, Wilma Pearl (A-ji-luhsgi, Asgaya-dihi [flower and protector of the village])

Wilma Pearl Mankiller, a western *Cherokee [III]* Indian, was the first female chief of the largest American Indian Nation today. Born in 1945, she served as chief of the Western Cherokee from 1985 to 1995.

Mankiller was born November 18, 1945, in the Indian Hospital in Tahlequah, Oklahoma, the capital of the Cherokee Nation. She was the sixth in a family of eleven children. Her father, Charley, was Cherokee, and her mother, Clara Irene Sitton, was Dutch Irish. Her father's family was directly descended from tribal members who were forced to march from the Cherokee homeland in the southeastern United States to what was supposed to be permanent Indian Territory, but later became Oklahoma

State. Their route became known as the *Trail of Tears [IV]* because one in four Cherokee died on the march.

Mankiller grew up in extreme poverty in Oklahoma in a home without electricity or running water. When she was 11 years old, her family relocated to San Francisco as part of the *Bureau of Indian Affairs [IV]* Relocation Program, which aimed to move large numbers of Indians from reservations to urban areas. The program was part of an official federal *termination policy [IV]* that sought to end the legal status of Indian tribes. In her case, the move caused her family to exchange living in rural poverty to living in urban poverty.

Mankiller entered the fifth grade and experienced difficulty in school when other children made fun of her accent and her name (a term for warriors who protected villages and that signifies Cherokee military ranking). The Mankiller family participated in events at the San Francisco Indian Center. Indian centers were an outgrowth of the mass migration of Indians from reservation to urban locations where they offered displaced tribal members from different Indian nations a gathering place and an outlet for cultural continuity.

Mankiller graduated from high school in San Francisco in the summer of 1963. Since no member of her family had ever gone to college, she did not consider that option. Mankiller took a dead-end clerical position after high school. She soon met and married Ecuadoran Hugo Olaya in Reno, Nevada, in November 1963. Their first child, Felicia, was born in August 1964 and another daughter, Gina, was born two years later. During that time, Mankiller suffered from kidney infections, an early sign of the polycystic kidney disease she was later diagnosed with, and which claimed her father's life in 1969. Although her husband wanted to restrict her activities to the home, Mankiller started attending Skyline Junior College and then San Francisco State College, where she studied sociology.

Mankiller continued her involvement in San Francisco Indian Center community projects and, at age 24, worked to raise funds and supplies for the 1969 American Indian *Alcatraz Island occupation [IV]*. Several of her siblings participated in the occupation, which drew national and international attention to the plight of American Indians. The occupation of Alcatraz, begun in November 1969, contributed to the end of the federal termination policy. When the occupation ended in June 1971, the termination policy had been formally rescinded. The involvement at Alcatraz started Mankiller's life of activism and service. She became a fundraiser and legal advocate for the Pit River tribe (see *Achumawi [III]*) in California. She also served as director of the Native American Youth Center in East Oakland.

After her divorce in 1977, Mankiller and her daughters returned to Oklahoma, where she began to work for the Cherokee Nation as their economic stimulus coordinator.

Mankiller earned a bachelor's degree in social work in 1979 from Flaming Rainbow University in Stillwell, Oklahoma. While commuting to the University of Arkansas, Fayetteville, for a master's program in community planning, she had a near-fatal car accident in November 1979. She crashed head-on into another car that was trying to pass from the oncoming lane. The driver of the oncoming car, her best friend Sherry Morris, was killed in the accident. Doctors predicted that Mankiller would spend the rest of her life in a wheelchair, but after 17 operations she regained her mobility. During 1980, a year after the car accident, she noticed an increasing muscle weakness that made it difficult for her to perform daily activities such as hair brushing. During the Labor Day telethon for muscular dystrophy, she realized she was experiencing the symptoms they were describing in the program. Mankiller was diagnosed with myasthenia gravis, a paralyzing nerve disease, and she underwent thymus surgery and steroid therapy in January 1981. A decade later, in 1990, she underwent a kidney transplant, with her brother Don serving as donor. Mankiller faced life-threatening illnesses with courage, and she believes her ordeals strengthened her spiritually.

Chief Wilma Mankiller. *Courtesy Wilma Mankiller.*

She returned to work in January 1981 as director of community development for the Cherokee Nation. She achieved great success with the nationally praised Bell Community Revitalization Project, which built homes and brought running water and utilities to impoverished communities. While working on this project, she met Cherokee Charlie Soap, whom she married in October 1986.

Cherokee chief Ross Swimmer selected Mankiller as his running mate for deputy chief in 1983. Mankiller expected some conservative backlash due to her liberal views and activist past, but she was surprised when campaign attacks focused on her gender. While her candidacy represented a "step forward," Mankiller acknowledged that it was also a "step backward" to precolonial times when the Cherokee were matrifocal and matrilineal, and when the women's council played an important political role.

Mankiller's successful election as deputy chief in August 1983 received national attention. She acknowledged, "Prior to my election, a young Cherokee girl would never have thought that they might grow up and become chief." Mankiller supervised the daily operation of an Indian nation that covered 14 counties. In September 1985, President Ronald Reagan offered Chief Swimmer a position as director of the Bureau of Indian Affairs in Washington, D.C. Consequently, in December 1985, Mankiller, then 40, was sworn in as the first female chief. She met much resistance at the start of her term. Some tribal members thought they just needed to wait two years to remove her from office in the next election, but changed their attitudes during her tenure. In 1987, she successfully ran for the position of chief and won another four-year term. In 1991, she again won reelection, receiving an overwhelming 83 percent of the vote. She decided not to run in 1995 due to poor health.

Mankiller holds honorary doctorates from Yale and Dartmouth Universities. In 1986, she was inducted into the Oklahoma Hall of Fame, elected to the National Women's Hall of Fame, and in 1987, named Woman of the Year by *Ms.* magazine. In 1996, she taught and lectured at Dartmouth College as a Montgomery Fellow. She also battled her lymphoma with chemotherapy and became a grandmother during that time. In 1998, President Bill Clinton awarded her the Presidential Medal of Freedom. Mankiller overcame a childhood of poverty and life-threatening illnesses to become one of the most respected leaders in the country.

Manuelito

Manuelito was chief when the *Navajo [III]* made the transition to reservation life. He was born around 1818 in southeastern Utah. Although he is known by his Spanish name (which means "little Manuel"), his Navajo name as a child was Ashkii Dighin, meaning "holy boy," and as an adult, he was called Hashkeh Naabah, meaning "the angry warrior."

The Navajo avoided major military conflicts with whites by remaining entrenched in their rugged terrain. They negotiated treaties with the United States government in 1846 and 1849. Peace lasted until disputes concerning the overgrazing of soldiers' horses on Navajo lands erupted in 1859. Soldiers destroyed Navajo crops, homes, and livestock. The following year, Manuelito began guerrilla warfare in the region.

After three years of sporadic attacks, Colonel Kit Carson was given orders to collect all the Indians in the state and move them to the desolate Bosque Redondo Reservation near Fort Sumner, New Mexico. In 1864, 8,000 Navajo surrendered, the largest group in all the Indian "wars." The surrendered Navajo were force-marched 350 miles to their new location on what they called the *Long Walk [IV]*. More than 200 Navajo died along the way. Those who made it to the Bosque Redondo Reservation found no food or clothing and overcrowding. More than 2,000 died of disease and starvation there.

In 1868, the Navajo were able to gain a new treaty allowing them to return to a reservation on their homeland. Manuelito served as chief of the Navajo during this transition period from 1870 until his death in 1884.

Navajo chief Manuelito. *National Archives.*

McCloud, Janet

Janet McCloud was one of the key leaders in the fish-in movement, which began in Washington State in the early 1960s. The fish-in movement took a stand regarding the rights of tribes to fish as promised in treaties (see *fishing rights [IV]*).

Janet McCloud was born on March 30, 1934, on the Tulalip Reservation in Washington State. Her childhood was turbulent, marked by alcohol, abuse, and foster homes. McCloud says that her first political action occurred at age six, when she gathered younger children behind her and kept a child molester at a distance.

She had an early first marriage and divorce and later married a Puyallup-Nisqually truck driver, Don McCloud, with whom she had eight children. The family lived in Yelm, a few miles south of the Nisqually River, near Olympia. McCloud's activism began with the issue of American Indian fishing rights in 1961, an activism spurred by an incident that year in which state game wardens broke into her home searching for deer meat.

Washington state officials routinely arrested American Indians for fishing, in direct violation of treaty rights. The 1854 Medicine Creek Treaty guaranteed Northwest Indian tribes unrestricted use of natural resources. With high poverty rates, the permission to fish was a significant contribution to a family's diet. Fish-in protests began as a response to Washington State policy, which tried to use state laws to restrict Indian fishing rights. When her brother-in-law and other men were arrested, McCloud and other women began fishing in their stead.

When McCloud turned to the large *Yakama [III]* tribe for support, she was ridiculed because she was a woman and a half-blood. In 1964, she founded a civil rights organization, Survival of American Indians Association (SAIA), to raise bail funds. She served as editor of the group's newspaper, *Survival News*, which gave an Indian view of the fishing rights controversy. Celebrities like Marlon Brando and Dick Gregory joined the ranks of those who were arrested.

After a decade of protest, the 1974 *United States v. Washington State* decision (more popularly known as the *Boldt* decision after Judge Hugh Boldt) recognized the treaty rights of tribes regarding fishing.

In the 1980s, McCloud established the Northwest Indian Women's Circle, which focused on issues like sterilization abuse and problems with the foster care placement and adoption of Indian children. McCloud was a founding member of *Women of All Red Nations [IV]* (WARN), an offshoot of the *American Indian Movement [IV]*.

McCloud has earned respect through her activism and her role as a mother of 8, grandmother of 35 (including 10 adopted grandchildren), and great-grandmother of 10. McCloud is an elder on whom American Indian communities continue to lean for encouragement, wisdom, and guidance.

Means, Russell

Russell Means, an Oglala *Lakota [III]*, was a founder of the *American Indian Movement [IV]* (AIM). After graduating from Arizona State University in 1967 with an accounting degree, he moved to Cleveland under the auspices of the *Bureau of Indian Affairs [IV]* (BIA) relocation program. The relocation program sought to move massive numbers of American

Indians from *reservations [IV]* to cities as part of a federal policy to terminate the legal status of tribes.

AIM was founded in 1968 in Minneapolis, Minnesota, with a format similar to the Black Panthers. AIM initially sought to address police harassment against American Indians in Minneapolis. Means started the next chapter of AIM in Cleveland, and he became a national spokesperson for the organization. The group drew its first national media attention with a Thanksgiving takeover of a replica of the *Mayflower*, located in Plymouth, Masachusetts. Several symbolic actions and the rapid growth of AIM chapters soon followed. In the summer of 1972, a group, including Means, organized a cross-country march to Washington, D.C., which they named the *Trail of Broken Treaties Caravan [IV]*. The group arrived in Washington in November, near the time of the presidential election, and occupied the BIA national office for six days. AIM acted as a response team, traveling when their assistance was requested.

One call in 1973 came from Gordon, Nebraska, to protest the brutal murder of Raymond *Yellow Thunder*. The two white perpetrators received a manslaughter conviction with probation but no jail time. Also in 1973, elders at the Pine Ridge Reservation in South Dakota called AIM to respond to the civil war being waged by corrupt tribal chair Dick Wilson and his goon squads against some residents. As a protest, AIM decided to occupy the Wounded Knee site—a protest that became a two-month standoff against the FBI and federal military forces. Following Wounded Knee, federal and state authorities charged Means with 37 felonies and 3 misdemeanors. All but 1 of the 40 charges were ultimately dropped.

Means ran for tribal chair in 1974 when Wilson sought reelection. Means won the primary election, but Wilson won the final election by fewer than 200 votes in balloting that the United States Commission on Civil Rights later found to be fraudulent.

Means remained an activist on several issues, including a call for the return of the Black Hills to the Lakota as well as the indigenous peoples' struggles in Central America.

In 1992, he appeared in the movie *The Last of the Mohicans* and, in 1995, a Disney production of *Pocahontas*. In spring 2001, Means announced his candidacy for governor of New Mexico. He remains a viable candidate in the 2002 race.

Momaday, Navarre Scott

N. Scott Momaday was born on February 27, 1934, in Lawton, Oklahoma. His father was *Kiowa [III]* and his mother *Cherokee [III]*. He attended reservation, public, and parochial schools. Momaday received a bachelor's degree in political science from the University of New Mexico in 1958 and a Ph.D. in English from Stanford University in 1963.

He taught English at several California universities, including the University of California at Santa Barbara, the University of California at Berkeley, and Stanford. In 1969, he was awarded the Pulitzer Prize for his novel *House Made of Dawn*. He has published many novels, including *The Way to Rainy Mountain* in 1969; *The Gourd Dancer* and *The Names* in 1976; and *Ancient Child* in 1985. He remains best known as a gifted novelist, and is also an accomplished poet.

Parker, Ely Samuel (Deioninhogawen, Donehogawa; Ha-sa-no-an-da)

Ely Parker (1828–c.1895) was the first American Indian commissioner of Indian affairs, a position he held under President Ulysses Grant. His father, William Parker, was a chief at Tonawanda; his mother was a descendant of both *Handsome Lake* and Red Jacket. Parker served in a *Seneca [III]* delegation to Albany, New York, and while he was there, he met anthropologist Lewis Henry Morgan. In 1851, Parker collaborated with Morgan on the published book *League of the Ho-de-no-sau-nee or Iroquois*.

IN THEIR OWN

Words

*I*t has of late years become somewhat common, not only for the press, but in the speeches of men of intelligence, and some occupying high and responsible positions, to advocate the policy of their (Indians') immediate and absolute extermination. Such a proposition, so revolting to every sense of humanity and Christianity, it seems to me could not for one moment be entertained by any enlightened nation.

—COLONEL ELY SAMUEL PARKER (DEIONINHOGAWEN, DONEHOGAWA; HA-SA-NO-AN-DA), MIXED SENECA CHIEF AND FIRST INDIAN COMMISSIONER OF INDIAN AFFAIRS (1828–C.1895). FROM AN 1871 REPORT BY PARKER ON INDIAN PEACE POLICY.

Parker became a chief in 1851 and led the successful struggle to save the Tonawanda Reservation.

Parker studied law and passed the bar examinations but was denied the right to practice law because he was an American Indian. He then studied engineering and had a successful career as a civil engineer, working on the Erie Canal. Parker served as a colonel in the Union army and as secretary to General Ulysses Grant, and wrote the surrender document at Appomattox that ended the *Civil War [IV]*.

When Grant was elected to the presidency in 1868, he appointed Parker as commissioner of Indian affairs. Parker oversaw the change in policy regarding American Indians called *Grant's Peace Policy [IV]*. Parker drew attention to the ruthless treatment of the Indians, especially those incidents that involved Plains Indians. When food rations promised in treaties were delayed by congressional actions, Parker bought supplies on credit and faced an impeachment trial as a result. Ultimately, he was cleared of all charges. Parker struggled against racial prejudice and people with business interests who sought access to Indian lands and resources during his tenure, as well as critics who wanted to continue their monopoly in appointments of Indian agents. Exhausted by the constant struggles, he resigned in 1871. He married a white woman and had one daughter.

After resigning as commissioner of Indian affairs, Parker was appointed to a position as building superintendent for the New York City Police Department in 1876. He served in this position until his death. He was buried in Buffalo, New York, near his grandfather, Red Jacket.

Peltier, Leonard

Leonard Peltier (b. 1944) was an *Anishinabe [III]* activist in the *American Indian Movement [IV]* (AIM) in the 1970s. In June 1975 he was involved in a shootout with FBI agents on the Pine Ridge Reservation, during which one Indian male activist and two FBI agents were killed. Peltier was convicted of killing the two FBI agents in a 1977 trial in Fargo, North Dakota. His conviction has sparked an international protest calling for his release. Two other codefendants were tried in a separate trial and acquitted by a jury in July 1976.

After the shootout on the Pine Ridge Reservation, Peltier fled to Canada. He was extradited under questionable circumstances. Three conflicting affidavits were collected from government witness Myrtle Poor Bear as the basis for his extradition. She later recanted these affidavits and claimed they were forced. Poor Bear told the court that she had never seen Peltier before meeting him at the Fargo trial, that she had not been allowed to read the three affidavits, and that FBI agents had threatened her and her children with physical harm if she did not sign them. At the trial the defense planned two weeks of testimony but the judge allowed two and one-half days. The only evidence against Peltier at the trial was the affidavits that Poor Bear recanted and one FBI agent who claimed he had seen Peltier from half a mile away. The defense team brought in experts who testified that it was impossible to identify anyone at the distance claimed by the FBI agent. Three teenage Indians testified under cross-examination that the FBI had also coerced their testimony.

Peltier's request for a new trial was turned down by the U.S. Circuit Court in 1978, and by the United States Supreme Court in 1978 and 1986. In 1985, the United States attorney admitted that he could not prove who shot the agents.

Peter Matthiessen published a book in 1983, *In the Spirit of Crazy Horse*, which made a case for Peltier's innocence. The FBI has still withheld more than 6,000 pages of documents from the public, claiming national security reasons. Robert Redford made a documentary in 1992 about the case, *Incident at Oglala*.

Peltier continues to serve two life terms. He was incarcerated first at Marion Federal Penitentiary in Illinois and is now at Leavenworth Federal Penitentiary in Kansas. Former United States Attorney General Ramsey Clark and attorney William Kunstler are among those who have worked on appeals for Peltier. The Eighth Circuit Court of Appeals turned down his third appeal for a new trial in 1993, thereby exhausting his remedies within the United States court system. In 1994, Dennis *Banks* organized a cross-country march on behalf of Peltier. The Walk for Justice ended in Washington, D.C., and asked President Bill Clinton to grant clemency to Peltier, but this appeal was unsuccessful. Leonard Peltier authored a book in 1999, *Prison Writings: My Life Is My Sun Dance*. Those who continue to call for Peltier's release include the European Parliament, Amnesty International, Archbishop Desmond Tutu, the *National Congress of American Indians [IV]*, Coretta Scott King, and the Kennedy Memorial Center for Human Rights.

Pocahontas

Pocahontas (c.1595–1617) was the daughter of the chief of the *Powhatan [III]* Confederacy, an alliance of 32 *Algonquin [III]* bands and more than 200 villages in Virginia. She became an important symbolic figure to white Americans of the friendship many indigenous peoples extended to European Americans. Her deeds of bringing food and supplies to starving white settlers is well documented, but she remains best known in the popular imagination for her alleged rescue of John Smith from execution. Captain John Smith was a leader of the Jamestown settlement. In 1608, when she was 13, she reportedly saved Smith's life by placing her body between his and the Powhatan executioner's. The story is suspicious to some historians because it did not surface in Smith's written accounts until many years later.

A fanciful 19th-century painting depicting the apocryphal (but popular) story of Pocahontas saving the life of English settler John Smith. *Library of Congress.*

In 1612, Pocahontas was taken hostage by whites who wanted to use her to bargain for the release of some Europeans held by the Powhatan. While in captivity at Jamestown, she converted to Christianity and took the name Rebecca. She married widower John Rolfe in 1613.

In 1616, she traveled to England with her husband and was received as the daughter of an emperor by King James I and Queen Anne. The royals reportedly objected to her marriage to Rolfe, not because it was interracial but because it was a union between a commoner, Rolfe, and a royal, Pocahontas.

In 1617, while waiting in Gravesend, England, to board a ship to Virginia, she died of a European disease, most likely smallpox. She was buried at St. George's Parish in Gravesend. Her father died a year later, in 1618. Her son, Thomas Rolfe, returned to Virginia in 1641 but had difficulty gaining permission from white authorities to visit his Powhatan relatives. There are Pocahontas memorials at both Gravesend and Jamestown.

Pontiac

Pontiac (c.1720–1769) worked to establish an intertribal confederacy to prevent a European American invasion of the Old Northwest. He was an early ally of the French in 1755 and was involved in the defeat of the British in the opening battles of the *French and Indian War [IV]*.

Pontiac was born in northern Ohio. His father was *Ottawa [III]* and his mother Chippewa. He had two sons. He was not a hereditary chief but rose to leadership by 1755 through his oratory and battle skills. By 1763, he had formed political alliances with 18 other nations in the area. The French surrendered to the British in 1763, and Pontiac began a rebellion that spring. He led combined forces of the Ottawa, *Huron [III]*, Delaware (see *Lenape [III]*), *Seneca [III]*, and *Shawnee [III]*. On a chosen date, each tribe was to attack the fort nearest to them. An Ojibwa woman betrayed the plans to the British, but Pontiac led a successful 15-month siege against Fort Duquesne that lasted into the spring of 1764. In the unsuccessful siege at Fort Pitt, smallpox–infected blankets and handkerchiefs were sent to the Indians, which started an epidemic.

IN THEIR OWN Words

Englishman, although you have conquered the French, you have not yet conquered us. We are not your slaves. These lakes, these woods, and mountains were left us by our ancestors. They are our inheritance; and we will part with them to none. Your nation supposes that we, like the white people, cannot live without bread and pork and beer. But you ought to know that He, the Great Spirit and Master of Life, has provided food for us in these spacious lakes and on these woody mountains . . .

—PONTIAC (PONTEACH), OTTAWA (c. 1720–1769), CONFRONTING ALEXANDER HENRY IN 1762.

After the rebellion began to disintegrate, Pontiac was forced to move to Illinois. In April 1769, Pontiac was murdered. Some suggest that a Peoria Indian, who had been bribed by the British with whiskey, stabbed him to death. A statue in his memory stands in the lobby of the city hall in Pontiac, Michigan.

Pretty-Shield

Pretty-Shield (1858–1938) was named by her grandfather after a medicine shield. She was born in southeastern Montana and became a well-known medicine woman of the Crow Nation.

She married a scout of Lieutenant Colonel George Armstrong Custer, Goes-Ahead, at age 16. Before marriage she had adopted an orphan baby girl but eventually had five children of her own as well. While mourning the death of a baby daughter, Pretty-Shield had a vision that told her to pursue training in Crow healing techniques.

When she was in her early 70s, Pretty-Shield told her life story to Frank Linderman, who was studying Plains Indians. Her book was published in 1932 under the title *Red Mother*. The title was later changed to *Pretty-Shield: Medicine Woman of the Crows* and is still in print. Her story told of the female experience of Plains Indian life and a medicine woman's practice.

Red Cloud (Mahpiua Luta, Makhpia-sha, Makhpiya-Luta [Scarlet Cloud])

Red Cloud (1820–1909) was a leader of the Oglala *Lakota [III]* during the late stage of the Plains uprisings. Red Cloud and his allies had several victories, compelling the United States to sign the Fort Laramie Treaty of 1868, which recognized Lakota lands that include the Black Hills.

Red Cloud's name refers to the scarlet clouds that appeared at his and his twin brother's birth in northcentral Nebraska. His father died while Red Cloud was an infant, and their maternal uncle helped raise the boys. Red Cloud's reputation as a warrior was well established by more than 80 feats of bravery, including his once returning from battle with an arrow through his body. He rose to the position of principal chief through his feats rather than hereditary lineage. He had five children.

A Dakota peace delegation to Washington, D.C. Seated left to right are Little Wound, Red Cloud, American Horse, and Red Shirt. *National Archives.*

In 1865, conflict heightened on the plains when Red Cloud and other allies refused to sign a treaty that would have granted access to *gold [IV]* fields in Montana through a trail on their lands. Part of the resistance to white encroachment included concerns about the impact such a trail might have on the *buffalo [I]* herds, a central component of the Lakota diet. When the army built forts on Sioux Territories without permission, the Lakota blocked food supplies for two years until an 1868 treaty was signed that resulted in removal of these forts. Various Lakota bands united in the struggle: the Oglala under Red Cloud; the Hunkpapa under *Sitting Bull*; the Brule under Spotted Tail; and the Northern *Cheyenne [III]* and *Arapaho [III]* led by *Dull Knife*. Young warriors of Lakota bands (including *Crazy Horse*) served under Red Cloud and his warriors, who used guerrilla tactics to harass the army.

In 1874, George Armstrong Custer violated the Fort Laramie Treaty by leading a gold-seeking expedition into the Black Hills. The trespassing wave of miners led to the 1875 War for the Black Hills. After the 1876 Indian victory at Little Big Horn, the United States government relentlessly rounded up American Indians onto *reservations [IV]*. Red Cloud was advocating peace with whites by the time of the Little Big Horn conflict, but his son Jack had fought in the battle, so the government accused Red Cloud of supporting the militants. The government relocated Red Cloud to Pine Ridge Reservation in 1878. When he asked for the dismissal of a corrupt Indian agent in 1881, the federal government instead dismissed him as chief at Pine Ridge.

IN THEIR OWN Words

I have heard that there are many troops coming out in this country to whip the Cheyenne, and that is the reason we were afraid and went away. The Cheyenne, Arapahos, and Kiowa heard that there were troops coming out in this country; so also the Comanche and Apaches, but do not know whether they were coming for peace or for war. They were on the lookout and listening and hearing from down out of the ground all the time. They were afraid to come in.

I don't think the Cheyenne wanted to fight, but I understand you burned their village. I don't think that was good at all.

—SATANTA (SET-TAINTE; THE ORATOR OF THE PLAINS; WHITE BEAR), KIOWA (1830–1878). SPOKEN AT THE TREATY OF MEDICINE LODGE.

When the Indian wars on the Plains ended, Red Cloud and his people were crowded onto a reservation with concentration camp conditions, where starvation and disease were rampant. Red Cloud was forced to move to the Red Cloud agency in Nebraska and later to Pine Ridge Reservation in South Dakota. Nearly blind in his old age, Red Cloud was baptized as a Roman Catholic and died in 1909.

Sequoyah (George Gist, George Guess, George Guest; Sequoia, Siwayi, Sogwili [principal bird, sparrow])

Sequoyah (c. 1770–1843) is best known for inventing the *Cherokee [III]* syllabary, a writing system that rapidly offered literacy to his nation. He was born in Taskigi near Fort Loudon, Tennessee. His mother was Cherokee, and some historians believe his father was the Revolutionary War soldier Nathaniel Gist. As a young man, Sequoyah permanently injured his leg during a hunting trip. The consequent arthritis caused him to walk with a limp for the rest of his life. He successfully battled alcohol abuse and became a skilled silversmith. He married a Cherokee woman, Sarah (Sally), in 1815 and had several children. Around 1818 he moved to Pope County, Arkansas, with Chief John Jolly's band.

Sequoyah, circa 1836. *Library of Congress.*

Sequoyah began to work on the Cherokee syllabary as early as 1809. First, he worked to create pictographs for the language but abandoned that method as too inefficient after he had developed 1,000 symbols. Next, he successfully reduced the Cherokee language to 200 symbols to represent syllables in the language, then further reduced that number to 86. He mixed English, Greek, and Hebrew letters in creating the symbols. His writing system was completed in 1821, making him the only individual in recorded history to invent an entire method of writing single-handedly. In 1821, he traveled to the East and demonstrated his system by carrying messages from the Arkansas Cherokee to their eastern relatives. The Cherokee Tribal Council adopted his syllabary in 1821, and awarded him a silver medal for his work. Within months, thousands of tribal members were able to communicate by using the written system. A bilingual newspaper, the *Cherokee Phoenix,* was established in northern Georgia in 1828. At that time, Sequoyah was a member of an Arkansas Cherokee delegation to Washington, D.C., where his invention was celebrated in the mainstream press.

In 1829, Sequoyah moved from lands in Arkansas to *Indian Territory [IV]* in the area of present-day Sequoya County, Oklahoma.

In 1842, he launched a linguistic expedition to find a group of Cherokee who had gone to Texas during the *American Revolution [IV].* He died in August 1843 in San Fernando, Tamaulipas, Mexico, but the exact location of his grave is unknown. His statue sits in the Capitol Hall of Oklahoma and his home is an Oklahoma State historical site. The giant coastal redwood trees known as sequoias were named after him.

Sitting Bull (Tatanka Iyotake, Tatanka Iyotank, Tatanka Yotanka)

Sitting Bull (c.1830–1890) was one of the primary chiefs who negotiated the Fort Laramie Treaty of 1868, which forced the United States to abandon forts and acknowledge *Lakota [III]* land claims, including claims to the Black Hills of South Dakota.

A Hunkpapa Lakota, Sitting Bull was born along the Grand River in the Dakotas near a site the Lakota called "Many Caches," near present-day Bullhead, South Dakota. He was the son of a chief who was also known as Sitting Bull or Four Horns. His name as a child was "Slow" because of his deliberate nature in making decisions, but he received his adult name, adopted from his father's name, at age 14 after counting coup (literally touching an enemy, not killing them). He assumed leadership of the Strong Heart Warrior Society in 1856 and in the same year received a bullet wound that caused him to limp for the rest of his life. He was a formidable warrior as a young man and became a spiritual leader and medicine man as he aged.

IN THEIR OWN Words

What treaty that the white man ever made with us have they kept? Not one. When I was a boy the Sioux owned the world; the sun rose and set on their land; they sent 10,000 men to battle. Where are the warriors today? Who slew them? Where are our lands? Who owns them . . . What law have I broken? Is it wrong for me to love my own? Is it wicked for me because my skin is red? Because I am Lakota, because I was born where my father died, because I would die for my people and my country?

—SITTING BULL, HUNKPAPA LAKOTA CHIEF (C. 1830–1890), TO 1883 SENATE INVESTIGATING COMMITTEE.

Following the 1862 Dakota uprising in Minnesota, whites trespassed on Hunkpapa lands in pursuit of fugitive *Dakota [III]*. Sitting Bull, in charge of the Strong Hearts, carried out guerrilla tactics against the army.

Even after some of the Lakota under Oglala *Red Cloud* and Brule Spotted Tail moved onto reservation lands, Sitting Bull refused to submit to reservation existence. The United States military ordered all Indian bands to report to tribal agencies by January 1876, but most of those who had not already surrendered did not comply.

Sitting Bull had a vision that predicted a victory for Indian forces before the 1876 battle with George Armstrong Custer at Little Big Horn. After performing a Sun Dance for three days, Sitting Bull had a vision of soldiers falling upside down into a Lakota village. The vision symbolized death for the soldiers.

In 1870, the white population in the Dakotas numbered fewer than 5,000. One decade later, the white population had increased to more than 130,000, with approximately 17,000 illegally panning for gold in the Black Hills.

In the 1870s, Sitting Bull and his followers escaped the deplorable conditions on the Great Sioux Reservation by fleeing to Canada, where he was treated as a visiting head of state. He surrendered in 1881 and returned to the United States, where he was taken to the Standing Rock Agency.

Sitting Bull was killed in December 1890, just days before the *Wounded Knee Massacre [IV]*. He was assassinated when 43 tribal police attempted to arrest him. One officer shot Sitting Bull in the head, and another officer shot him through the thigh. The riot that followed his death resulted in the deaths of six police officers and eight of Sitting Bull's followers, including his son.

Sitting Bull. *State Historical Society of North Dakota.*

Squanto (Tisquantum)

Squanto (c. 1580–1622) is remembered by white historians as one of the first Indians to come to the aid of English colonists. He was a member of the Patuxet band of *Wampanoag [III]* on Cape Cod, in Massachusetts. He was kidnapped from New England in 1614 by the English and sold with 20 others at a slave market in Malaga, Spain. A Christian friar reportedly brought Squanto to England to work for a merchant, where Squanto learned English. He was able to return to America on a trading ship before the Pilgrims arrived in 1620. Few Patuxet had survived European epidemics, especially smallpox, which killed thousands of Indians from 1616 to 1619.

Squanto greeted the Pilgrims in English and helped them to survive their first winter in America. The colonists brought barley, peas, and wheat seeds from England. However, the seeds would not grow in the New England area. Squanto taught them how to plant corn and to use fish as fertilizer. He made the first Thanksgiving feast, an Indian tradition, possible in the fall of 1621. He died of an European disease, probably smallpox, in November or early December 1622.

Standing Bear (Mo-Chu-No-Zhi, Mochunozhi)

Standing Bear (c. 1829–1908) came to national attention in 1878 when he led some of his people on a 40-day, 500-mile march from *Indian Territory [IV]*, now the state of Oklahoma, to their lands in northern Nebraska. He

further pressed his claim to live on his traditional lands in the white man's court. The judge decided that the army could not forcibly relocate Indians, and that American Indians were human beings under United States law. The army ignored the ruling.

In 1875, Congress passed an act to forcibly relocate the *Ponca [III]* from Nebraska to Indian Territory. Ponca lands had been erroneously signed over to the *Lakota [III]* in the Fort Laramie Treaty of 1868. In 1877, the army rounded up the Indians and began a forced relocation march. Many Ponca died during the forced marches to Indian Territory as well as after they reached the site. Many tribes and bands were being force marched to Oklahoma as the army rounded them up.

Standing Bear, circa 1905. *Library of Congress.*

One year after their removal from northern Nebraska, one-third of the Ponca had died, including the son of Standing Bear. Standing Bear resolved to bury his son on Ponca traditional lands in Nebraska, so he began the trek northward. After two months of marching, their footprints left a bloody trail in the snow. The Ponca took refuge on *Omaha [III]* land. The army tracked them to Omaha lands and began to force march them southward again.

When they reached Omaha, local citizens obtained a writ of habeas corpus. Federal attorneys argued that Indians were not persons under the United States Constitution and should not be afforded legal protections. In federal court, the judge ruled against the army. Protest letters to Congress resulted in a Senate investigation.

In 1879, Standing Bear conducted a lecture tour in the East to garner further support on behalf of his people. Afterwards, his band was allowed to return home. Standing Bear died in his homeland in 1908.

The Ponca had their tribal status terminated in 1965, although it was restored by an Act of Congress in 1990.

Tecumseh (Tecumtha)

Tecumseh (1768–1813) was a military leader who attempted to create an intertribal response to the invasion of the Ohio Valley by European Americans. He was born near present-day Springfield, Ohio. His father was a *Shawnee [III]* war chief, his mother of *Cherokee [III]* and *Creek [III]* ancestry. Both his father and his mentor, Shawnee chief Cornstalk, were murdered by whites. Before the *American Revolution [IV]*, the British had tried to limit European American expansion to the east of the Appalachian Mountains through royal proclamations and treaties. White settlers, however, ignored these agreements and trespassed into the Ohio Valley and Great Lakes around 1790. At this time a confederation that included the Shawnee, Delaware (see *Lenape [III]*), *Miami [III]*, *Ottawa [III]*, and *Wyandotte [III]* warned the United States government against continued trespassing on their lands. Conflicts between whites, the Indian confederacy, and federal forces broke out. In 1794, the Indian confederacy was defeated at the Battle of Fallen Timbers. In 1795, Ohio and Indiana were ceded at the Treaty of Greenville, a treaty Tecumseh refused to sign.

Tecumseh next attempted to establish a permanent Indian state with the confederation group members. He hoped for a nation that would stretch from Canada to the Gulf of Mexico and serve as a buffer between the different European territories. Territorial governor William Henry Harrison attacked the Indians and burned their village of 12,000 at Prophetstown, or Tippecanoe. Tecumseh was killed in 1813 at the Battle of the Thames in Kentucky. A group of Kentuckians skinned a body they thought was Tecumseh's for souvenirs, although it may be that his warriors hid his body from enemies.

Thorpe, Grace

Grace Thorpe, a member of the Sac and Fox tribes, rose to national prominence as an American Indian leader during the late 1960s Red Power movement of young urban Indians. She continued her activism into the 1990s as a leader of the Native American Environmental Movement.

Thorpe descended from Chief Black Hawk, a leader in the 1832 *Black Hawk Conflict [IV]*. Her father was the 1912 decathlon and pentathlon Olympic athlete Jim *Thorpe*. Her father's medals were confiscated by the Olympic Committee a year after his victory for a technical transgression involving his brief involvement with semipro baseball prior to the Olympics. Many suspected he had been targeted because he was Indian.

The youngest of three daughters, Grace Thorpe was born in Yale, Oklahoma, to Jim and Iva Thorpe in 1921. Also known as No Ten O Quah ("Wind Woman"), she went to the same Indian boarding school that her father attended in Carlisle, Pennsylvania; during World War II, she joined the Women's Army Corps (WACs). Thorpe was a U.S. corporal stationed in New Guinea and Japan at the end of the war, where she served on General Douglas MacArthur's staff. She was married to Fred Seeley for a brief time while in Japan. With two children, a daughter, Dagmar, and a son, Thorpe, she returned to the United States to live in Pearl River, New York, in the 1950s, where she worked selling Yellow Pages ads to businesses.

Thorpe moved to California and began her activism with the 1969 *Alcatraz Island occupation [IV]*. The nineteen-month occupation, which began in November 1969 and ended in June 1971, garnered national and international coverage and became the spark that ignited the Red Power movement. As Thorpe recalled, "Alcatraz made me put my furniture into storage and spend my life savings." Many incorrectly believe that the *American Indian Movement [IV]* (AIM), formed in Minneapolis in 1968, led the occupation. Although some members of AIM, as well as other young Indians from throughout the country, participated in Alcatraz, the occupation was led by young, urban American Indian students from California campuses.

Thorpe was 48 years old at the time of the Alcatraz occupation, an elder compared to the student occupiers. She negotiated with the government for a power generator, water barge, and ambulance service for the island. The ambulance service was in great demand, since numerous injuries occurred due to the crumbling of the building. She also coordinated publicity for the occupation, handling press releases and arranging visits by Hollywood stars such as Jane Fonda, Marlon Brando, Anthony Quinn, and Candice Bergen.

Seventy-four shorter-lived occupations by American Indians followed Alcatraz. Thorpe continued her activism by serving as a press liaison for the March 1970 occupation at Fort Lawton, Washington, which was successful in securing land for the Daybreak Star Cultural Center. She also served as press liaison for an occupation near Davis, California, in November 1970. That occupation resulted in the building of an Indian university, something the earlier occupiers of Alcatraz had hoped to establish. The Davis occupation of the 640-acre old Nike missile base successfully secured the site of Deganawidah-Quetzalcoatl (DQ) University by April 1971, the first university for American Indian and Chicano students.

While residing in California Thorpe also participated in the struggle of Pit River Indians to hold their sacred land in northern California, against the wishes of the federal government and the large Pacific Gas and Electric Company. Pit River Indians had refused a $29.1 million settlement by the government for their traditional lands. In 1972, a settlement was reached that included partial land restoration and a monetary payment.

Thorpe left California to work as a lobbyist for the National Congress of American Indian (NCAI), the largest American Indian civil rights organization in the nation. In that position she tried to get factories to open on reservations in order to provide more Indian jobs while allowing families to remain on the land. In 1971, she cofounded the National Indian Women's Action Corps. In 1974, the U.S. Senate Subcommittee on Indian Affairs hired her as its legislative assistant. She later served for two years in the House of Representatives on the *American Indian Policy Review Committee [IV]*. During this time, she also furthered her education, receiving a paralegal certificate from the Antioch School of Law in 1974 and a bachelor's degree from the University of Tennessee, Knoxville in 1980.

Thorpe returned to the Sac and Fox Reservation in Oklahoma in 1980 and served as a district court judge for the Five Tribes of Oklahoma and also as a health commissioner.

Thorpe served as vice president of the Jim Thorpe Foundation and, with her sister Charlotte, lobbied for restoration of her father's Olympic medals. In 1983, 30 years after her father's death, the International Olympic Committee annulled its previous decree and presented Jim Thorpe's gold medals to the family.

Thorpe has remained an activist throughout her life. In her 60s, with money only from her social security checks, she started a fight against what she called "radioactive racism" when her own tribal government considered storing nuclear waste on tribal land. The federal government and private industry were exerting pressure and making money offers to numerous tribes, trying to persuade them to store nuclear waste on their reservations. Thorpe and other community members convinced their tribal council to withdraw their application for consideration of a nuclear waste repository on reservation land, though it could have brought millions of dollars a year to the reservation.

In 1993, she founded the National Environmental Coalition of Native Americans (NECONA), which urged tribes to establish nuclear-free zones on their reservations. Thorpe's organization was so successful that by 1998 only two tribes, the Ft. McDermitt Paiutes and Skull Valley Goshutes, were still considering nuclear waste storage.

By building on the proud heritage of her father's accomplishments, Grace Thorpe changed environmental policy across the nation and remains a powerful voice for American Indian rights today.

Thorpe, Jim Francis

Jim Thorpe was born in 1888 near Prague, Oklahoma, of Irish, French, and *Potawatomi [III]* ancestry. His mother was a granddaughter of Sauk leader *Black Hawk*.

At *Carlisle Indian School [IV]*, Thorpe became a national football hero, while winning letters in 10 other sports there. After finishing school, Thorpe went on to the 1912 Olympics in Stockholm, Sweden, where he won the decathlon and pentathlon. His medals were taken away when it was revealed that he had played professional baseball during part of a summer in 1911. Some in the general public suspected that his race had been a factor in the decision.

Jim Thorpe in his football uniform at the Carlisle Indian School.
National Archives.

Thorpe played professional baseball for the New York Giants and the Boston Braves for six years beginning in 1913. In the 1920s, he played professional football with the Chicago Cardinals and other teams. He also formed an all-Indian team, the Oorang Indians, which played two seasons for the National Football League.

In the 1930s, he appeared in some movies and then returned to Oklahoma, where he became involved in tribal politics. He joined the Merchant Marines during World War II. In 1951, Burt Lancaster starred in the movie *Jim Thorpe—All American*.

In a 1950 poll of sports writers, Thorpe was named the best athlete of the first half of the twentieth century. He was inducted into college and professional football halls of fame.

Jim Thorpe died in 1953. In 1983, 30 years after his death, his Olympic medals were presented to the Thorpe family.

Victorio (Beduiat, Bidu-Ya)

Victorio was a leader in the *Apache [III]* uprisings of the 1870s. Born in 1825 in southern New Mexico, he served with Apache leader *Mangas Coloradas* and, after Coloradas's death in 1863, assumed tribal leadership.

In 1877, the Mimbreno band of the Apache were given a reservation at Warm Springs in southwestern New Mexico, but that same year the United States government ordered them to move to the San Carlos Reservation in Arizona. Victorio escaped with 300 followers and eluded capture for several years. An 1878 agreement with the United States allowed the Mimbreno to return to Warm Springs Reservation, but they were then moved to the Mescalero Reservation. Victorio escaped again. Victorio and 80 of his Mimbreno followers died in an October 1880 battle with Mexican forces.

Ward, Nancy (Nanye-Hi, "One Who Goes About," Tsistunga-gis-ke, "Wild Rose")

Nancy Ward was the last Ghighua, or "Beloved Woman," an honorary leadership position in the *Cherokee [III]* Nation.

Nanye-Hi was born in 1738 in Chota, the sacred capital, or "mother town," of the Cherokees. Her mother was Tame Deer; her father, Fivekiller, was part Delaware or Leni *Lenape [III]*. Her nickname was Tsistunga-gis-ke or Wild Rose because her skin color was a delicate pink.

Ward married another Cherokee, Kingfisher, while in her teens, and had two children with him. She often accompanied her husband to battle and prepared firearms at his side. In 1755, she went with her husband as part of a group of 500 warriors to the Battle of Taliwa against Muskogean *Creeks [III]* in northern Georgia. When her husband was killed, 18-year-old Ward picked up his weapon and led a charge against the enemy. The Cherokee viewed her brave leadership as the determining factor in their victory. In recognition, she was named Beloved Woman, a lifetime distinction and the highest office to which a Cherokee woman might be selected. It was believed that the Great Spirit used the voice of the Beloved Woman to speak to the Cherokee.

The Cherokee were matrilineal, and their women had a great deal more status and power than European American women of the time. Americans referred to them as a "petticoat government" because of the prominent role women had in civil and war councils. As a Beloved Woman, Ward held a voting position on the general council, leadership of the women's council, decision-making rights regarding the fate of prisoners, and served as the tribe's ambassador and negotiator. Ward spoke for her nation in negotiations with the United States government and counseled against land cessions and removal to the West.

In 1781, when Ward entered peace talks with state representatives at Little Pigeon River in Tennessee, she asked the officials to take the treaty back to their women for ratification. The white men were upset that a woman had been sent to negotiate with them; Ward, in turn, was disappointed that they had not brought their women to the meeting as, among the Cherokee, women had veto and ratification power regarding decisions of war and peace. Ward stated further, "This peace must last forever. Let your women's sons be ours; our sons be yours. Let your women hear our words." Ward negotiated the first treaty the Cherokee made with the new United States government in 1785, the Treaty of Hopewell.

In 1808, under Ward's leadership, the women's council made a statement protesting the sale of tribal lands and instructing the men to keep their "hands off white man's paper talks." In an 1817 document she sent to the general council she wrote, "We do not wish to go to an unknown country, which we have understood some of our children wish to go over the Mississippi, but this act of our children would be like destroying your mothers."

Ward married Irish Scots trader Bryant Ward and the couple had one child. They ran an inn near Chota, on the Ocowee River in eastern Tennessee, and eventually separated. Ward returned to live in Chota in 1824 and was cared for in her old age by her son.

Nancy Ward died on November 19, 1818. As she died, people reported seeing a white light leave her body. She was buried in Polk County near Benton, Tennessee, near the grave of her father, Fivekiller. Ward didn't live to see her people removed to western lands—a removal she fought against in her lifetime—on the forced march called the *Trail of Tears [IV]*.

Winnemucca, Sarah Hopkins (Sally Winnemucca; Thocmetone, Thoc-me-tony [shell flower])

Sarah Winnemucca served as an interpreter and negotiator for the Northern *Paiute [III]* Nation. Her lecture tour inspired others to support American Indian issues.

Sarah Winnemucca was born in 1844 at Humboldt Sink in what later became the state of Nevada. Her father was chief of the Paiute. Her grandfather Winnemucca had escorted Captain John Fremont across the Sierra Nevada to California in 1845.

In 1860, at age 16, Winnemucca was sent to a convent school in San Jose, California. Her school days ended abruptly three weeks later, when white parents complained about the presence of an Indian child, so the nuns sent her home. After attending the convent school, she converted to Christianity and took the name Sarah. She was fluent in English, Spanish, and three American Indian languages.

In 1865, when some white men's cattle were stolen, soldiers massacred the Paiute, including Winnemucca's mother, sister, and baby brother.

Winnemucca worked as an interpreter at Camp McDermitt in Nevada from 1868 to 1871 and later at the Malheur Agency in Oregon. In 1871, she married Lieutenant E. C. Bartlet, whom she left because of his alcoholism. She later married an Indian man, but she left him shortly afterward because he abused her.

In 1872, a new reservation in Oregon was established for the Paiute. Winnemucca accompanied her tribe to the Malheur Reservation, where she worked as an interpreter and taught at the agency school. After the *Bannock Conflict [IV]* in 1878, the Paiute were moved to the *Yakama [III]* Reservation in Washington State.

In 1881, she taught for a year in Vancouver, Washington, where she met and married Lieutenant L. H. Hopkins. Her husband accompanied her on lecture tours in which she sought support for the retention of tribal lands. She spoke in cities throughout New England and the East Coast. Her lectures led to a book published in 1883. *Life Among the Paiutes* was part autobiography, part tribal history, and part political activism. It concluded with a petition that readers could sign and send to Congress. More important, the book was the first volume written in English by an American Indian woman. She continued touring and collecting thousands of signatures on petitions that she sent to Congress, asking that the government fulfill its promised land allotment to the Paiute. Congress passed a bill ordering this action in 1884, but the secretary of the interior refused to sign it.

Starting in 1886, she taught for three years at government-run schools for Paiute students in Nevada. Contrary to the established white-centered curriculum, Winnemucca taught Indian history, culture, and language.

Sarah Winnemucca died of tuberculosis on October 16, 1891, in Monida, Montana. She was buried with Paiute rites, and her obituary appeared on the front page of the *New York Times*. She had been the most famous American Indian woman of her time, though the cause she devoted her life to, reclamation of her tribe's lands, was never achieved.

Wovoka (Jack Wilson)

Wovoka was born in 1856 in Mason Valley, Nevada. His father was a Northern *Paiute [III]* spiritual leader. An earlier Paiute shaman, Wodziwob, had originated the first *Ghost Dance [I]* movement in 1870. As an adolescent, Wovoka lived with a Christian family on a ranch in western Nevada and adopted the name Jack Wilson among whites.

Wovoka caught a severe fever in 1888 and was delirious during a solar eclipse on January 1, 1889. In his delirium, he saw a vision that the dead would return to those who were in mourning if they revived the Ghost Dance, a ritual involving meditation, prayers, singing, and dancing in large circles. His spiritual message, which also advocated the avoidance of white habits (especially alcohol), spread rapidly among Indian boarding schools and reservation communities including the *Arapaho [III]*, *Cheyenne [III]*, *Shoshone [III]*, and *Lakota [III]*. Some considered Wovoka to be the Red Messiah and called him the Red Man's Christ. Other adherents believed that special Ghost Dance shirts could stop bullets.

White authorities felt threatened by the dances, which they saw as revolutionary, and summoned the military to forcibly stop them. These interventions resulted in the assassination of *Sitting Bull* and the massacre of *Big Foot*'s band at Wounded Knee, South Dakota, in December 1890. Wovoka was shocked by the bloodshed and called for peace with whites. The Ghost Dance religion gradually subsided under continued suppression.

Wovoka died in 1932 on the Walker River Reservation in Nevada.

Yellow Thunder, Raymond

In death, Oglala *Lakota [III]* Raymond Yellow Thunder (1921–1972) became a symbol of several American Indians who were murdered in reservation border towns by white locals who were never fully prosecuted for their crimes. The *American Indian Movement [IV]* (AIM) staged a protest over his death that brought national scrutiny of the law enforcement practices of white officials.

Raymond Yellow Thunder was kidnapped by whites in Gordon, Nebraska, on February 12, 1972, stuffed into the trunk of a car, taken to an American Legion Hall, stripped from the waist down, and forced to dance there and later at a Laundromat. Yellow Thunder spent the night in jail for intoxication and was released the next day. Several days later his dead body was found in the cab of a pickup truck on a used-car lot. He had died from blows to the head. Four local whites were arrested, charged with manslaughter—not murder—and given bail. Two men were eventually convicted of the manslaughter charge and were sentenced to one only year's probation but no jail time.

Fifteen hundred AIM supporters participated in a march in Gordon to protest the official unresponsiveness to the murder.

PART III

Nations

American Indians have a different status from other racial minority groups in the United States. They not only have a land base (4 percent of total U.S. land) but are members of sovereign nations within the boundaries of the United States. There are more than 500 Indian nations in the United States today: 229 in Alaska and 329 in the lower 48 states. Other nations and tribes, such as the Colusa, Timuca, and Coohuiltecs, no longer exist, due to a combination of epidemics, wars, enslavement, and the encroachment of white colonizers onto Indian lands.

Of the 500 nations in existence today, many faced harsh challenges to cultural continuity during forced removals from their lands. On the other hand, a few nations (such as the Zuni, Hopi, Pima, Lakota, Mohawk, Onondaga, Seneca, and Penebscot) have been able to continue to live on parts of their traditional sacred lands.

One hundred Indian languages are still spoken today, although at contact there were more than 300 languages from at least eight language groups: the Algonquian language family, Athapaskan, Caddoean, Iroquoian, Muskogean, Penutian, Siouan, and Uto-Aztecan. One-third of American Indians are able to speak their nation's language. Among the nations with the highest percentages of speakers are the Navajo, Iroquois, Inuit, Apache, and Lakota. Only 20 languages, however, are expected to survive the 21st century. The biggest challenge many nations face is that Indian children are no longer raised speaking their language. This English-only trend began when Christian-run American Indian boarding schools in the 19th century forbade the use of native languages. As a result, fluency for many was lost within one generation.

About a third of all Indian nations live on reservations that contain mineral resources, including one-half of the uranium, one-sixth of the natural gas, and one-tenth of the total coal reserves in the United States. Despite this apparent wealth, American Indians remain one of the poorest groups, with one of the lowest standards of living in the United States. Forty-one percent of residents on reservations live below the poverty line.

There are 310 reservations in all, meaning that many tribes do not have reservations. Many reservations are small in size: California, for example, has the highest number of reservations with nearly a hundred, but most are under 200 acres. Only 45 percent of reservation land is actually owned by tribes, with the balance owned by non-Indian individuals and businesses. Today, less than half of the 26 states east of the Mississippi have a reservation; west of the Mississippi, all states except three have reservations. With or without reservations, Indian nations have continued to work to maintain sovereignty.

Any discussion of Indian nations must also address the question of who is an Indian. As is well known, "Indian" is a misnomer, first used by Columbus, who, on arriving in the Caribbean, believed he had reached islands off India. Before European contact, nobody was an Indian.

In the 19th century, the federal government imposed tribal membership based on blood quantum on nations. Tribal membership requirements vary among tribes: some require one-half blood ancestry; others simply proof of descent or residency requirements on the reservation for enrollment. This last requirement has become more problematic since the majority of American Indians do not live on reservations today. In addition, some tribal enrollment is allowed only through a maternal line, or only through a paternal relationship.

In its heyday between 1953 and 1968, the federal government's termination policy drastically affected the questions of what was considered a nation and who qualified as a tribal member. Some tribes lost their status during termination and are still petitioning to regain it. The petition can cost millions and take decades. Some tribes have state recognition or no recognition at all.

The very term American Indian has been criticized for erasing the huge diversity among Indian nations in languages, geographies, traditions, and political organizations. On the other hand, one could argue that intertribal identities are a centuries-long tradition among some, dating back to intertribal leagues, confederacies, and councils. Some individuals identify primarily as members of a particular nation; others seem to have dual identities as both Indians in the intertribal sense and as members of particular nations.

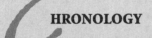

CHRONOLOGY · Nations

1803 *The Louisiana Purchase extends United States land claims west of the Mississippi River. The federal government begins plans to move eastern tribes west of the Mississippi.*

1804–1806 *The Lewis and Clark expedition encourages further white settlement in the West. Their guide is Sacagawea, a Shoshone who, with her infant son in tow, successfully leads their caravan.*

1809 *The Treaty of Fort Wayne, Indiana, is signed. Fraudulent treaties are signed under pressure from Territorial Governor William Henry Harrison.*

1809–1823 *Sequoyah becomes the first person to invent a written language by himself when he develops the Cherokee syllabic alphabet.*

1811 *The Battle of Tippecanoe; Governor William Henry Harrison, who has presidential aspirations, takes a militia of 1,000 members and attacks the intertribal settlement of Prophetstown, which was founded by Tecumseh.*

1812–1815 *The War of 1812 is fought against the United States by the English and their Indian allies led by Tecumseh, who is killed in battle in 1813.*

1813–1814 *The Creek are removed from their lands in the Southeast at the end of the Creek (Red Stick) War.*

1817 *Cherokee lands in Georgia are exchanged for lands in Arkansas Territory. By 1820, several thousand Cherokee migrate west into Arkansas Territory.*

1817–1818 *The First Seminole War.*

1820–1824 *The Kickapoo resist removal from their lands in Illinois Territory.*

1824 *The United States Bureau of Indian Affairs is established within the War Department.*

1827 *The Winnebago uprising in Wisconsin; the Cherokee adopt a constitution; the state of Georgia refuses to acknowledge Cherokee sovereignty.*

1828 *The Cherokee Phoenix, a bilingual weekly publication, is established.*

1829 *Gold is discovered on Cherokee lands.*

1830 *Congress passes the Indian Removal Act, which mandates the removal of eastern tribes to Indian Territory west of the Mississippi (now the states of Arkansas, Kansas, and Oklahoma); the Choctaw cede their lands in Mississippi and are forcibly removed to western Arkansas; influenza decimates tribes in British Columbia, California, and Oregon.*

1831–1839 *The Five Civilized Tribes (Cherokee, Chickasaw, Choctaw, Creek, and Seminole) are force marched from their lands to Indian Territory west of the Mississippi River. The Cherokee march, during which one in four members die along the way, becomes known as the "Trail of Tears."*

1832 *The Black Hawk Rebellion is fought in Illinois and Wisconsin between the united Sauk and Fox tribes led by Black Hawk and the United States military; the United States Supreme Court rules in favor of the Cherokee legal challenge to forced removal from their lands to lands in the West. President Andrew Jackson ignores the ruling and verbally challenges Supreme Court Chief Justice John Marshall to enforce the decision.*

1834 *Mexico secularizes Spanish missions.*

1835–1842 *The Second Seminole Resistance. The Seminole refuse to cede their lands and are forcibly removed from Florida.*

1837 *A smallpox epidemic decimates the Arikara, Hidatsa, and Mandan, leaving fewer than 100 Mandan survivors; the Chickasaw are removed from Mississippi and Alabama to Oklahoma.*

1846–1848 *The U.S.-Mexican War.*

1846–1868 *Apache Wars in New Mexico, led by Mangas Coloradas and Cochise.*

1847–1850 *The Cayuse rebellion in Oregon.*

1848–1849 *The gold rush begins with the discovery of gold in California. The California Indian population drops from more than 120,000 in 1850 to fewer than 20,000 by 1880.*

1849 *The Metis rebellion in Canada.*

1849–1850 *The Pomo are massacred in California. Five Pomo men kill two abusive ranchers. Soldiers cannot find the five males, so they kill an entire village of 130 Pomo men, women, and children who were fishing.*

1850–1851 *The Mariposa rebellion in California, fought by the Miwok and Yokuts tribes against white miners.*

1850–1860 *A cholera epidemic spreads among tribes in the Great Basin and southern Plains.*

1851 *The Treaty of Fort Laramie acknowledges tribal territory of the northern Plains Indians, including the Lakota, Cheyenne, and Arapaho in exchange for an agreement to let whites pass through their lands on the way to California, Washington, and Oregon. Lands* guaranteed to Indian Nations in this treaty eventually form the states of Colorado, Kansas, South Dakota, North Dakota, Montana, Nebraska, and Wyoming; the Yuma and Mojave uprisings in California and Arizona.

1852 Quechan Indians of southern Arizona rebel against United States troops building Fort Yuman on Quechan lands.

1853–1854 The northern portion of Indian Territory is dismantled and Kansas and Nebraska are created from the lands.

1853 The Gadsden Purchase transfers land claimed by Mexico in California, Arizona, and New Mexico to the United States.

1853–1856 The United States signs and breaks a series of 52 treaties.

1854 The United States Indian Affairs commissioner calls for an official end to the Indian removal policy.

1855–1856 The Yakama rebellion in Washington unites the Walla Walla, Umatilla, and Cayuse with the Yakama.

1855–1858 The third Seminole rebellion in Florida.

1858 The Coeur d'Alene or Spokan rebellion, fought in Washington by an alliance of the Coeur d'Alene, Spokan, Palouse, Yakama, and northern Paiute tribes.

1860–1864 The Navajo rebel against forced removals to Bosque Redondo. Kit Carson and his troops burn every Navajo village,

poison Navajo wells, and destroy all Navajo livestock and crops. In 1864, the Navajo are force marched on what becomes known as the "Long Walk." Many die on the way.

1861–1863 Apache uprisings in the Southwest, led by Mangas Coloradas and Cochise.

1861–1865 The Civil War; most Indian tribes remain neutral, but some remnant of the tribes in the Confederate states assist the South after receiving promises of statehood; after the war, these tribes are forced to cede half their lands in Indian Territory as a punishment, though no similar punishment is wielded against Southern states.

1862 A smallpox epidemic on the northwest coast kills more than 200,000 Indians.

1862–1863 Dakota uprising in Minnesota; in the largest mass execution in United States history, 38 Dakota are hanged the day after Christmas (December 26, 1863) in Mankato, Minnesota.

1864 The Sand Creek Massacre (called the Cheyenne-Arapaho War by whites) takes place, when a volunteer force of whites massacres more than 300 Cheyenne and Arapaho, mainly women, children, and elders, who are camped at Sand Creek under a flag of peace; gold is discovered in Colorado; a new federal law allows Indians to testify in court against whites.

1865–1873 The Mexican Kickapoo Uprising in the Southwest.

1866 The United States Congress appropriates Indian lands for construction of a transcontinental railroad; Choctaw chief Allen Wright proposes the name Oklahomaa, meaning "red people" in the Muskeogean language, for Indian Territory.

1866–1868 War over the Bozeman Trail in Montana and Wyoming; united Cheyenne, Lakota, and Arapaho forces led by Chief Red Cloud are successful in battle and secure favorable terms in the 1868 Fort Laramie Treaty.

1867 The Treaty of Medicine Lodge results in the removal of the Cheyenne and Arapaho to reservations in Oklahoma that were created by lands taken from the Five Civilized Tribes; the United States purchases Alaska from Russia.

1868 The Fourteenth Amendment to the United States Constitution gives African American males the right to vote but specifically excludes American Indians; the Fort Laramie Treaty guarantees the Black Hills to the Lakota.

1869 The Treaty of Bosque Redondo returns the Navajo to a reservation on their traditional lands, but on less than one-tenth their original size; President Ulysses S. Grant's Peace Policy is implemented—control of Indian agencies is transferred from army officers to Christian groups; Seneca chief Ely Parker becomes the first American Indian to serve as head of the Bureau of Indian affairs (BIA). He serves two years before resigning. The First Riel Rebellion by Metis occurs in Canada. The transcontinental railroad is completed.

1869–1870 A smallpox epidemic occurs among Canadian Plains tribes, including the Blackfeet, Blood, and Piegan.

1871 Congress formally abolishes the treaty process. The United States Senate had approved 372 treaties previously. Later agreements will not have treaty status or recognize tribes as sovereign nations; western Indians are forbidden to leave reservations without permission from the Indian agent; white hunters begin the indiscriminate slaughter of buffalo herds as a part of a plan to eradicate Indians by eliminating their food source. By the late 1880s, 30 million buffalo have been slaughtered, and fewer than 1,000 buffalo remain.

1872–1873 The Modoc Conflict in California and Oregon.

1873–1874 The Buffalo War is fought by the Cheyenne, Arapaho, Comanche, and Kiowa in an attempt to save remaining buffalo herds from destruction in Oklahoma and Texas.

1874 A United States Army expedition party under George Armstrong Custer trespasses on Lakota lands and discovers gold in the Black Hills. White miners invade the Lakota Territory.

1874–1875 *The Red River War on the southern Plains unites the Comanche, Kiowa, and Cheyenne under Quanah Parker and Santana.*

1875 *Comanche under Chief Quanah Parker surrender at Fort Sill after losing their fight against buffalo hunters backed by the United States Army.*

1876 *The Canadian Indian Act grants Canadian citizenship to Indians willing to relinquish their status as Indians.*

1876–1877 *The War for the Black Hills unites the Lakota, Cheyenne, and Arapaho under leaders Sitting Bull and Crazy Horse. In June 1876, Custer's Seventh Cavalry is defeated at the battle of Little Big Horn. Sitting Bull flees to Canada; Crazy Horse is assassinated while in police custody.*

1877 *The Nez Perce Conflict: The Nez Perce flee more than 1,000 miles toward the Canadian border, after refusing to relocate to a reservation in Oregon per the mandates of a fraudulent treaty. Though promised return to their homeland, the Nez Perce are relocated to Oklahoma and held as prisoners of war for more than eight years before being allowed to return to the Northwest.*

1877–1880 *Victorio leads Apache resistance in the Southwest.*

1878 *The Bannock Conflict in Idaho and Oregon unites the Bannock, Cayuse, and northern Paiute.*

1878–1879 *Northern Cheyenne under Dull Knife flee to their homeland in the Dakota Territory from lands in Oklahoma to which they were forcibly removed.*

1879 *The Carlisle Indian School is founded in order to assimilate Indian students; Ponca chief Standing Bear wins his case in federal court that Indians have a right to sue whites in court.*

1879–1885 *Many white Indian reformer groups are founded, including the Indian Rights Association, Women's National Indian Association, and the National Indian Defense Association.*

1881 *Sitting Bull surrenders at Fort Berthold, North Dakota; white Indian reformer Helen Hunt Jackson publishes* A Century of Dishonor, *which details the unfair and brutal treatment of Indians by the United States government.*

1881–1886 *Geronimo leads Apache resistance in the Southwest.*

1883 *Congress allows tribes to administer judicial decisions in all areas except major crimes, where federal courts have jurisdiction; Paiute tribal member Sarah Winnemucca publishes* Life Among the Paiute *and lectures throughout the East on behalf of her people.*

1885 *Canada outlaws the potlatch ceremony. The law is not repealed until 1951; the last large herd of buffalo is exterminated in the*

Nations (continued)

United States; the Second Metis Rebellion; Indian police units are established by the Bureau of Indian Affairs to enforce government policies.

1886 Geronimo and his band of Chiricahua Apache surrender after more than two decades of struggle.

1887 Congress passes the General Allotment Act (Dawes Act), dividing tribal lands among individual owners and selling surplus land to whites. Tribes lose two-thirds of their land under this act.

1889 Congress splits the Great Sioux Reservation into six smaller reservations, with the surplus land sold to whites.

1890 Paiute religious leader Wovoka founds the Ghost Dance movement; Sitting Bull is assassinated at Pine Ridge Reservation on December 15; More than 200 Lakota preparing for a Ghost Dance are massacred at Wounded Knee on December 28.

Abenaki

Abenaki (AB-eh-nah-kee) meant "easterners, those living at the sunrise," or "dawn land people." They referred to themselves as *Wapanahki* (other spellings included *Abeneaki, Wahanaki,* or *Wapanaki*) and spoke an Eastern Algonquian language. They were an Algonquian tribe with two divisions: the Eastern Abenaki in Maine (Arosagunticook, the Kennebec, *Penobscot,* and Pigwacket) and Western Abenaki in Vermont (the Penacook, Sokoki, and Winnipesaukee). The 17th- and 18th-century Abenaki Confederacy also included the *Maliseet, Micmac,* and *Passamaquoddy.* Descent was patrilineal. Wampum belts recorded treaties and council decisions.

According to their oral history accounts, the Abenaki originally came from the Southwest. However, in the early 17th century, Abenaki were living in northern New England and southern Quebec. At that time there were an estimated 15,000 members: 10,000 Eastern Abenaki and 5,000 Western Abenaki. Today approximately 5,300 Abenaki reside in northern Vermont and southern Quebec.

Spirituality was an important element in Abenaki culture. Sacred sites included the Champlain Valley and Mount Katahdin in Maine. At puberty, boys could seek a guardian spirit by going on a vision quest. Abenaki buried their dead in bark coffins with weapons and tools to use in the afterlife. Triangular structures facing east were placed over graves.

The Eastern Abenaki lived in dome-shaped and square houses with pyramid roofs shingled with bark. Birchbark and elm bark mats were used. In winter, interior walls were lined with bearskins or deerskins for insulation. Smoke holes were created on the roofs, and doors were covered by deerskins. Protective log walls surrounded some villages. The Western Abenaki lived in birchbark longhouses with several families housed in each structure.

A harsh climate meant that the Abenaki produced fewer crops than the more southern Algonquians. The western group grew corn, beans, squash, and tobacco; they hunted caribou, deer, bear, and moose. Maple and birch sap were used to make syrup and sugar. The Abenaki used birchbark and dugout canoes, snowshoes, and toboggans for transportation.

One of the first Europeans they had contact with was Samuel de Champlain in the early 17th century. Contact with Europeans introduced the Abenaki to *diseases [I]* to which they had no resistance; thousands of

Abenaki died from a plague epidemic in 1617 and then from a smallpox epidemic in 1633.

Europeans used Abenaki clothing, canoes, and farming techniques. Many Abenaki became involved in the fur trade and intermarried with the French. In the 19th century, many of the Abenaki spoke French and some even attempted to pass as French in order to avoid racial discrimination. The Abenaki allied themselves with the French in colonial wars. In the *American Revolution [IV]*, however, they were divided and fought for both sides.

The Western Abenaki never signed a treaty with the United States. In 1941, the state of Vermont appropriated traditional hunting grounds and established a wildlife refuge. In 1954, the state of Maine rescinded legislation that prevented American Indians from voting. In the 1960s, fish-in protests were held, as the Abenaki struggled to gain official recognition. State recognition was gained in 1976 but withdrawn the following year.

A traditional harvest dinner is still held every October. Abenaki language is taught in some public schools in Canada, and a handful of native speakers reside in Quebec. The Odanak and Wolinak Reserves in Quebec are provincially and federally recognized.

Achumawi

Achumawi (A-ch-u-ma-we) are also known as the Pit River tribe. Their name means "river people." Numerous petroglyphs dating as far back as 1000 B.C. record tribal events. Their language, Atsugewi, derives from the Palaihnihan branch of the Hokan language. They are classified as part of the Great Basin cultural group.

Their traditional lands were in northeastern California. In the mid-19th century, the Achumawi population was estimated at 3,000. By 1910, their numbers had been reduced to 1,000. Their current population is approximately 1,350.

The Achumawi shared belief structures with some other California groups, including rituals related to adolescence and death. At puberty, boys sought guardian spirits through vision quests. Girls were given a 10-day ceremony at the time of their first menstrual cycle. In their second month of menses, the ceremony was repeated for nine days, with a declining number of days spent on the ceremony in subsequent months. The dead and their possessions were cremated. It was thought that the soul departed for the western mountains.

Houses were cone shaped with tule mats stretched over a pole frame. Wood-frame winter houses were built partly underground. A ladder through the smoke hole at the top served as an entrance.

The Achumawi's allies included the Atsugewi, *Paiute*, Shasta, and Yana. They had some conflicts with the *Modoc*. One of their weapons included arrows poisoned with rattlesnake venom. They used tule-fiber balsa rafts and juniper and pine dugout canoes for transportation and made clothing from shredded juniper bark.

Their first contact with whites was an encounter with American trappers around 1828. But it wasn't until the 1849 gold rush in California that large numbers of whites began occupying their lands. State and private vigilantes hunted Indians throughout California beginning around this time in order to clear the lands of other tenants. Their lands were broken into individual allotments in 1897 by the federal government. Most of these allotments were lost between 1917 and 1930 to the Pacific Gas and Electric Company. Seven small rancherias were created between 1915 and 1938.

The Pit River tribe gained federal recognition in 1976 and adopted a constitution in 1987. Today, unemployment remains high at 60 percent. Recent activism has focused on stopping development on the sacred Mount Shasta in northern California.

Alabama–Coushatta

Alabama (al-uh-BAM-uh), or Alibamu, meant "medicine gatherers, weed gatherers," or "plant." They were culturally related to their neighbors the *Creek* and *Choctaw*. Alabama were part of the Creek Confederacy. Traditionally they had more than 50 clans, but today there are only 12 matrilineal clans in existence. Alabama speak a Muskogean language. The Coushatta were once a neighboring tribe which merged with the Alabama.

Their traditional lands are in Alabama and Mississippi. Although the Alabama population was estimated between 700 and 1,000 in the 18th century, currently there are approximately 2,100 (400 in Louisiana, 800 in Texas, and 900 in Oklahoma enrolled as part of the Creek Nation).

The Alabama and Coushatta most likely descended from the Mound Builders. They may have originated north and west of the Mississippi.

Alabama legend recounts their emergence from a great underground cave. Because of a large tree at the cave's entrance, the group split. Those who emerged on one side became the Alabama, and those who emerged on the other side became the Coushatta.

The sun and other deities were important in Alabama spiritual practices. Other traditions included the Green Corn ceremony, the stomp dance, and the consumption of "black drink" (a purging tea). As with other Creek tribes, their villages were divided between red and white clans: red villages were associated with games and war, and white villages with civic affairs. Chiefs (mikos) came from the white clan and were chosen by merit to head a democratic council, which made decisions by consensus. Adultery was punishable by public whipping and exile. The dead were buried with their heads to the east.

Towns were planned in a square and surrounded by log walls up to several hundred feet long. Towns included a central plaza and a ball-field for team sports. Housing was composed of pole-framed structures with plastered walls and bark-covered or shingled roofs with smoke holes. The outer covering was of mud and grass or mats.

Men hunted with blowguns. Woman made pottery and baskets with geometric designs. Both genders used body paint and pierced their ears and noses. Women parted their hair in the middle and tied each section. Men had four braids: two in front and two in back.

They first encountered Europeans in 1540 when Hernando de Soto arrived in their lands. De Soto found the "Alibamo" tribe in central Mississippi and attacked and killed many of them in a fierce battle. Later, they moved east into present-day Alabama, where they lived at the junction of the Coosa and Tallapoosa rivers. De Soto also found the Coushatta living on the Tennessee River. During the colonial period, the Alabama were allies of the French. Some left their traditional lands after the French were defeated by the British following the *French and Indian War [IV]* in 1763; others left their traditional lands and moved to Louisiana and Texas or joined the *Seminole* in Florida. By the 1780s, the Americans wanted the land in Alabama and the tribe was forced to move west across the Mississippi River into Louisiana around Opelousa. Around 1803, they moved west again, across the Sabine River into northeast Texas. They were settled in the region of the Hasinais Caddo Indians, where they still live today. In 1858, they were given 1,280 acres of land where their reservation is today. Those who remained in Alabama fought with the Creek in the 1813–1814

Creek Rebellion (Creek War). Most survivors of this conflict were resettled by the U.S. government in *Indian Territory [IV]* (Oklahoma) with their Creek allies in the 1830s. Alabamas in Texas helped the Texans in their war with Mexico and were granted land in 1836, which was soon taken away by white settlers. Sam Houston worked to gain a new reservation of 1,280 acres for them in 1842. Three thousand additional acres were added in 1928.

They remained a part of the Creek Nation until 1938 when the Alabama-Quassarte gained federal recognition and several hundred acres of land. The Coushatta tribe in Louisiana gained federal recognition in 1971. Today, the Alabama-Coushatta are one of three federally recognized Indian tribes in Texas. They live on 1,800 acres of tribally owned land in east Texas near Livingston. There are 1,100 enrolled members, of whom 500 live on tribal lands.

Both the Alabama and Coushatta languages are still spoken by elders in Texas and Oklahoma. Some tribal members also continue the practice of pine-needle basket weaving. They hold an annual powwow in June. More recently, in 1993 they won a federal court case that allows their children to wear long hair as an act of religious freedom.

Aleut (see Alutiiq)

Algonquin

Algonquin (Al-GON-kin) is derived from a *Micmac* word meaning "at the place of spearing fish and eels from the bow of a canoe." Algonkin is the term for the original tribe and Algonquian for a language group of tribes. Alternate spellings include Algonquian, and Algonkian. They refer to themselves as *Anishinabeg*, meaning "true men." Descent was patrilineal.

In the 17th century, the Algonquin lived near Quebec and Ontario. Today, they live on reserves in the same area and in New England. There were an estimated 6,000 Algonquin in the early 17th century; today there are approximately 8,000 members.

The Algonquin believed in a creator spirit, Manitou. Adolescent boys and girls went on vision quests to seek guardian spirits who could assist them in hunting or healing. Wooden roof-shaped structures having images of the deceased were placed over some of their graves. An annual feast of the dead was celebrated, as well as a Green Corn festival.

They built rectangular birchbark shelters as well as wigwams. The large rectangular structures were similar to the longhouses of the *Iroquois*. Walls of upright logs often surrounded the village for defense purposes. To construct a wigwam, a number of small trees were tied together in a domed shape, then covered with birch bark that had been sewn together. Swamp grass and furs were used for insulation. Tree branches covered with hides were used to cover floors and served as beds. The roofs had smoke holes.

Because of the harsh climate, their crops played a small role in their diets. They fished year-round and made maple sugar. Watertight containers made of birch bark were used for storing water. They also made unpainted pottery with geometric designs pressed into the clay. They used birchbark canoes, snowshoes, and toboggans for transportation. Wood was used for armor and shields. Birchbark items were decorated with templates of zigzag bands or floral patterns. Clothing was usually made of buckskin or moose skin and was often decorated with fringes. Both genders wore long, braided hair, although women sometimes wore a small cap or band of shells.

The Algonquin were part of many confederacies, including the *Abenaki* Confederacy, the *Powhatan* Confederacy, and the Wappinger Confederacy. They began trading with the French in the early 16th century and later had contact with Samuel de Champlain when he came to North America in 1603. Their numbers were sharply reduced by a smallpox epidemic in the 1670s. After the final French defeat in 1763, they and the British became allies.

Sixty percent of Algonquin in Quebec still speak their language. Tribal records are recorded on wampum belts, which were once used as a form of currency. They are provincially and federally recognized by Canada.

Alutiiq

The term Alutiiq (A-lu-tek) was the name given by Russian colonizers to the peoples living on the Alaskan coast. The Alutiiq refer to themselves, however, as *Unangan* or *Sugpiaq*, meaning "real person." The plural form of the name is Alutiit. They are also referred to as Pacific Eskimos, Pacific Yup'ik, South Alaska *Inuit*, Yuit, or Aleut. Descent was matrilineal. The maritime Alutiit speak the Sugcestun or Suk dialect of the Pacific Gulf Yup'ik branch of Eskimo, an EskAleut language.

Traditionally they inhabited coastal southern Alaska. In the mid-18th century, the population was estimated between 10,000 and 20,000; in 1850, there were just 2,000 Alutiit left. Currently there are approximately 5,000 enrolled members, living in 15 Alutiiq villages. They are comprised of three subgroups: the Chugachmiut of Prince William Sound, the Unegkurmiut of lower Kenai Peninsula, and the Qikertarmiut of Kodiak Island.

The term "Alutiiq" is relatively new. Native speakers and scholars have used it since the early 1980s to refer to both the language and culture of the group of Alaska native people indigenous to Kodiak Island. Beginning in Russian colonial times, most Alutiiqs were called, and have called themselves, Aleuts, although their language is not very similar to the language spoken by Aleuts on the Aleutian Islands. The Russians recognized the differences between the people on the mainland (now called Alutiiq) and those on the islands (Aleuts) but used one blanket term, Aleuts, to distinguish them from other native groups. In addition to a common language and traditional culture, Alutiiqs share a history of Russian colonization and the lasting influence of the Russian Orthodox religion.

Alutiiqs believed that human spirits were reincarnated in new births, and names often reflected this. Ceremonies included memorial feasts, a Messenger's Feast similar to a potlatch, and rituals for whale hunts. Carved and painted masks were used in some ceremonies. Both genders practiced medicine. *Berdaches*, men who cross-dressed as women, were often thought to have special spiritual powers. In addition, some girls were raised as boys and lived as men. There were class divisions of noble, commoner, and slave in Alutiiq society, as in some Northwest groups.

Girls were secluded during the first menstrual period for a few months. Women continued to be secluded in huts during their menses and at the births of their children. Women also tattooed their chins at puberty. Marriages were recognized when gifts were given to the bride's family, and the groom went to live with them. Both genders could have more than one spouse and were allowed to divorce. The dead were wrapped in seal or sea lion skins and kept in a special death house. Nobles were sometimes mummified. Mourners cut their hair and blackened their faces.

Houses were built partly underground and had planked walls. Side sleeping rooms were heated with hot rocks. Several families occupied each house. In temporary hunting or fishing camps, skin boats provided shelter. Chiefs (toyuq) and secondary chiefs (sukashiq) were chosen by elders.

Salmon was a staple of their diet, as were a variety of sea mammals. They hunted whales using a 12-inch poisoned dart. For transportation, they made kayaks of sealskin stretched over a frame of branches, as well as dugout canoes and toboggans pulled by dogs. Clothing included long parkas in cold weather. The conical woven hats worn by men at sea may have been influenced by the *Tlingit*.

The Alutiiq had lived in their traditional lands for at least 7,000 years before the Russians arrived in 1741. However, it was not until 1784 that Russians established their first permanent settlement on Kodiak Island. The Russians forced the Alutiiq to hunt sea otters for pelts for them by holding their wives and children as hostages. The United States took control of Alaska from the Russians in 1867.

In 1989, the Exxon *Valdez* oil tanker spilled 11 million gallons of crude oil, an environmental disaster that affected nearly all Alutiiq villages. In 1991, 756 skeletal remains of ancestors were returned by the Smithsonian after a 50-year battle by the Alutiiq to have them returned.

Many villages can be reached only by air or water. Most Alutiiq today practice the Russian Orthodox religion. Some elders still speak Russian as well as English and Alutiiq. Many still have Russian surnames, and Russian foods are part of the diet. Most villages are small in population, generally having only 100–200 residents. They are federally recognized under the *Alaska Native Claims Settlement Act [IV]*.

The term "Aleut" (pronounced a-LOOT or AL-ee-oot) refers to the people of the Aleutian Islands, which number about 100 bodies of land off the coast of Alaska in the North Pacific. The word Aleut may have been a native word for island. Ancestors of the Aleut and Inuit came to North America around 2500 to 1000 B.C., much later than other Indians who had been in the Americas since before 35000 B.C. The name Alaska came from an Aleut phrase *alaeksu* or *alachka* meaning "mainland." Like the Northwest Coast Indians, Aleut society placed great importance on wealth and rank (more so than the Inuit did). However, the Aleut do not practice potlatch like the Northwest Coast Indians.

The Aleut are coastal people who rely on the sea as their food source. Aleut kayaks, or baidarkas, are made of walrus or seal skins stretched over wooden frames. They lived in barabaras, large group houses built over pits with beams made from driftwood or whale bones.

Anishinabe

The Anishinabe (ah-nish-ih-NAH-bey) are also known as Chippewa, Ojibway, Ojibwa, or Ojibwe. They refer to themselves as *Anishinabe,* meaning "first people." The Anishinabe were comprised of 15 to 23 patrilineal clans. They speak dialects of Algonquian languages.

In the 17th century, they were estimated to number between 35,000 and 70,000. Currently, there are 48,000 enrolled members in Minnesota, 30,000 in Michigan, 25,000 in North Dakota, 16,500 in Wisconsin, and 60,000 in Canada. The Anishinabe are one of the largest tribes in North America.

Like other Algonquian, the Anishinabe believed in a creator spirit, Manitou. Spirits were thought to exist in animate and inanimate objects. Boys sought guardian spirits in four-day fasts or vision quests. Girls could also have visions, but they were not required to go on a vision quest to receive them. Dreams, in general, were considered important.

Other spiritual traditions included the Anishinabe Midewiwin, or medicine dance society, which may have developed in response to European epidemics that decimated the populations. Members wore special medicine bags, called mide. The Midewiwin held secret meetings lasting several days once a year. The proceedings were recorded on bark scrolls using bone instruments and red paint.

Men could have more than one wife, and divorce was easy to obtain. The dead were wrapped in birch bark and buried with tools. They believed the soul of a dead person traveled for four days before reaching a location in the West. Mourning lasted a year.

Housing consisted of a domed wigwam made of mats or birch bark stretched over a pole frame. Each wigwam had a smoke hole in the roof. Larger wigwams housed several families and had a fireplace at each end.

Women raised corn, beans, and squash and used canoes to harvest wild rice, a staple of their diet. Meat was dried and mixed with fat and cherries to make pemmican. They also collected maple sap for sugar that was used in water and as a seasoning.

They decorated their clothing and medicine bags with quillwork and used their teeth to punch designs into birchbark sheets. Most of their clothing was made of buckskin and dyed with red, yellow, blue, and green colors. In the south, women wore woven fiber shirts. Allies included the *Ottawa* and *Potawatomi*, and later, the French. They had conflicts with the *Iroquois* and Kakotas.

The Anishinabe migrated to the Great Lakes region from a more northeastern location before 1200. The fur trade launched by Europeans encouraged tribes to try to expand their boundaries or to relocate as they depleted hunting in their traditional lands. As a result the Iroquois invaded Anishinabe lands from the east, and subsequently, the Anishinabe drove the *Dakota* further west toward the Plains. The Plains Anishinabe, who moved to North Dakota and Montana, adopted many aspects of Great Plains culture. Some bands followed British and French trading posts as they expanded westward.

Many Anishinabe intermarried with the Cree and the French and became known as Metis, meaning "mixed." Anishinabe fought the British in the *French and Indian War [IV]* and in *Pontiac's Rebellion [IV]*, and they fought as allies of the British in the *American Revolution [IV]*. Later they fought against Americans in *Little Turtle's War [IV]*, Tecumseh's Rebellion, and the War of 1812. Plains Anishinabe took part in the Metis Rebellion led by Louis Riel in 1869 (see *Riel Rebellion [IV]*).

Anishinabe ceded most of their eastern land to the United States in 1815 after the final defeat of the British. They then settled on reservations in Minnesota and Wisconsin. Those groups, with the exception of Red Lake, lost 90 percent or more of their lands through allotment and fraud. In 1968, a group of urban Anishinabe founded the *American Indian Movement [IV]* (AIM) in Minneapolis.

Today, there are approximately 30,000 Anishinabe speakers and Anishinabe communities in Michigan, Minnesota, Montana, North Dakota, Wisconsin, and southern Ontario.

Apache

Apache (U-pa-che) comes from the *Zuni* word Apachu meaning "enemy." The Apache name for themselves is *Ndee*, or *Dine'e* (Di-ne) meaning "the people." Residence was matrilocal and descent was by matrilineal clans.

Some scholars argue that the Apache's ancestors, the Athapascans, came from Asia to North America as late as 1000 B.C. One branch of the Athapascans, ancestors of the Apache and *Navajo*, migrated southward. In any case, it seems that the Apache arrived in the Southwest from Canada around A.D. 850. There, the Apache settled in mountains surrounding valleys where earlier *Pueblo* settlements were. Apache bands included the San Carlos, White Mountain, Tonto, and Cibecue in Arizona; the Chiricahua and Mimbreno in Arizona and New Mexico; the Mescalero in New Mexico and Mexico; the Lipan in Texas and Mexico; and the Jicarilla in New Mexico and Colorado.

Apache spirituality recognized protective mountain spirits (ga'an), and a creator, Ussen or Yusn, a giver of life. Mountain spirits were represented by masked dancers, a possible Pueblo influence. They wore masks and body paint and carried wooden swords in their ceremonies. Headdresses of dancers used four colors: white symbolizing pollen, black symbolizing eagle feathers, yellow symbolizing deerskin, and blue for turquoise. They believed that other living things were once people.

According to Apache tradition, White-Painted Woman was the first human. She was celebrated in a four-day puberty ceremony for girls. Both genders learned to ride and how to use the bow and arrow, sling, and spear. Marriages were noted with rituals that confirmed the allegiance a man owed to his wife's family. Once married, men did not speak directly with their mothers-in-law out of respect. However, divorce was easy to obtain. The deceased had their faces painted red and were buried immediately. Their possessions were burned, including their houses and horses, possibly due to a fear of ghosts returning to claim them. Some Apache viewed the afterlife as having two realms: a happy realm for good people and a barren realm for evil ones such as witches.

In 1540, Francisco de Coronado arrived in their land. The Spanish sold the Apache into slavery. After acquiring horses from the Spanish through trade and raiding, the Apache both raided and traded with Spanish and Pueblo settlements.

Mexico won independence in 1821 and, soon after, put a bounty on Apache scalps. The Apache were allies of the Americans in the 1848 Mexican War because of long-standing disputes with Mexico. Following each discovery on Apache lands of valuable resources such as *gold [IV]*, copper, silver, and coal, however, the United States took the lands in forced treaties. Conflict with the United States began in 1860, when, after being bullwhipped by

American miners, Mimbreno chief *Mangas Coloradas [II]* began an uprising. He was captured in 1862 and killed by guards while imprisoned.

In 1871, citizens of Tucson marched to a peaceful camp under the protection of the military and massacred more than 100 Apache there, mainly women and children. Following this incident, President Ulysses Grant implemented a "peace policy" that consisted of force marching Indians to remote reservations to separate them from white settlers. (See *Grant's Peace Policy [IV]*.)

Cochise [II], son-in-law of Mangas Coloradas and leader of the central band of Chiricahua, also engaged in guerrilla warfare against the U.S. Army. Cochise surrendered in 1874. Beginning in 1877, *Victorio [II]* (a Mimbreno Apache) and *Geronimo [II]* (a Chiricahua Apache) led rebellions on the San Carlos Reservation, where starvation and disease had claimed many lives. Victorio's rebellion lasted from 1877 to 1880 and ended with his death in battle in Mexico.

In 1881, Geronimo, a southern band shaman, fled with a group of followers from San Carlos after soldiers had killed a medicine man. Geronimo's rebellion was the last Indian uprising in the United States. After being pursued by one-fourth of the United States Army, Geronimo finally surrendered in 1886. Following that, the federal government sent all Chiricahua, including those who had remained at San Carlos, to prisons in Alabama and Florida. One-fourth of them died during the next few years. After his final surrender, Geronimo and his followers were shipped in chains by train to Fort Pickens, Florida. They were also briefly imprisoned in Alabama. The state of Arizona opposed the return of Apache, so Geronimo and his followers were eventually taken to Fort Sill, Oklahoma, where Geronimo died in 1909, still a prisoner of war.

The Fort Sill Apache today are descended from the 87 who chose to remain in Oklahoma rather than to relocate with more than 100 others to the Mescalero Reservation. The population of Fort Sill Apache today is just under 100. The largest Apache population can be found at White Mountain with approximately 12,500 members, followed by San Carlos with 7,500 members, the Mescalero with 3,500, the Jicarilla with 3,100 members, and the Tonto with 90 members. Elected tribal councils were installed in compliance with the 1934 Indian Reorganization Act (IRA).

Most Apache still participate in many traditional ceremonies, including the girls' puberty ceremony called Na'ii'es, or Sunrise Ceremony, which is held in the summer. Traditional food such as agave or mescal, cactus fruits, acorns, and pine nuts or pinons are still eaten on ceremonial occasions. The Camp Grant Massacre of 1871 is remembered on Apache Memorial Day. The Mescalero Apache, the Apache Tribe of Oklahoma, and the Fort Sill Apache are all federally recognized.

Apache, Chiricahua

Chiricahua (Che-re-ka-wa) is a name taken from the Chiricahua Mountains in southeast Arizona. In the early 1600s, the Chiricahua were living in southwestern New Mexico, southeastern Arizona, and northern Mexico. Current Chiricahua communities include the Mescalero Apache Reservation in southeastern New Mexico and Fort Sill, Oklahoma. In the early 17th century, the Chiricahua population was estimated at 3,000. Today, of approximately 25,000 Apache, 3,500 are Chiricahua and live on the Mescalero Reservation.

There were three Chiricahua bands: the eastern, or Cihene, also known as Mimbreno; the central (Chokonen) band; and the southern Nednai (Enemy People), who lived mainly in Mexico.

Eastern Chiricahua used tipis for some of their housing. They hunted *buffalo [I]* like some Plains tribes and they raised corn. They wore buckskin clothing and moccasins. Women carried knives and, later, ammunition belts. Girls wore their hair shaped around two willow hoops over their

Chiricahua Apache prisoners on an embankment outside their railroad car in Arizona. Among them is Geronimo, seated in the first row, third from the right. *National Archives.*

123

ears. Older women wore their hair parted in the middle in two braids, a common Plains style.

Most Chiricahua live on the 460,000-acre Mescalero Reservation in southeastern New Mexico with the Mescalero and Lipan Apache. The tribal council began functioning after 1934, and a new constitution was adopted in 1964. The majority still speak Apache, though the dialect is more Mescalero than Chiricahua. Traditional puberty rituals for young women are still practiced. The July Fourth rodeo includes the dancing of costumed mountain spirits.

Apache, Jicarilla

Jicarilla (Hee-ka-re-a) is Spanish for "little basket" or "chocolate basket." Descent was matrilineal and residence was matrilocal. In the early 17th century, there were an estimated 1,800 Jicarilla Apache. The population declined to 815 by 1900. Currently, of 25,000 Apache, approximately 3,000 are Jicarilla.

The tribe was divided into two bands: the Ollero, who claimed affinity to the sun and animals, and the Llanero, who identified with the moon and plants. More than other Apache, the Jicarilla were influenced by both Pueblo and Plains cultures. The Llanero lived closer to Pueblos and picked up many of their customs, including farming and pottery making. The Ollero lived closer to the Plains and exhibited elements of that culture, including buffalo hunting and the use of tipis. Both groups wore Plains-style moccasins. Traditional allies for both groups included the *Ute* and Pueblo people. They had conflicts with the *Comanche, Cheyenne, Arapaho*, and *Navajo*.

After the 1848 war with Mexico, the Jicarilla came under the control of the United States. Because the Jicarilla practiced raiding, an 1851 treaty mandated that the Jicarilla remain at least 50 miles from all white settlements. The food and protection that were offered in exchange for their relocation never materialized, so some Jicarilla returned to raiding. By 1873, they were the only southwestern tribe without a reservation. Tribal representatives traveled to Washington, D.C., to lobby for land, but in 1883 they were forced onto the pre-existing Mescalero Reservation. In 1887, they gained an official Jicarilla Reservation of 742,000 acres in northwest New Mexico with a reservation capital of Dulce. However, by 1914, 90 percent of the Jicarilla had tuberculosis. About 400 survived. Many left to live in and blend into local Latino communities.

A constitution was adopted in 1937 as part of the Indian Reorganization Act, which mandated a tribal council composed of 10 positions with a chair and vice chair.

Seventy percent of the Jicarilla are still involved in traditional spiritual practices. Ceremonial relay races between the Ollero and Llanero, symbolizing the race between the sun and moon, are held in mid-September. Most enrolled members live on the reservation, although less than half the tribe, mainly elders, speak Jicarilla.

Apache, Lipan

Lipan (Le-pan) probably meant "warriors of the mountains." Residence was matrilocal, and descent was matrilineal. Before 1700 the Lipan lived in southcentral Texas, but today they live on the Mescalero Reservation in southeast New Mexico. Their population was estimated at 100 Lipan Apache in 1900, though there were likely 10 times that number prior to contact with Europeans.

The Lipan believed death returned one's spirit to the underworld to the site where the people originally emerged. The Lipan Apache lived in hide tipis and sometimes in dome-shaped brush houses called wikiups. They exhibited some aspects of Plains cultures. For example, they used hide containers rather than baskets or pottery for storage. Males wore hard-soled, low-cut moccasins. Both genders braided their hair and plucked their eyebrows. As in Plains cultures, the highest military achievement was to touch an enemy (count coup) rather than to kill.

Before 1700, the Lipan separated from the Jicarilla Apache and migrated southward. With the acquisition of horses brought by the Spaniards, they began hunting buffalo. After the war with Mexico in 1848, Americans living in Texas implemented an extermination policy regarding Indians residing in their state; Lipan who survived went to live in Mexico. In the late 1870s, some Lipans fought with Chiricahua leader Victorio, who was killed with his followers in Mexico.

The Mescalero Apache gained a reservation in 1873 and accepted other Apache refugees, including 37 Mexican Lipan in 1903. The majority of residents still speak Apache, though the dialect is more Mescalero than Lipan. The Lipan language is no longer spoken.

Apache, Mescalero

The name Mescalero (Mes-ka-le-ro) is derived from the mescal plant, or agave, an important part of the Mescalero diet. The Mescalero, who traditionally lived in west Texas, now live on the Mescalero Reservation in southeast New Mexico.

Treaties with Mexico in 1801 and 1832 acknowledged the Mescalero right to land in Mexico and New Mexico. Despite this, however, the Mescalero sided with the Texans and the United States in the 1848 war with Mexico. By 1863, they were forced into a concentration camp at Fort Summer at Bosque Redondo on the Pecos. The land they shared with 9,000 Navajo was overcrowded; starvation and disease claimed many lives. Survivors escaped after two years and went to live in the mountains for seven years. In 1873, the Mescalero gained a reservation on their traditional summer territory, though it was too small to sustain hunting and gathering. In 1880 some Mescalero joined the Chiricahua in guerrilla wars against the United States. The military responded by placing all Mescalero under martial law in penned corrals filled with manure.

From 1895 to 1898, a repressive Indian agent implemented a policy of forced labor, haircuts, and "civilized" clothing and houses. To undermine the power of older women in a matrilocal and matrilineal society, the Indian agent imprisoned grandmothers if their grandchildren did not attend boarding school.

Near the turn of the 20th century, efforts were made by the federal government to take the Mescalero Reservation and make it into a national park. The Mescalero accepted other refugee Apache, hoping that increased numbers would strengthen their struggle to retain their reservation lands. In 1903, 37 Lipan Apache arrived, joined in 1913 by 187 Chiricahua from Fort Sill, Oklahoma. They eventually gained title to the reservation in 1922.

The tribal council consists of a president, vice president, and eight council members elected for two-year terms. The majority speak a Mescalero dialect of Apache.

Apache, Western

A number of Apache bands living in Arizona are classified as Western Apache. These bands include the San Carlos, White Mountain, Tonto, and Cibecue.

Traditionally, Western Apache bands lived in the northwestern corner of Arizona, but most Western Apache today live on two reservations, the White Mountain and San Carlos, each with populations of more than 10,000. Reservations today include the 1.66-million-acre Fort Apache, comprised primarily of Cibecue and White Mountain bands, and the 1.87-million-acre San Carlos Reservation, comprised primarily of the San Carlos band. Both reservations were established in 1871. Camp Verde Reservation in Arizona covers 640 acres and comprised of the Tonto and the Yavapai.

Western Apache were agriculturalists, which they learned from the Pueblo. At least one-quarter of their diet came from the crops they raised, which included corn, beans, and squash. Their allies included the *Quechan*, *Chemehuevi*, *Mojave*, and Yavapai. They had conflicts with the Maricopa, Pai, *Tohono O'odham*, and Navajo.

In the 1850s, most of the repressive government policies against the Apache were focused on the Chiricahua. The White Mountain and Cibecue bands did not live near mines and white settlements, so they were able to avoid most conflicts.

The Tonto faced massacre following the influx of whites after a gold strike at Prescott, Arizona, in 1863. The army and local vigilantes massacred a group of San Carlos in 1871, mainly women, children, and the elderly. The people were force marched onto the San Carlos Reservation. In 1930, the government displaced the San Carlos again when the new Coolidge Dam flooded their entire reservation, including their farmlands. Activists at San Carlos opposed a planned telescope observatory by the University of Arizona on sacred Mount Graham.

The San Carlos Reservation, which is primarily desert, has one of the highest poverty rates in the United States. It is run by a 12-member tribal council adopted in 1934.

Arapaho

Arapaho (uh-RAP-uh-ho) probably came from the *Pawnee* word tirapihu meaning "trader." The Arapaho refer to themselves as *Inuna-ina*, meaning "our people" or *Hinono'eno* meaning "sky people." Arapaho is an Algonquian language.

The Arapaho population was estimated between 3,000 and 5,000 in 1800; currently, the population is about 6,500. More than 3,000 years ago, the Arapaho may have lived in the western Great Lakes region with the *Gros Ventre*, where they farmed in permanent settlements. They might also have been related to the *Blackfeet* and *Cheyenne*. The Gros Ventres migrated westward with the Arapaho in the early 1700s and then migrated to northern Montana and southern Saskatchewan. In the early 18th century, the Arapaho migrated from regions in Minnesota and North Dakota westward to Wyoming, eastern Colorado, and western Kansas. In the 19th century, the group divided into the Northern Arapaho, who settled in Wyoming, and the Southern Arapaho, who settled in Colorado. By this time, they were *buffalo [I]* hunters living in tipis and exhibiting other signs of Great Plains culture such as secret societies, medicine bundles, and the Sun Dance.

They cooked their primary food, buffalo meat, by boiling it in a hole in the ground filled with hot rocks and water. Buffalo could also be preserved by drying it and mixing it with fat and cherries to make pemmican. Women decorated clothing and tipis with porcupine quills and paintings made with vegetable coloring. Designs included diamond shapes with appendages. Arapaho society included eight organized military societies based on age.

The most sacred object of the Arapaho was a long tobacco pipe with a stem the length of a man's arm; that sacred pipe, now centuries old, is today kept by a Northern Arapaho family. The most highly regarded military feat was to touch enemies with the hand or a stick (counting coup) rather than to kill them. The *Lakota, Comanche, Kiowa,* and Southern *Cheyenne* were Arapaho allies. They had sporadic conflicts with the *Shoshone, Ute,* Pawnee, and *Crow*.

The Sun Dance ritual made use of a sacred tree trunk in the center of the ceremony gathering. People danced around the sacred trunk, going without food or sleep for several days while gazing at the sun. Both genders served as spiritual leaders.

Fur traders began entering their lands in the 1730s. Arapaho signed the 1851 Fort Laramie Treaty, but when *gold [IV]* was found in 1858, whites broke the treaty. In 1864, a peaceful group of Southern Arapaho and Cheyenne, mainly women and children, were massacred by United States Army troops at Sand Creek, Colorado, as part of an effort to rid the entire state of Colorado of Indians.

By the 1880s, the buffalo had been hunted to near extinction by whites. The Arapaho were one of many tribes that adopted the *Ghost Dance [IV]* religion, which prophesied the return of the buffalo and the tribe's ancestors. Most of the Ghost Dance songs recorded by historians were those sung by the Arapaho.

The Arapaho signed the 1867 *Treaty of Medicine Lodge [IV]* and were placed on a reservation in Oklahoma. The 1868 Fort Laramie Treaty granted the Northern Arapaho the right to settle with the Lakota on the Pine Ridge Reservation in South Dakota. They remained in Wyoming, hoping to gain their own reservation, but in 1878 they agreed to move to the Eastern Shoshone Wind River Reservation. The Cheyenne-Arapaho Reservation was established in 1869 and about 1,600 Southern Arapaho moved there. The 4-million-acre reservation was opened to white settlement, however, with the 1890 Allotment Act.

Today, the Wind River Reservation of 2,268,008 acres, established in 1863, is comprised of Shoshone and Arapaho tribes in Wyoming. Their current population is approximately 5,700. The 3,000 Southern Arapaho in Western Oklahoma have no tribal land. Unemployment among the Northern Arapaho is about 78 percent, and unemployment among the Southern Arapaho is about 70 percent. Often the National Forest Service tries turning sacred Indian sites into tourist attractions, as it tried to do in 1989 with a site that included a medicine wheel at Big Horn National Forest. The July Sun Dance in Wyoming is intertribal. A few Southern Arapaho still speak the language, and a language program has been implemented at Wind River.

Arikira

Arikira (uh-RICK-uh-ruh) translates as "horn" and refers to the traditional hairstyle of wearing two bones in the hair. Other possible translations are "elk people," or "corn eaters." They call themselves *Tanish* or "Original People." They are sometimes called the Arikaree or Ree. Residence was matrilocal and descent was matrilineal. Arikira is a Caddoan language. They are classified as a Great Plains culture but were more settled than other Plains tribes.

The Arikira may have originated in eastern Texas and parts of Oklahoma, Arkansas, and Louisiana. They migrated farther north than other Caddoan-speaking tribes. They split from the *Pawnee* to move to the central plains into central South Dakota in the 17th century, near two Siouan speaking tribes, the *Hidatsa* and *Mandan*. Today, most Arikira live in western North Dakota. In the late 18th century, the Arikira population was estimated between 3,000 and 4,000, although current enrollment in the

Three Affiliated Tribes (Arikira, Hidatsa, and Mandan) is approximately 6,000.

Most of the Arikira religious festivals were associated with the spirit of "mother corn," a symbol of female fertility and spiritual nurturing. Spiritual practices included vision quests and the use of personal sacred bundles. The keeper of the sacred tribal medicine bundles position was hereditary. Social rank in Arikira culture also had a hereditary component. Arikira had a number of burial rituals in common with other Plains tribes. For example, they wrapped their dead in animal skins and painted their faces red. The deceased were then buried in a sitting position. A mourning period of one year followed each death.

For purposes of defense, villages were surrounded by log walls. The Arikira lived in earth lodges about 40 feet in diameter that housed two or more extended families. Family lodges were grouped around a central, larger, community, ceremonial lodge. Skin tipis were later used during buffalo hunts. Women cultivated corn, squash, beans, sunflowers, and some tobacco. Main sources of transportation included boats constructed of buffalo hides stretched over a willow frame, snowshoes, travois pulled by dogs, and horses. Clothing included winter turbans made of animal skins. Their traditional enemies were the *Lakota*.

The Arikira's first contact with Europeans was with French traders in the 1730s. After acquiring the *horse [I]* in the mid-18th century they ranged farther to hunt *buffalo [I]*. A smallpox epidemic in the 1780s dramatically reduced their numbers and a second smallpox epidemic in 1837 brought them to the brink of extinction. Around 1845, they moved farther north near the Mandan and Hidatsa. The Fort Laramie Treaty of 1851 recognized 12 million acres held among the three tribes. However, in 1870 the Fort Berthold Reservation was established with only 8 million acres. Allotment policies during the 1880s reduced tribal lands even further, to 1 million acres.

In 1934, under the Indian Reorganization Act (IRA), the Arikira merged with the Hidatsa and Mandan and became known as the Three Affiliated Tribes. In the 1950s, the Garrison Dam on the Missouri River flooded their farms, homes, and sacred sites.

The current population of the Fort Berthold Reservation is 3,000. More than half of the land is owned by whites. The local Fort Berthold Community College allows tribal members to continue their education without having to leave tribal land. Each community holds an annual powwow. Some elders still speak native languages. There is a museum at New Town and the tribes publish a weekly, the *Mandan, Hidatsa, and Arikira Times*.

Assiniboine

Assiniboine (uh-SIN-uh-boin) means "those who cook with stones" in the Algonquian language spoken by the *Anishinabe*. It refers to the practice of heating stones and then placing them in water to heat food. The Canadian Assiniboine are also called Stoneys. Today, there are 30 bands in both Canada and the United States. They speak a *Dakota* dialect of the Siouan language. Assiniboine were a Plains culture group.

The Siouan people had migrated north from Ohio into Minnesota. The Assiniboine split from other Siouan groups (such as the Dakota, *Lakota* and *Nakota*) in the 1600s. By the 18th century, they lived in Montana and Saskatchewan. Their population was estimated at 10,000 in 1780, though today nearly 8,000 Assiniboine, **Gros Ventre**, and Yanktonai live on two Montana reservations.

By the 18th century, the Sun Dance had become an important ceremony for the Assiniboine, though their version did not include self-mutilation. Their primary deity was Wakonda. Another important element of Assiniboine culture was vision quests or dreams that could offer visions of guardian spirits. Girls were secluded for four days at their first menses. Marriage was formalized by giving gifts to the bride's family.

The dead were placed in tree scaffolds with their feet to the west. After the scaffolds collapsed, the bones were buried. The Assiniboine also practiced cremation and believed that the dead spent their afterlife in a paradise in the south. Signs of mourning included cutting hair, dressing in ragged clothing, and sometimes self-inflicted cuts on limbs.

Tipis were made for two to four families and could be as large as 30 feet in diameter, with 12 sewn *buffalo [I]* hides stretched over a three-pole foundation. Women accompanied men on buffalo hunts in order to butcher and dry the meat. Buffalo meat was also boiled in skin-lined holes filled with hot rocks. Decorative work included quillwork and designs on tree bark. Men wore long hair coiled on the tops of their heads. The most highly regarded military feat was touching enemies with a hand or a stick (counting coup) rather than killing them. They were allies of the *Cree* and Anishinabe and had conflicts with the *Blackfeet*, *Hidatsa*, and Lakota.

Smallpox epidemics struck in 1737, 1780, and 1836. The near extinction of buffalo herds by white hunters led the Assiniboine to sign the 1851 Fort Laramie Treaty. In 1887, the Assiniboine and Gros Ventres were confined to the Fort Belknap Reservation. The lower division of *Assiniboine* was confined to the Fort Peck Reservation in 1873 with the Yanktonai. Several hundred Indians soon died there.

The Fort Belknap Reservation in Montana, established in 1887, is comprised of 616,000 acres, although only one-quarter of that land is tribally owned. The current population is around 2,300. Fort Peck Reservation in Montana, established in 1873, is comprised of 981,000 acres; again, only one-quarter of it is tribally owned. The population there is around 5,700. Unemployment is 33 percent at Fort Peck and 55 percent at Fort Belknap.

Beaver

Beaver comes from Tsattine meaning "dwellers among the Beaver." Today, they refer to themselves as *Deneza* or *Dunne-za,* meaning "real people." They are culturally similar to the Sekani, with whom they may once have been united and the Chipewyan. They speak a Northern Athapascan language.

Traditional Beaver lands in the mid-18th century were in Alberta and British Columbia. In the 17th century, the Beaver population was estimated at between 1,000 and 1,500, though today there are only 800 enrolled members. Ancestors of the Beaver have been on their traditional lands for at least 10,000 years.

As with other tribes, Beaver culture included vision quests. They also held a twice-yearly festival involving a fire sacrifice of food. Men could have more than one wife. Descent was patrilineal, but newly married couples lived with the woman's family for a time. Corpses were placed on platforms in trees. Mourners gave away the possessions of the deceased, cut their own hair, and sometimes made cuts on their bodies.

Housing was a structure of three-pole conical tipis covered with moose or caribou hides. They also built winter earth lodges. They hunted *buffalo [I]* in groups by driving them into enclosures. Food was cooked with hot rocks in spruce or birchbark containers. Both sexes painted their bodies. Spruce and birchbark canoes, snowshoes, and toboggans drawn by women (and, later, by dogs) were their main means of transportation. The Beaver experienced conflict with Sekani and *Cree.*

The tribe began to control its land holdings in the 1980s, although disputes with Canada over land continue today. They still use dream songs in ceremonies and hold a summer gathering each year, known as Treaty 8 Days after the eight treaties the Beaver signed with Canada. Beaver remains the first language of many.

Bella Bella

Bella Bella is a term coined around 1834 to refer to a number of bands including the Kokaitk, Oelitk, Oealitk, Heiltsuk, and Heisla. They speak a Wakashan language.

The Bella Bella lived north of Vancouver Island and the *Kwakiutl* people in British Columbia. Their population was estimated at 1,700 in 1835. By 1901, their numbers were reduced to 330, although current survivors number about 1,870 enrolled members.

Bella Bella culture featured a number of secret societies, invitation into which was hereditary. Wealthy members sponsored feasts and potlatches in which one gained status by redistributing goods. There were four "crest groups" or clans: the raven, eagle, orca, and wolf. Society was divided into classes of nobles, free commoners, and slaves. Tattoos denoted symbols of high rank. Marriage was accompanied by gifts from the groom's family to the bride's family.

The Bella Bella lived in rectangular cedar-plank houses with interior posts, adjustable smoke holes, mat-lined walls, and gabled roofs. Salmon was a staple in their diet as was other marine food. Totem poles and masks were carved and painted. Cedar dugout canoes and sometimes bark canoes were the primary means of transportation. Women wore cedar-bark aprons. Blankets were woven of cedar bark, mountain-goat wool, and dog hair. Abalone nose and ear pendants were worn by those with some resources. They painted their faces and bodies to protect themselves from sunburn. They experienced conflicts with the *Bella Coola*, *Haida*, Tsimshian, and Kwakiutl.

The first European contact with the Bella Bella was probably in 1793, when Canadian explorers George Vancouver and Alexander Mackenzie expanded the fur trade into their region. An 1862 smallpox epidemic devastated the population. In 1880, the government established the Bella Bella Reserve (Canadian term for reservation) in British Columbia that was run by Methodist *missionaries [IV]*. The Bella Bella today have 22 reserves.

Bella Coola

The Bella Coola refered to themselves as the *Nuxalkmx*. In 1980, they changed their name to the Nuxalt Nation. Bella Coola is a Salishan language.

They may have arrived in British Columbia around 1400. The population of Bella Coola in British Columbia in 1780 was estimated at 1,400. By the 1970s, there were 600 enrolled members, whereas today there are about 1,100 enrolled members.

Potlatches allowed Indians to display social status by the amount of wealth they gave away. Bella Coola society had class divisions, but mobility was possible even among slaves. Girls were secluded for a year following their first menses. They traditionally celebrated the first game caught by boys and the first berries gathered by girls each year. Cruelty and infidelity were grounds for divorce. The dead were buried in a sitting position in wooden boxes, along with any property they owned.

The Bella Coola lived in large homes built of red-cedar planks. Sometimes the homes were built on stilts as a defense against floods or attacks. Fish and salmon were staples of their diet. The first salmon of the season was consumed in a ritual that carefully returned its bones to the water. Masks and carved poles were decorated with painted crests, though they had no full-size totem poles. They also used pictographs and made petroglyphs. Several types of canoes decorated with crests or painted black were used for transportation, including seagoing canoes. Both genders were tattooed. They experienced conflict with the *Carrier, Chilcotin*, and *Kwakiutl*.

They recognized the existence of four or five worlds, with the human world at the center. They worshipped a supreme female creator and other deities who resided in the sky. The Bella Coola had two secret societies, entrance to which was based on heredity. Most of their ceremonies were held in winter.

Like the *Bella Bella*, they first encountered Europeans in 1793 when George Vancouver and Alexander Mackenzie arrived to expand the fur trade. After *gold [IV]* was discovered on their land in 1851, they experienced more violence at the hands of whites. Whole villages were decimated in the smallpox epidemic of 1863. Protestant *missionaries [IV]* arrived in the 1870s. A group of Bella Coola traveled to Germany, where they performed music and dances for more than a year and inspired one audience member, anthropologist Franz Boas, to begin a lifelong study of Northwest coastal Indians. People were able to relearn old songs in the 1960s by listening to earlier recordings made by anthropologists such as Boas. Today the Bella Coola live on seven reserves (Canadian term for reservation) in British Columbia.

Beothuk

The Beothuk (BAY-uh-thuk) name was thought to mean "human body." With the *Inuit,* they were the only Indians on the Atlantic coast of the northeastern United States and Canada who did not speak an Algonquian language, though the Beothuk language shares some word roots. Like the Algonquin, they lived in birchbark wigwams, used birchbark canoes, and cooked in birchbark containers. They painted their skin with red ocher as an insect repellant. The *Micmac* called them Macquajees, for "red people," referring to that Beothuk practice.

The Vikings were the first Europeans who may have encountered the Beothuk in A.D. 1000, though there is some uncertainty, since the encounter may have been with the Micmac. The Beothuk did encounter a number of Europeans, including John Cabot from England in 1497, Giovanni da Verrazano of France in 1523, and Jacques Cartier of France in 1534.

A misunderstanding with the French led to the Beothuk extinction. The idea of ownership was more fluid in Beothuk culture than among the French. The French accused the Beothuk of theft and attacked them. They also gave the Micmac guns and offered a bounty on Beothuk scalps. The few Beothuk who survived hid among the Naskapi and other Indians. The last known Beothuk, Shanawdithit, or Nancy April, died in 1829.

Blackfeet

The Blackfeet referred to themselves as *Amskapi Pikuni,* meaning "spotted robes." The Blackfeet were a confederacy of three tribes: the Pikuni, meaning "small robes," the Kainah, meaning "blood of many chiefs," and the Siksika, a *Cree* word meaning "Blackfoot People." Their name, Blackfeet, may have referred to their moccasins blackened by dye or ashes from prairie fires. They are generally called "Blackfeet" in the United States, and "Blackfoot" in Canada. Their language is an Algonquian language.

The Blackfeet may have originated in the Great Lakes region and moved westward sometime before the 17th century. They were part of an alliance with the *Assiniboine, Arapaho*, and *Gros Ventre*. Around 1800, the Blackfeet lived near Saskatchewan, though today they live in Montana and southern Alberta. The Blackfeet population was estimated at 15,000 in 1780; today, the population numbers about 13,000.

One of the ceremonies they practiced, the Sun Dance, was probably acquired through the Arapaho or Gros Ventres. In the Blackfeet version, women as well as men participate. Boys usually earned a new name at puberty. Divorce could be attained on grounds of laziness, infidelity for men, or cruelty for women. They placed their dead on platforms in trees. Mourners cut their hair and made cuts on their own limbs; male mourners left the band temporarily.

Women built tipis from pine poles and as many as a dozen buffalo skins. Tipis faced east and were often painted with depictions of stars and battles. *Buffalo [I]* was a staple, as was the camas root. Women wore their hair loose, while men had one lock of hair down their foreheads to their noses and plucked their faces. Allies included the Gros Ventres and Sarcee. They experienced conflict with the *Salish*, Flathead, *Nez Perce, Kootenai, Assiniboine, Shoshone, Crow, Lakota*, and *Cree*. The highest military honors were awarded for getting weapons away from enemies rather than killing them.

The numbers of Blackfeet were drastically reduced by repeated epidemics in 1781, 1837, 1864, and 1869. In fact, the Pikuni were exterminated entirely by disease. Treaties signed between 1851 and 1878 ceded land to the United States and Canada.

The Blackfeet Reservation was established in northern Montana in 1855. Hundreds of Blackfeet died of starvation in 1883 after the buffalo herds had been hunted to near extinction by whites. All but 3,000 of the original reservation's 2 million acres were lost to allotment.

The Blackfeet Reservation in Montana today consists of 3,000 square miles, of which 70 percent is owned by the tribe. There are three Canadian reserves: Siksika, Blood, and Peigan. Unemployment is around 50 percent in Montana and 80 percent on the reserves in Canada. Blackfeet in the

United States adopted a constitution in the 1930s. The reservation also contains Blackfeet Community College, established in 1976.

Caddo

Caddo (CAD-o) meant "true chiefs" in the language of one of the Caddo tribes, the Kadohadacho. The Caddo included the Natchitoches Confederacy in Louisiana, the Hasinai or Tejas (Texas) Confederacy, and the Kadohadacho Confederacy in Texas and Arkansas. They were the westernmost tribes among those in the Southeast region. They spoke a Caddoan language. Other tribes in the Caddoan language family included the *Arikira, Pawnee,* and *Wichita.*

The Caddo are believed to have originated in the Southwest. Anthropologists estimated that the Caddo reached the Great Plains in the mid-12th century and migrated to the Southeast shortly afterwards. Their population was estimated at 8,000 in the late 17th century. By the turn of the 18th century, their population was reduced to 4,000. Today, there are about 3,300 enrolled Caddo. The largest group currently lives in Oklahoma.

The Caddo supreme spirit was Ayanat Caddi. The original legend tells of a man and woman emerging from below the earth near the Red River. The man had a pipe and a flint; the woman had seeds of corn and pumpkins that produced crops to feed the tribe.

Traditional dances included the Turkey Dance, the Drum Dance, which recounted the legend of their origin, and the Morning Dance. Premarital sex was not condemned, and divorce was easy to obtain. The dead were buried with food, water, and tools. It was believed that six days after death, the spirits of the dead went to a pleasant house in the south. The Turkey Dance is still performed by women accompanied by songs that retell tribal history.

Some of their settlements had hundreds of houses, and some villages were surrounded with log walls for defense. Temples were built on top of platform mounds. Houses in the East were 40 feet high and made with a pole frame covered with grass thatch. Houses were as large as 60 feet in diameter and resembled a beehive. The Western Caddo built earth lodges. They slept in cane beds raised three feet off the ground. Women raised corn, beans, pumpkins, sunflower, and tobacco.

The first European the Caddo encountered was Hernando de Soto in 1541. The Caddo kept repeating the word *tejas,* which meant "friends." The Spanish gave this name to the province that later became Texas. The Caddo began trading with the French in the early 17th century.

In 1835, the Caddo ceded their land in Louisiana to the federal government and moved to Texas. In the 1850s, they were driven out of Texas during a move by vigilantes to rid the state of all Indians. They were granted a small reservation in Oklahoma in 1859. Most of the reservation was allotted and broken up into small individual lots around 1900. The "surplus" land was sold to whites. A constitution outlining the basis of their tribal government was adopted in 1938 and revised in 1976.

The reservation in Oklahoma is comprised of 42.5 acres. An eight-member tribal council and chair govern the tribe. Unemployment is around 40 percent.

Cahuilla

Cahuilla (Ka-hw-e-la) referred to themselves as *Iviatim*, meaning "speakers of their native language." Descent was patrilineal. They spoke Cahuilla, part of the Cupan subgroup of the Uto-Aztecan language.

The Cahuilla population, estimated at 10,000 in the 17th century and 5,000 by the late 18th century, has about 1,200 enrolled members today who live on 10 reservations in southern California.

Among traditional Cahuilla ceremonies were an annual mourning ceremony and an eagle ceremony. They also believed that the dead stayed involved in the lives of the living. Women (as well as men) practiced medicine and led active lives, competing in foot races and other sports. Divorce was not easy to obtain in Cahuilla society. Their weapons included poison-tipped arrows.

They built rectangular houses of thatch. Acorns were a staple in their diet, although they also developed agriculture. Petroglyphs predating 1000 B.C. have been discovered that depict the hunting of big game. Pictographs also exist of the girls' puberty ceremony.

One of the first Europeans the Cahuilla encountered was explorer Juan Bautista de Anza in 1774. The Spanish established missions in the area, which is why the Cahuilla are predominantly Catholic today. Many Cahuilla worked on Spanish ranches as well, although exposure to Europeans led to a smallpox epidemic among the Cahuilla in 1863. They came under U.S. control after the Mexican War of 1848. They were able to establish reservations with the passage of the 1891 Act for the Relief of Mission Indians but faced termination in the 1950s. One group, the Mission Creek Reservation, was terminated as late as 1970.

None of the 10 reservations have Indian Reorganization Act constitutions. The 1934 Indian Reorganization Act allowed tribes to resume self-government only if they adopted constitutions that followed the United States model. This was not a seamless fit with traditional forms of governing in some tribes, and so most Cahuilla reservations continue to operate through a general council of members of voting age and a business committee. They hold two powwows annually. The Maiki Museum at Morongo Reservation, which opened in 1964, highlights Cahuilla culture and sponsors an annual fiesta. Clans of the Cahuilla are no longer in existence and few traditional ceremonies are practiced. Only a few dozen people still speak Cahuilla.

Carrier

Carrier came from a Sekani word that referred to the custom of some women who carried their dead husbands' bones in a birchbark container on their backs. They referred to themselves as *Takulli,* meaning "people who go upon the water." Descent was matrilineal. They were culturally similar to the Sekani, Nahane, Tahltan, Tsetsaut, Tutchone, and **Chilcotin**, and spoke dialects of a Northern Athapascan language.

Their lands are located in the southwestern portion of the Subarctic cultural area in present-day British Columbia. Their population, estimated at 8,500 in the late 18th century, today has about 9,800 enrolled members.

The Carrier had 20 clans and distinct social classes of nobles, commoners, and slaves, although commoners could gain noble rank though accumulation of wealth. Crests were displayed on totem poles and houses. Potlatches were held to mark important life events among the nobles. To display their status, nobles would give elaborate feasts and give gifts to guests. The higher the value of the gifts, the more respect a noble could garner.

Gifts were given to the bride's mother to mark a marriage. During the first year of marriage, the couple lived with the bride's family and the groom provided for his new in-laws.

Their homes were rectangular and were built with pole frames and spruce-bark covering. Each home housed several families. Some southern groups built underground winter lodges. Salmon and caribou were staples of the diet. Noble males wore special blankets for special occasions. Armor was made of wooden slats or moose hide embedded with pebbles.

The Carrier were a mixture of cultures. Like other Northwest coastal cultures, they lived in plank houses, had social classes, and held potlatches. With the Plateau culture they shared dependence on fish, winter pit houses, and summer spruce-bark shelters. Unlike other Subarctic cultural groups, however, they did not use snowshoes or toboggans.

Their first encounter with Europeans probably occurred in 1793 with Alexander Mackenzie, a Scots trader who worked for the North West Company. In 1806, a local trade fort was established in their area. Widespread death from diseases followed contact with Europeans, including an outbreak of smallpox, which exterminated an entire band in 1837. In addition to disease there was also a suppression of cultural practices. The Catholic Church, which arrived in the 1840s, worked to suppress traditional celebrations, including the potlatch. More whites moved into their area once the Canadian Pacific Railway, completed in 1885, ran through their land.

Carrier bands today live on a hundred small reserves in British Columbia. Clans still exist and many still speak Carrier.

Catawba

Catawba (cuh-TAW-buh) is possibly derived from the *Choctaw* word *katapa* or *katapu* meaning "divided," or from the Yuchi word *kotaha* meaning "robust men." They refer to themselves as *Issa* or *Essaw*, meaning "people of the river." Catawba is a Siouan language.

The Catawba, who may have migrated to the Carolinas from the Northwest and lived along the border of North and South Carolina, today live in South Carolina or Oklahoma. The Catawba population, estimated at 6,000 in the 17th century and at 500 by 1760, today has 1,400 members.

Under Catawba social practices, divorce was easy to obtain. The dead were buried under bark and earth. Their round homes were constructed of pole frames covered with bark. They also constructed temples, as other Southeast tribes did.

They practiced agriculture and hunted with blowguns, which were 5 to 6 feet long and had a range of more than 30 feet. Catawba pottery was highly developed. Pottery was stamped with carved pieces of wood in order to imprint designs. They experienced conflict with the *Cherokee*, Delaware, *Iroquois*, and *Shawnee*.

The first Europeans the Catawba had contact with were the Spanish in the 1500s. A series of epidemics (in 1698, 1718, 1738, and 1759) later decimated the tribe. The 1759 epidemic, for example, killed two-thirds of their members. They incorporated other tribes who had also grown smaller due to epidemics, including the Cheraw, Congaree, Eno, Pedee, Santee, Saponis, Wateree, and Waxhaw. In 1743, a visitor wrote of hearing more than 20 languages spoken in their villages.

They fought against forced labor and slave raids by the British in the Yamasee War of 1715. By 1763, they were confined to a 15-square-mile reservation. The Catawba supported the rebels in the *American Revolution [IV]*. Later some Catawba joined the Cherokee in western Carolina in the 1830s. In the 1840s, they were displaced from their lands when the state of South Carolina promised them a new reservation outside the state in the Treaty of Nation Ford. The promise was never kept and many Catawba drifted back to their former lands in South Carolina. In the 1850s, some Catawba families moved to Arkansas and to the *Indian Territory [IV]* in Oklahoma. Those who remained in South Carolina gained a reservation of 630 acres. Most Catawba were sharecroppers. The Catawba Indian School opened in 1896 and remained open until 1962.

The Catawba were able to gain federal recognition in 1943. In 1962, the tribe lost its federal status because of its dwindling numbers. The 650-acre Catawba State Reservation is located near Rock Hill, South Carolina. The last speaker of Catawba, Samuel Blue, died in 1959, and the last full blood, Hester Louisa Blue, died in 1963. In 1993, the federal status of the tribe was reinstated, and today there are 120 members left.

Cayuga

The name for the Cayuga (kah-YOO-guh) comes from their native language and means "people of the place where the boats were taken out." They were one of the first five tribes to join the *Iroquois League [IV]*. Wampum belts recorded events and were later used as trade money. Descent was matrilineal. They spoke a northern dialect of the *Iroquois* language.

Their ancestors lived in upstate New York since before 800 B.C. They lived near Cayuga Lake, with the *Seneca* to the west and the *Onondaga* to the east. They had 13 main villages. Anthropologists estimate that there were approximately 1,500 Cayuga of the 20,000 total population of the Iroquois Confederacy in 1660. Today, there are about 6,000 Cayuga: 500 live in New York, 3,000 live in Canada, and 2,500 live in Oklahoma.

The Cayuga believed in a creator called Orenda. One of their most important festivals occurred in midwinter, with an eight-day New Year's celebration. There were nine matrilineal clans. Women had a higher status in Cayuga society than did women in white society. Cayuga women chose leaders and decided when war would occur. The dead were buried in a sitting position with food and tools. Both genders tattooed their bodies.

In the early 18th century, there were at least three Cayuga villages with populations of 500 per village and 30 longhouses per village. Longhouses were 50 to 100 feet long and held as many as 20 families. They were covered with elm bark and had smoke holes in the roofs. People slept on mats on raised platforms. In the 18th century, the Cayuga accepted members from smaller nations into their ranks, including the Tutelos, Saponis, Nanticoke, and Conoys. Log walls surrounded some villages. Women raised corn, beans, and squash, and grew orchards of peaches, pears, and apples. Corn, a staple in their diet, was stored in bark-lined cellars.

The Cayuga had closer relationships with the French than did the other Iroquois tribes, who were allies of the British. Later, the Cayuga and other Iroquois groups supported the British in the *American Revolution*

IN THEIR OWN Words

I appeal to any white man to say if he ever entered Logan's cabin hungry and he gave him not meat; if he ever came cold and naked and he clothed him not. During the course of the last long and bloody war, Logan remained idle in his cabin, an advocate for peace. Such was my love for the whites that my countrymen pointed as I passed and said, "Logan is a friend of the white man." . . . The last spring in cold blood and unprovoked, whites murdered the relatives of Logan, not even sparing his wives and children. There runs not a drop of my blood in the veins of any living creature.

—JAMES LOGAN (LOGAN THE MINGO, JOHN LOGAN; SOYECHTOWA; TACHNECHDORUS, TAHGAHJUTE [HIS EYELASHES STICK OUT, SHORT DRESS]), CAYUGA (C.1725–1780). LOGAN SENT A SPEECH TO A COUNCIL WITH LORD DUNMORE, GOVERNOR OF VIRGINIA, 1774.

[IV]. After the war, some Cayuga migrated northward to the Six Nations Reserve in Canada; others went to live with the Seneca in New York.

Many Cayuga adopted the *Handsome Lake [II]* religion in the early 18th century. Handsome Lake was a Seneca who preached a blend of traditional and Christian practices.

The Cayuga were governed by sachems who were chosen by the women. The Cayuga sent 10 sachems to represent them at the Iroquois Confederacy Council. The founders of the United States government modeled their system after that of the Iroquois Confederacy. Benjamin Franklin specifically cited the Iroquois as a model he followed in creating a new nation. In 1869, Canadian law mandated that tribal descent be changed to patrilineal. Canada terminated the tribes' traditional forms of government in 1924 and imposed an all-male elected system on the reserves.

Some of the Cayuga in New York were moved to *Indian Territory [IV]* in Oklahoma in 1831. Their lands in Oklahoma were reduced from a 65,000-acre reservation to a mere 140 acres by 1936, but the tribe was able to resist termination in the 1950s.

Cayuse

Cayuse (ki-YOOS) was from the French word *cailloux* that meant "people of the stones or rock." They referred to themselves as *Waiilatpu,* meaning "superior people." They were similar in culture to the *Nez Perce* and Walla Walla. Their language was part of the Sahptian division of the Penutian language. Their neighbors, the Molala, were the only other people who spoke their Cayuse dialect, called Waiilatpuan.

Although their traditional lands were in northeast Oregon and southeast Washington, most Cayuse currently live in Oregon. The population, estimated at 500 in the 18th century, today numbers about 1,000. They live on the Umatilla Reservation, which they share with the Umatilla and Walla Walla.

While the Cayuse condemned adultery, wealthy men could have more than one wife. They built summer homes covered with woven reed mats; winter homes were oblong earth lodges. Salmon and fish were staples in their diet. They constructed their clothing of bark, and later of tanned hides.

After they acquired the *horse [I]* in the 18th century, the Cayuse adopted many aspects of the Plains culture, including tipis, moccasins, clothing made of tanned skin, and hunting *buffalo [I]*. The Nez Perce were their allies; indeed, in the 19th century, many Cayuse spoke the Nez Perce language. They fought sporadically with the Western *Shoshone*.

Among the first Europeans they met were Lewis and Clark in 1806. More whites migrated to their lands when the Oregon Trail opened in 1843. *Missionaries [IV]* Marcus and Narcissa Whitman grew wealthy from the sale of Indian lands and were prejudicial in their interactions with the Cayuse. When European *diseases [IV]* decimated the Cayuse community, the Indians blamed the missionaries, since Cayuse children attending the missionary school were the first to catch smallpox. Consequently, a group of Cayuse Indians destroyed the mission and killed the Whitmans in 1847. This attack was the beginning of the white-Indian conflict known as the Cayuse War, which lasted until 1850. After the white militia murdered 30 Cayuse in their camp in retaliation, the Palouse and Walla Walla joined the conflict on the side of the Cayuse. The federal government eventually hanged two Cayuse. The Cayuse joined later uprisings, including the *Yakama* in 1855, the Nez Perce in 1877, and the Bannock in 1878 (see *Bannock Conflict [IV]*).

In 1855, the Cayuse were removed to the 92,273-acre Umatilla Reservation in Pendleton, Oregon. They lost more land and fishing sites when the Dalles Dam was constructed in the 1950s. A nine-member tribal council governs the tribe. The Cayuse hold an annual Pendleton round-up and festival of the arts and celebrate a traditional ceremony for the first salmon.

Chemehuevi

Chemehuevi is a Yuman word that means "nose in the air like a roadrunner." The phrase refers to a running style the tribe practiced. They refer to themselves as *Nuwi*, meaning "the people," or *Tantawats*, meaning "southern men." They are the most southern group of the Southern *Paiute*.

Since at least the 19th century they have lived in the Chemehuevi Valley in southwestern California. Their traditional lands were located in this area and also the Mojave Desert and southwestern Utah. It is estimated that the population was 500 in 1600. Today, there are approximately 700 members. They speak Paiute, a dialect of the Shoshonean branch of the Uto-Aztecan language.

They practiced flood-plain farming. Allies included the *Mojave*, *Quechan*, Yavapai, and Western **Apache**. They experienced conflict with the *Cocopah*, *Pima*, *Tohono O'odham*, and *Pee Posh*.

Their 270,000-acre Colorado River Reservation was established in 1865, followed by the 36,000-acre Chemehuevi Reservation in Chemehuevi Valley, California, in 1907. The Hoover Dam, built in 1935, cut off the water the Chemehuevi had used to farm. The Parker Dam, built in 1939, placed 8,000 acres of Chemehuevi lands under water. By the end of World War II, about 100 *Navajo* and Hopi joined the Chemehuevi and Mojave, and they became the Colorado River Indian Tribes. They became formalized when they established a constitution in 1971.

The Mojave tribe dominates the group politically. There are approximately 90 Chemehuevi at the Chemehuevi Reservation and 600 at the Colorado River Reservation.

Cherokee

Cherokee (CHAIR-uh-kee) is derived from the *Choctaw* word *Tsalagi*, meaning "people of the land of caves," or possibly from the *Creek* word *Tciloki*, meaning "people who speak differently." They referred to themselves as *Ani-yun-wiya*, meaning "red people." They spoke Cherokee, an Iroquoian language. The Cherokee, who are related to the *Iroquois*, were the most southern of Iroquoian speakers. Three dialects were divided by region: the lower towns spoke Elati; the middle, Kituhwa; and upper, Atali. Descent was matrilineal.

The Cherokee were one of the groups whites classified as the five "civilized" tribes, along with the *Chickasaw*, Choctaw, Creek, and *Seminole*. In the 19th century, those tribes dressed, farmed, and governed themselves in very similar ways to the whites.

The Cherokee were the largest tribe in the Southeast. About 100 villages were located in southern Appalachia, which included parts of Alabama, Georgia, Kentucky, North Carolina, South Carolina, Tennessee, and Virginia. Towns were divided into lower, middle, and upper regions. Today most Cherokee live in northeastern Oklahoma or North Carolina. The Cherokee population, estimated at 29,000 in the mid-16th century, is now more than 300,000, making the Cherokee the largest Indian nation in the United States.

The Cherokee probably originated around the Ohio Valley or Great Lakes region and were possibly descended from the Mound Builders. The town of Echota in present-day Georgia was their ancient capital. (It is now an archaeological site.) Spiritual practices focused on the sun, which was considered female in nature. The Cherokee believed in an upper world on earth and a lower world beneath the land. One of their most important ceremonies was the annual Green Corn festival, celebrated when the last of the corn crop ripened. Dreams were an important part of their culture. Medical practices included the use of herbs, sweats, changes in diet, rubbings, and the use of *beads [I]* and crystals.

Cherokee villages were united in a confederacy. There were two chiefs in every village: a red (war) chief, and a white (peace) chief who held the title Beloved Man or Woman. White chiefs supervised civil functions; red chiefs supervised the competitive games and war. Women could not only be chiefs, but they also sat in on village councils and had their own women's council as well. Whole towns could also be considered red or white. There were seven matrilineal clans. Divorce could be attained and was formalized when women placed men's belongings outside the home, which the women owned. The high status of women was reduced with changes imposed by white society. Twins were sometimes raised as shamans. The dead were buried underground or beneath stones.

Log walls surrounded villages. Summer homes were rectangular structures built of pole frames and walls of cane matting and clay plaster with thatched roofs. Houses were approximately 70 feet by 15 feet and usually divided into kitchen, dining, and bedroom areas. Some homes were two stories high. Winter homes were smaller and circular in shape. They were 20 feet high and cone shaped. Built over a pit, and framed by poles covered with earth, they also functioned as sweathouses. The Cherokee also constructed seven-sided temples on raised mounds in the center village plaza, which held as many as 500 people. The inside held tiered seats around a central fire.

Women raised three kinds of corn as well as beans, squash, sunflowers, and tobacco. Corn was baked into bread. They also collected maple

Title page of the 1827 Constitution and laws of the Cherokee Nation. *Library of Congress.*

sap, which they made into syrup. Nine-foot-long blowguns with a range of 60 feet were used to hunt small game and birds. They sometimes fished by using poison in a small area of water to bring fish to the surface.

Pottery was stamped with carved wooden designs. Ovens were made of hot, flat stones covered with rounded lids. Dugout or birchbark canoes held as many as 20 people. Both genders wore nose ornaments and body paint. Ceremonial turkey and eagle feathers were used for headdresses and capes. Men slit their ears and stretched them with copper wires.

The first European they encountered was Hernando de Soto in 1540. In 1760, they fought for two years with the British over unfair trade practices but were ultimately defeated when the British carried out a scorched earth policy against them. They lost most of their eastern lands in the subsequent treaty. Between 1721 and 1835, they made more than three dozen land cessions to the British and, later, to the United States. The Cherokee supported the British in the *American Revolution [IV]* rather than the rebels, who were land hungry and the source of many Indian/white conflicts. Mid-18th century epidemics, however, decimated the population. The Cherokee supported the United States in the Creek War in 1813.

The Cherokee Nation was formally founded in 1827 with a written constitution, which, like the American Constitution, disenfranchised African Americans and women. Some Cherokee also owned slaves. *Sequoyah [II]* (George Gist) invented a written language for the Cherokee in 1821. The written language was so successful that within months the majority of the Cherokee Nation were literate in it. In fact, the Cherokee literacy rates were higher than those of their white neighbors. In the late 1820s, they began publishing their own newspaper, the *Cherokee Phoenix.*

The *Indian Removal Act [IV]* of 1830 was motivated by the greed of whites once *gold [IV]* was discovered in Cherokee territory. The Act demanded the removal of the Cherokee and other southern tribes to live west of the Mississippi River in what was to be *Indian Territory [IV]* forever but is today the state of Oklahoma, the northwest corner of Arkansas, and the states of Kansas and Nebraska. Many prominent Americans sided with the Cherokee cause, including Davy Crockett, Henry Clay, and Daniel Webster. Whites demolished the printing press and offices of the *Cherokee Phoenix* because it published articles opposing the Indian removal. The Cherokee pressed their case through the United States Supreme Court and were ultimately successful. President Andrew Jackson willfully ignored the court decision, stating, "Justice John Marshall has made the ruling, let him enforce it."

The Cherokee were rounded up by militia and placed in stockades that served as internment camps, where many died. More than 1,000 Cherokee managed to escape and flee to the mountains of North Carolina. They gained recognition in 1889 as the Eastern Cherokee Nation.

Beginning in 1838, the majority of Cherokee were force marched 800 miles to Indian Territory. One in four Cherokee died along the way in a journey that became known as the *"Trail of Tears" [IV]*. More Cherokee died once they reached the territory due to lack of provisions, clothing, and shelter. The Western Cherokee established two bilingual newspapers, the Cherokee *Advocate* and the *Cherokee Messenger*. They also opened schools, including a male and female seminary to provide higher educational opportunities. The Cherokee Nation was split during the *Civil War [IV]* between those members who supported the Confederacy, and those who supported the Union.

Those living in Indian Territory were repeatedly removed as lands continued to be reduced. Indians were removed from the northern region of the territory to make room for the new states of Kansas and Nebraska. The *Dawes Act [IV]* in the late 1880s forced allotment of Cherokee lands; as a result, more than 2 million acres of Indian land were sold as "surplus" to white settlers. When the Cherokee and Choctaw refused allotment and pressed their cases in federal courts, Congress passed the *Curtis Act [IV]* of 1898 to dissolve tribal governments and courts. In 1902, they terminated Indian governments. Oklahoma became a state in 1907.

In the 1930s, a group of full-bloods separated from the Western Cherokee and formed the United Keetoowah Band. The Keetoowah continued to recognize the seven traditional clans and cultural practices such as establishing white (peace) towns. The Keetoowah received federal recognition in 1946.

IN THEIR OWN Words

The whites have passed the mountains and settled upon Cherokee lands, and now wish to have their usurpation sanctioned by the confirmation of a treaty. New cessions will be required, and the small remnant my people will be compelled to seek a new retreat in some far distant wilderness. There they will be permitted to stay only a short while, until they again behold the advancing banners of the same greedy host. When the whites are unable to point out any farther retreat for the miserable Cherokees, they will proclaim the extinction of the whole race.

—DRAGGING CANOE (CHEUCUNSENE; KUNMESEE; TSIYU-GUNSINI; TSUNGUNSINI), CHEROKEE CHIEF OF THE CHICKAMAUGA BAND (c. 1730–1792). STATED AT THE TREATY OF FORT STANWIX COUNCILS, 1768.

Today, the Western Cherokee capital is located in Tahlequah, Oklahoma, with nearly 200,000 enrolled members and 61,000 acres of tribal land. (Indian lands in Oklahoma are called Trust Areas, not reservations as they are in other states.) The Western Cherokee adopted a tripartite form of government with the new constitution in 1975.

The Eastern Cherokee population of approximately 10,000 lives on the 56,000-acre Qualla Boundary Cherokee Reservation, established in 1874 in western North Carolina. Land is owned by individuals but can only be sold to other tribal members. The government is also tripartite in form.

The United Keetoowah Band in Northeastern Oklahoma has approximately 7,000 members and currently no land base. The Western Cherokee Nation celebrates the Cherokee National Holidays over Labor Day weekend. Wilma *Mankiller [II]*, chief of the Western Cherokee for the decade beginning in 1985, was one of the first women to head a major tribe. Since 1984, the Eastern Band and Western Cherokee have met as a joint body every two years.

The Atali dialect of Cherokee is still spoken by 13,000 members; the middle Kituhwa dialect is spoken by about 1,000 in North Carolina, mainly in ceremonies. More than 14,000 tribal members speak Cherokee, making them the seventh largest group of speakers of a native language north of Mexico. The Keetoowah Society maintains traditional religious practices. The Cherokee Nation of Oklahoma, Eastern Band of Cherokee, and United Keetoowah Band are federally recognized. Bands in other states, including Arkansas, Alabama, Georgia, and Tennessee, are recognized by their states and are currently seeking federal recognition.

Cheyenne

Cheyenne (shy-ANN) is a *Dakota* word meaning "red talkers" or "foreign talkers." They refer to themselves as *Tse-tsehese-staestse*, meaning "people, our people," or "beautiful people." Cheyenne is an Algonquian language that had two dialects.

In the late 18th century, their population was estimated at 3,500. Today, there are around 11,000 enrolled members, most of whom live in southeastern Montana and western Oklahoma.

The Cheyenne originally lived in Minnesota. They believed in a creator and that the universe had seven levels. They believed that guardian

149

spirits could be obtained in dreams or on vision quests. Ceremonies included the Renewal of the Sacred Arrows (Mahuts), the Sun Dance, and the five-day Sacred Buffalo Hat (Isiwun) ceremony. The Renewal of the Sacred Arrows was an important four-day-long ceremony in which four arrows given by the creator to a cultural figure, Sweet Medicine, and then to the people, were removed from a sacred bundle.

Traditional governing was conducted by the council of 44, composed of 4 leaders from each of the 10 bands and 4 religious leaders. Council terms lasted for 10 years. There were six military societies. There was more prestige in touching enemies (counting coup) than for killing them among many tribes. Murderers were ostracized or exiled. Most societies, or social groups, were gender specific, such as the Medicine Women. The high-status buffalo society was composed of women who had embroidered 30 buffalo hides. After marriage, the couple lived with the bride's family. The dead were wrapped in robes and placed on platforms, usually in a tree, with their weapons and tools.

Before migrating westward from the northern Mississippi Valley, the Cheyenne lived in bark and earth lodges. As they moved on to the Plains they lived in buffalo-hide tipis. They raised corn, beans, and squash, gathered wild rice, and made pottery before migrating westward.

One of their first encounters with Europeans was with René-Robert La Salle in 1680. When furs became scarce due to the huge demand, Indians who hunted for fur pushed farther westward. As a result, the Cheyenne were displaced by *Lakota* and *Anishinabe* and migrated westward. They moved to North Dakota and then farther west to Nebraska and Wyoming. Once on the Plains they stopped farming and became *buffalo [I]* hunters. They eventually allied with the *Arapaho* and Lakota. Around 1832 the tribe split into Northern and Southern Cheyenne when some bands moved south.

In 1849, a cholera epidemic killed about 200 Cheyenne, nearly half their population. The surviving Cheyenne signed the 1851 *Treaty of Fort Laramie [IV]*, which offered tribes a yearly compensation to allow whites to travel through their country on their journeys to lands farther west. The discovery of *gold [IV]* at Pike's Peak in 1859 brought more whites into Southern Cheyenne territory. The Southern Cheyenne were later forced to give up their lands in Colorado after the territory of Colorado decided to remove all Indians from its region. The Cheyenne suffered an even greater setback in

1864 with the *Sand Creek Massacre [IV]*, one of the worst atrocities of the Cheyenne-Arapaho War. Two hundred Indians were murdered at Sand Creek, as many as at the subsequent *Wounded Knee Massacre [IV]*.

Some Northern Cheyenne fought with the Lakota under *Red Cloud [II]* in the successful campaign to close the Bozeman Trail from 1866 to 1868. The United States Army caught 1,000 Northern Cheyenne and force marched them to the Cheyenne-Arapaho Reservation in Oklahoma. Food was scarce and two-thirds of the Northern Cheyenne caught malaria in the new location. They decided they would rather die trying to return home than to stay where they were. Three hundred escaped with *Dull Knife [II]* and headed north. It took six weeks and 13,000 soldiers, but eventually, the escapees surrendered at the Pine Ridge Reservation in South Dakota in 1881.

In 1868, the Southern Cheyenne settled with the Arapaho on a 4-million-acre reservation in Oklahoma. The reservation was later eliminated through allotment. The 436,948-acre Northern Cheyenne Reservation was formed in 1884. The Northern Cheyenne were among the last tribes to accept allotment. They were able to hold off until 1926. Eight years later, the Indian Reorganization Act ended the practice of allotment, so the Cheyenne's loss of lands was less than many other tribes.

The Northern Cheyenne, as signers of the 1868 Fort Laramie Treaty, joined the Lakota in refusing financial compensation and instead sought the return of the Black Hills. The 1868 treaty was signed at the close of the Red Cloud war. It promised possession of the Black Hills to the signers. The hills had been confiscated by the United States government when gold was discovered in the area. A congressional bill asking for return of the land was introduced in 1985 but withdrawn in 1990.

A 5-member tribal council and a president govern the Northern Cheyenne. A 28-member council, half of whom are Cheyenne and the other half Arapaho, governs the Southern Cheyenne-Arapaho. Most of the 5,000 Southern Cheyenne live in western Oklahoma.

The Sacred Buffalo Hat is kept by the Northern Cheyenne and the Sacred Arrow is kept by the Southern Cheyenne. The Northern Cheyenne hold a spring rodeo and Memorial Day and Fourth of July powwows. Ninety-seven percent of the land remains in tribal ownership. Tribal headquarters is located at Lame Deer, Montana. There are approximately 3,500 enrolled members, and the unemployment rate is around 50 percent.

Chickasaw

Chickasaw (CHICK-uh-saw) was a Muskogean word for sitting down. The Chickasaw were culturally similar to the *Choctaw* and *Creek*. They were one of the *Five Civilized Tribes [IV]*, according to whites, meaning that they had integrated aspects of white culture with their own. The other four tribes were the *Cherokee*, Choctaw, Creek, and *Seminole*. Descent was matrilineal.

Chickasaw traditional lands were in eastern Arkansas, western Kentucky, western Tennessee, and the northern parts of Mississippi and Alabama. Today, most Chickasaw live in Oklahoma. Their population, estimated at 5,000 in 1600, now consists of 35,000 members.

According to their oral history, the Chickasaw migrated north from Mexico. On their journey, they placed the same sacred leaning pole into the ground each day until they came to a place where it no longer leaned, indicating they should settle there. Their creator was Ababinili. Men could have more than one wife and avoided their mothers-in-law to show respect. Although men were not punished for adultery, women were beaten or had an ear or nose cut off. The dead, buried in a sitting position, were interred with their possessions in graves under their houses.

Log walls surrounded Chickasaw villages. Homes were rectangular pole frames covered with cypress or cane. They were whitewashed inside and outside and had small, east facing doors. Circular winter homes were partly underground and measured approximately 25 feet in diameter. Winter homes were plastered with clay. Furniture included couches and raised wood-frame beds.

The Chickasaw grew corn, beans, squash, and sunflowers, and collected sassafras root to make tea. Clothing was made of deerskin and cloth from mulberry bark. Both genders sometimes wore nose rings and painted their bodies. Like the Cherokee, young men slit their ears and stretched them with inserted copper wire. Warriors were often tattooed with the picture of an animal.

In 1541, they encountered their first Europeans, the Spanish, who had accompanied Hernando de Soto. The Spaniards tortured them and tried to enslave them along with other Southeastern tribes. In the late 17th and early 18th centuries, the Chickasaw engaged in the fur trade with the British. The Chickasaw dependence on fur trade led them into conflicts with other tribes in the region when they tried to expand their hunting grounds.

The tribe was split in loyalty during the *American Revolution [IV]*. Some Chickasaw owned cotton plantations, and the tribe as a whole owned nearly 1,000 African-American slaves. By 1830, as one of the Five Civilized Tribes, they adopted a written code of laws that included the creation of a police force and the banning of alcohol. They ceded land to the federal government in several treaties from 1805 to 1818 and in 1832, under the *Indian Removal Act [IV]*, they ceded all their lands east of the Mississippi.

In 1837, they were forcibly removed to *Indian Territory [IV]*, today's state of Oklahoma. The approximately 3,000 Chickasaw who began the forced march fared somewhat better than the Cherokee, who lost one-fourth of their members on the way. The Chickasaw established a reservation and a government in Indian territory in 1855. They fought on the side of the Confederacy in the *Civil War [IV]*. Due to the Chickasaw plantation and slave-owning past, the tribe never adopted freed slaves, a practice of other Oklahoma tribes. Their reservation lands were allotted in 1900. Congress dissolved all tribal governments in Oklahoma in 1906; the Chickasaw government, however, was not dissolved until 1907. In 1970, Congress returned to the Chickasaw the right to elect their own government.

Approximately 9,000 Chickasaw continue to live in southern Oklahoma, with their headquarters in Ada. Their poverty rates in Oklahoma run about 20 percent, somewhat lower than among other groups, because many Chickasaw reside closer to towns and jobs than groups in remote rural locations where economic opportunities are few. Most members are Baptists or Methodists. The Chickasaw operate a tribal museum and newspaper, the *Chickasaw Times*. An annual festival is held in September. About 500 elders still speak the language.

Chilcotin

Chilcotin means "inhabitants of Young Man's River" in their language. They were culturally similar to the *Bella Coola*, *Carrier*, *Kwakiutl*, and interior *Salish* tribes. Chilcotin was a Northern Athapascan language. Descent was bilateral.

Their traditional lands were in the interior of British Columbia, near the headwaters of the Chilcotin River and the Anahim Lake district. Their population was estimated at 1,500 in the 17th century and approximately 3,500 in the late 18th century. Today, there are about 500 enrolled members.

Both genders went into temporary seclusion at adolescence in order to seek guardian spirits. Girls were also secluded at the onset of their first menses. Social classes consisted of nobles, commoners, and slaves. Those with wealth gave potlatches, a feast with gift giveaways, to gain status. When nobles died, most of their possessions were given away at a large potlatch. The dead were cremated or buried in the ground or under rocks.

Homes were rectangular earth lodges with a smoke hole at the top. Basketry had human, animal, or geometric designs. Men wore their hair at shoulder length; women wore long braids. Both genders painted and tattooed their faces, and red and black face paint during wartime. Killing a tribal member was punishable by temporary isolation from the tribe.

Fort Alexandria was established in their region in 1821. A *gold [IV]* strike near the Fraser River in 1860 led to a mass invasion of whites, who also looted Indian graves. A smallpox epidemic in 1862 killed hundreds of Chilcotin.

Chinook

The name Chinook (shi-NOOK) was derived from a word in the language of their neighbors, the Chehalis, for a particular village site, which itself may have referred to the moist sea breezes that came from their area. The Chinook had two divisions: the upper Chinook and the lower Chinook. They lived on the Pacific coast in what is now Washington State. The Chinook language, which has an upper and a lower dialect, is a Penutian language. The lower dialect incorporated the language of the neighboring Cathlamet, Mulnomah, and Kiksht. Other tribes who spoke Chinook included the Cathlapotle, Chilluckittequaw, Clackamas, Clatsop, Clowwewalla, Skilloot, Wasco, and Watlala. Chinook also referred to an Oregon trade language that was used along the Pacific coast from Alaska to California. It was a mixture of Chinook, Nootkan, French, and English.

Today there are about 2,000 enrolled members, down from an estimated population of 22,000 in 1780, but more than the fewer than 100 Chinook living at the end of the 19th century.

Fish was a staple of the Chinook diet and the first salmon caught each year was consumed in a ritual ceremony that returned the bones of the fish to the water.

The Chinook lived in more than 30 villages along the coastline of Washington State; winter villages each had 20 or more 50-foot-long houses. Winter homes were rectangular and clad in cedar planks, like their Northwest Coast neighbors, but partly underground in the style of the Plateau culture. Floors were covered with matting or wood planks. Elevated beds ran along the walls.

Society was divided by classes. To communicate with the lower-ranked people, Chinook chiefs would use an orator as an intermediary. Imported dentalium shells from coastal tribes and, later, *beads [I]* from China, were used for money. The word potlatch was Chinook in origin and meant "giving." The dead were wrapped in mats and buried with their possessions in canoes.

Chinook musical instruments included long poles with bunches of deer hooves attached. They had six types of carved canoes, including some that held as many as 30 people. Women wore skirts of cedar bark and silk grass. Both genders wore rainproof cedar hats and tule-mat rain capes.

The first Europeans the Chinook encountered were the Spanish in the 1500s, who arrived by boat. Smallpox had spread among them by 1792. As the disease decimated neighboring tribes, they were absorbed by the Chinook. In 1811 John Jacob Astor, the owner of the American Fur Company and the Pacific Fur Company, founded Astoria, a fur-trading outpost on the coast. The Chinook were central negotiators between whites and Indians in the area; thus their language formed the basis of the Chinook trade language used widely throughout the region. Chinook women had traditionally played a more active role in trade than men, so the expanding development of trade increased their status.

By the 1850s, the Chinook had ceded most of their land to the United States for fishing rights in treaties that were never ratified. Their traditional lands were taken without treaty or payment when Oregon gained statehood in 1859 and Washington in 1889.

In 1913, they joined other tribes and formed the Northwestern Federation of American Indians, a pan-Indian group that sought treaty compliance. In 1925, they established a business council and pursued court cases regarding their rights. The United States Supreme Court ruled in 1931 that the Chinook and some of the other tribes had rights to the 340-square-mile Quinault Reservation in Taholah, Washington, which had been established in 1855 for a number of other tribes. Once on the reservation, the Chinook accounted for 60 percent of its population. In 1951, Chinook who did not live on the reservation were treated as a terminated tribe. They organized in 1952 to press for land claims, but the final decision in 1971 gave them no land.

Today, many Chinook live on the 2,076-acre Chehalis Reservation. Established in 1864, it has a population of approximately 300 Indians and is governed by an elected tribal council. Approximately 69 Chinook also live on the 335-acre Shoalwater Reservation, established in 1866. The last fluent speakers of Chinook died at the start of the 20th century, and the language is not spoken today. A few tribe members still speak the Chinook trade jargon, however. In 1979, the Chinook of Klamath Falls, Oregon, and another group in Chinook, Washington, applied for federal recognition based on their unratified 1851 treaty and 1953 termination. Their petitions were rejected in 1986. They plan to continue seeking federal recognition.

Chipewayan

Chipewayan (chip-uh-WHY-an) was from the *Cree* word meaning "pointed skin," which referred to the method of drying beaver skins that left them pointed at the bottom. They referred to themselves as *Dene*, meaning "the people," and spoke an Athapascan language. The Chipewayan were the largest group of Athapascans living in Canada and Alaska.

The Chipewayan may have originated in the Rocky Mountains, although their traditional lands were along the northern edge of the Sub-arctic in western Canada, northern Manitoba, Alberta, and Saskatchewan. Although there were about 4,000 to 5,000 Chipewayan in the 17th century, the population today is approximately 1,000.

They communicated with the spirit world through dreams and visions. At adolescence, women married older men, who could have more than one wife. In their funeral tradition, they destroyed property that had belonged to the dead and left them exposed to the elements. The dead were thought to inhabit an island full of game if they had lived a good life.

Chipewayan homes were conical caribou-skin tents with spruce branches and caribou skin for flooring, similar to the dwellings of the Plains Indians. They tattooed their cheeks in parallel lines, and some men grew beards. They also made many tools from copper found in their region.

In 1717, the *Hudson's Bay Company [IV]* established a post in Chipewayan territory. Ninety percent of the Chipewayan population died in a 1781 smallpox epidemic. They signed several treaties from 1876 to 1906 and moved to reserves. They are provincially and federally recognized in Canada.

Chitimacha

Chitimacha (chid-uh-MA-shuh) probably meant "those who have pots" but may have meant "those living on Grand River" or "men altogether red." They were comprised of three subtribes: the Chitimacha, Chawasha, and Washa. The Chitimacha language may be related to Tunican.

They resided in their traditional land in the southern part of Louisiana for at least 2,500 years. They probably migrated from the south, around the Natchez region. The tribe, estimated at 3,000 members in 1700 and just 51 by 1930, today has approximately 700 enrolled members.

In their religious practices, the Chitimacha recognized a sky spirit who may have been female. They had a 12-foot-square temple and an annual six-day festival held at midsummer. They practiced a male puberty rite involving fasting and many hours of dancing. A man also became known by his son's name when he became a father. Women could hold any spiritual or political positions in Chitimachan society.

Their homes were pole framed and covered with thatch. Crops included sweet potatoes, melons, beans, squash, sunflowers, and corn. Both genders had long fingernails. Some men decorated their hair with feathers and lead weights. Men used blowguns that were accurate up to 60 feet.

In 1682, René-Robert La Salle claimed Chitimacha lands for France and named that area Louisiana after King Louis XIV. Most Indian slaves of the French were Chitimacha. By 1881, a small group was living near Chareton, Louisiana. In 1917, they gained federal recognition and their lands were purchased privately and sold to the United States. A 250-acre Chitimacha Reservation was established in 1930 in Louisiana. They fought against termination from 1949 to 1969.

A council governs the approximately 200 reservation residents. Their language is no longer spoken. The only Indian school in Louisiana is operated on the Chitimacha reservation.

Choctaw

Choctaw (CHAHK-taw) were also known as Chahta and Pafallaya, a *Chickasaw* word meaning "long hair." Most men in Southeastern tribes shaved their heads, but Choctaw men wore their hair long. They were culturally similar to the Chickasaw and *Creek* and were one of the *Five Civilized Tribes [IV]*. Descent was matrilineal. Choctaw was a Muskogean language.

Their oral history accounts tell that the Choctaw originated at Nanih Waiya, the Mother Mound, a location near Noxapater, Mississippi. They descended from the *Mississippian [I]* Temple Mound Builders and once may have been united with the Chickasaw. Some Choctaw descended directly from the inhabitants of a large village in northwestern Alabama now called Moundville. In the 16th century, they lived in the southern half of Mississippi and parts of Alabama, Georgia, and Louisiana. Today, most Choctaw live in southeastern Oklahoma. In the mid-16th century, the Choctaw population was approximately 15,000 to 20,000. Today, approximately 20,0000 live in Oklahoma, and 4,000 live in Mississippi.

They recognized sun and fire spirits and celebrated the Green Corn ceremony in the fall. They had a national council and were one of the most democratic of Southeastern tribes. Both genders competed in lacrosse teams. Women who committed adultery were punished; some had to live as prostitutes. Homosexuality was accepted in Choctaw culture. Both parents observed food taboos—abstaining from certain foods—following the birth of a child. Maternal uncles were very involved in raising nieces and nephews. Boys received tattoos at adolescence.

The Choctaw wrapped the bodies of their dead in skins and placed them on platforms with food and tools. Raising the dead on platforms was believed to be the way to return their spirits to the sun. At designated times throughout the day, ritual mourning and crying occurred for the dead. Bones were then buried under mounds.

Log walls often surrounded towns, which contained pole-framed houses covered with grass or cane thatch. Winter homes were circular and insulated with clay. They also made bread from corn and sweet potatoes and used sassafras root for tea. They spun fabric with buffalo wool and twisted turkey feathers into thread to make blankets. Women wore skirts of buffalo and plant fiber. A regional trade language was mixed with sign language to enable communication. Both genders tattooed their bodies, the men with records of their war exploits.

One of the first Europeans they encountered was Hernando de Soto, who burned their villages in 1540. The French arrived in Choctaw territory by the late 17th century. During the colonial period, they usually allied with the French, but some bands were friendly to the British. In 1763, the French ceded to Britain all their claims to lands east of the Mississippi, though it is debatable how much of those Indian lands the French could claim to possess.

The Choctaw sided with the Americans against the British in the *American Revolution [IV]* but were shown little consideration by the new government afterwards. The Choctaw began ceding their lands to the federal government in 1801 through treaties in which tribes were often promised lands that did not belong to the federal government or that the government did not intend them to settle upon. By the 1820s, whites regarded the Choctaw as a "civilized" tribe.

The Choctaw never fought the United States, but they were nevertheless force marched west of the Mississippi along with other tribes when President Andrew Jackson carried out the 1830 *Indian Removal Act [IV]*. The Choctaw had fought with President Jackson in the Creek War but, ironically, they were the first tribe to be removed. The arrangements were sealed in an 1830 Treaty of Dancing Rabbit Creek, which was signed by a few Choctaw after the majority had already voted to reject the treaty and had headed home. For those who chose to remain in Mississippi, their tribal government was declared illegal by the state.

About 12,000 Choctaw were removed between 1831 and 1834. One-fourth of the Choctaw died on the forced march of several hundred miles to *Indian Territory [IV]*, which is today the state of Oklahoma. Most Choctaw fought for the Confederacy during the *Civil War [IV]*. Before and during the Civil War, some African Americans who had ecaped from slavery lived as citizens with the Choctaw. After the war, the Choctaw paid for the removal of some of them; others they adopted into the tribe. Some Choctaw today are descended from these African Americans.

The General Allotment Act and the *Curtis Act [IV]* removed lands in Oklahoma (meaning "red people" in Choctaw) from Indian control. By the 1920s, the federal government recognized the Mississippi Choctaw. However, in the 1950s, the Mississippi Choctaw fought against termination. The South's segregation policies aimed at African Americans, known as Jim Crow laws, were also applied to the Choctaw.

The 145,000-acre Choctaw nation has its headquarters in Durant, Oklahoma. The 17,819-acre Mississippi Choctaw Reservation was established in 1930. In 1907, there were approximately 7,000 full-bloods in both Mississippi and Oklahoma. This number declined to 5,000 in 1973 and then to just more than 2,000 today. Most Oklahoma and Mississippi Choctaw are Baptists. In Oklahoma, the Choctaw have a museum and a monthly newspaper, *Bishinik*. An annual festival is held on Labor Day. Games of stickball are still played at powwows. A few Mississippi Choctaw still speak the language. Choctaw communities in Louisiana and Alabama have petitioned for federal recognition, but a southern Alabama band was denied federal recognition in 1998.

Chumash

The Chumash (CHOO-mash), who have also been referred to as the Santa Barbara Indians, speak six different dialects of the Hokan language. They have lived along the Pacific coast from San Luis Obispo to Malibu and inland to the western part of the San Joaquin Valley since before A.D. 1000. Large Chumash villages existed at Syuhtun, Santa Barbara, Shisholop, and Ventura. Their population was estimated to be between 10,000 and 18,000 in the late 18th century, but by 1940 there were only 85 members. Today just more than 200 live on the Santa Ynez Reservation, although approximately 2,000 others identify themselves as Chumash.

Among their religious practices the Chumash recognized spirits called sup, achup, or chupu. They also used charm stones for healing. In ceremonies, they sometimes ingested a hallucinogen called tolache. The head chiefs of their villages could be either male or female. Cross-dressing was not uncommon and denoted enhanced spiritual powers.

Their houses were dome structures 50 feet in diameter built of poles covered with grass. Reed mats were used to cover floors and to cover frame beds. Acorns and marine life were their diet staples. They used abalone and shell for inlay work and carved sea animals out of wood and soapstone. They also made rock paintings, the earliest of which date from A.D 1000. They were the only known North American tribe who built plank boats that had 12- to 30-foot hulls and could carry crews of four for fishing and transportation among islands. Plank boats were made of split cedar logs sewn together with plant fibers and then caulked with asphalt.

Women wore buckskin skirts decorated with abalone shells. Long hair was tied with strings. Both genders pierced noses and ears and painted their bodies.

Their first contact with Europeans occurred in 1542 with Juan Cabrillo of Spain. Contact with Europeans was minimal, however, until the Franciscans built a mission in 1722 at San Luis Obispo and used Indians for slave labor. Some Chumash, however, managed to escape to the hills. In 1824 major rebellions occurred at several missions. After winning its independence from Spain, Mexico took over the missions in 1834 and released the Indians from servitude. Fifteen years later, white settlers arrived in great numbers in the wake of the California gold rush of 1849 and ended up stealing most Chumash land. By 1855, just 100 Chumash remained. By 1900, death from disease and intermarriage had erased most aspects of Chumash culture.

Today a five-member council governs the 120-acre Santa Ynez Reservation established in 1901 in Santa Barbara County. The tribe is working to retain traditional ceremonies such as the Dolphin Dance. The last fluent speaker of Chumash, Mary Yee, died in 1965.

Cocopah

The word Cocopah comes from the *Mojave* word kwi-ka-pah, their word for "neighbors." They referred to themselves as *Xawil Kunyavaei,* meaning "those who live on the river." Descent is patrilineal. Cocopah speak a language called River Yuman, from the Hokan-Siouan language.

Today, many members live in northwestern Mexico and on a reservation near Somerton, Arizona. By the 17th century, the population was estimated at 5,000 to 6,000. In the 19th century, there were approximately 3,000 members. At the end of World War II, about 50 members remained on the reservation. Today, there are approximately 7 members and another 200 living in Baja and Sonora, Mexico. They are known as Cucapa in Mexico.

A Cocopah creation myth tells of twin gods living underwater who emerged to create the world. The Cocopah cremated their dead with their possessions so they would not return to look for their belongings. A six-day mourning ceremony called "karuk" featured song cycles given in dreams.

In winter, they lived in conical, semi-subterranean dwellings. In summer, they constructed brush-covered huts. Crops included corn, beans, black-eyed peas, pumpkins, and melons. They also collected wild wheat that grew in seawater and built earthen dikes for irrigation. Seeds were planted in holes rather than rows to protect topsoil. Both genders made basketry; women also made pottery. Women wore willow-bark skirts and both genders painted their faces. Allies included the *Tohono O'odham*, Pai, and *Pee Posh*. They experienced conflict with the Mojave and *Quechan*.

The 1853 Gadsden Treaty separated the four bands of Cocopah into two in Mexico and two in Arizona. The railroad arrived in 1877. In 1905, the federal government diverted the Colorado River, which led to their displacement.

The 1,700-acre Cocopah Reservation was established in 1917. It adopted a constitution and elected a five-member tribal council in 1964. Unemployment runs at about 90 percent. The Cocopah are trying to attain dual citizenship for their kin in Mexico. They still burn possessions of the dead and continue to speak their native language.

Coeur d'Alene

Coeur d'Alene (kur-duh-LANE) was a French word for "awl heart" or "pointed heart," reportedly a term a chief used to insult traders who misunderstood the term to be the tribe's name. They referred to themselves as *Skitswish*, which possibly meant "foundling." There were three geographical divisions: the Coeur d'Alene River, Spokane River, and Coeur d'Alene Lake. They spoke an interior Salish dialect and used sign language in trading.

The Coeur d'Alene and other *Salish* people, which included the neighboring Flathead, *Kalispel*, and *Spokan*, originated in British Columbia. They migrated from the Pacific coast to the Plateau in prehistoric times. By 1760, they had acquired the *horse [I]* and began to hunt *buffalo [I]* Plains-style. In the 19th century, they lived in central Idaho, eastern Washington, and western Montana. Today, their reservation is located in Idaho. Their population was estimated at 2,000 in the early 18th century. By 1850, their numbers had declined by three-quarters to just 500. Today, there are approximately 1,200 enrolled members. Seven hundred reside on the reservation.

Both genders could seek guardian spirits on vision quests. The dead were wrapped in blankets and buried. The Coeur d'Alene practiced giveaways, similar to coastal potlatches. They had more than 30 village communities.

Between one and three families lived together in semi-underground, conical mat houses. As the tribe adopted some of the lifestyles of the Plains culture after acquiring the horse, they began to live in skin tipis. Salmon and fish were dietary staples, supplemented by buffalo in later times. They had occasional conflicts with the *Nez Perce* and Spokan and eventually allied themselves with the Flathead, *Kootenai*, and Nez Perce. Following that, their conflicts were generally with the *Crow, Lakota*, and *Blackfeet*.

Following the establishment of a Jesuit mission on their lands in 1842, most Coeur d'Alene became Catholic. In 1858, they fought the Coeur d'Alene War with the Northern *Paiute*, Palouse, and Spokan. The "war" was caused by whites' violations of treaties and occurred in the context of a resistance struggle by the Plateau Indians at that time.

The tribe ceded 2.4 million acres to the United States in 1873 in exchange for a 600,000-acre reservation. Pressure from miners forced them to cede 90 percent of these lands. In 1875, Oregon Governor Isaac Stevens failed to make a promised treaty with the Coeur d'Alene, so they had no protection against an onslaught of white miners and settlers. Miners' interests forced them to cede more land to the United States in the late 1880s. Most of their remaining land was lost to allotment, which divided tribal lands into small individual lots, with the surplus sold to whites, in the early 20th century.

IN THEIR OWN Words

I am a red man. If the Great Spirit had desired me to be a white man he would have made me so in the first place. He put in your heart certain wishes and plans, in my other and different desires. Each man is good in his sight. It is not necessary for eagles to be crows. We are poor . . . but we are free. No white man controls our footsteps. If we die . . . we die defending our rights.

—SITTING BULL (TATANKA IYOTAKE, TATANKA IYOTANKA, TATANKA YOTANKA), HUNKPAPA LAKOTA CHIEF (C. 1830–1890). STATED WHILE A REFUGEE IN CANADA IN 1877.

The Coeur d'Alene Reservation (now reduced to 69,176 acres) is located in Kootenai County, Idaho. They adopted their constitution in 1949.

A seven-member tribal council, elected for three-year terms, governs the tribe. Unemployment is usually about 50 percent. Traditional games are celebrated in July at the Whaalaa Days. Currently, the Coeur d'Alene are pressing a claim to ownership of Coeur d'Alene Lake. Few speak the language but language programs are in place on the reservation.

Colville

The name Colville is derived from the whites' naming of the Colville River and the Colville Fort after Eden Colville, governor of the *Hudson's Bay Company [IV]*. Whites also called the Colville "basket people," after their large salmon fishing baskets. They referred to themselves as *Shuyelpee*. They were culturally similar to the Okanagon and Sanpoil and spoke a language from the Okanogan group of the Interior dialect of *Salish*.

In the 18th century, most Colville lived in what is today northeastern Washington State. At that time, their population was estimated at 2,000. They were reduced to only 6 or 7 members by 1882. Today, approximately 3,700 live on the reservation.

The Colville believed that all things, both animate and inanimate, had spirits. Tribal members could seek guardian spirits through feats of endurance. They consumed the first salmon of the season in a five-day ritual and returned the bones to the water at the ritual's conclusion. A first fruit rite was also observed. The Colville sometimes practiced gift giveaways, or potlatches. Girls were secluded for 10 days at puberty. The dead were wrapped in tule mats or deerskin and buried with their possessions. Mourners cut their hair and wore old clothing.

IN THEIR OWN

Words

I will follow the white man's trail. I will make him my friend, but I will not put my back to his burdens. I will be cunning as a coyote. I will ask him to help me understand his ways, and then I will prepare the way for my children, and their children. The Great Spirit has shown me—a day will come when they will outrun the white man in his own shoes.

—MANY HORSES (DOG; LITTLE DOG; SITS-IN-THE-MIDDLE), PIEGAN WAR CHIEF (?–1867). CONFIDED TO A WHITE FRIEND IN 1890 AFTER FEELING THAT THE GHOST DANCE HAD FAILED TO REMOVE THE ARMY.

Their winter homes were semi-underground, circular pit lodges with flat or conical roofs and could be entered through the smoke hole. They also camped in mat or skin tipis. Salmon and other fish were staples of their diet. Weapons included rawhide or wooden armor. They were allies of the Okanagon and had conflicts with the *Nez Perce* and *Yakama*.

In 1782, a smallpox epidemic killed many Colville. They did not participate in the Plateau conflicts of the 1850s, but like many tribes, they were forced to accept treaties in 1855. In 1872, two Colville reservations were established. Whites later thought the lands on the first reservation were too valuable to be given to Indians, so it was replaced with another reservation with less desirable lands. In 1885, Chief Joseph of the Nez Perce and his followers joined the Colville Reservation. They were also joined by the Chelan, Entiat, Lake, Methow, Moses, Nespelem, Okanogan, Palouse, San Poil, Sinkiuse, and Wenatchee tribes. Many Colville converted to Catholicism in the late 19th century. In 1900, their reservation lands were reduced to 1.5 million acres, half their former size. The Confederated Tribes of the Colville Reservation were formed in 1938 and adopted a constitution that year. The tribe struggled with the issue of termination in the 1950s but eventually remained intact. Construction of the Grand Coulee Dam in the 1950s destroyed their traditional fish runs.

The Confederated Tribes are governed by a 14-member council with its tribal headquarters in Nespelem. The 1,011,495-acre reservation, one of the largest in the Northwest, has a total population of approximately 3,700. They are members of the Affiliated Tribes of Northwest Indians. They host an annual powwow and circle celebration.

Comanche

Comanche (cuh-MAN-chee) was derived from the *Ute* word Komanicia, meaning "one who wants to fight me," or possibly the Spanish word *camino ancho* meaning "main road." They referred to themselves as *Nermurnah,* meaning "true human beings," or "people." Variations of the Comanche language were used as a trade language on the Plains. Their language was similar to *Shoshone* and to languages spoken in Central America. Comanche was part of the Uto-Aztecan language.

The Comanche were originally joined with the Eastern Shoshone in Arizona's Gila River region from at least 3000 B.C. until 500 B.C. At that point, a group migrated north toward Utah and raised a type of corn that had been developed in Mexico. The Comanche lived in the Rocky Mountain regions of Wyoming and northern Colorado. In the middle to the late 17th century, they moved into the central and southern Great Plains. By 1719, they had moved to Kansas. Today, most Comanche live in Oklahoma. In the late 18th century, their population was estimated between 7,000 and 12,000. By 1900, their numbers had been reduced to 2,000. Today, they number approximately 8,500 members.

Significant elements of Comanche culture and tradition included the Eagle Dance and Beaver ceremony, both of which were important observances. In 1874, they also adopted the Sun Dance, an annual summer renewal rite. The dance was adopted at a time when the buffalo were being hunted to extinction by whites and the Comanche way of life was changing with pressure to move to reservations. Young Comanche men traditionally sought guardian spirits on vision quests. Men could have more than one wife. The dead were buried in their best clothing with their faces painted red and red clay on their eyes, and their possessions were given away. Mourners cut their hair and made cuts on their limbs.

Buffalo [I] was a staple of their diet. Both genders were excellent riders, and children were taught to ride by age five. For battle they used red paint on their faces and on the heads and tails of their horses. Their allies included the *Pawnee*. They joined a confederacy in 1840 with the Southern Cheyenne and Southern *Arapaho*. They occasionally fought the *Kiowa* and *Apache*.

From 1780 to 1781, the Comanche lost half their population to a smallpox epidemic. A cholera epidemic in 1849, brought by whites traveling through their territory on the way to the California gold rush, took an even heavier toll. In the 1840s, the Comanche fought with Texans who had implemented a policy of extermination of all Indians in the area.

IN THEIR OWN *Words*

You said that you wanted to put us on a reservation, to build our houses and make us medicine lodges. I do not want them. I was born upon the prairie where the wind blew free and there was nothing to break the light of the sun. I was born where there were no enclosures and where everything drew a free breath. I want to die there.

—TEN BEARS (PARIA SEMEN; PARIASEAMEN; PAROOWAY SEMEHNO; PARRA-WA-SAMEN; PARRA-WA-SEMEN; PARRYWASAYMEN; PARYWAHSAYMEN;), COMANCHE SPOKESPERSON (1792–C. 1872). SPOKEN TO THE U.S. COMMISSIONERS AT THE 1867 COUNCIL AT MEDICINE LODGE CREEK.

166

They signed an 1865 treaty that reserved lands for them in western *Indian Territory [IV]*, which today is the state of Oklahoma. The 1867 *Treaty of Medicine Lodge [IV]* assigned them to lands in Oklahoma but they eluded roundup by the military until 1875. In 1875, mixed-blood Chief Quanah Parker surrendered to the army and settled on lands in Indian Territory. Parker was an astute leader who was able to gain favorable land leases. He was involved in establishing the Peyote religion.

Allotment of reservation lands began in 1892. Sixteen years later, in 1908, nothing remained of the reservation. During World War II, the Comanche served with other Oklahoma Indians in the Forty-fifth Thunderbird division. The Comanche language was used as the basis of a signal code. About two dozen Comanche served as code talkers.

The Comanche had been confederated with the Kiowa and Plains Apache in the 1867 Treaty of Medicine Lodge. However, in 1963 they separated from the confederation and became the Comanche Tribe of Oklahoma. They adopted a constitution in 1967. They have no reservation. Approximately 5,000 Comanche live near the tribal headquarters at Lawton, Oklahoma. Just over 200 elders speak the language, and the tribe has joined efforts with the University of Oklahoma to preserve the language. A Comanche Homecoming Powwow is held in July at Walters, Oklahoma.

Coosan

Coosan is an Athapascan word that refers to the Coos Bay area in Oregon. The Coosan are actually composed of two groups, the Coosan and Siuslaw. They speak two Coosan languages, Hanis and Miluk. Both the Coosan and Siuslaw languages are part of the Penutian language group.

The Coosan continue to live around their traditional lands in Coos Bay, Oregon. Their population numbered 4,000 in the mid-18th century. By 1870, this number had been reduced to 465. Today the Confederated Tribes of Coos, Lower Umpqua, and Siuslaw have 500 enrolled members.

The Coosan believed they could gain power through dreams and vision quests. They conducted ceremonies after catching the first salmon and first elk of the season in order to celebrate the return of game and to honor the salmon and elk on which their diet depended. Residence was patrilocal. The role of chief was hereditary and was open to women as well as men.

The Coosan were divided into four classes: noble, commoner, poor, and slave. All classes shared the same subsistence levels but differed in the amount of nonfood wealth they accumulated. Men paid a bride-price at marriage. Possessions of the dead were broken and placed around their graves.

Homes were built partially underground and could be 50 feet long and 25 feet wide. Walls and roofs were constructed of planked cedar. Tule mats lined the inside walls and covered the floors, and raised bed platforms ran along the walls. Salmon and other fish were staples of the diet. In the 1870s, they practiced the Dream Dance, a variation of the *Ghost Dance [IV]*.

The tribe and reservation were terminated in the 1950s. Federal recognition was restored in 1977, and in 1980 the Coosan gained a 3,630-acre reservation.

The Confederated Tribes of Coos, Lower Umpqua, and Siuslaw Indians in Coos Bay, Oregon, have a six-acre land base and cemetery.

Costanoan

Costanoan is a Spanish word meaning "coast people." They are sometimes referred to by the name of one subgroup, Ohlone. Eight dialects of the language were spoken: Awaswas, Chalon, Chohenyo, Karkin, Muutsun, Ramaytush, Rumsen, and Tamyen. Costanoan is a Penutian language.

Since before 500 B.C. the Costanoan have inhabited the central California coast from San Francisco Bay to south of Monterey Bay. Today, many Costanoan live in that same area. Their population was estimated at 10,000 in the mid-18th century. That number was reduced to 200 by the 1970s.

Costanoan lived in conical homes constructed of pole frames covered with tule or grass. Important Costanoan dances included the Coyote Dance, Devil's Dance, Dove Dance, Medicine Man's Dance, and Puberty Dance. Traditionally, girls were secluded at puberty, while boys sought guardian spirits in vision quests. Marriage was formalized with gifts to the bride from the groom, and newlyweds lived in the groom's family home. Men could have more than one wife. Some men grew beards; others tweezed their faces with wooden tweezers or a pair of mussel shells. Both genders tattooed and painted their bodies. The dead were buried or cremated with their possessions. Souls of the dead were thought to journey across the sea.

By the late 18th century, the Spanish had built seven missions in Costanoan territory and forced religious conversions on the Indians. Between 1770 and 1832, the population had been reduced more than 80 percent. The California gold rush brought a flood of white settlers into the area.

The Costanoan have never had a reservation. In the 1960s, Costanoan descendants of the Mission San Jose were able to prevent the destruction of a burial ground that was in the path of a proposed freeway. This group organized as the Ohlone Indian tribe and gained title to a cemetery in Fremont, California. A similar situation in 1975 at Watsonville, California, led to the founding of the Pajaro Valley Ohlone Indian Council after activists formed a human barricade to prevent destruction of *burial grounds [IV]*. In 1989, Stanford University returned skeletal remains for reburial.

The Costanoan language has been extinct since the 1930s. However, the Costanoan have been recognized by the state of California and are seeking federal recognition.

Cree

Cree is from the French word Kristeneaux, a designation for a particular Cree band. They referred to themselves as *Ininiw*, meaning "person," or, among the Woodland Cree, as *Atheneauwuck*, meaning, "people." They spoke a dialect of a central Algonquian language.

The Cree and *Anishinabe* were once probably united. Their traditional lands were in Ontario and Quebec, where they lived for at least 4,000 years. Their population was estimated at 20,000 in the 16th century. Today, there are about 120,000 Cree. Most live in Ontario and Quebec, but some reside on the Rocky Boy Chippewa-Cree Reservation in Montana.

Woodland Cree had a number of important aspects to their religious practices. They believed in a creator spirit, Manitou. Adolescents sought guardian spirits on vision quests. Social customs included the practice of grooms working for their in-laws for a period of time. The dead were wrapped in bark with their tools and buried in the ground. They also held an annual feast of the dead.

In southern areas, people lived in dome-shaped birchbark wigwams. Further north and west, lodges were covered with caribou or moose skins. Houses were occupied by extended families of 10 or more people. Southern groups also hunted *buffalo [I]*. Meat was boiled by adding hot stones to containers or was dried and mixed with fat and berries to make pemmican. They made cooking vessels of birch bark and decorated clothing with geometric (and later, floral and beaded) designs.

One of the first Europeans they encountered was Henry Hudson in 1610. Later, French and Scottish trappers intermarried with the Cree. The mixed-race children of those unions were known as the Metis. The Metis led two rebellions in the late 19th century over land rights.

A large part of their tribal lands was flooded in 1971 as a result of the construction of the James Bay hydroelectric project. The flood produced by the project released mercury from the soil that polluted the water, making fish in the region unsafe to consume. A second James Bay project that was planned would have flooded an additional 2,000 square miles. However, that project was blocked by activists in 1994.

About half the Cree still speak the language. Canada provincially and federally recognizes the Cree.

Creek

Creek Indians were designated so by the British, who named them for Ochesee Creek. The Creek were composed of a number of subtribes, of which the Muskogee was the largest. Whites called the Creek one of the five "civilized" tribes that included the *Cherokee, Chickasaw, Choctaw*, and *Seminole*. Descent was matrilineal. Beaded belts recorded tribal history, as did pictographs. They used Choctaw as a trade language, although their own language was Muskogean. Other Muskogean-speaking groups included the Alabama, Chickasaw, Choctaw, Coushatta, and Seminole.

The Creek probably descended from the *Mississippian [I]* Temple Mound Builders. The Creek Confederacy was formed before 1540 and continued to thrive through the 18th century. It was comprised of a number of subtribes including the Muskogee. Their traditional lands were in Alabama, eastern Georgia, and southern Tennessee. The Upper Creek in Alabama had two main towns: Abihkba and Tukabahchee. The Lower Creek in eastern Georgia had two main towns, Coweta and Kashita, and were considered to be more assimilated into white society.

Today, most Creek live in east central Oklahoma. The population was estimated at 22,000 in the mid-16th century, of which 80 percent were Muskogean. In 1900, there were approximately 10,000 members. Today, the Creek have about 30,000 enrolled members, more than half of whom live in Oklahoma.

Creeks marked the New Year with a Green Corn ceremony, a type of thanksgiving feast. A black caffeine drink that caused vomiting was consumed during ceremonies in order to purify the body. Another feast that took place in late fall was the Dance of the Ancient People. Creek tradition involved spiritual beings such as dwarfs, fairies, and giants.

Creek culture permitted premarital sex and allowed men to marry more than one wife. Both parties could be killed or punished in cases of adultery, and rape and incest were capital offenses. Widows could not remarry for four years, but widowers could remarry in four months. Men avoided their mothers-in-law out of respect. Infanticide was allowed during the first month of a child's life. They buried their dead beneath their houses, along with their possessions. The Creek believed that the land of the dead beyond the Milky Way was reserved for the worthy.

The Creek dwelled in tribal towns where populations ranged from 100 to 1,000. A town crier announced tribal council decisions. Elders known as Beloved Men and Beloved Women were part of the council. As with the Cherokee, red towns were associated with games and war, and white towns were associated with civic affairs. Creek society was divided into 40

> **IN THEIR OWN** *Words*
>
> When the first white man came over the wide waters, he was but a little man . . . very little. His legs were cramped by sitting long in his big boat, and he begged for a little land . . .
>
> When he came to these shores the Indians gave him land, and kindled fires to make him comfortable . . .
>
> But when the white man had warmed himself at the Indian's fire, and had filled himself with the Indian's hominy, he became very large . . .
>
> Brothers! I have listened to a great many talks from our Great Father. But they always began and ended in this—"Get a little farther; you are too near me." I have spoken.
>
> —SPECKLED SNAKE, CREEK CHIEF. STATED IN 1829 DURING CREEK DEBATES ABOUT REMOVAL TO WEST OF THE MISSISSIPPI.

clans, each of which was named for an animal. Towns were organized around a central plaza built upon a mound. Homes were 12 feet high and had beds built along the walls. Beams that supported the structure were often painted or carved with human and animal designs. Walls were plastered with grass or mats on the outside. Families had two-story granaries. Corn, beans, and squash were staples of their diet. They also hunted with blowguns of eight to ten feet in length. Some Creek men wore moustaches. They had conflicts with the Apalachee, Cherokee, and Choctaw.

A 19th-century cigar advertisement showing American Indians welcoming Hernando de Soto and his crew, as de Soto's men plant a large cross on Indian land. *Library of Congress.*

The first European the Creek encountered was Hernando de Soto in 1540. They were allies of the British, although they joined in the Yamasee Rebellion in 1715 to protest British practices of Indian slavery and brutality. In the *American Revolution [IV]*, the white stick (Lower Creek division) supported the United States, and the red stick (Upper Creek) supported the British. After the Revolution, both groups were forced to cede 23 million acres to the new American government in the Treaty of Horseshoe Bend. In 1825, a handful of chiefs illegally signed a treaty that ceded all tribal lands in the state of Georgia to the state.

President Andrew Jackson signed the *Indian Removal Act [IV]* in 1830 that called for all Indians in the Southeast to live west of the Mississippi. Forced relocation began in 1836. Four thousand of the 14,000 who were forcibly marched to *Indian Territory [IV]* (now Oklahoma) died on the way. During the *Civil War [IV]*, their allegiance was split between the Confederacy and the Union. The Upper Creek, being more traditional, supported the Union.

They adopted a constitution in 1867 but lost their political independence and all their lands when Oklahoma became a state in 1907. In 1900, Chitto Harjo (Crazy Snake) led a rebellion against allotment. The short-lived rebellion was ultimately unsuccessful, and Harjo was arrested and imprisoned. In 1917, the Upper Creek joined the Green Corn Rebellion, a movement of poor rural Indians, African Americans, and white sharecroppers who sought federal assistance and an end to World War I.

The Creek constitution was revised again in 1975. The Upper Creek today are mainly Baptists, and the Lower Creek are generally Presbyterians and Methodists.

The Creek still celebrate a Green Corn ceremony in July. There are Creek communities in Alabama and Georgia who do not yet have federal recognition.

Crow

The Crow referred to themselves as *Absaroke*, a Siouan word for "bird people." Descent was matrilineal. Crow is a Siouan language.

Originally the Crow were united with the *Hidatsa* in Ohio. Around the 17th century, they split off from the Hidatsa and moved westward when *Anishinabe* and *Cree*, armed with guns, pushed them off their lands in order to hunt for the fur trade. By the late 18th century, they lived in southwestern Montana and northern Wyoming. At that point, they split into two divisions. The mountain group settled in southern Montana and northern Wyoming, and the river group settled in Yellowstone. Their population was estimated at 4,000 in the late 18th century. Today, the Crow have about 8,400 members, who live mainly in Montana.

An important part of Crow culture were guardian spirits who could be acquired in dreams or though vision quests. Three primary traditions were the Sun Dance, the Medicine Lodge, and the Tobacco Society.

A delegation of Sioux Indians to Washington in 1891. *Library of Congress.*

A dance and a feast followed the planting of tobacco. Premarital or extramarital sex was allowed, but female chastity was valued. As in Creek and other cultures, males avoided mothers-in-law out of respect. They placed their dead on a platform and later buried the bones. Mourners cut their hair, gave property away, and made cuts on their limbs to indicate their grief.

When the Crow lived with the Hidatsa they built earth lodges. Later, when they moved to the prairies, they constructed skin tipis. Most tipis held about 12 people, but the largest tipis could hold as many as forty. Before moving to the Plains, corn was a staple of the diet. After moving westward, *buffalo [I]* became more important. The Crow wore their hair which, with horsehair extensions, could reach the ground, parted in the middle. Some traders called the Crow the "long-haired Indians." They occasionally fought the *Blackfeet*, *Lakota*, and *Shoshone*. Allies included the *Mandan*, *Nez Perce*, and *Salish* (Flathead). They believed that touching an enemy (counting coup) was a higher honor than killing.

Major smallpox epidemics reduced their number by more than half in 1781 and 1833. In 1851, they signed the *Treaty of Fort Laramie [IV]*, retaining 38.5 million acres in the Yellowstone region. These lands were

IN THEIR OWN Words

Their Wise Ones said we might have their religion, but when we tried to understand it, we found that there were too many kinds of religion among white men for us to understand, and that scarcely any two white men agreed which was the right one to learn. This bothered us a good deal until we saw that the white man did not take his religion any more seriously than he did his laws, and that he kept both of them just behind him, like helpers, to use when they might do him good in his dealings with strangers.

We made up our minds to be friendly with them, in spite of all the changes they were bringing. But we found this difficult, because the white men too often promised to do one thing and then, when they acted at all, did another. They spoke very loudly when they said their laws were made for everybody, but we soon learned that although they expected us to keep them, they thought nothing of breaking them themselves.

—PLENTY COUPS (ALAXCHIIAAHUSH, ALEEK-CHEA-AHOOSH [MANY ACCOMPLISHMENTS]), CROW CHIEF (C. 1848–1932). QUOTED IN *PLENTY COUPS, CHIEF OF THE CROWS*, BY FRANK LINDERMAN, UNIVERSITY OF NEBRASKA PRESS, 1962.

reduced in 1868. They served as scouts for the United States in the conflicts of the 1860s and 1870s against the Lakota and Nez Perce. Their traditional giveaways and the Sun Dance were outlawed in 1884. In the 1950s, they relinquished their rights to Bighorn Canyon, where the Yellowtail Dam was built. In 1981, they ceded ownership of the Bighorn River to the state of Montana.

The 1.5-million-acre Crow Reservation in Montana was established in 1868. Less than a third of this land is tribally owned. About 4,700 people reside on the reservation. All adults participate in the general council, which elects four tribal officers.

Although Little Big Horn College offers higher educational opportunities, unemployment among the Crow runs about 50 percent. Today, there are 10 clans, and the Crow language is still spoken by the majority. They hold an annual fair in August that includes a rodeo and giveaways.

Dakota

The Dakota (da-KO-tah) take their name from the word in their own language meaning "ally." *Dakotah Oyate,* meaning "Dakota people," and *Ikce Wicasa,* meaning "free people," are also used. They are often called Sioux, but the word "Sioux" is an outdated term that was used by whites to refer to the Dakota, *Lakota*, and *Nakota* people. French in origin, Sioux refers to the *Anishinabe* word for the Dakota, *Nadowe-is-iw,* meaning "snake" or "enemy." Today, Lakota or Dakota is sometimes used to refer to all three groups. The Dakota language is a Siouan dialect of the eastern group.

The Dakota may have originated in eastern Texas or in the Ohio Valley as descendants of the *Hopewell [I]* Mound Builder culture. They were the last group to move westward to search for *buffalo [I]*, and as a result, they retained many Eastern *Woodland [I]* and Great Lakes cultural traits. The Yankton and Santee bands exhibited signs of Prairie Indian culture. In the late 17th century, the Dakota lived in Wisconsin and north central Minnesota. By the 19th century, they had been pushed onto the prairies and eastern plains of Minnesota and eastern South Dakota as other tribes, armed with guns, moved into their territory to hunt for furs. At that time, their population was estimated to be 5,000. In 1839, the population was just under 4,000. Today, there are around 6,000 Dakota out of 25,000 total among the three groups: Dakota, Lakota, and Nakota. Originally, there were 13 subdivisions of Siouan speakers. Their seven political divisions included: the Dakota, who were the eastern group (Sisseton, Wahpeton, Wahpekute, and Mdewakanton); the Lakota, who were the western group (Teton); and the Nakota, who were the central group (Yankton and Yanktonai). The lifestyle of the Lakota (Teton) became the stereotyped image of all American Indians: tipis, war bonnets, and buffalo hunting.

Among the Dakota, descent was patrilineal. They believed in a creator spirit called Wakan Tanka. They retained Woodland-type traditions, such as the Medicine Lodge Society, although the Dakota later adopted some Plains ceremonies like the Sun Dance. The Dakota were divided into seven bands, each of which represented at the Seven Council fires, which served as a national deliberating body. The dead were wrapped in skins or blankets with their tools and placed on platforms. After a few months the bones were buried in mounds.

Little Crow, a leader of the 1862 Dakota uprising in Minnesota. *Library of Congress.*

Log walls surrounded some villages. While in Wisconsin and Minnesota, they lived in wood-framed bark houses, which men and women built together. Some used tipis after their move to the prairies. Women decorated items with geometric designs; men decorated items with realistic forms. Most clothing was made from buckskin. On the Plains, they decorated clothing with *beads [I]* and quillwork in geometric and animal patterns. Their traditional enemies were the Anishinabe. As with other groups, touching an enemy (counting coup) brought more honor than killing.

The Dakota ceded their lands in Minnesota and Iowa to the United States in 1837 and 1851 in the Mendota (Mdewakanton and Wahpekute Santee) and Traverse de Sioux Treaties (Sisseton and Wahpeton) in exchange for a small reservation. A rebellion started in the summer of 1862 when whites continued to trespass on their lands, while many Dakota were starving because promised food and payments did not arrive.

After the short-lived conflict, the military sentenced more than 300 Dakota to death. Lincoln, however, pardoned more than 250 of them. Thirty-eight Dakota were hung in a mass execution on the day after Christmas in Mankato, Minnesota; this remains the largest mass execution in

U.S. history. Surviving Dakota were force marched to Fort Snelling and transported east. Dakota land and property were confiscated. Mdewakanton and Wahpekute survivors were forced to relocate to Crow Creek, South Dakota, where hundreds died within the first year due to starvation and disease. Little Crow, who had been a leader of the uprising, was hunted and killed in 1863. His scalp and skull remained on display at the Historical Society in St. Paul, Minnesota, until the 1970s. Small numbers of Dakota remained in the state of Minnesota after the conflict.

Today, many Dakota reservations exist in Minnesota and South Dakota. There are more than 10,000 enrolled tribal members. Unemployment rates vary by reservation, from a high of 60 percent to a low of 20 percent. The Sisseton Wahpeton Community College opened in South Dakota in 1975. Many tribal members still speak Dakota.

Dogrib

Dogrib is an English translation of the Thlingchadinne word meaning "dog flank people," which refers to their legend of descent from a dog. They also refer to themselves as *Dine*, meaning "people." Dogrib is a northeastern Athapascan language.

Dogrib traditionally lived in the northwest territories and may have migrated from lands in the south and east. Their population was estimated at 1,250 in the late 17th century. Today, they have approximately 3,000 enrolled members.

Spirits that inhabited bodies of water were a focal point of some Dogrib traditional practices. Parents often changed their own names at the birth of children. Men served their in-laws for a period of time after marriage and could have more than one wife. They placed their dead on platforms. Mourners destroyed the property of the deceased and made cuts on their own bodies. A memorial feast was held on the first anniversary of their lost relatives' death. They lived in tipis made of as many as 40 caribou skins, and boiled meat by placing hot stones in caribou stomach-lined holes. They exported some copper from their region. Musical instruments included caribou hoof rattles. They had conflict with the Yellowknife, Chipewayan, and *Cree*.

Trading posts were established in their region by the 1790s. Fort Rae, the first permanent local fort, was built in 1852. The tribe suffered from epidemics in 1859. Most converted to Catholicism by 1870. They signed their first treaty with Canada in 1900. Some Dogrib language is still in use, and tribal bands are still recognized.

Gros Ventre

Gros Ventre (grow-VAHN-truh) was the French word for "big bellies." The Gros Ventre tribe gained this name from Europeans because of the hand movements they used in their sign language. They referred to themselves as *Ah-ah-nee-nin,* meaning "white clay" people. According to their creation myth, they were shaped out of clay by the creator. Descent was patrilineal. Gros Ventre is an Algonquian language.

More than 3,000 years ago they may have been united with the *Arapaho* and lived in the western Great Lakes region in permanent villages. The *Anishinabe* pushed them westward in the early 18th century. During this migration, the Gros Ventre and Arapaho separated. After acquiring the *horse [I]* in the mid-18th century, they adopted many of the cultural traits of the Plains Indians, such as living in tipis and hunting *buffalo [I].* In the late 18th century, most Gros Ventre lived in north-central Montana. Today, most continue to reside in that area. Their population was estimated at 3,600 in the 18th century. By 1895, there were less than 600 members left, but their numbers have grown to an estimated 2,900 enrolled members today.

The Gros Ventre observed Plains spiritual practices such as vision quests, medicine bundles, and the Sun Dance. They still own two sacred pipes, given to them by the creator: the Feathered Pipe and the Flat Pipe. Men could have more than one wife and divorce was common among them. They wrapped their dead in robes and placed them on a platform. Food was cooked with heated rocks in a hole filled with water.

They signed the 1851 *Treaty of Fort Laramie [IV]* and another treaty in 1855 that ceded lands to the United States. The smallpox epidemic of 1870 greatly reduced their numbers. In 1888, the Gros Ventre were placed on the Fort Belknap Reservation in northern Montana, which they shared with the *Assiniboine.* An 1884 *gold [IV]* rush in the area forced the tribe to cede more lands. Tuberculosis claimed more than 90 percent of the tribe in the 20th century.

The 616,000-acre Fort Belknap Reservation is run by a 12-member tribal council composed of half Gros Ventre and half Assiniboine. One-quarter of the lands today are tribally owned, and unemployment runs about 50 percent. Their language is still taught in schools, but few speak fluently today. The Gros Ventre are considering officially changing their name to Ah-ah-nee-nin.

Haida

Haida (HI-duh) is derived from the name the tribe called themselves meaning "people." Descent was matrilineal. The Haida speak dialects of the Athapascan language group.

The Haida settled on their lands, which include the Queen Charlotte Islands and parts of British Columbia, more than 9,000 years ago. Today, most Haida continue to live on Queen Charlotte as well as on Prince Wales Island in Alaska. Their population was estimated at 9,000 to 10,000 in the late 18th century, but had dropped by 95 percent to just a few hundred by 1915. Today, there are approximately 1,800 enrolled members.

The Haida believed that animals possessed souls like humans, lived in villages, and changed shapes. They believed in the existence of three separate worlds: sea, sky, and land. They gave potlatches—feasts and gift giveaways by people with wealth—so they could confirm their status. Crests carved on totem poles identified lineage and rank. These crests were also engraved on other wooden items and tattooed on the bodies of the wealthy. Crest figures were painted in black, red, and blue-green and portrayed mythological characters and events. Haida believed children were reincarnated ancestors. Girls were secluded for a month at their first menses. Marriages were arranged in childhood and marked by gift exchanges. As part of their funeral tradition, the dead lay in state for several days and were then buried. Burial was followed with a potlatch. The wealthy had memorial poles erected in honor of their loved ones.

They lived in red-cedar-planked houses with cedar-bark roofs. Houses could be as large as 60 by 100 feet and had terraced tiers that served as sleeping areas. Salmon, halibut, and other fish were staples of their diet. Unlike their southern neighbors, the *Nootka* and *Makah*, the Haida did not hunt whales. Clothing was made from cedar bark or animal skins.

They experienced conflict with the Coast Tsimshian, *Bella Bella*, Coast *Salish*, *Kwakiutl*, Nootka, and Southern *Tlingit*.

One of the first Europeans they encountered was Juan Perez Hernandez in 1774. Methodist *missionaries [IV]* arrived in the area in 1829. In the 1830s, the *Hudson's Bay Company [IV]* established a trading post in their area. Smallpox epidemics in 1791 and 1862 eliminated entire village populations.

In 1884, Canada passed the Indian Act, which provided for the continued establishment of reserves, including 3,500 acres for the Haida. That same year, however, the potlatch was outlawed.

In 1936, the Haida were the first Indian group in Alaska to adopt a constitution on American territory. They gained a reservation in 1949, but the salmon industry lobbied against it and a judge invalidated it within a few years. Under the terms of the 1971 *Alaska Native Claims Settlement Act [IV]*, the Haida set up hundreds of corporations, such as Sealaska and the Tlingit-Haida Central Council, to administer the money and land settlement. They elect tribal councils every two years, and they still observe potlatches at deaths.

Hare

Hare was the English name given to the tribe because of its dietary consumption of snowshoe hare. They are also called Pai Indians. In their own language, the Hare refer to themselves as *Kawchottine*, meaning "people of the great hare." The Hare are culturally similar to the *Dogrib* and *Kutchin*, with whom they were traditionally allied. The Hare language is of the Northern Athapascan group.

The Hare believed that guardian spirits could appear in dreams and that souls were reborn after death. Grooms served a bride's family after marriage. Their funeral ceremonies included a memorial feast one year after death.

Hare lived in pole-framed houses. Later, in the 19th century, some used caribou-hide tipis. They boiled meat by placing hot stones in liquid. They traveled by toboggans, which were pulled by women before dogs were used in the 20th century. Body decorations included tattooing and face painting. Their traditional enemies were the *Inuit* and Yellowknife.

One of the first Europeans they encountered was Alexander Mackenzie in 1789. The North West Company built Fort Good Hope in their region in 1806. Their population was estimated at approximately 800 in the early 18th century. Today, the number of enrolled members is slightly below that number.

Havasupai

Havasupai (hah-vah-SOO-pie) means "people of the blue-green water." They are a branch of the Hualpal Indians. Residence was patrilocal. They speak Upland Yuman, part of the Hokan-Diouan language group.

Since the 1100s, 13 bands of Havasupai have lived near the Grand Canyon in Arizona. Their population was estimated at 250 in the 17th century, but epidemics had reduced their numbers to just over 100 by 1906. Today, there are about 400 enrolled members.

Their seclusion in canyons allowed them to avoid contact with and attacks from Europeans until the 1800s, when a trail to California was cut through their lands. Mines opened in the territory in 1863. They gained a reservation of 518 acres in 1880 and often invited *Hopi*, *Hualapai*, and *Navajo* neighbors to their ceremonies. Their lifestyle was more similar to the Hopi than to the Yuman group to which they were related. They cremated the dead, and by the late 19th century began to bury them. They used masked dancers in ceremonies—a practice they may also have adopted from the Hopi. Like other tribes, they participated in the *Ghost Dance [I]* in the 1890s. Marriage was formalized when the groom moved in with the bride's family. After the birth of a child, couples moved into their own homes, which were owned by men. Both genders tattooed and painted their faces. Girls went through a formal puberty ritual.

Homes consisted of conical wikiups of thatch over a pole frame. They raised corn, beans, squash, sunflowers, and tobacco. They produced brown, unpainted pottery and finely woven baskets that could serve as water containers. Most of their clothing was made of buckskin or yucca fiber and was trimmed with hoof bells. Allies included the Hopi and Hualapai. They had conflict with the Tonto *Apache*, Western Apache, and Yavapai.

The Havasupai were forced off their traditional lands in 1934 when the National Park Service confiscated their lands and destroyed their homes. In response, a tribal council was created in 1939. After active lobbying by the tribe, some of their confiscated lands were returned in 1975, when the Grand Canyon National Park Enlargement Act was signed. Concerns with contamination from uranium mines, especially of their sacred site in the Kaibab National Forest, led the tribe to ban mining on their lands. They have resisted proposed mines on the basis of the *American Indian Religious Freedom Act [IV]* in order to protect their sacred sites.

Today, many never leave their canyon area; as a result, intermarriage with other groups is rare. The nearest shopping facilities are 100 miles away. Horses are still used by some as their primary source of transportation. Most children entering the tribal school speak Pai. They still hold a traditional fall peach festival.

Hidatsa

Hidatsa (hee-DOT-suh) was the name of a former village and may have meant "rows of lodges" or "original people." French traders called them Gros Ventres of the Missouri. Descent was matrilineal. Hidatsa is a dialect of the Siouan language.

Originally, the Hidatsa may have lived on the lower Mississippi River, migrating north through Tennessee, Kentucky, and Ohio. They were originally united with the *Crow* tribe but separated from them in the late 17th century. The Hidatsa increasingly became associated with the agricultural

A Hidatsa winter village in North Dakota in the 1840s. *State Historical Society of North Dakota.*

Arikira and *Mandan* tribes. In the late 18th century, their population was estimated at 2,500. Today, the Hidatsa have approximately 6,000 enrolled members of the Three Affiliated Tribes (Arikira, Hidatsa, and Mandan). By the 18th century, most of the Hidatsa were living in western North Dakota, where they continue to reside today.

Some of the Hidatsa's rituals included the Corn Dance feast of the Women, and later the Sun Dance. They also had a White Buffalo Society, a society consisting only of women members, who lured the buffalo to the hunters.

The Hidatsa lived in circular earth lodges that were about 40 feet in diameter and could house as many as 40 people from two or three families. The house's wooden frame was covered with clay and sod, and could last as long as 10 years or more. Furnishings included rawhide platform beds and buffalo robe couches. They used portable tipis when traveling on a hunt. Women raised corn, beans, squash, pumpkins, and sunflowers. Men grew tobacco. Once the tribe acquired the *horse [I]* in the 18th century, they hunted *buffalo [I]* on the plains. Body decorations included tattoos. They were allies with the Mandan and experienced conflict with the *Dakota* and *Shoshone*.

Among the first Europeans they encountered were Meriwether Lewis and William Clark, who lived among them for several weeks during their expedition in the early 1800s. Smallpox epidemics reduced their population to just a few villages by 1800. Another smallpox epidemic in 1837 reduced their numbers to fewer than 100. The survivors moved to a single village with the Mandan near Fort Berthold, North Dakota. The Arikira joined them in 1862. The Fort Berthold Reservation was established in 1871 for the three groups. The 1851 *Treaty of Fort Laramie [IV]* had recognized their land claims to 12 million acres. That was reduced to a reservation of 8 million acres in 1871, then further reduced to 1 million acres by 1886. The Hidatsa unsuccessfully opposed the Garrison Dam built in the 1950s, which submerged most of their farmlands and homes.

Today, they live on the 900,000-acre Fort Berthold Reservation with the Arikira and Mandan, although the tribes own less than half of that land. The reservation population is just under 3,000, of which Hidatsa are the largest group. Most Hidatsa live in the town of Mandaree. A few elders speak the language. Each tribe sponsors an annual powwow. There is a tribal museum at New Town and a newspaper, the *Mandan, Hidatsa, and Arikira Times.*

Hopi

The name Hopi (HO-pee) comes from the term *Hopituh Shi-nu-ma*, meaning "peaceful people." Descent was matrilineal and residence was matrilocal. Hopi is a *Shoshone* dialect of the Uto-Aztecan language group. They are the only *Pueblo* people to speak a dialect of the Uto-Aztecan language group.

The Hopi are the most western group of Pueblo people. They are descendants of the ancient *Anasazi [I]* culture and have lived in the same location for at least 10,000 years. One settlement, Oraibi (Third Mesa), has been occupied since 1100. Other major settlements include Walpi (First Mesa) and Shungopavi (Second Mesa). They reside in northeast Arizona in the center of *Navajo* lands. Their population was estimated at 2,800 in the late 17th century; today, the Hopi have approximately 7,000 enrolled members.

According to their oral history, the Hopi are caretakers of the fourth world, the earth, in exchange for permission to live there. The Hopi have two major ceremonial cycles: the masked cycle, which lasts from January until July, and the unmasked cycle, which lasts the rest of the year. During the winter period, kachinas (supernatural beings symbolized by masks worn in tribal ceremonies) traveled to the human world and lived in people's bodies until summer.

Their staple crop of corn and their need for rain are the focus of many ceremonies, which can last up to nine days. Ceremonies are conducted in a kiva, a below ground area that is symbolic of a doorway to the underworld from which they emerged. A stone-lined hole in the floor represents the entrance to the cave world of their ancestors.

The Hopi ceremony that is probably most familiar to outsiders is the August Snake Dance. The August Snake Dance is a rain ceremony in which the kachinas dance with live snakes around their necks, arms, and in their mouths.

A mask of raw cotton that symbolized the clouds covered the face of their dead, who were wrapped in blankets and buried with food and water. Prayer sticks for a spirit ladder were also placed in graves.

Women built and owned houses, and the men farmed. Pueblo housing was sometimes four or five stories high and built of adobe. The houses were entered through ladders in the roofs. The ladders represented the trees they climbed when emerging from the underworld. In addition to corn, they raised beans, squash, cotton, and tobacco. Accurate calendars were used to mark planting and harvest cycles. Men wove clothing, and women made pottery. Single girls wore their hair in the shape of a squash blossom that protruded from both sides of their heads; the hairstyle meant that a girl was ready for marriage. After marriage, the women wore braids.

Their first encounter with Europeans was with Francisco de Coronado in 1540. The first missionary arrived in 1629, but the Spanish did not colonize the Hopi, because of the difficulty in reaching their settlements. The Hopi joined the Pueblo Rebellion of 1680 led by Popé, who had reacted against enslavement and religious persecution. The Hopi accepted refugees from other pueblos when the Spanish reoccupied Santa Fe and the surrounding area in 1692. In 1700, the Hopi destroyed the mission at Awatovi, thus managing to remain free of European contact and Christianity for more than 200 years.

Five Hopi children, circa 1900. *Library of Congress.*

The 1.5-million-acre Hopi Reservation was established in 1882. When surveyors arrived to allot their lands to individual tribal members, they were met with armed resistance. Hopi leaders were imprisoned for resisting allotment. The Hopi who refused to send their children to boarding schools run by whites were also imprisoned. The United States military sometimes kidnapped Hopi children and moved them miles away to boarding schools.

Following the establishment of the Hopi Reservation, the Navajo began to settle on Hopi land. Navajo presence on Hopi territory began a dispute over land that continues today. In 1943, the federal government formally divided Hopi and Dine (Navajo) lands, resulting in the loss of most Hopi land to the Navajo. The Hopi moved to their side of the divided lands, but many Navajo remained where they were on the Hopi half of the lands.

Today, there are 13 Hopi villages on three mesas, all of which are governed by a tribal council. In 1966, the council signed leases for coal strip mining and nuclear testing despite the protests of many tribal members. Seventy percent of the tribe's budget is drawn from coal leases. Strip mining, however, has caused radiation contamination and pollution of water resources.

Arizona state universities have developed a new Hopi written language. Most Hopi speak both English and Hopi and continue to live in traditional pueblos. Partly as a result of their long avoidance of outside influence, they retained more of their traditional ceremonial life than most other United States tribes.

Houma

Houma meant "red" in the *Choctaw* and *Chickasaw* languages, but it may also be an abbreviation of "red crawfish." Today, most Houma live in the southeastern Louisiana marshes. In 1650, there were an estimated 1,000 Houma, but by 1700 that number had been reduced to about 600. Today, the Houma have 11,000 enrolled members.

The Houma had temples that contained carved wooden figures and earthen images. Among the spirits of the natural world that they worshipped were the sun, fire, and thunder. Some young people sought guardian spirits on vision quests. Women in Houma society sometimes served as war chiefs.

Homes were square framed structures with adobe walls and were generally 15 to 30 feet in width, although doors were less than 4 feet high. For food, the Houma raised corn and gathered shrimp. Among the weapons they used were blowguns.

The first Europeans encountered by the Houma were the French, who soon became their allies. Intermarriage with the French integrated the French language and the Catholic religion into Houma culture. They also intermarried on occasion with other whites and with African Americans. In the early 18th century, they welcomed smaller neighboring tribes such as the Acolapissa, Bayogoula, Biloxi, and *Chitimacha* to their ranks. However, they never formally entered a treaty with the United States. Some Houma relocated to Oklahoma, but most stayed in isolated communities where their children did not attend public schools. In the 1930s, oil companies took advantage of Indian illiteracy to gain their lands. Most Houma did not attend school until after World War II, and local schools were not desegregated until late 1969.

Today, the Houma have no tribal land base. They are governed by a tribal council and are the largest tribe in Louisiana. French is their first language, and English their second. Only a few words of Houma are still known. The Houma were denied federal recognition in 1998.

Hualapai

The Hualapai (WAH-lah-pie), meaning "pine tree people," are culturally similar to the Havasupai. The Havasupai are also known as the Eastern Pai, and Hualapai are the Western Pai. They spoke Upland Yuman, a dialect of the Hokan-Siouan language group.

Since about 1100, the Hualapai have resided on lands near the Grand Canyon. They are descended from the ancient Hakataya culture. In the 17th century, of the estimated 2,000 Pai Indians, approximately 1,000 were Hualapai. By the early 20th century that number had been reduced to about 100. Today, the Hualapai have approximately 1,800 enrolled members.

Hopi and *Navajo* neighbors often participated in Hualapai feasts at harvest time and for other ceremonies. The Hualapai cremated their dead with their belongings and feared ghosts. Hopi influence was apparent in the tribe's use of masked dancers. Medicine people believed that they acquired power from dreams. After the birth of a first child, a Hualapai couple usually moved into their own home. Body decorations included tattoos and painting, and women tattooed their chins.

IN THEIR OWN Words

We knew that this land beneath us was composed of many things that we might want to use later such as mineral resources. We knew that this is the wealthiest part of this continent, because it is here the Great Spirit lives. We knew that the White man will search for the things that look good to him, that he will use many good ideas in order to obtain his heart's desire, and we knew that if he had strayed from the Great Spirit he would use any means to get what he wants. These things we were warned to watch, and we today know that those prophecies were true because we can see how many new and selfish ideas and plans are being put before us. We know that if we accept these things we will lose our land and give up our very lives.

—DAN KATCHONGVA, HOPI (1865–1972).
TESTIMONY BEFORE CONGRESSIONAL COMMITTEE IN 1955.

Homes were built of thatch over a pole frame in conical or domed shapes. They raised corn, beans, squash, sunflowers, and tobacco. Women wore yucca fiber dresses trimmed with hoof rattles. Their closest allies were the kindred Havasupai. They experienced conflict with the Yavapai and *Mojave*.

Few Europeans moved into their remote lands, although a trail from the Rio Grande to California passed through Pai lands in the mid-1800s, and mines opened in their area in 1863. In 1874, they were interned with the Mojave, then allowed to return to their traditional lands two years later. White cattlemen opposed their return, but mine owners supported the move since the Hualapai represented a source of cheap mining labor.

Their reservation of one million acres was established in 1883. They were forced off most of those lands in 1934 when the National Park Service destroyed their homes. In 1938, they adopted a nine-member tribal council and constitution. (A new constitution was adopted in 1970.) Tribal headquarters are located at Peach Springs, Arizona. Unemployment runs at 80 percent.

The tribe has banned mining on tribal lands due to fear of contamination from local uranium mines of a sacred site in the Kaibab National Forest.

Most children speak only Pai until they enter public schools. Their elementary school offers a bilingual program. They hold an annual summer memorial powwow that coincides with an annual mourning observance in which they bury the clothes of the dead. (Traditionally, they burned clothes as part of this mourning ceremony.) Some Hualapai never leave the canyon where the tribe resides, and others travel outside no more than a few times a year. Many still ride horses for transportation.

Hupa

The Hupa (HOOP-uh) take their name from the Yurok word for Hoopa Valley. They referred to themselves as *Natinookwa*, meaning "people of the place where the trails return." The Hupa were divided into northern and southern groups. Descent was patrilineal. Hupa is an Athapascan language. They were culturally similar to their neighbors the Chilula *Karuk*, Whilkut, and Yurok, although they did not share the same language group: Karok is a Hokan language, and Yurok an Algonquian language.

The Hupa arrived in northwestern California some time before 1000 B.C.; one of their sacred houses has in fact been carbon dated to more than 7,000 years ago. Their population was estimated at 1,000 in the early 19th century. Today, the Hupa have about 2,000 enrolled members.

The Hupa celebrated traditional dance ceremonies such as the Brush Dance, the White Deerskin Dance, and the Jumping Dance. These ceremonies lasted as long as 10 days in summer or fall and included lengthy oral accounts of tribal history. The start of the salmon run was also marked with a ceremony. Most of their medical practitioners were women. Hupa society was ranked by wealth, and wealthy men who could afford it were allowed more than one wife. They wrapped their dead in deerskins and buried them with their tools on top of their graves. They believed that souls departed for the underworld after five days. Marriages were marked by a feast and an exchange of gifts. If children were not born, the bride price was returned and the marriage ended. Children were not formally named until age five.

Their cedar-planked homes with small round doorways were similar to those of the Northwest Coastal tribes living to their north. Women and children slept in the family home, men in sweat houses that were also used for ritual purification through exposure to heat and sometimes doubled as clubhouses. Acorns, acorn bread, salmon and other fish were staples of the diet. Women had three vertical striped tattoos on their chins, and both genders wore earrings.

Their contact with Europeans was limited until the mid-19th century due to their isolated location in the California highlands. Settlers flooded onto their lands only after the 1849 California gold rush. A fort was built on their lands in 1858. Their reservation was established in 1864 and their boarding school in 1893.

The 85,445-acre Hoopa Valley Reservation—the largest and most populous in California—is located in Humboldt County. Other groups who live on their reservation include the Chilula, Karuk, Whilkut, and Yurok. They adopted a constitution in 1950 and amended it in 1972. In 1988, the tribe was selected by the federal government to participate in the Tribal Self-Governance Demonstration Project.

They continue to practice traditional dances and acorn gathering, and some elders still speak their original language. One Hupa group, the Tsnungwe, has 300 enrolled members and is currently seeking federal recognition.

Iglulik

The name of the Iglulik people is derived from their snow houses, or igloos. They speak a dialect of *Inuit*, of the EskAleut language group. Descent was bilateral.

Their traditional lands are in the central Arctic. Their population was estimated at 500 in the early 19th century. Today, the Iglulik have approximately 2,400 enrolled members.

The Iglulik recognized female creative spirits associated with natural forces and cycles. Their doctors (who could be male or female) diagnosed a number of illnesses, including soul loss, violation of taboos, and anger of the dead, whom the Iglulik feared. Grooms served their in-laws for a short time, and men could have more than one wife. Babies were often named after ancestors. The dead were wrapped in skins and buried with their tools in the snow. All activities ceased in a family for six days following a death.

For part of the winter, their homes were domed snow dwellings accessible through a tunnel. They used ice or animal gut for windows and sometimes lined the snow house with sealskins. Snow houses could be built together for multiple family living arrangements. In the summer they lived in sealskin tents. Oil-soaked bones were used as cooking fuel. Clothing was made of caribou and sealskins.

Among the first Europeans they encountered were Scottish whalers in the early 19th century. In 1999, Canada established a new, mainly Inuit territory of 36,000 square kilometers. This area, called Nunavut, meaning "our land," makes up nearly one-fifth of the landmass of Canada. Many Iglulik still speak their language, which is taught in schools (especially in the early grades) and is broadcast on local radio and television stations. However, high school dropout rates are about 50 percent and unemployment hovers at around 30 percent.

Illinois

Illinois, or Illini, were a group of Algonquian bands that included the Cahokia, Kaskaia, Michigamea, Mmoingwena, Peoria, and Tamaroa. They referred to themselves as *Inoca*, meaning "people." (The state name of Illinois is an English pronunciation of the French spelling of their name.) They were an Eastern *Woodland [I]* group with many similarities to the *Miami*. Descent was patrilineal. Illinois is an Algonquian language.

The Illinois may have originated in the Northeast and mixed with descendants of the *Mississippian Culture [I]* before moving south. In the early 17th century, they lived south of Lake Michigan, but by the end of the 17th century they had moved to present-day Illinois and corners of Iowa, Missouri, and Arkansas. Today, most Illinois Indians live in northeastern Oklahoma. Their population was estimated at 10,000 in 1650, but at just 1,800 by 1750.

Their creator spirit, Manitou, lived to the east and may have symbolized the sun. Both boys and girls in their tradition sought guardian spirits on vision quests, and a feast celebrated a boy's first hunting success. Certain Illinois men, known as *berdaches*, lived and dressed as women; they were believed to possess special spiritual powers. Men were allowed to have more than one wife, although female adultery was punished harshly by death, mutilation, or rape. They painted the faces and hair of their dead, wrapped them in skins, and buried them in the ground or placed them on platforms with their tools. The souls of the dead were believed to travel to an afterlife.

They lived in large rectangular lodges that could house as many as 12 families. Lodges were constructed of pole frames covered with woven mats. Mats also covered the floors and were spun from buffalo and bear hair. Body decoration included painting and tattoos. They experienced conflict with the *Dakota*, *Iroquois*, *Osage*, *Pawnee*, and *Quapaw*. Their traditional allies included the *Otoe* and Miami. Capturing prisoners was a higher honor than killing them.

Similar in structure and concept to the *Iroquois League [IV]*, the Illinois Confederacy united the Cahokia, Kaskakia, Michigamea, Mmoingwena, Peoria, and Tamaroa. It is not known exactly when it was founded, but the confederacy was defeated by the *Kickapoo*, Ojibwa, *Ottowa*, Sauk, and Fox in the early 18th century. Some Illinois joined *Pontiac's Rebellion [IV]* against the British in 1763. An Illinois Indian, hired by Britain, was responsible for the assassination of Chief *Pontiac [II]* in 1769. During the *American Revolution [IV]*, the Illinois supported the American rebels, but this did not result in favorable treatment from the new government.

Their name was adopted by Illinois Territory and then the state of Illinois in 1818. They were moved to the northern part of *Indian Territory [IV]* (Kansas) in 1833, where they lived with the Miami until 1867, when they bought land in northeastern Oklahoma. In 1873, they adopted the tribal name of the United Peoria and Miami. Tribal lands were lost through allotment in 1893 and, later, through Oklahoma's transition to statehood in 1907. They reorganized as the Peoria Tribe of Oklahoma in 1940. The tribe was terminated in 1950 but its federal status was reinstated in 1978.

Today, tribal headquarters are located in Miami, Oklahoma, on 40 acres of land. Unemployment among the 2,000 enrolled members runs at 90 percent.

Ingalik

The name "Ingalik" is a Russian translation of an *Inuit* word for "Indian." The Ingalik referred to themselves as *Deg Hit'an*, meaning "people from here." They spoke a northern dialect of the Athapascan language, although today many speak Inuit.

The Ingalik originated in Canada and moved westward to settle in Alaska around 1200. Historians estimated their population to be 1,500 in the 19th century. Today, the Ingalik have about 650 enrolled members.

In their spiritual views, the world consisted of four levels: one above the earth's surface, two below the earth's surface, and the earth itself. The dead could travel to any level, while the living were confined to the earth itself. Their ceremonies included four types of potlatches: the Bladder ceremony; the Doll ceremony; a two- to three-week Animal ceremony; and a death potlatch to honor the deceased. The wealthy held potlatches to redistribute possessions to others and to increase their own status. Social position was not inherited and could be changed. If the first wife allowed it, a wealthy man could have two wives. The dead were buried in wooden coffins in the ground, which was followed by a 20-day mourning period in which the possessions of the deceased were given away.

Their winter homes were partially below ground, dome shaped, and covered with sod; summer homes were built of spruce planks. Men, however, slept in a communal house, a cultural trait possibly borrowed from their Yup'ik neighbors. Caribou and fish were staples of the diet. They also ate a kind of ice cream made of snow, oil, and berries. Women wore moccasins that were attached to their pants. Their traditional enemies were Koyukon and other Athapascan tribes.

The first Europeans they are known to have encountered were Russian explorers in 1833. Epidemics in 1838 reduced their numbers. A trading post was constructed in their region in 1867, the same year that the United States took possession of Alaska. Under Alaskan territorial law, the natives were only entitled to land they held as individuals and not to lands they held in common. Since little farming is possible in the Arctic, most Ingalik survived by hunting on lands held in common, which meant this restriction was particularly harsh for them. Natives in the Arctic received little official land or recognition. The Yukon gold rush brought a flood of whites into their area in the late 1890s.

Today, most villages range in population from 50 to 500 people. The village administers the corporation formed under the *Alaska Native Claims Settlement Act [IV]* (ANCSA).

Inuit

The Arctic culture of the Inuit extends from eastern Siberia to northern Alaska, Canada, and as far as Greenland. People who settled this region arrived between 2500 and 1000 B.C.—much later than other American Indians. Although they have also been called Aleut and Eskimo, today the term Inuit, meaning "the people," is preferred. ("Eskimo" is an Algonquian term meaning "raw meat eaters.") Related tribes include Inuk, Inupiaq, Inupiaw, and Yupik. The Inuit language is part of the EskAleut language group.

The Inuit can be divided into three regional groupings: the Alaskan Inuit of North Alaska, which includes the Inupiaq and Yupik; the central Inuit of Canada; and the Greenland Inuit. Subgroups include the Baffinland, Caribou, Copper, and Labrador Inuits.

Depiction of Inuit life on Baffin Island. *Library of Congress.*

The Northern Inuit lived in igloos, hide tents, and huts. Southern groups lived above ground in wooden houses or in partially underground wood and sod houses, while the Central Inuit built igloos in winter. Igloos were constructed as domes with holes in the roofs for ventilation. Outer walls were covered with soft snow, and a clear block of ice served as a window. Inuit in Alaska and Greenland built permanent domed or rectangular houses called karmak, made from stones and sod or from logs. Sometimes whale ribs were also used.

Clothing consisted of parkas, pants, mittens, stockings, and boots made from seal and caribou skin. Boots had as many as four layers of caribou fur, down, and moss for insulation. Some Inuit wore ivory armor sewn together with rawhide. Women often wore ear pendants and nose rings or chin plugs made of ivory, shell, wood, or sandstone. Marine mammals and caribou were staples of their diet.

The Inuit believed that spirits could be found in nature and that souls were reincarnated after death. Their spiritual leaders included both men and women. Spiritual ceremonies included the use of masks that represented the spirits of animals and nature. In ceremonies, men wore face masks representing animal sprits, and women wore finger masks. Believing that animals' souls resided in their bladders, they practiced a ceremony known as the Bladder Dance, in which inflated bladders of sea mammals were returned to the sea.

Infants were given the name of ancestors and seen as a vehicle for the rebirth of the spirits of the deceased. Infants were thought to possess the characteristics of the deceased, as well, regardless of their gender.

The Inuit used kayaks, sleds (called *komatik* in the Inuit language), and dog teams for transportation. Some Inuit hunted whales in 40-foot-long boats called umiaks. Like the Makah, the Alaskan Inuit used harpoons to tire the whales before coming closer with spears. In addition to spears and bows and arrows, the Inuit also used bolas, which were weighted ropes thrown to entangle the animals. Today, most Inuit communities are incorporated as villages.

One notable subgroup is the Baffinland Inuit, who refer to themselves as Nunatsiaqmiut, meaning "people of the beautiful land." They speak Inuit-Inupiaq, a dialect of the EskAleut language group. They have been settled on their traditional lands on Baffin Island for more than 4,000 years. Their ancestors, the Thule, were a pre-Inuit group who inhabited the region around the second millennium A.D. and spoke an antiquated form of the Inupiat language. The Baffinland Inuit population was estimated at 2,700 in the mid-18th century; today, they have approximately 11,300 enrolled members.

Baffinland Inuit homes were stone huts covered with skins, or domed snow houses. Beds were raised platforms covered with branches and skins. They used skin tents for shelter in summer. They practiced a form of singing known as throat singing. Women's sealskin parkas had extra large hoods in which to carry infants. Men were allowed to have more than one wife, and divorce was easy to obtain. The dead were wrapped in skins and buried under rocks. Mourners brought food to the graves during four days of mourning.

The first Europeans they encountered were the Norse around 1000. Whaling centers brought European diseases and economic change. Later, the *Hudson's Bay Company [IV]* established a trading post in the region in 1711 and involved the people in fur trading. During the 1950s, there was outside interest in mineral resources on their lands. Baffin Island is part of the new territory of Nunavut, a new Inuit territory comprised of one-fifth of the land base of Canada. Many are hopeful that Nunavut will allow more self-determination in Inuit affairs. Many people still speak Inuktitut, which is taught in their schools and is broadcast on local radio and television.

An Inuit family on Baffin Island. *Library of Congress.*

Caribou Inuit (so-called because of the reliance on caribou in their diet) also inhabit the new territory of Nunavut. They refer to themselves as Nunamiut, meaning "inlanders," and also speak the Inuit-Inupiaq dialect.

Like the Baffinland Inuit, the Caribou Inuit descended from the ancient Thule people. The Caribou Inuit have resided on their traditional lands since before the 12th century. The Hudson's Bay Company first visited the Caribou Inuit lands in 1717. Their population was estimated at approximately 500 in the late 18th century and at 1,500 by 1915. Today, the Caribou Inuit have about 6,900 enrolled members.

Their creative spirit was symbolized by a female caribou. Their winter houses were traditionally made of stone, covered with moss and snow; around 1880, they began to build domed snow houses. Furniture consisted of platforms covered with skins and mats. They experienced conflict with the Chipewayan and Dogrib.

Also based in Nunavut are the "Copper Inuit"—so called by whites because of the copper that the Inuit mined and used in their tools and weapons. Descent was bilateral. Speaking a dialect of Inuit-Inupiaq, they are descended from ancient pre-Dorset, Dorset, and Thule cultures. Their population was estimated at 1,300 in the late 18th century. Today, the Copper Inuit have approximately 2,000 members.

Finally, the Labrador and Ungava Inuit are two northeastern groups who once spoke different dialects. They now refer to themselves as Inuit Kapaimiut, meaning "people of Quebec." They are descendants of the ancient Dorset people and have occupied their traditional lands in the northern half of the Labrador Peninsula since before 1500 B.C.

They shared many cultural traditions with other Inuit groups. They also sometimes raised children to assume the roles of the other gender. Kapaimiut culture also included adult cross-dressers, who could marry other tribe members. Their homes were partly below ground and constructed of stone, whalebone, and wood frames with skin roofs; windows were made of gut. Houses were large enough to hold 20 people. They also used domed snow houses and conical or domed skin tents. Their umiaks (skin-covered boats) could hold 30 people and were usually rowed by women. Some of their clothing was made of buckskin, although most was made of caribou or sealskin.

The first Europeans they encountered were probably the Norse around 1000. Basque and other European whalers arrived in the late 15th century. Their population was estimated at 3,000 in the mid-18th century; today, there are approximately 12,000 members.

Inupiat

Inupiat is an *Inuit* name meaning "the people." The Inupiat speak a dialect of Inupiaq, of the EskAleut language group.

Their traditional lands were in the interior of northern Alaska, although today they have spread across northern Canada and into Greenland. Canadian relatives are known as the Inuit. Related groups also live in the Siberia area of Russia. Their population was estimated at 9,500 in the mid-19th century. Today, the Inupiat have an estimated 12,000 members.

Their culture shared a number of similarities with the Inuit. Their Messenger Feasts, held in fall and winter, for example, were similar to the Inuit practice of potlatches. They also carved wood and ivory.

Houses were domes about 15 feet in diameter and constructed of driftwood and sod. Moss and sod were used for insulation and stretched animal gut or ice served as windows. Homes held two families with as many as 12 people. In larger communities, men lived in separate houses.

Russians were the first Europeans the Inupiat encountered in early to mid-18th century. Epidemics struck in the 1870s and 1880s, sometimes accompanied by a famine. Famines often accompanied disease because there was no one to hunt or farm due to illness or the caretaking of others. Gold miners arrived in 1898.

In 1961, the Inupiat held a "duck-in" to protest the ban on their hunting of waterfowl between March and September, the only time the birds are in northern Alaska. At the time of the duck-in, Inupiat Paitot, a political organization to address land and hunting issues, was formed. In the late 1960s, the Inupiat learned that 15,000 pounds of radioactive material from Nevada had been dumped on their land. The waste was not put into containers but had simply been poured into holes in the ground. The discovery of oil on the North Slope in 1968 led to the passage of the *Alaska Native Claims Settlement Act [IV]* (ANCSA) in 1971.

Since there were no high schools in their villages, Inupiat children were sent to boarding schools for four years. When they returned, they often no longer knew the Inupiat language. After lawsuits in the 1970s, however, high schools were built in several villages. A Native Trade Fair is held after the Fourth of July, and the Messenger Feast is held in January. There are approximately 11 permanent villages today, each governed by elected mayors and city councils.

Ioway

Ioway (I-oh-way) comes from a *Dakota* word, *ayuhwa*, meaning "sleepy ones." They referred to themselves as *Pahoja*, meaning *dusty noses*. They are also referred to as Iowa. Descent was patrilineal. Their language, Iowa-Otoe-Missouria, is a dialect of the Chiwere branch of the Siouan language and is very similar to the Winnebago tongue.

According to their oral history, the Ioway once lived with the Winnebago, Missouria, and Otoe north of the Great Lakes. By the 17th century, however, most Ioway were living in the prairies of northern Iowa and southern Minnesota, where they had migrated from the Great Lakes region. Today, most of the Ioway live in central Oklahoma and northeast Kansas. Their population was estimated at 1,100 in 1760. Today, the Ioway have approximately 2,300 enrolled members.

The Ioway practiced a ceremony similar to the Grand Medicine Dance of *Woodland cultures [I]*. They lived in earth lodges or bark-covered pole-framed lodges and in skin tipis when hunting. They raised corn, beans, squash, melons, sunflowers, and pumpkins. When they adopted the *horse [I]* around 1720, *buffalo [I]* also became a staple of their diet.

They worked in the fur trade with the French in the 18th century, but a smallpox epidemic reduced their numbers in 1803. The tribe signed several treaties, beginning in 1824, which eventually ceded all their lands to the United States. In 1836, they were assigned a reservation in the northern part of *Indian Territory [IV]*, in what is now southeastern Nebraska and northeastern Kansas. That land, however, was further reduced. In the 1870s, they divided into two groups; the Southern Ioway went to live in Oklahoma and the Northern Ioway remained in Kansas and Nebraska. The southern group preferred to live in more traditional ways on communally held land, and the northern group accepted individual allotments. The Southern Ioway obtained a reservation in 1883, but it was opened to white settlement just a few years later.

The Ioway in Oklahoma belong to the United Indian Nations of Oklahoma. Few people today speak the language. Blood quantum, determined by the enrollment records of ancestors, only require descent from an enrolled member in the Kansas group and one-sixteenth in the Oklahoma group. There are only about a dozen full-bloods. Each tribe has an annual powwow and the Kansas group also has a rodeo. The Ioway of Kansas, Nebraska, and Oklahoma are federally recognized.

Iroquois

Iroquois (IR-uh-koy) was derived from the French translation of the Algonquian word *ireohkwa,* meaning "real adders" or "snakes." They refer to themselves as *Haudenosaune* (ho-dee-no-SHOW-nee), meaning "people of the longhouse." Iroquois refers to a group of six nations—the *Cayuga, Mohawk, Oneida, Onondaga, Seneca,* and *Tuscarora*—who share a common language. Several other tribes besides the Six Nations spoke Iroquois, including the *Wyandotte/Huron* and Susquehannok. The *Cherokee* in the Southeast also spoke Iroquoian. Descent among the Iroquois was matrilineal. Although they lived among the more numerous Algonquian tribes, they might have been descendants of one of the more ancient *Woodland cultures [I]* such as the Owasco.

Five of the Six Nations formed the *Iroquois League [IV]*, or Iroquois Confederacy, sometime before 1400, and possibly as early as A.D. 1100. The Tuscarora became the sixth member nation after they migrated from North Carolina to New York in the 1700s. Two men are cited as responsible for bringing the nations together: *Deganawida [II]*, a Huron prophet from the north, and *Hiawatha [II]*.

Log walls surrounded Iroquois villages. Within the walls, longhouses of 50 to 100 feet housed as many as 20 families. Using quills, the Iroquois wrote public records on wampum belts. Their society was divided into several clans, which included the beaver, deer, wolf, bear, turtle, hawk, heron, snipe, and eel.

In Iroquois society, women owned the crops and chose the tribal leaders. Annual festivals included the Green Corn, Maple Sugar, and Strawberry festivals, but the most important was the New Year festival held at the first new moon of the year. Orenda was the name of their creator spirit.

The Iroquois were allies of the Dutch and, later, the British. They were also strong enough to stop the French from expanding southward from Canada. The Iroquois fought with the British, and the Algonquin fought with the French in the French and Indian War from 1689 to 1763. However, the League had divided loyalties in the *American Revolution [IV]*. Two tribes, the Oneida and Tuscarora, sided with the Americans, while the other four Iroquois tribes sided with the British. General George Washington sent an invading army into Iroquois lands in 1779, which defeated the Iroquois not through direct warfare but by the burning of their homes and crops. Among the Iroquois, Washington was called the Town Destroyer. After the Revolution, some Iroquois moved to Canada. In 1799, the Seneca sachem, *Handsome Lake [II]*, preached a return to traditional practices mixed with Christianity. His message was formalized as the Code of Handsome Lake. He also restored the Confederacy council fire to Onondaga in central New York State. The council fire had burned in their traditional lands and then was transported to Canada when the League dissolved. Handsome Lake's restoration of the fire to New York signified renewed cultural determination. In the 20th century, the Confederacy resisted the 1924 Indian *Citizenship Act [IV]* and selective service.

Today more than 10,000 Iroquois live on reservations in New York, Ontario, and Quebec. In 1989, the state of New York returned 12 wampum belts to the Onondagas, who are the traditional wampum keepers in the Confederacy. The belts had been held by New York since the conclusion of the American Revolution. The Six Nations still meet in council and regularly recite the Great Law, a ceremony that can take more than a week.

Kalispel

Kalispel (KAL-uh-spell) means "camas people." (Camas was a staple plant of the tribe's diet.) The French also referred to them as the *Pend d'Oreille* (pon-duh-RAY), meaning "earrings." They were divided into lower and upper divisions and spoke a dialect of Interior *Salish*.

Most Salish people, including the Kalispel, are believed to have resided in British Columbia before migrating southward. Their traditional lands were around Pend d'Oreille Lake, Oregon, where some of them still live today. Their population was estimated at 1,600 in the 18th century. Today, the Kalispel have about 250 enrolled members, half of whom reside on the reservation.

The Kalispel believed that guardian spirits could be gained through dreams or vision quests. Marriage was usually monogamous. After they adopted the *horse [I]*, the tribe took on some cultural traits of Plains Indians, including the *buffalo [I]* hunt. They dressed their dead in robes, or sewed them into blankets, before placing them on raised platforms and eventually burying them; the deceased's possessions were then given away.

Their homes were constructed of a wood frame covered with mats or cedar bark. They used tipis only when hunting. Fish and camas bread were staples of their diet. Allies included the *Kootenai* and *Spokan*.

The Kalispel assisted the Lewis and Clark Expedition in 1805. The North West Trading Company opened a trading post on their lands in 1809. In 1855, they were forced to cede lands to the United States, and the upper division was moved to the Flathead Reservation in Montana, but the lower division refused to move and negotiated for a reservation of its own. The Confederated Salish, which included the upper and lower Kalispel and Kootenai tribes, were placed on the Flathead Reservation in western Montana. The British Columbia gold rush in 1863 brought white miners into their lands. The Kalispel Reservation was established in 1914 and comprised of 4,629 acres. The tribe adopted a constitution in 1938. A Kalispel powwow is held in August.

Karuk

Karuk means "upstream" in their language, which is part of the Hokan language group. Today most Karuk live in southern Oregon and northwestern California. Historians estimated their population at 1,500 in the 18th century. In 1905, their numbers were approximately 500. Today, the Karuk have about 2,900 enrolled members. They are one of the largest tribes in California but have a small land base of only 300 acres.

Their ceremonies were centered on staple foods of their diet. The Jumping Dance, for example, was held in conjunction with the salmon run, and the Deerskin Dance celebrated the acorn harvest. They shared cultural traits with the *Hupa* and Yurok. Both women and men practiced medicine. They buried their dead with shell money and their possessions; clothing and tools that belonged to the dead person were then hung around the grave. They believed that five days after death, the soul rose to the sky, and that a person's happiness in the afterlife depended to some degree on the wealth he possessed on earth. Premarital sex and having children before marriage were accepted in Karuk society. Newlyweds resided with the groom's parents.

The Karuk lived in rectangular homes constructed of cedar planks. Doors were small; porches and fireplaces were paved in stone. After the age of three, males slept in a separate communal house. The Karuk grew tobacco and fished using nets cast from platforms.

The Karuk were able to avoid contact with outsiders until the *gold [IV]* rushes of the 1850s, when conflicts with prospectors led to whites burning Karuk villages and massacring them. Many Karuk were moved to the Hoopa Valley Reservation in California in the 1850s, where the majority today continues to reside. They adopted a constitution in 1985 and are governed by a nine-member tribal council. The 300-acre Quartz Valley Reservation has a population of just over 100 members. Ceremonies are held at three religious centers: the town of Clear Creek, the town of Orleans, and the town of Somes Bar. Many of their villages have been inhabited since before contact with Europeans, including Cottage Grove, Ike's, Oak Bottom, and Tea Bar. The Karuk gained federal recognition in 1979.

Kaw

Kaw referred to themselves as *Hutanga,* meaning "by the edge of the shore," which was a reference to their origin story of residence on the Atlantic Ocean. Descent was patrilineal. They spoke a dialect of the Dhegiha group of the Siouan language.

They once may have been united with other Siouan groups including the *Omaha, Osage, Ponca*, and Quapaw, although the Kaw had split off from the other tribes by the early 16th century. They arrived in present-day northeastern Kansas from the lower Ohio Valley some time before the mid-17th century. Today, most Kaw live near Kaw City, Oklahoma. Their population, estimated at 5,000 in 1700, had less than 700 a century and a half later. Today, the Kaw have approximately 1,600 enrolled members, including a mere handful of full-bloods.

Their creative spirits dwelled in nature. Adolescent boys sought guardian spirits on vision quests. Kaw society was organized into 16 clans, as well as 2 tribal divisions, the Nata and Ictunga. More than other tribes, the Kaw placed a high value on female chastity. Their funeral custom involved painting the body of the deceased, covering it with bark, and burying it with his or her possessions. The mourning lasted a year.

The Kaw lived in wood-framed circular or oval lodges covered with mats. The dwellings were as large as 60 feet in diameter and had five or six families living in them. Beds were made of skin-covered wood platforms. Women raised corn, beans, squash, and sunflowers. Men plucked or shaved all their hair. Their traditional enemies included the *Cheyenne*, Mesquaki, *Ioway*, Omaha, Osage, *Otoe, Pawnee*, and Sauk.

In the 1700s, the Kaw moved onto land in western Kansas that the *Apache* had left. With the introduction of the *horse [I]* in the 1700s, the Kaw began to exhibit cultural traits of the Plains Indians. They ceded Missouri lands to the United States in 1825 in exchange for a reservation in Kansas. William Clark of the Lewis and Clark Expedition of 1804 to 1806 negotiated many of their early land cessions. Their Kansas reservation was originally in the northern part of *Indian Territory [IV]*, which Congress confiscated in 1852 to form the states of Kansas and Nebraska. Other lands were confiscated in 1873 and the Kaw were moved again, this time to Indian Territory in Oklahoma. Their lands were allotted and their government disbanded in 1902. Vice President Charles *Curtis [II]*, who served under President Herbert Hoover from 1929 to 1933, was one-eighth Kaw. In 1959, the tribe reorganized itself with a land base of 260 acres. In the 1960s, however, most of those lands were flooded when the United States Army built the Kaw Reservoir.

The Kaw today have 135 acres of trust lands. Their tribal headquarters are in Kaw City, Oklahoma, where they hold a tribal powwow every August. They adopted a new constitution in 1990 and are governed by a seven-member council. Fewer than a dozen elders still speak the language.

Kickapoo

Kickapoo (KICK-a-poo) is derived from the word *Kiwegapaw* in their language, meaning "people who move about." They were culturally similar to the Sauk and Mesquaki. Descent was patrilineal. Events and history were recorded on prayer sticks. They spoke one of three dialects that make up the Sauk-Mesquaki-Kickapoo branch of the Algonquian language.

They were originally a Western Great Lakes group closely related to the Sac and Mesquaki (*Mesquakie*) and other Algonquian tribes. They may have originated in southeast Michigan and were possibly united with the *Shawnee* in the past and then with the *Miami*. By the mid-17th century, they lived in Michigan and Ohio, as well as in northeast Kansas. Their population was estimated at 3,000 in the mid-17th century, the same number as today.

Their primary creative spirit was Manitou. They believed that spiritual insight could be gained from dreams and personal names. Sacred bundles given by Wisaka, the son of Manitou, are the basis of their ceremonials. Their most important ceremony was a weeklong thanksgiving in early spring, but they also celebrated Green Corn and Buffalo dances. Girls were secluded at their first menses and boys were honored with a feast after they killed their first game. Marriage was marked by a gift exchange between families. They buried their dead in log vaults with tobacco, spoons, food, and water, and believed that the land of the dead lay to the west.

Wood-framed houses were covered with bark or tule mats. Bed platforms were lined along the sides.

The first Europeans they are known to have encountered were French fur traders in the 1600s. After the French were defeated in 1763, the Kickapoo became allies of the Spanish. They participated in *Pontiac's Rebellion [IV]* of 1763 and in *Little Turtle's War [IV]* from 1790 to 1794; some bands also supported *Tecumseh's [II]* Rebellion from 1809 to 1811. They were forced to move several times, which eventually resulted in three separate communities: Kansan, Oklahoman, and Texan/Mexican. After their defeat in the *Black Hawk War [IV]*, the majority of Kickapoo accepted a reservation in Kansas in 1832. Kenekuk, the Kickapoo prophet, preached a combination of Kickapoo spirituality mixed with Christianity, a central tenet of which was an edict against ceding lands to whites. The Kansas Kickapoo are descendants of Kenekuk. In the 1870s, the U.S. Army illegally crossed into Mexico to destroy a Kickapoo village and returned with women and children whom they held as hostages in *Indian Territory [IV]* (Oklahoma). In 1883, the Kickapoo gained a 100,000-acre reservation in Oklahoma. That reservation was allotted 10 years later and many of the Mexican Kickapoo then returned to northern Sonora in Mexico. They were able to resist termination in the 1950s.

The 6-by-5-mile, 19,200-acre (originally 768,000 acres) Kickapoo Reservation in Kansas has a population of approximately 350. Tribal members own about one-third of the land. Oklahoma Kickapoo have a tribal headquarters in McCloud and are governed by a five-member council. Approximately 1,900 members reside on 6,000 acres of land. Texas Kickapoo live on 17,000 acres of land and have a population of 650 near the international bridge over the Rio Grande. A small group of Kickapoo also lives in Sonora, Mexico. The Texas band was given federal recognition in 1983 and has the right to move freely across the Mexico-United States border, one of the few tribes with this right. About one-quarter of this group are United States citizens. Some tribe members in Oklahoma still speak the language. Their spiritual practices remain intact, especially in Mexico. Unemployment runs about 40 percent, and approximately one-third live in poverty.

Kiowa

Kiowa (KI-uh-wuh) was derived from *Kaigwu*, a name they called themselves that meant "principal people." They may have originated in Arizona or western Montana. Some historians have surmised a possible ancient connection with Mesoamerican groups such as the Aztec, since the Kiowa kept tribal records in the form of pictographic calendars. Tribal history was recorded on *buffalo [I]* skins. When whites hunted the buffalo to near extinction, the Kiowa began recording their history on manila paper. The Kiowan language is related to the *Pueblo* language, Tanoan.

In the late 17th century, the Kiowa lived near the *Crow* Indians in western Montana. In 1790, a band of *Apache* joined the Kiowa and became known as the Kiowa Apache. Today, the Kiowa live in southwest Oklahoma. In the late 18th century, their population was estimated at 2,000. By the 19th century, there were just 1,000 members remaining, their numbers reduced by smallpox. Today, the Kiowa have approximately 10,000 enrolled members.

Among their most important sacred items were the Ten Grandmother Bundles. The bundles contained a number of ancient objects that were considered to be sacred to the tribe. The Kiowa adopted the Sun Dance in the 18th century from northern Plains tribes, though their form of the Sun Dance did not involve self-mutilation. The Kiowa experienced conflict with the *Cheyenne, Dakota,* and *Osage.*

When they acquired the *horse [I]* in 1730, they adopted many cultural traits of the Plains Indians, including hunting buffalo and living in tipis, which Kiowa women traditionally built and owned. In 1867, they ceded land to the United States in the Medicine Lodge Treaty in exchange for a shared reservation with *Comanche in Indian Territory [IV]* (Oklahoma). The federal government was impatient with the pace of

> ## IN THEIR OWN *Words*
>
> *I love this land and the buffalo and will not part with it. I want you to understand well what I say. Write it on paper . . . I hear a great deal of good talk from the gentlemen the Great Father sends us, but they never do what they say. I don't want any of the medicine lodges (schools and churches) within the country. I want the children raised as I was.*
>
> *I have heard you intend to settle us on a reservation near the mountains. I don't want to settle. I love to roam over the prairies. There I feel free and happy, but when we settle down we grow pale and die.*
>
> —SATANTA (SET-TAINTE; THE ORATOR OF THE PLAINS; WHITE BEAR), KIOWA (1830–1878). SPOKEN AT TREATY OF MEDICINE LODGE.

Kiowa migration to their reservation, so in 1869, they kidnapped Kiowa leaders Satanta (White Bear) and Lone Wolf. The government threatened to put them to death unless the Kiowa were incarcerated on their reservation. The last of the Kiowa surrendered in 1875 and were herded into corrals. Two thousand Kiowa were placed on a reservation at Fort Sill with an equal number of Comanche. Many died of starvation, overcrowding, and disease.

A Kiowa calendar written on buckskin. The Kiowa "Anko" calendar was a tribal chronicle begun in 1832 and covered the years up to 1885. *National Archives.*

Further epidemics decreased their numbers in the late 1870s, 1895, and 1902. Many Kiowa practiced the *Ghost Dance [IV]* in the 1880s and 1890s. Their reservation lands were allotted in 1901. One of the most famous Kiowa is the novelist N. Scott *Momaday [II]*, who won the 1969 Pulitzer Prize for *House Made of Dawn.*

The 208,396-acre Kiowa Reservation in southwest Oklahoma, established in 1867, currently has only 7,000 acres that are owned by tribal members. Tribal headquarters are located in Carnegie, Oklahoma, where 9,000 of 10,000 enrolled tribal members reside. Today, about 200 elders still speak the language.

Klamath

The origin of the name Klamath (KLAM-uth) is unknown, although they referred to themselves as *Maklaks*, which means "people" in their language. The Klamath dialect of the Penutian language group is similar to the *Modoc* language.

Their ancestral lands were located around Klamath Lake and the Klamath River near the Oregon-California border. Women sometimes served as chiefs.

In 1829, Peter Skene Ogden was one of the first Europeans the Klamath encountered. By 1864, they had signed a treaty that placed them on the Klamath Reservation in Oregon. Several smaller tribes were also put on their reservation, including the Modoc, Northern *Paiute*, Pit River, Shasta, and Snake Indians. The Klamath were able to retain only 1.18 million acres from their original lands of 20 million acres.

The Modoc were forced onto their own reservation in the 1870s. However, tensions between the two groups caused the Modoc to flee and return to California, and that sparked the Modoc War of 1872. Congress terminated the Klamath in 1954 and their lands were allotted. The federal government paid the Klamath less than 85 cents an acre and paid them nothing for the timber resources on it. The Klamath were left landless.

Today, 70 percent of the Klamath live below the poverty level. Their powwow, held on December 31 each year, ushers in the New Year. Treaty Days in August celebrate their restored tribal status. They are still without a land base but have had federal recognition since 1986.

Klikitat

Klikitat is taken from a *Chinook* word meaning "beyond." The Klikitat referred to themselves, however, as *Qwulh-hwai-pum,* meaning "prairie people." They were culturally similar to the *Yakama* and spoke a Sahaptian dialect of the Penutian language group.

Before their contact with Europeans, their population was estimated at 700. Today, they live in the area around Mount Adams in southcentral Washington. They lived in circular houses built partially below ground, as well as in above-ground mat houses. Salmon and other fish were staples of their diet. According to Klikitat tradition, boys traditionally sought guardian spirits on vision quests. The dead were buried with their tools in gravel pits lined with cedar planks.

Among the first Europeans they encountered were Meriwether Lewis and William Clark in 1805. In 1855, they signed a treaty ceding more than 10 million acres of their land in exchange for a 1-million-acre reservation. They were supposed to have two years to relocate to the reservation, but the governor of Washington allowed whites to begin moving onto Indian lands just 12 days after the treaty was signed. By the start of the 20th century, whites owned 80 percent of the Klikitat Reservation.

The Klikitat continue to reside near their traditional lands in south-central Washington. A 14-member tribal council governs the reservation. Three-quarters of the population lives in poverty. Today the Klikitat comprise 8 percent of the 8,000-member Yakama Indian Nation.

Kootenai

Kootenai (KOOT-uh-nay) referred to themselves as *San'ka*, meaning "people of the waters." Their language, Kutenaian, was most likely related to the Algonquian language group.

They may have originated as far east of the Rockies as the Lake Michigan area. By the late 18th century, however, they lived near the Washington-Idaho border. Before their contact with Europeans, their population was estimated at 1,200 divided into an upper and lower group. Today, there are 900 enrolled members in the United States and 500 in Canada.

The Kootenai believed that spirits resided in all aspects of the natural world and they may have believed in a creator spirit symbolized by the sun. Guardian spirits were sought on vision quests at adolescence. Both women and men served as religious leaders and practiced medicine. Some of the most important ceremonies were the midwinter festival, the Sun Dance, and the War Dance. They wrapped their dead in robes and blankets, then temporarily placed them on platforms before burial; the possessions of the deceased were given away.

They traditionally lived in pole framed mat-covered structures, although some of the tribe switched to the use of skin tipis during the 18th century. The upper division of Kootenai adopted Plains culture lifestyles while the lower division remained more entrenched in the Plateau culture. The lower division Plateau culture group wore bark, mat, and hemp clothing; the upper division wore buckskin Plains-style clothing. They occasionally fought the *Assiniboine, Blackfeet, Cree*, and Lake.

In the 18th century, they acquired the *horse [I]* and began hunting *buffalo [I]*. The establishment of the United States-Canadian border in 1846 divided the tribe in two. In 1855, the Flathead Reservation in Montana was established for the *Salish* and Kootenai people. The Kootenai Reservation in Idaho was established in 1974.

The 2,680-acre Kootenai Reservation has 200 tribal members, of whom approximately 60 live on the reservation. Most of the lands are allotted. A constitution, adopted in 1947, allows a four-member tribal council to govern them.

The 627,070-acre Flathead Reservation, established in 1855 for Salish and Kootenai, today has a population of 5,000. Tribal members own almost half the land. Unemployment runs at approximately 50 percent.

Kutchin

Kutchin Indians (kuch-IN) refer to themselves as *Kindjie*, meaning "person." They spoke Kutchin, a dialect of the Northern Athapascan language, and their culture reflected strong *Inuit* and *Tlingit* influences. Descent in their society was matrilineal.

Their territory is in Alaska and the Yukon. Their population was estimated at 5,000 in the 18th century. By the mid-19th century, that number had been reduced to 1,300. In 1970, there were just 700 members. Today the Kutchin have approximately 2,000 enrolled members in Canada and 600 in Alaska.

The Kutchin believed guardian spirits could be acquired through dreams or fasting. They may have prayed to moon-related deities. They believed that people, bears, and caribou shared similar hearts, and they belonged to animal-associated matrilineal clans. Men did the cooking but women ate last. A young woman's mother chose her husband for her. Babies were carried in birchbark containers. According to Kutchin tradition, the dead were cremated and their property was destroyed. Mourners made cuts on their own limbs. The wealthy gave potlatches, primarily at funerals.

They lived in dome-shaped bark-covered structures or in caribou-skin tents with branches for flooring. Women tattooed lines on their chins; men wore their hair in a ball at the neck and covered their hair with grease, down, and feathers. The tribe experienced conflict with the Inuvialuit, Inupiaq, Koyukon, and Tanana. They faced devastating epidemics in the 1860s, 1870s, and in 1897. The Klondike gold rush in 1896 brought white settlers to their lands.

Today, the native Doyon Corporation controls their lands. Under the 1971 *Alaska Native Claims Settlement Act [IV]*, most villages organized as corporations in order to control their resources. Today, most Kutchin are fluent in English. They are working to save endangered caribou herds from the resource destruction that accompanies development.

Kwakiutl

Kwakiutl (KWAH-kee-oo-tel), which may have meant "beach on the other side of the water," spoke a dialect of the Wakashan language group. Their neighbors to the south, the *Makah* and *Nootka*, also spoke Wakashan dialects.

Originally, their lands, which have been occupied for at least 10,000 years, were on the central coast of British Columbia. Their population, estimated at 8,000 in the early 19th century, today has approximately 4,000 enrolled members.

They believed guardian spirits could be obtained through prayer and fasting. Their most important ceremonies, held in winter, included the Cedar Bark Dance, the Weasel Dance, and potlatches. They called their potlatch *pasa,* which means to "flatten" and refers to the flattening of guests under the weight of gifts they received. Northern bands cremated their dead and southern groups buried their deceased.

Their cedar-plank houses, some as long as 60 feet, faced the sea. House posts were carved and painted with crests. Sleeping platforms ran along the walls. Red and black were the basic colors used for artistic decorations. Like the *Haida*, the Kwakiutl were skilled wood carvers. They wore long cedar-bark robes and painted their bodies against sunburn. Some men grew facial hair. They occasionally fought with the Coast *Salish*. Salmon and other fish were staples of their diet.

In the 1880s, Canada established reserves for the Kwakiutl. Legislation, passed in 1885, outlawed the potlatch but the Kwakiutl continued to hold the ceremony secretly. In 1921, 45 chiefs and their wives were arrested for violating this law. Twenty-two people served prison sentences, while the rest received suspended sentences on the condition that their villagers surrender all their sacred and ceremonial objects, including their masks. That collection was housed in the National Museum of Man. In 1975, the museum agreed to return the objects to the tribes if they built museums in which to house the artifacts. Potlatching ceremonies grew again in the 1970s. The Canadian government returned sacred objects to the Kwaguilth Museum and U'Mista Cultural Center in 1978.

The Kwakiutl still live in British Columbia, where their tribal councils have municipal powers. English is the first language of most members.

Lakota

Europeans mistakenly referred to the Lakota by the incorrect name of Sioux, an outdated term derived from the French translation of an *Anishinabe* word, *Nadowe-is-iw*, which meant "adder" or "snake" and implied an enemy. They called themselves Lakota, meaning "ally," as well as *Ikce Wicasa*, which meant "free people." The Lakota were related to the *Nakota* and *Dakota* to their east. The western Lakota subgroup, the Teton, had seven subdivisions. They included the Hunkpapa, Itazipco, Mineconjou, Oglala, O'ohenonpa, Sicangu, and Sihapsa. Lakota is a western dialect of the Siouan language group. Descent was patrilineal.

The Lakota may have originated along the lower Mississippi River or in eastern Texas. They migrated northward to the Ohio Valley and may have been related to the Mound Builder culture of the 9th to 12th centuries. About A.D. 1000 they migrated from the Southeast to northcentral Minnesota and parts of the Dakotas. By the mid-19th century, they resided in parts of Nebraska, Wyoming, and Montana. Today, most live on reservations in South Dakota. The Lakota population was estimated at 12,000 members during the late 18th century; today, there are approximately 55,000 enrolled members. The Oglala, the largest group, live at Pine Ridge Reservation, and the Sicangu live at Rosebud Reservation, both of which are in South Dakota.

According to oral traditions, White Buffalo Calf Woman brought the Lakota many ceremonies for their spiritual practices. Those ceremonies included the sweat lodge, vision quests, girls' puberty rituals, and the Sun Dance. Guardian spirits, usually animals, appeared to people who were on vision quests or they could come in dreams. Women could seek visions or quests but generally received their visions through their dreams. Women may have been thought to have had inherent spiritual power due to childbirth and thus had no need to search for guardian spirits as men did. Guardian spirits provided information about which items were to be kept in personal medicine bundles. Those bundles were worn on the individual and provided special protection. Cross-dressing *berdaches* sometimes served as spiritual leaders.

One of their most important ceremonies, the 12-day Sun Dance, involved dancing, praying, fasting, and mutilating the body. Premarital sex was frowned upon and girls sometimes slept wearing chastity belts, although men with wealth could have more than one wife. Men were usually older than the women when they married, since males needed time to acquire goods to distribute at their marriages. Monogamy in women was valued, and unfaithful wives might have their noses cut off. When they were about four, children had their ears pierced. Girls and women were secluded during their menses. The dead were buried on high hills or on platforms in trees.

While in the woodlands, the Lakota lived in bark-covered, pole-framed lodges. When they migrated westward onto the plains, they lived in buffalo-skin tipis erected by the women. The average tipi was made of 12 buffalo skins placed over pole frames and was painted with depictions of special events. Skin flaps at the top served as smoke holes, and buffalo robes covered the floors.

By the mid-19th century, war leaders wore long, eagle-feathered war bonnets for ceremonies. The war bonnet signified achievements in battle. Whites, however, adopted it as a cliched symbol of all Indians. Status among the Lakota was based on acts of bravery more than wealth. Touching enemies (counting coup) carried more prestige than killing them. Their allies included the *Arapaho* and *Cheyenne.*

They had conflicts with the Anishinabe and the *Cree*, who were armed by their French allies. The Black Hills (Paha Sapa) had become their spiritual center by 1775. In 1792, they defeated the *Arikira* Confederacy and expanded to the west. By the 1830s, most Teton lived on the plains and were part of the Plains culture that used *buffalo [I]* as a staple of the diet. They signed the *Treaty of Fort Laramie [IV]* in 1851, agreeing to allow whites to pass through their lands in exchange for official recognition of their tribes. When *gold [IV]* was discovered in Montana later in the 1850s, whites violated the treaty by establishing the Bozeman Road. In the mid-1860s, led by the Oglala *Red Cloud [II]*, the Lakota won a battle to force the United States to close the road. The 1868 Fort Laramie Treaty closed the Bozeman Trail, agreed to keep whites off Lakota lands, and established the Great

IN THEIR OWN *Words*

Father: I wish all to know that I do not propose to sell any part of my country, nor will I have the whites cutting our timber along the rivers, more especially the oak. I am particularly fond of the little groves of oak trees. I love to look at them, and feel a reverence for them, because they endure the wintry storm and summer's heat, and, not like ourselves—seem to thrive and flourish in them.

—SITTING BULL (TATANKA IYOTAKE, TATANKA IYOTANKA, TATANKA YOTANKA), HUNKPAPA LAKOTA CHIEF (C. 1830–1890), ANSWERING TO JESUIT FATHER PIERRE JEAN DE SMET AT POWDER RIVER CAMP, WHO WAS ADVISING SALE OF LAKOTA LANDS, 1868.

Sioux Reservation. During an illegal military expedition led by Lieutenant Colonel George Armstrong Custer in 1874, gold was discovered on Lakota lands in the Black Hills. Gold miners and European settlers then flooded Lakota lands in violation of the treaty. Younger leaders, like the medicine men *Sitting Bull [II]* and *Crazy Horse [II]*, fought to protect their sacred lands and rejected United States offers to purchase the Black Hills. In 1876, Lakota and Cheyenne led by Crazy Horse and Sitting Bull defeated the United States Seventh Cavalry under Custer. In 1877, Sitting Bull led his people north to Canada to escape military harassment. Crazy Horse surrendered in 1877 and was assassinated while under arrest. When threatened with removal to *Indian Territory [IV]* (Oklahoma), the Lakota ceded the Black Hills to the United States, but not enough adult Lakota males signed it to make it binding.

A portrait of Sioux (Lakota, Dakota, and Nakota) delegates on a visit to Washington, in 1888, along with U.S. commissioners, taken on the steps of the U.S. Capitol building. *Library of Congress.*

In the 1880s, railroad companies and land speculators broke up the Great Sioux Reservation. In 1888, the great reservation was divided into six smaller ones and the remaining lands were opened to white settlement. More than half the former reservation lands formed the state of South Dakota. The government cut off rations to the tribe in 1889. The Lakota joined the *Ghost Dance [IV]* religion, which had predicted the return of the buffalo and the return of Lakota ancestors. Many believed the Ghost Shirts they wore could stop bullets.

In 1890, Sitting Bull was arrested and assassinated while in captivity. During that same year, Chief Big Foot led 350 of his people to Pine Ridge to join Red Cloud. The army ordered Big Foot to surrender at Wounded Knee Creek. While the soldiers were disarming the Lakota, a rifle fired, perhaps accidentally. Soldiers opened fire with four cannons, killing 300 Lakota, most of whom were women and children. Known as the *Wounded Knee Massacre [IV]*, the event marked the end of large-scale Indian resistance.

The Lakota adopted a constitution in 1934. Many prominent leaders in the Red Power movement of the 1960s and 1970s were Lakota, including *American Indian Movement [IV]* (AIM) leader Russell *Means [II]*. In 1973, AIM had a 71-day standoff with the FBI at Pine Ridge, which became known as Wounded Knee II (see *Wounded Knee occupation [IV]*.) Under a corrupt tribal government at Pine Ridge and endorsed by the FBI, a reign of terror and violence had begun in 1972. In 1975, a gunfight on the reservation resulted in the controversial conviction of Anishinabe-Dakota Leonard Peltier, who was sent to a federal prison to serve two life sentences.

The Lakota pressed their case contending the illegal seizure of the Black Hills by the United States government. In 1980, the United States Supreme Court ruled in favor of the Lakota treaty, citing violation complaints, and ordered financial compensation of 17.5 million dollars. The Lakota refused that money and remained committed to the return of the land. Another compensation bill, opposed by the South Dakota delegation, failed in the Senate in 1990.

The Oglala today live on Pine Ridge Reservation (population 23,000), the largest of the Lakota reservations and second in size only to the *Navajo* reservation. Lakota lands comprise 18 percent of the state of South Dakota. The Sicangu live on the Rosebud Reservation (population 18,000), and the Hunkpapa live on the Standing Rock reservation (population 6,700). Some Lakota also live at the Cheyenne River, Crow Creek, and Lower Brule Reservations. Half the Lakota live off the reservation. Unemployment on Lakota reservations ranges from 50 to 80 percent. The Sun Dance is still practiced, and it usually lasts four days. Giveaways, based on the Keeping of the Soul ceremony taught by White Buffalo Calf Woman, are still held. The Lakota sacred pipe is kept at the Cheyenne River Reservation. The Oglala Nation Powwow is held on the first weekend in August.

Lenape

Lenape or Leni Lenape (len-ee len-AH-pay) means "human beings" or "real people" in their language. The English referred to them as the Delaware because of their nearness to the Delaware River. (Both the river and the state were named after Lord De La War, the second governor of Virginia.) Other Algonquin tribes claimed descent from the centrally located Lenape, whose lands were considered the original homeland of all

Algonquin groups. Descent was matrilineal. Their history and legends were recorded on engraved and painted wood.

In the Northeast, the Lenape may have resided originally around Labrador, where they were united with the *Shawnee* and *Nanticoke*. They eventually migrated to the eastern Great Lakes region, where they encountered the ancient *Hopewell culture [I]*. Like the *Iroquois*, the Lenape were comprised of numerous Algonquin bands, also known as the Delaware Confederacy. By the time of European contact, their lands extended from North Carolina to New York. The northern bands in the Confederacy spoke the Munsee dialect, and the southern bands spoke the Unami dialect of Algonquian. Historians estimate their population to have been 10,000 in 1600, a number that had shrunk to only 1,000 members by 1900. Today the Lenape have approximately 16,000 enrolled members.

They referred to the Great Spirit as Manitou. An important ceremony, the Big House, lasted 12 days and involved a log structure that symbolized the universe and the lighting of a new sacred fire. They believed that guardian spirits could be acquired in adolescence. Both genders practiced medicine. The dead were believed to travel to an afterlife. Each Lenape belonged to one of three clans: the turkey, turtle, or wolf. Premarital sex was accepted but adultery was not. They buried their dead with their personal possessions in a sitting position, and mourners visited the graves of the deceased annually.

An 18th-century depiction of treaty negotiations between Quaker William Penn and the Lenape. *Library of Congress.*

Lenape houses were circular grass- or bark-covered structures up to 100 feet in diameter. Multiple families lived in those structures, which were similar to Iroquois longhouses. Wall platforms served as beds and seats. The floors and walls were covered with woven reed mats. Log walls surrounded villages. They used a mixture of bear grease and onion on their hair and their bodies as protection from the sun and insects.

Among the first Europeans they encountered was Henry Hudson in 1609. In 1626, the Dutch gave the Manhattan band of Lenape $24 worth of goods. The Dutch believed they had purchased Manhattan, but the Lenape probably understood the exchange as a lease, a misunderstanding that led to a series of conflicts between the two groups. In 1683, the Lenape signed a treaty of friendship with Quaker William Penn, the first treaty Indians signed with Europeans. William Penn supported Indian land rights and their rights to their spiritual practices, but most whites were not so fair. The Peach Wars, for example, started in 1655 when a farmer killed an Indian woman for picking peaches from his orchard. In 1782, Pennsylvanians massacred a band of Lenape over a stolen plate. The Lenape lived in 10 different states and over the years signed 45 different treaties with the colonists. They fought against the British in the *French and Indian War [IV]* and were divided in their loyalties in the *American Revolution [IV]*. Some Lenape participated in *Little Turtle's War [IV]* from 1790 to 1794 and in *Tecumseh*'s *[II]* Rebellion from 1809 to 1811. By 1835, they were forced onto northern *Indian Territory [IV]* in Kansas. Later, in 1867, they were forcibly moved to Oklahoma.

The Delaware Tribe of Western Oklahoma, established in 1866, resides on 63,600 acres (only 3,000 acres of which are tribally owned) along with Wichita and *Caddo* tribes near Anadarko, Oklahoma. Each Oklahoma community holds a powwow in the summer. The Delaware Tribe of Indians and the Delaware Tribe of Western Oklahoma are federally recognized, but Delaware groups in New Jersey, Kansas, Colorado, Pennsylvania, and Delaware have been denied official recognition.

Lillooet

The Lillooet, whose name means "end of the trail," have lived in southwest British Columbia, Canada, for more than 9,000 years. Lillooet is an interior dialect of the *Salish* language. Their population was estimated at

4,000 in the 18th century. Today, there are approximately 4,500 enrolled members.

The Lillooet carved wooden masks to represent mythological ancestors. Adolescents in Lillooet tradition sought guardian spirits on vision quests or in dreams. Girls were secluded during their first menstrual period. Like other coastal groups, they had a class system of nobles, commoners, and slaves. Potlatches were given by the wealthy to attain status and redistribute resources through feasts and giveaways. They wrapped their dead in woven mats or fur robes and placed them in painted boxes or in graves lined with bark or mats. Graves were marked with clan totem poles. The totem pole was a carved post painted with the spiritual and mythological symbols from tribal legends and the histories of particular families or clans. In addition to being used to mark graves, the clan totem also appeared on the center pole or an outside pole of Lillooet homes.

Lillooet men built circular cedar-bark lodges on wooden frames. The lodges were dug in to a depth of 6 feet and were up to 35 feet in diameter. Larger log and plank houses could hold as many as eight families. Salmon and other fish were staples of their diet. They made clothing from cedar bark or animal skins; women also wore abalone in their braids and tattoos on their wrists and arms. The Lillooet experienced conflict with Thompsons and other Salish groups.

Gold rushes in the mid-19th century were followed by white land invasions and smallpox epidemics. Famine in the 1860s followed the epidemics, since no one was well enough to grow the crops. They are currently provincially and federally recognized in Canada.

Luiseno

Luiseno is the name of a southern California tribe and is derived from the nearby Mission San Luis Rey. The Luiseno spoke a Cupan dialect of the Takic division of the Uto-Aztecan language group.

They lived in coastal southern California, where they might have migrated from the Great Basin area more than 8,000 years ago. In the 18th century they resided south of Los Angeles, but today most Luiseno live on reservations in San Diego and Riverside. Their population was estimated at 10,000 in the late 18th century; today, the Luiseno have approximately 1,700 enrolled members.

Luiseno religious practices involved sandpainting for ceremonies. Women sometimes served as chiefs and medical practitioners, although descent in their society was patrilineal. Their homes were built partially underground and covered in bark. Acorns and fish were staples of their diet.

Among the first Europeans they encountered was Gaspar de Portolá, who founded the Mission San Diego in 1796. English-speaking whites flooded into their lands in the 1840s following the California gold rush. The Luiseno and other Indians at the time could not testify in court regarding the theft of their lands, so miners and settlers were relatively free to dispossess Indians of anything they desired. Several Luiseno reservations were established in 1875; the Act for the Relief of Mission Indians in 1891 established five more Luiseno reservations and brought federal police, schools, and courts to support assimilation. In 1895, a Luiseno school was burned by tribal members, and the teacher was assassinated. By the early 20th century, Luiseno land could not support agriculture due to Whites' control of water resources. Two dozen Luiseno still speak the language.

Lumbee

The Lumbee are a racially mixed tribe with Cheraw Indian, African American, and white ancestors. The Cheraw are a Siouan group who lived in northwestern South Carolina, where they first had contact with the Spanish. Historians surmise that Lumbee ancestors may have included British survivors of the lost colony of Roanoke, Virginia, which was founded in 1587. That hypothesis seems to be supported by the fact that more than 20 surnames of Roanoke colonists exist among the Lumbee. Their ancestors may also include other Indian groups including the *Cherokee*, Croatoan, and *Tuscarora*. Their first language is English.

Today, they live in southeastern North Carolina and northeastern South Carolina and have approximately 48,000 enrolled members.

By the early 18th century, although they had no observable Indian traditions, their skin color led whites to identify the Lumbee as Indian. Beginning in the 1760s, they lost large areas of their lands to white settlement. In 1835, the state of North Carolina denied the Lumbee land, the vote, and other civil rights; in other words, they were treated like other "persons of color."

During the *Civil War [IV]*, the Lumbee resisted Confederate attempts to use them as forced labor. Lumbee tribal member Henry Berry Lowry raided wealthy plantations to feed the poor of all races and led a Lumbee resistance. His father and brother had been killed for reportedly assisting Union troops. Lowry continued his raids after the war but disappeared in 1872.

Following the war, the Lumbee pressed for state and federal recognition. In the South, their status was classified as a third racial group between African Americans and whites. As a result, their schools were segregated from both whites and African Americans. In 1885, North Carolina recognized them as Croatoan Indians but reclassified them in 1911, first as Robeson County Indians, then as Cherokee Indians of Robeson County, until the Cherokee protested use of their name. They were finally recognized by the state as Lumbee Indians in 1953 and partially recognized by the federal government in 1956. In 1958, thousands of Lumbee confronted the Ku Klux Klan at a planned rally and drove them out of the area, an incident that received national and international attention. Tribal members largely govern the town of Pembroke, North Carolina. They are the largest tribe east of the Mississippi and the largest nonfederally recognized tribe.

Maidu

The Maidu were culturally similar to the Miwok, Wintun, and Yokut. Their language, Maiduan, is of the Penutian language group. Maidu (MY-doo) is their word for "person."

Traditional Maidu lands were in the Sierra Nevada region of northern California, near the Nevada border. Today they live on small reservations in northern California. Their population was estimated at 9,000 in the early 19th century; there are about 2,500 enrolled members today.

There were three divisions among the Maidu: the Maidu, Konkow, and Nisenan, which comprised the largest group. The Maidu believed that spirits could be found in nature. Both genders were permitted to practice medicine. Marriage was marked by gift exchanges. Newlyweds lived with the bride's family at first and then moved to their own home near the groom's family. The Nisenan cremated their dead; the other groups buried their dead with food and gifts.

They lived in pole-framed houses that were covered with brush in the summer or skins in winter. Acorns were a staple of their diet. Their weapons included poisoned arrows, which they used in their occasional conflicts with the *Achumawi.*

During Spanish and Mexican rule, they were able to avoid religious conversions. However, the California gold rush of 1849 brought an influx of whites onto their lands. They purchased rancherias between 1906 and 1937 with funds from legislation that mandated that lands be found for landless California Indians. In 1906 the last traditional Maidu headman died and their ceremonial objects were bought by a local museum.

Unemployment today is high. A few Maidu still speak their original language. Three rancherias are seeking to regain their recognition, and four groups have filed for federal recognition. The Maidu Nation and North Maidu Tribe do not have federal recognition. The Mechoopda Tribe of Maidu Indians won recognition in 1992.

Makah

Makah (mah-KAW) is a Klallam word meaning "the people." The Makah referred to themselves as *Kwe-net-che-chat*, meaning "people of the point." Descent was patrilineal. They were culturally similar to the *Nootka* of Vancouver Island, who were also whalers. Makah is a Nootkan dialect of the Wakashan language group; the Makah were the southernmost group of Wakashan speakers.

The Makah live on the northwest tip of the Olympic Peninsula in Washington State, where they have been for more than 4,000 years, having originally migrated from Vancouver Island. Some of their villages were occupied as early as 1500 B.C. Their population was estimated at 2,000 in the late 18th century; today the Makah have approximately 1,900 enrolled members, 900 of whom live on the Makah Reservation.

Both genders in Makah society could serve as spiritual leaders and practice medicine. Most of their ceremonies took place in the winter and involved the use of carved wooden masks. Like other Northwest Coast groups, they had a class system and a potlatch tradition. Marriage was marked by gifts given to the bride's family. When the dead were buried, their possessions were put into boxes and buried with them.

Their houses, each of which held several families, were made of cedar planks and built on wooden frames as large as 60 feet long by 15 feet high. The fronts of houses and support posts were generally carved and painted. Sea mammals and fish were staples of the diet. They spun wool from dog hair and fibers and used shells for utensils. Clothing was made from cedar bark. They experienced conflict with the Hoh, Klallam, and *Quileute*.

The Makah first encountered the British and Spanish around 1790. By the 1850s, whole villages were decimated by *diseases [I]* introduced by Europeans. They signed the Treaty of Neah Bay in 1855, ceding lands to the United States in exchange for fishing rights and a reservation. The reservation was not easily accessed by the outside world until 1930, when a road was built. In 1932, a Makah tribal member donated land to build an elementary school and a high school so Makah children would not have to be removed to boarding schools.

The 27,244-acre Makah Reservation is governed by a five-member tribal council. Unemployment runs at 50 percent. Their cultural heritage has a strong presence in their modern life, including the airing of some local radio programs in the Makah language and the annual Makah Days celebration at the end of August. They are the only tribe in the United States with treaty rights to hunt whales. In 1998, they hunted whales for the first time in 80 years despite protests by animal rights groups. Traditional

IN THEIR OWN

Words

The first subject to which we would call attention of the governor is the depredation daily committed by the white people upon the most valuable timber on our reservation. . . . This has been the subject of complaint for many years. . . .

Our next subject of complaint is the frequent thefts of our horses and cattle by the whites, and their habit of taking and eating them when they please, and without our leave.

Another evil arising from the pressure of the whites upon us, and our unavoidable communication with them, is the frequency with which our Indians are thrown into jail . . . and for the most trifling causes. . . . The greatest source of all our grievances is that the white men are among us.

—RED JACKET (SAGOYEWATHA [HE KEEPS THEM AWAKE]), SENECA (c. 1755–1830). LETTER SENT TO GOVERNOR DEWITT CLINTON OF NEW YORK IN 1821.

potlatches are still practiced and a dozen members still speak the original language.

Maliseet

Maliseet is a *Micmac* word meaning "broken talkers." The ancestors of the Maliseet may have included the *Passamaquoddy*, since both the Maliseet and Passamaquoddy spoke a dialect of the Algonquian language.

They may have originated in the Southwest and had contact with the Ohio Mound Builders, but their traditional lands were in New Brunswick, Canada, and northeastern Maine. Their numbers were estimated to be under 1,000 in the early 17th century; there are approximately 3,000 enrolled members today.

Both genders in Maliseet society practiced medicine. Grooms served their in-laws' family for a year before marriage. While divorce was rare, sexuality was restricted.

Their homes were birchbark-covered wigwams that were rectangular in shape and framed in wood. They also had council houses that could hold as many as 100 people. Corn, a staple of their diet, was stored in bark-lined pits. Birchbark was also used to make dishes, boxes, and raincoats.

Samuel de Champlain was one of the first Europeans they encountered in the early 17th century. From an early date, they were involved in the French fur trade and joined the pro-French *Abenaki* confederacy in the mid-18th century. Because of their extensive trading relationship, they often intermarried with the French and sided with them in the colonial wars.

The Jay Treaty of 1794 gave the Maliseet and other tribes with members on both sides of the United States–Canadian border, such as the *Mohawk*, free border-crossing rights. Today, they live on reserves in south-

IN THEIR OWN Words

I am about to leave you, and when I am gone and my warning shall no longer be heard or regarded, the craft and avarice of the white man will prevail. Many winters I have breasted the storm, but I am an aged tree, and can stand no longer . . . Think not I mourn for myself. I go to join the spirits of my fathers, where age cannot come; but my heart fails when I think of my people, who are soon to be scattered and forgotten.

—Red Jacket (Sagoyewatha [he keeps them awake]), Seneca (c. 1755–1830). Spoken in 1830, near death.

east Canada, where unemployment runs about 50 percent. A few people in New Brunswick still speak the native language. They participate in the Wabanaki Aboriginal Music Festival every Labor Day weekend and celebrate Saint Anne Day in July.

Mandan

Mandan (MAN-dun) is a *Dakota* word. The Mandan, however, referred to themselves as *Numakiki*, meaning "people" in the Siouan language they spoke. Descent was matrilineal in their society.

The Mandan arrived in the Missouri River region from the southeast Ohio Valley as early as the 7th century and were one of the first groups to reside on the plains. Their neighbors were the *Hidatsa* to the north and the *Arikira* to the south. Their population was estimated at 3,600 in the early 18th century. By 1837, their numbers had dropped to just over 100; today there are 6,000 members in the Three Affiliated Tribes: the Mandan, Hidatsa, and Arikira. Most Mandan now live in North Dakota.

The Mandan possessed sacred medicine bundles called "mother," which were handed down from generation to generation. According to tradition, one of these bundles, the Lone Man medicine bundle, was given to the Mandan by the first human. The sacred shrine of Lone Man, the creator of the earth, stands on the reservation today. There was also the Sacred Canoe medicine bundle, made from the planks of a canoe on which tribal ancestors survived a great flood. The Mandan practiced a four-day Okipa ceremony that may have been the precursor of the Sun Dance. The ceremony involved fasting and self-mutilation, through which participants hoped to receive a vision. Other festivals included the women's Corn Dance and men's Buffalo Dance. There were nine Mandan villages in the early 19th century, divided into 13 clans. Status was confirmed through giveaways and acts of bravery.

Villages contained as many as 150 earth lodges and were surrounded with log walls. The partly underground earth lodges were up to 40 feet in diameter and housed as many as 50 people. Furniture inside the homes included raised rawhide beds lined against the walls, willow backrests, and buffalo robe couches. They used burned trees to fertilize the soil and stored crops in deep pits. Mandan allies included the *Crow* and Hidatsa. They experienced conflict with the Dakota.

In the mid-18th century, they acquired the *horse [I]*, but unlike other tribes in the Plains area, they did not give up their agricultural lifestyle. Lewis and Clark lived among the Mandan in 1804 and wrote about them. The painter and writer George Catlin lived among them from 1830 to 1836. German Prince Maximilian zu Wied also lived among them from 1833 to 1834, painting their portraits and keeping journals on their activities. A major smallpox epidemic in 1837 decreased their population by more than 90 percent, from 1,600 to just over 100 people. Their reduced numbers led to a cultural merger with the Hidatsa, whom they joined in 1845 at Like-a-Fishook village. The Arikira joined them as well in 1862.

The 1851 *Treaty of Fort Laramie [IV]* recognized their lands of more than 12 million acres. However, when the Fort Berthold Reservation was established in 1870 for the Three Affiliated Tribes, it consisted of only 8 million acres. Those lands were reduced by allotment to only 1 million acres by the 1880s. In 1910, the federal government again appropriated large sections of land. In 1934, Mandan tribal representatives traveled to New York City to lobby for the return of their sacred Water Buster medicine bundle from the Heye Foundation Museum, now part of the Smithsonian. The bundle was finally returned many years later. In the 1950s, the Garrison Dam flooded much of their land, farms, and homes.

A Mandan village scene. *State Historical Society of North Dakota.*

Today, the 900,000-acre Fort Berthold Reservation in western North Dakota has a population just under 3,000, although whites own more than half the reservation. A casino was opened in 1993. Each of the Three Affiliated Tribes holds an annual powwow. A few elders still speak the original language. The largest settlement on the reservation, New Town, is home to a tribal museum as well as the offices of the tribal newspaper, *Mandan, Hidatsa and Arikira Times.*

Menominee

Menominee (muh-NOM-uh-nee) is a corruption of the *Anishinabe* word Manomini, meaning "wild rice people." The English called them Rice Indians, but they referred to themselves as *Mamaceqtaw*, meaning "the people who live with the seasons." They were culturally similar to the Anishinabe and Winnebago and speak an Algonquian language.

They are descendants of the *Old Copper culture [I]* people. Their traditional lands were in central Wisconsin, including their largest village, which was near Green Bay. Today, most Menominee live in northern Wisconsin. They have the distinction of being one of the few tribes east of the Mississippi able to continue living on part of their ancestral lands. Their population was estimated at 3,000 in the early 17th century; there are approximately 7,000 enrolled members today.

The Menominee believed in a great spirit, Mecwetok, who may have been associated with the sun. Dreams, which revealed sacred songs, dances, and ceremonies, also played an important role among the Menominee. A medicine society, the Midewiwin, was open by invitation. Status could be achieved through dreams or acts of bravery. Men could have more than one wife. They placed their dead on platforms, and in later periods buried them with their belongings in birchbark coffins.

The Menominee alternated between housing styles during the course of the year. Summer homes were rectangular pole structures covered with bark; winter homes were wigwams covered with mats. Most villages also had a lacrosse field. As their name suggests, wild rice (as well as fish) was a staple of their diet. Women raised corn, beans, squash, and tobacco and could participate in hunting and fishing. Both genders wore copper jewelry. Historically, the Menominee were allies of the Winnebago and experienced conflict with the Sauk and *Mesquakie*.

The Menominee were involved in the fur trade in the late 17th century and intermarried with the French. They avoided participation in most of the colonial wars, although some sided with the British in the *American Revolution [IV]* and the War of 1812. By 1820, whites were living on their lands. In the *Civil War [IV]*, a regiment of Menominee fought for the Union. By the 1950s, they were a stable and prosperous tribe due to their management of timber resources. Because of this prosperity, they were deemed acculturated, and President Dwight Eisenhower signed the Menominee Termination Act in 1954, which took effect in 1961. After termination, their hospital was forced to close and many Menominee sank into poverty, as they could not afford to pay property taxes and so were forced to sell large portions of their lands. Their once-prosperous reservation became the poorest county in Wisconsin. A new organization, the Determination of Rights and Unity for Menominee Shareholders (DRUMS), successfully lobbied in 1973 to regain their federal status with passage of the Menominee Restoration Act. Ada Deer, a founder of DRUMS, became the assistant secretary for Indian Affairs in the *Bureau of Indian Affairs [IV]* in the Clinton administration in 1992. She was the first woman to hold this position.

The 230,000-acre Menominee Reservation in Wisconsin was established in 1848. Its current population is about 3,000. The Menominee adopted a constitution in 1977 and are governed by a nine-member tribal council. The Menominee Nation Powwow is held on the first weekend in August and the Veterans Powwow on Memorial Day weekend. The Menominee also celebrate Menominee Restoration Day on December 22.

Mesquakie (Fox)

Mesquakie (mes-KWAK-ee) means "red earth people." The Mesquakie Indians have also been referred to as the Fox, the name of a clan once used by whites to refer to the whole tribe. They were culturally related to the *Kickapoo* and Sac and spoke dialects of an Algonquian language called Sauk-Mesquakie-Kickapoo.

Before modern times, the Mesquakie may have lived near Lake Erie before the *Iroquois* drove them westward. In the 17th century, they were located in eastern Wisconsin, but by the 18th century the *Anishinabe* had forced them westward into southwest Wisconsin and northern parts of Illinois and Iowa. Today, most Mesquakie live in central Iowa. Their tribal headquarters is located in Lincoln County, Oklahoma. Their population, estimated at 2,500 in the mid-17th century, is today approximately 1,000 enrolled members.

Mesquakie cosmology recognized upper and lower worlds: the lower world was beneath the earth's surface, while the Mesquakie lived in the upper world, on earth. A creative spirit called Manitou oversaw the upper world. Mesquakie newlyweds lived with the bride's family during their first year of marriage; men could also have more than one wife, and divorce was permitted in cases of adultery. Important ceremonies included the Midewin, Green Corn, and Adoption ceremonies, through which a deceased relative could have his or her position in the family replaced by an adopted family member. As adults, people could gain additional names related to dreams or feats of bravery. The dead were wrapped in bark or mats and buried. Mourning lasted at least six months.

Families of 10 or more people lived in longhouses covered with bark measuring about 50 feet by 20 feet in length. Women raised corn, beans, squash, pumpkins, melons, and tobacco. Body decorations included tattoos and body painting. Their traditional allies included the Sauk and Kickapoo. They experienced conflict with the Anishinabe and *Dakota*.

The Mesquakie participated in the fur trade but, unlike other tribes, they did not settle near trading posts or missions. In the mid-18th century, armed with British weapons, they fought the French during the French and Indian War. In fact, they were the only Algonquin tribe who were not allied with the French, primarily because their enemies, the Anishinabe, were closely aligned with the French. Those who survived both war and European *diseases [I]* went to live with the Sauk in 1733 and remained there until the 1850s. The Sauk refused to release the Mesquakie survivors to the French and both tribes escaped to Iowa. After the French pardoned them in 1737, both tribes returned to Wisconsin.

The Mesquakie were active in *Little Turtle's War [IV]* from 1790 to 1794 and in *Tecumseh*'s *[II]* Rebellion from 1809 to 1811. They also fought on the side of Sac chief Black Hawk in the *Black Hawk War [IV]* of 1832, the final war in the Old Northwest. In 1842, after ceding their remaining lands to the United States, the Sauk and Mesquakie were relocated to Kansas. The tribes were further removed to Oklahoma in 1869. Many Mesquakie left the Sauk and returned to Iowa in the 1850s, where they lived on lands purchased in 1857 from the state of Iowa.

The 5,000-acre Mesquaki (Sac and Mesquakie) Reservation in Iowa has a population of just over 500, and sits on part of the lands the tribe purchased in 1857. Their annual powwow is held in August.

> **IN THEIR OWN Words**
>
> You know I have a little boy who was lost among the mountains. I want you to find that boy, if he is not dead, and tell him the last words of his father were that he must never go beyond the Father of Waters, but die in the land of his birth. It is sweet to die in one's native land and be buried by the margins of one's native stream.
>
> —TSALI, CHEROKEE MARTYR (C. 1795–1838). SPOKEN WHILE FACING A FIRING SQUAD IN 1838.

Miami

The name Miami (my-AM-ee) comes from the *Anishinabe* word *Omaumeg*, meaning "people of the peninsula." They referred to themselves as *Twaatwaa*, an imitation of the sound of a crane. They were culturally similar to the *Illinois* and spoke an Algonquian language.

The Miami are descendants of the prehistoric Ohio Mound Builders. By the mid-17th century they were living in northern Illinois and southern Wisconsin. Today, however, most Miami live in Oklahoma and Indiana. Their population, estimated at 10,000 in 1650, was approximately 4,500 in the mid-17th century and barely 600 in 1846. Today, there are about 7,000 Miami; 2,500 live in Indiana and 4,500 live in Oklahoma.

The sun was the focus of Miami worship. Miami society was headed by peace and war chiefs, who could be either male or female. Peace chiefs organized feasts, while war chiefs provisioned war parties and made decisions to cease wars. As adolescents, both genders sought guardian spirits

IN THEIR OWN Words

I have heard talk and talk, but nothing is done. Good words do not last long unless they amount to something. Words do not pay for my dead people. They do not pay for my country, now overrun by white men . . . Good words will not give my people good health and stop them from dying. Good words will not get my people a home where they can live in peace and take care of themselves. I am tired of talk that comes to nothing. It makes my heart sick when I remember all the good words and broken promises . . .

You might as well expect the rivers to run backward as that any man who was born a free man should be contented when penned up and denied liberty to go where he pleases . . .

Let me be a free man—free to travel, free to stop, free to work, free to trade where I choose, free to choose my own teachers, free to follow the religion of my fathers, free to talk and think and act for myself—and I will obey every law, or submit to the penalty.

—JOSEPH (CHIEF JOSEPH; EPHRAIM; HEINMOT TOOYALAKET, HIN-MAH-TOO-YAH-LAT-KEKT, HINMATON YALATIK, IN-MUT-TOO-YAH-LAT-LAT [THUNDER COMING FROM WATER OVER LAND]; YOUNG JOSEPH), NEZ PERCE (1841–1904). STATEMENT OF SURRENDER TO GENERAL NELSON MILES, OCTOBER 1877, U.S. SECRETARY OF WAR REPORT, 1877.

on vision quests. Naming children was the prerogative of female elders, who chose names based on dreams. Adults, however, could change their own names as a way to influence their luck. Adult status was marked by face painting. Abusive husbands or adulterous wives were punished, and the punishment could culminate in death. Like a number of other tribes, the Miami accepted male cross-dressing.

The Miami lived in oval homes made of a pole framework covered with mats. They raised corn, beans, squash, and melons and hunted *buffalo [I]*. Red was a popular color for decorative use. Historically, they were allied with the *Kickapoo* and fought the *Chickasaw* and *Dakota*.

Among the first Europeans the Miami encountered were the French in the 1650s. Although they traded with the French, they occasionally sided with the British in colonial wars, especially in the *American Revolution [IV]*. They supported the French against the English and *Iroquois* in the French and Indian War from 1689 to 1763. They fought against the English in *Pontiac's Rebellion [IV]* of 1763, after which they were forced to cede most of their Ohio lands to the British.

From 1790 to 1794, Michikinikwa, or Little Turtle, led *Little Turtle's War [IV]*, also known as the Miami War—one of the first wars for the Old Northwest. A coalition of groups joined the Miami in that war, including the Anishinabe, Illinois, *Lenape*, *Ottawa*, *Potawatomi*, and *Shawnee*. They were decisively defeated, however, at the Battle of Fallen Timbers in 1794. The subsequent Treaty of Greenville forced the Miami to cede all of Ohio and most of Indiana to the federal government. Around 1803, Governor William Henry Harrison wanted to press for statehood status for the Indiana Territory. He pressured the Miami to cede their remaining lands in Indiana to the United States. During the War of 1812, Harrison ordered attacks on neutral Miami villages. They were forced to cede more land in a series of treaties from 1818 to 1840. Half the Miami, about 600 members, were forcibly removed to Kansas in 1846 and later relocated to Oklahoma. They lost their federal recognition in 1897.

Tribal headquarters today are located in Miami, Oklahoma, where the tribe owns only 35 acres of land. The northern group is located near Peru, Indiana. Although the Miami Tribe of Oklahoma is federally recognized, the Miami Nation of Indiana's request for reinstatement of federal recognition was rejected in 1992.

Micmac

Micmac (MICK-mack) means "allies"; the Micmac also referred to themselves as *Souriquois*. They were culturally similar to the *Maliseet*, *Penobscot*, and *Passamaquoddy*. In the 18th and 19th centuries, they were members of the *Abenaki* Confederacy. Their earliest written language was a hieroglyphics recorded on birch bark or animal hides. They also used this language to record historical events on wampum belts. Micmac was an Algonquian language, which, interestingly, is nongendered.

The Micmac originated around the Great Lakes area and had some contact with the Ohio Mound Builders. They have resided on their traditional lands in southeast Quebec and northern Maine for at least 10,000 years. Tribal legend predicted the arrival of blue-eyed people from the east. Today, they continue to live near their traditional lands. Their population was estimated at 5,000 in the 16th century. Currently, there are around 27,000 enrolled members, 20,000 in Canada and 7,000 in the United States.

Pages from a Micmac prayer book, most likely from the 17th century. *Library of Congress.*

The Micmac believed in a creative spirit, Manitou, who may have symbolized the sun. They also respected bears, who they believed could change into other species. Micmac social structure involved three social classes: nobles, commoners, and slaves. According to Micmac custom, boys passed into adulthood after they killed their first large game. Grooms spent two years working for their in-laws prior to marriage, which was marked with a feast. The birth of children formalized a marriage. They mourned their dead for three days and then wrapped them in bark and buried them with their belongings or placed them on platforms. Mourners cut their hair and observed a one-year mourning period.

Homes were wigwams covered with birch bark, skins, or woven mats. Floors were covered with boughs. Piles of boughs covered by fur served as beds. They made butter from pounded moose bones. They also ate marine animals, which were a staple of their diet. They were allied with southern Algonquin in the Abenaki Confederacy and experienced conflict with the *Beothuk*, *Inuit*, *Iroquois*, and Labrador.

They may have been one of the first groups of Indians to encounter Europeans when the Vikings arrived around A.D. 1000. Centuries later, they came in contact with John and Sebastian Cabot in 1497, Jacques Cartier in 1523, and Samuel de Champlain in 1603. By the 17th century, they were involved in the fur trade and had become allies of the French. By the mid-18th century, many Micmac had become Catholics. Forty percent of the Canadian Micmac still speak their original language. As agreed in the 1794 Jay treaty, tribal members can freely cross the U.S.–Canadian border. In 1992, the Micmac in northern Maine gained federal recognition from the U.S. government.

Missouria

Missouria (miz-OAR-ee-uh), or Missouri, is an Algonquian word meaning "people with dugout canoes." The Missouri Indians referred to themselves as *Niutachi,* meaning "people of the river mouth." They were culturally similar to the *Ioway, Otoe, Ponca*, and Winnebago (Ho Chunk) and spoke a language that belonged to the Southern Siouan group.

The Missouria may have originated north of the Great Lakes and had been united with the Ioway, Otoe, and Winnebago (Ho Chunk). We know that in the 16th century they migrated southward to the junction of the Missouri and Grand Rivers and that the Otoe and Missouria divided around 1600 due to an affair between two chiefs' children. Today most Missouria live in Oklahoma. Their population was estimated at 1,000 in the late 18th century, but by 1829, following an 1820 epidemic, there were fewer than 100 left. Today, there are approximately 1,500 members, 800 of whom reside in Oklahoma.

The Missouria recognized a creative spirit named Wakonda, with whom communication was possible through vision quests. Socially, each Missouria belonged to 1 of 10 clans. The dead were buried or placed in a tree followed by a four-day mourning period.

They lived in farming villages of 40 to 70 lodges. Their homes were partly underground earth lodges as large as 40 feet in diameter, although they used skin tipis on hunting trips. Once they were relocated to the plains they relied more on *buffalo [I]* than on crops. Historically, the Otoe were their allies, and they experienced conflict with the *Dakota, Mesquakie, Omaha, Pawnee,* and Sauk.

They ceded their lands to the United States in treaties in the 1830s and in 1854 and were eventually relocated to a reservation in northern *Indian Territory [IV]* on the Kansas-Nebraska border. In 1876 and 1881, they made further land cessions and were moved to southern Indian Territory (Oklahoma). The reservation in northcentral Oklahoma was allotted by 1907. After oil was discovered on their land, they were forced to give up their remaining allotments. They have no reservation today. They adopted a constitution in 1984 and are governed by a tribal council. An annual powwow is held in July.

Modoc

The name Modoc (MO-dock) is derived from the *Klamath* word *Moatokni* meaning "southerners." They referred to themselves as *Maklaks,* meaning "people." They were linguistically related to their Klamath neighbors and spoke a dialect of the Lutuami division of the Penutian language.

The Modoc traditionally lived in northern California and southern Oregon. Today they live in Oregon and Oklahoma. Their population was estimated at 500 in the 18th century and 150 in 1954. Today, there are 600 enrolled members, two-thirds of whom reside in Oregon.

The Modoc lived in partially below ground lodges constructed of wooden poles covered with mats and earth. Salmon and other fish were staples of their diet. Charcoal was used to blacken the face to protect against sun and snow. They wrapped their dead in deerskin and cremated them with their belongings. Mourners cut their hair and covered their faces with pitch and ash.

Their numbers were reduced by epidemics in 1833 and 1847. Whites began arriving in their area in the 1840s, but when *gold [IV]* was discovered on their lands in 1851, miners arrived in droves, often killing Indians on sight. In 1864, they ceded most of their land to the United States and moved to the Klamath Reservation in Oregon. There they faced starvation as they continued to petition for their own lands. In 1870, 300 Modoc, under the leadership of Kintpuash (*Captain Jack [II]*), returned to their traditional lands in defiance of their cessions in 1864. Conflicts with white settlers were followed by conflicts with the military, who eventually captured and hung some Modoc leaders; others were imprisoned at Alcatraz Island. (See *Modoc Conflict [IV].*) Surviving Modoc were relocated to the *Quapaw* Reservation in *Indian Territory [IV]* (Oklahoma). In 1890 their lands in Oklahoma were allotted, and a small group returned to the Klamath Reservation around 1905. The Klamath Reservation was terminated in 1954. The Oklahoma Modoc lost their federal recognition in 1956 but had it restored in 1978.

Today, the Modoc Tribe of Oklahoma is located in Miami, Oklahoma, on just nine acres of land. They adopted a constitution in 1991. Some Modoc also live on the Klamath Reservation in Chiloquin, Oregon.

Mohawk

Mohawk (MO-hawk) is an Algonquian word for "eaters of men." They referred to themselves as *Kaniengehawa,* meaning "people of the place of flint." They were one of the five original member tribes of the *Iroquois League [IV],* the most eastern in location. Descent was matrilineal and residence was matrilocal. Wampum belts recorded historical events. They spoke a northern dialect of Iroquois.

The Mohawk have lived in New York since at least A.D. 800. Today, they live in southern Quebec, Ontario, and northern New York. The Mohawk population was estimated at 4,000 in the mid-17th century. Today the Mohawk have about 28,000 enrolled members: 13,000 in Canada, and 15,000 in the United States.

Their creative spirit was named Orenda. Some of their major ceremonies included the Maple Sap, Strawberry, and Green Corn ceremonies. They also held an eight-day New Year's observance, a festival of great importance. Individual Mohawks belonged to one of three clans: wolf, bear, and turtle. Women held a high status in Mohawk culture, and they were included in the decision making regarding war. Food was shared among all members. The dead were buried in a sitting position with food and tools.

In the 17th century, the Mohawk had three main villages and several smaller ones having populations of as many as 1,000 residents. They lived in elm bark covered longhouses that could be as long as 100 feet. Usually two or three maternally related families lived in each dwelling. They experienced conflict with the Algonquin, *Anishinabe, Cree,* and Montagnais.

The first of many epidemics struck in 1634, reducing Mohawk numbers by two-thirds within ten years. The Dutch were early trading partners, a role the English took over when they supplanted the Dutch in 1664. When the Iroquois League split its loyalties during the *American Revolution [IV]*, the Mohawk primarily supported the British. The British in Canada established the Six Nations Reserve for their Mohawk allies after the war. The establishment of the Six Nations Reserve encouraged Mohawks to move to Canada in great numbers after the war. Today the Jay Treaty of 1794 guarantees them free crossing of the U.S.–Canadian border.

The *Handsome Lake [II]* religion of the 19th century taught a combination of traditional and Christian teachings. Fifteen percent of the Canadian Mohawk still speak the language; a smaller number speak it on reservations in the United States.

IN THEIR OWN Words

Brother: We have borne everything patiently for this long time past; we have done everything we could consistently do with the welfare of our nations in general— notwithstanding the many advantages that have been taken of us, by individuals making purchases from us, the Six Nations, whose fraudulent conduct toward us Congress never has taken notice of, nor in anyway seen us rectified, nor made our minds easy. This is the case to the present day; our patience is now entirely worn out; you see the difficulties we labor under, so that we cannot at present rise from our seats and attend your council seat, agreeable to your invitation. The boundary line we pointed out, we think is a just one, although the United States claim lands west of that line; the trifle that has been paid by the United States can be no object in comparison to what a peace would be.

Brother: We are of the same opinion with the people of the United States; you consider yourselves as independent people; we, as the original inhabitants of this country, and sovereigns of the soil, look upon ourselves as equally independent, and free as any other nation or nations. This country was given to us by the Great Spirit above; we wish to enjoy it, and have our passage along the lake, within the line we have pointed out.

—JOSEPH BRANDT AT A COUNCIL MEETING IN ONONDAGA VILLAGE ON BUFFALO CREEK, ON APRIL 21, 1794.

Mojave

Mojave (mo-HAV-VEE) is a Spanish translation of the Uman word *Aha-makave*, meaning "people who live along the river." The Mohave were culturally similar to their neighbors the Foothill Yokuts and spoke River Yuman of the Hokan-Siouan language group.

They have lived in the Mojave Valley since before A.D. 1150 on lands that border Arizona, California, and Nevada. Their population was estimated by historians at 20,000 in the early 16th century, although only 3,000 members remained by 1770. Today, there are approximately 3,300 enrolled members.

The Mojave oral tradition tells of their emergence into this world from a place near Spirit Mountain, Nevada. Dreams held special importance for them and offered a setting where ancestors might visit. Both genders tattooed and painted their bodies. They cremated their dead along with their possessions. They raised corn, beans, and pumpkins and made red coiled pottery. Their allies included the *Chemehuevi, Quechan*, Western *Apache*, and Yavapai. They experienced conflict with the *Cocopah, Tohono O'odham, Pee Posh*, and *Pima*.

In 1865, Congress created the 270,000-acre Colorado River Reservation primarily for the Mojave and Chemehuevi. Some Mojave moved there, but the majority (70 percent) remained in the Mojave Valley, where they finally gained a reservation in 1880. Allotment of their lands began in 1904. During World War II, Japanese-American citizens were interned on the Colorado River Reservation. The army took more than 25,000 acres of Indian land for that purpose. After the war, the government opened those confiscated lands to *Hopi* and *Navajo* settlement.

The Mojave today reside on two reservations: the Colorado River Reservation and the much smaller Fort Mojave Reservation on their traditional lands. Several hundred Mojave also live on the Fort McDowell Reservation in Arizona. More than half speak their original language.

Mono

Mono is derived from the Yukut word for "fly-people," so named for the alkali flies around Mono Lake that were part of the Mono Indians' diet. The Mono, however, referred to themselves as *Nimi*, meaning "people." Descent was patrilineal.

Their traditional lands were in central California in the Sierra Nevada region of Madera and Fresno counties. Today, most Mono live on rancherias in northern California. Their population was estimated at 2,500 in the late 18th century, but today there are only about 200 enrolled members: 38 on Big Sandy Rancheria in Fresno County, 159 on Cold Springs Rancheria in Fresno County, and a few others among the 700 mixed Indians on the Tule River Indian Reservation in Tulare County, California.

Mono ceremonies included the Bear Dance and annual Mourning Ceremony. They brought the *Ghost Dance [IV]* religion of 1870 west of the Sierra Nevada but did not participate in the 1890 revival. They believed the dead traveled west for two days to the land of the dead. Wealthy men could have more than one wife. They intermarried with the Yokuts. Acorns were a staple of their diet.

Since they lived in isolated mountain regions, the Mono survived in higher numbers than other California Indians who had greater contact with whites. In 1910, they gained three rancherias. Today, the Mono Tribal Council is located in Dunlap, California, although the other two rancherias were terminated in the 1950s.

Nakota

The Nakota are the central group among the three related *Dakota* tribes, of which the other two are the Dakota in the east and the *Lakota* in the west. There were two divisions among the Nakota: the Yankton (meaning "end village"), and Yanktonai (meaning "little end village"). Descent was patrilineal. Nakota is a dialect of the Siouan language.

The Nakota may have originated on the lower Mississippi River or in eastern Texas. They migrated to the Ohio Valley and may have been related to the Mound Builder culture of the 9th through 12th centuries. In the early 17th century, the Nakota migrated from northcentral Minnesota to eastern North and South Dakota. Today, they reside on reservations in the Dakotas and Montana. The Nakota population was estimated at 5,000 in the late 17th century. There are approximately 10,000 enrolled members today.

Their creative spirit was known as Wakan Tanka. They believed guardian spirits could be sought in dreams and on vision quests. By the mid-18th century, they had moved to the plains and had adopted many traditions of the Plains cultural group, including the Sun Dance. The dead were wrapped in skins and placed on platforms with their belongings. Mourners cut their hair and caked their faces with white clay.

While in Minnesota, they lived in bark-covered or mat-covered lodges. On the plains, they lived in earth lodges and tipis. In the Great Lakes region, women raised corn, beans, and squash, and gathered wild rice. When they moved westward onto the plains, *buffalo [I]* became a staple of the diet. They experienced conflict with the *Anishinabe.*

Among the first Europeans they encountered were the French in Minnesota in the late 17th century. The Yankton and Yanktonai separated around that time. Beginning in 1830, the Yankton gradually ceded their Iowa lands to the United States. By 1860, they had ceded all their remaining lands and moved to South Dakota. The Yanktonai ceded their lands in 1865 and moved to reservations in South Dakota (Standing Rock and Crow Creek), North Dakota (Devils Lake), and Montana (Fort Peck).

Many Nakota still perform traditional ceremonies and speak the language. A powwow at Devils Lake is held each July. Standing Rock Community College was established in 1973, and there is also a community college at Fort Peck. Ella Cara *Deloria [II]* and Vine *Deloria, Jr. [II]* of the Standing Rock Reservation are nationally known Indian intellectual figures.

Nanticoke

Nanticoke is a variant of the tribe's actual name, *Nentego*, which means "tidewater people." They were culturally similar to other Algonquin tribes, including the Assateague, Choptank, Conoy, Patuxent, Piscataway, and Pocomoke. Descent was matrilineal. They spoke an Algonquian language.

The Nanticoke may have originated in Labrador and may have been united with the *Lenape* and *Shawnee.* It is possible they migrated through the Great Lakes region and Ohio Valley, where they had contact with the mound-building *Hopewell culture [I].* In the 17th century, they lived on the peninsula between the Delaware and Chesapeake bays. Today, they reside in Canada, Oklahoma, and Delaware. Their population was estimated at 160 in 1600. Today the Nanticoke have about 1,000 members in Delaware alone.

In the early 17th century, there were five or more Nanticoke villages, each one surrounded by log walls. Houses were rectangular in shape and covered with bark or mats. Some Nanticoke chiefs had been female.

Among the first Europeans they encountered was the English Captain John Smith in 1608. After seven decades of white settlement and encroachment onto Nanticoke lands, the English granted the tribe a reservation in 1684. By 1707, whites had trespassed to settle on the original reservation lands, so the Nanticoke were given another 3,000 acres. (The new reservation was in turn sold to the colonists in 1768.) In 1754, the Nanticoke merged with the Piscataway. They remained neutral in the French and Indian War but were allied with the British during the *American Revolution [IV]*. In 1778, 200 members moved to the Six Nations Reserve in Canada. Others moved west with the Lenape to northern *Indian Territory [IV]* (Kansas), and then were relocated again in 1867 to southern Indian Territory (Oklahoma). The federal government has never officially recognized many eastern tribes, including the Nanticoke, who are still petitioning to gain federal recognition.

Narragansett

The Narragansett (nah-ruh-GAN-sit) may have originated in the Southwest, but by the 1600s, they were located in southcentral Rhode Island and were one of the most powerful tribes in the New England area. Their population at that time was estimated at 3,000. In 1990, the Narragansett had about 2,400 enrolled members. They spoke an eastern dialect of the Algonquian language.

They believed in a central creative spirit, Cautantowwit, who resided in the Southwest. Other spirits communicated with people through dreams and visions. A dual administration headed by both a junior and senior chief and a spiritual leader ruled the tribe. Women sometimes held the position of spiritual leaders. They wrapped their dead in skins or woven mats and buried them with their tools. Good persons joined the creator, Cautantowwit, in the Southwest after their deaths.

The Narragansett lived in villages surrounded by log stockades. Their circular wigwams had diameters of up to 20 feet; they were covered with bark in the summer and with woven mats in the winter. Women, who performed most of the agricultural tasks, raised corn, beans, squash, and sunflowers.

The Narragansett began trading with the British and Dutch by 1623, a relationship that led to their first smallpox epidemic 10 years later. They fought as British allies in the Pequot Conflict of 1636. In the same year, they sold land to Roger Williams, which became the foundation for the state of Rhode Island.

Because of the continuing trespassing on their lands by whites, they joined the *Wampanoag* and Nipmuc in *King Philip's War [IV]* of 1675. Their participation in that war resulted in the deaths of 600 Narragansett and the enslavement of more than 400 others. In the aftermath, many were dispersed among other tribes in the area. The fewer than 100 Narragansett who remained in Rhode Island worked as servants or slaves of the white colonists.

The last fluent speaker of Narragansett died in the early 19th century. The remaining members adopted a constitution in 1849. All the reservation except three acres was sold at public auction in 1880, and the tribe was then terminated.

They were able to reconstitute themselves in 1934 under the Indian Reorganization Act. In 1971, they were one of the first tribes to gain reburial of ancestral remains from an anthropological excavation in the 1960s. They reobtained their tribal recognition from the United States federal government in 1983.

> ## IN THEIR OWN Words
>
> *rothers, we must be one as the English are, or we shall all be destroyed. You know our fathers had plenty of deer and skins and our plains were full of game and turkeys, and our coves and rivers were full of fish.*
>
> *But, brothers, since these Englishmen have seized our country, they have cut down the grass with scythes, and the trees with axes. Their cows and horses eat up the grass, and their hogs spoil our bed of clams; and finally we shall starve to death; therefore, stand not in your own light, I ask you, but resolve to act like men.*
>
> —MIANTUNNOMOH, NARRAGANSETT. 1642 SPEECH ON THE EAST END OF LONG ISLAND.

In 1978, they settled a lengthy court suit for the return of lands taken from them in 1880, winning back two pieces of land of approximately 900 acres each. Today, the Narragansett Reservation in Charlestown, Rhode Island, comprises 1,800 acres. Their annual powwow in August has been held for more than 250 years.

Naskapi-Montagnais

The Naskapi-Montagnais (NAS-kuh-pee/Mon tunn ya) refer to themselves as *Nenenot,* meaning "the people." Both *Algonquin* groups have language similarities, speaking dialects of the Cree and Algonquian languages. They have occupied their traditional lands on the Labrador Peninsula for more than 5,000 years. The two bands have united in recent years as the Innu nation.

Historians estimated their population to be 4,000 Montagnais and 1,500 Naskapi during the 15th century. The entire Innu population in 1990 was approximately 16,000.

The French founded Quebec in 1608, and the Naskapi-Montagnais soon began participating in fur trade with them. Missionaries urged the relocation of tribes to the coast; epidemics and lack of game followed such transitions.

Tribal societies consisted of 25 to 30 bands having as many as 300 people each. Both men and women in their societies practiced medicine. Family hunting grounds were inherited patrilineally. Sexual relations were somewhat relaxed, and divorce was easy to obtain, although men could have more than one wife. Men performed bride service for at least a year, doing tasks for the woman's family.

Their homes, which held as many as 20 people, were covered in birch bark (Montagnais) and caribou skins (Naskapi). Their interiors were covered, first with branches, then with woven skins or mats. They also built A-frame and rectangular lodges as community halls.

In their daily lives, they hunted moose and caribou and stone-boiled or roasted the meat. Some Montagnais had gardens, while others made maple syrup. Making use of Labrador's flora, they made diapers out of moss and storage containers from birch bark and animal skins. Red paint was applied to clothing in geometrical patterns with bone pens or stamps. Decorating with parallel lines, triangles, and leaf shapes was also popular. Their traditional enemies were the *Inuit*, *Micmac*, and *Iroquois*; allies included the Algonquin and *Maliseet*.

The Naskapi-Montagnais, like other nearby tribes, have been affected by the contruction of hydroelectric projects near their traditional lands. Since 1940, the Canadian government has built more than 20 hydroelectric dams in Labrador. In 1975, the Eastern Cree and Inuit were required to cede more than 640,000 square kilometers of land for an enormous hydroelectric project at James Bay. The James Bay Project has been widely criticized by environmentalists and indigenous groups. Phase One of the project, completed in 1984, created the world's largest underground hydroelectric powerhouse, with spillways three times the height of Niagara

Falls. The completion of the James Bay project was suspended in 1994 after the New York State Power authority refused to sign a purchase contract.

Natchez

The Natchez (NATCH-is) were the largest tribe on the Mississippi River in the mid-16th century. Their direct predecessors were likely the *Mississippian [I]* Mound Builder culture, which may have had Mesoamerican influences. Their Natchezan language seems to have been related to the Muskogean language.

Their traditional lands were near present-day Natchez, Mississippi, although they may have originated in the Northwest. Their population was estimated at 4,500 in 1650, but was only 300 by 1731. Today, they are extinct.

The sun was their central deity and they obeyed a monarch who represented the spirit of the sun. Large adobe mounds in the main village included a sun temple. They also celebrated the Great Corn ceremony in mid to late summer.

The Natchez had two social classes: nobles and commoners. Nobles in Natchez society were required to marry commoners; the offspring of such unions kept the social status of the mother. In general, they practiced sexual freedom before marriage, although fidelity was expected after marriage. Divorce was rare. Part of their culture also included cross-dressing men, *berdaches*, who could assume a female gender role.

Their homes were constructed of square adobe walls lined with platform beds and covered with thatched roofs. Their diet was based on agriculture, primarily corn, pumpkins, and beans. Deer and buffalo hunting supplemented with fishing also determined their diet. Women made fabric from the inner bark of mulberry trees. Both genders painted and tattooed their faces and bodies.

One of the first Europeans they encountered was Hernando de Soto in 1542. However, it was the French who proved to be their most persistent enemy. Their battles with the French began in 1716, culminating in the Natchez Revolt of 1729 when the French ordered an evacuation of their Great Village. In 1731, the French sold those who survived the wars into slavery in the Caribbean. Some members were able to escape to local tribes such as the *Chickasaw, Creek,* and *Cherokee*. Those local tribes were removed to *Indian Territory [IV]* with the *Five Civilized Tribes [IV]* in the 1830s.

The last fluent speaker, Watt Sam, died in 1965, and their last formal ceremony was held in 1976.

Navajo

The Navajo (NAH-vuh-ho) refer to themselves as *Dine'e'* (dee-NAY), meaning "the people." Like the *Apache*, the Navajo are of Athapascan descent. Anthropologists believe that the Athapascan groups came to the Southwest area later than other groups, probably before A.D. 1400. Navajo, an Athapascan language, is related to the Na-Dene language group spoken in northern and central Canada. They are classified as part of the Southwest cultural group.

JUDICIAL BRANCH

OF THE

NAVAJO NATION

Rules of Court
Rules Of Civil Procedure
Rules of Criminal Procedure
Rules Of Probate Procedure
Rules Of The Court Of Appeals
Rules Of Evidence

Title page of the Navajo Tribe court rules, displaying the Great Seal of the Navajo Tribe. *Library of Congress.*

Today, the 28,800-square-mile Navajo Reservation, an area larger than the state of West Virginia, is located in northern Arizona, New Mexico, and southern Utah. It is the largest reservation in the United States. The Navajo themselves are the largest Indian nation in the United States, numbering about 200,000 members, including 144,000 on reservation lands.

Navajo oral tradition tells of their emergence from the underworld about 800 years ago. Spiritual beings such as Coyote, Hanging Woman, Spider Woman, and the Hero Twins assisted the transition to this world. Their ceremonies include the use of masked dancers, feathered prayer sticks, sandpainting, and cornmeal; some of their ceremonies were borrowed from *Hopi* and *Pueblo* people. The singers who usually conduct ceremonies employ one or more of twenty-four groups of incantations known as the chantway systems. Each chantway group might have 50 or more chants and hundreds of songs or prayers.

Women owned most of the property in Navajo society, including homes, crops, and livestock. A four-day puberty ceremony for girls was one of the tribe's most important tribal ceremonies. Their homes were known as hogans, six- or eight-walled structures covered with stone and adobe.

The Navajo joined the Pueblo people in the 1680 revolt against the Spanish. In the 1860s, war Chief *Manuelito [II]* led the Navajo in a fight against forced removal. Kit Carson finally defeated them in 1864 through a scorched-earth policy, and Manuelito surrendered two years later. As punishment, the Navajo were forcibly marched to Bosque Redondo (Fort Sumner) in eastern New Mexico. Hundreds of Navajo died on the 400-mile trek known as the *Long Walk [IV]*. Two thousand more Navajo died during a smallpox epidemic the following year. In 1868, the Navajo re-

IN THEIR OWN

Words

I was 18 when I entered the service, on very short notice. I didn't even have time to go back to see my parents. All I did was write them a letter. I was working at the hospital in Fort Defiance when I suddenly made up my mind to join the Marines. I filled out my application, had my physical and was on my way. I had been exposed to the Catholic religion a little but I admit I hadn't taken it very seriously.

I did pray many times when I was exposed to danger on the main battleline, as a code talker and as a signalman. I prayed as my mother and father had taught me—to the Heavenly Being as well as to Mother Earth.

Now when I came back, surprisingly my mother told me, "Son, do you know that since you left, almost every morning, I have gone to my sacred hill and prayed, using my sacred corn pollen, that you would come back with your whole physical being and a good mind." Maybe that is the reason I came back all in one piece.

Now I did have a hell of a time with malaria; I got it on Guadalcanal. Out of about 6000

Marines over there, I was among the last 16 to get it. Some of the colonels and generals asked, "How is it with you Navajoes? Are you so tough that you don't even need to take quinine?" I always said, " I don't know. I had a tough life when I was a little boy."

I came back to San Francisco, where they sent me to a rehabilitation center, then to a hospital, then home for a month's leave. I was skin and bones. I came back to Gallup where my father met me. He said, "Son, I'm glad you came back alive, I don't want you to go to town and try to have some fun; I want you to come home with me. I have something for you there." So I said, "O.K." Well, they had a medicine man there for me. They had a sing over me.

My mother and father were so happy to have me back that they killed a little nine-months pet goat; it was real tender. They wanted to feed me, I was so thin. But it didn't have any taste to it. I just couldn't eat it. I had to set it aside. There was something about the malaria, the things I had gone through, the difference in the wind and air. . . well, I just couldn't eat it.

But I got well. I think my mother's prayers on her sacred hill helped me through the war and after I got back home.

—ANONYMOUS NAVAJO CODE TALKER.

quested to return to their traditional lands, obtaining 3.5 million acres of land for a reservation. Manuelito returned home and served as chief.

During World War II, several Navajo served in the Marines, using their language to transmit a code that was never broken by enemy forces. On July 26, 2001, President George W. Bush awarded the gold Congressional Medal of Honor to the five surviving Navajo code talkers. The other 24 Navajo code talkers received medals posthumously.

In 1955, the United States divided Navajo lands into six districts, with whites as superintendents. Massive strip mining of coal and uranium, begun in the 1950s, caused severe pollution problems on Navajo lands. In 1976, 25 energy-producing tribes, including the Navajo, created the *Council of Energy Resource Tribes [IV]* in order to gain more control over the business practices of companies interested in Navajo mineral resources. The Navajo had a particular concern, given their long history of exploitative leases with energy companies.

In 1936, the Navajo adopted a set of rules that acted as a constitution, under which a Navajo tribal council is elected every four years. Unemployment today runs about 30 percent. In 1974, Congress passed the Navajo-Hopi Land Settlement Act that aimed to force relocation movements and formally divide jointly held lands. A second settlement act, passed in 1996, allows a longer time period for the two groups to relocate but still orders their separation.

Some of the curriculum in tribal schools is taught in the Navajo language, which is spoken by more than 100,000 members. Approximately 25,000 people, mainly elders, still speak only or mostly Navajo. Local radio stations broadcast programs in Navajo. In 1969, the Navajo Community College became the first tribally controlled college in America.

Nez Perce

Nez Perce (nes-PURSE) is the French term for "pierced nose." Ironically, while some of the neighboring tribes pierced their noses, the Nez Perce generally did not. They referred to themselves as *Nimipu,* meaning "the people." Their early culture contained a mixture of Great Plains and Northwest coastal cultures. The Nez Perce language is part of the Sahaptian dialect of the Penutian language group.

Their traditional lands were in southeast Washington, northeast Oregon, and southwest Idaho. Historians estimated their population at 6,000 in the early 19th century. In 1990, there were 3,000 enrolled members.

In the winter, people dressed as their guardian spirits and sang their spirit songs. Nez Perce chiefs were usually elected. Women and most men married by age 14. Men, who usually paid a bride price, could have more than one wife. Divorce was rare, but adultery was a capital crime. In the event of a divorce, the property went to the husband.

Chief Joseph. *State Historical Society of North Dakota.*

Their funeral ceremony involved painting the faces of their dead and wrapping them with their tools in deerskins. Boulders and wooden stakes marked their graves. Those in mourning cut their hair and wore torn clothing.

Nez Perce homes were partially below ground, circular, wood-framed structures with mat coverings. Mats also covered the floors. Older boys and single men slept in a separate communal lodge. Mattresses were made of inner bark or dry grass; folded animal skins were used for pillows. Salmon and other fish were staples of their diet, as were dried meat and berries.

They experienced conflict with the *Blackfeet, Gros Ventre,* and *Crow.* Allies included the *Flathead, Coeur d'Alene, Spokan, Cayuse, Umatilla, Yakama,* and Walla Walla.

An 1879 bird's-eye view of the Nez Perce Agency in Idaho. *National Archives.*

The Nez Perce obtained the *horse [I]* around 1730 and adopted some aspects of Plains culture, including hunting *buffalo [I]*. Some of the first Europeans they encountered were members of the Lewis and Clark expedition in 1805. In 1855, the Nez Perce ceded several million acres of land to the United States. A flood of white miners arrived after the *gold [IV]* strikes in the Nez Perce area in the 1860s.

IN THEIR OWN Words

I am tired of fighting, our chiefs are all killed, the old men are all dead, the little children are freezing to death. I want to have time to look for my children see how many of them I can find; maybe I shall find them among the dead. Hear me, my chiefs, I am tired; my heart is sick and sad. From where the sun now stands, I will fight no more forever.

—CHIEF JOSEPH, NEZ PERCE (1841–1904). SPOKEN AT HIS SURRENDER NEAR THE BEAR PAW MOUNTAINS TO GENERAL NELSON A. MILES, 1877.

In 1863, one minor chief with no authority signed a treaty to cede more than 75 percent of the remaining Nez Perce lands, ultimately evicting his people. In 1877, resistant bands were given 30 days to leave their homes. *Chief Joseph [II]* sided with the resisters. When he learned that whites planned to take his lands, Chief Joseph reportedly tore up his Bible. The group endured a 2-month flight, traveling 1,700 miles while army troops pursed them. Many died on the journey. They were forced to surrender in early October, just 30 miles from the Canadian border. At the surrender, Chief Joseph spoke his famous words, "I will fight no more forever." Those who survived were exiled to desolate reservation lands in Kansas and in Indian Territory (Oklahoma), and eventually to the Colville Reservation in Washington.

Chief Joseph died in 1904, never having been allowed to return to his homelands. A dramatic rise in death rates from tuberculosis after the 1870s was partially connected to the replacement of traditional mat houses with conventional, white-style housing.

Today, the 92,685-acre Nez Perce Reservation is located in northcentral Idaho. In 1990, the tribal population was 1,860. In accordance with their 1948 constitution, tribal elections are held every three years. Few members today are fluent in Nez Perce. The Nez Perce National Historic Trail, which follows the route taken by Chief Joseph and his people, was established in 1986. In 1992, after a 15-year battle, the Nez Perce were successful in having the Bear Paw Mountain Battleground where Chief Joseph surrendered declared a national historical site.

Nootka

The tribal name Nootka (NOOT-kuh) means "circling about," and is widely used to refer to more than 20 tribes. All of these groups speak dialects of the Wakashan language group. They have been classified as part of the Northwest Coast culture group.

They have lived on their ancestral lands on the western half of Vancouver Island, British Columbia, for at least 5,000 years. Their population was estimated by historians to be 15,000 in the mid-18th century. In 1990, there were approximately 4,800 Nootka.

In their spiritual practices, one did not seek to establish a relationship with a spirit but was instead seized by it. Two of their primary ceremonies were the Wolf Dance and the Curing Ceremony.

Nootka society was divided into the classes of chief (an inherited position), commoner, and slave. When a chief accumulated a surplus of resources, he held a potlatch, or gift giving ceremony. Potlatch comes from the Nootka word for sharing, *Patshatl.* Large potlatches were also held by wealthy families to celebrate the onset of female puberty among their daughters. Nootka society allowed for divorce and sometimes overlooked adultery. The dead were placed into boxes or canoes, which were then placed in trees or caves with their belongings. When a chief died, the Nootka erected a memorial totem pole for him.

They lived in multifamily cedar houses that could be as large as 150 feet long and 10 feet high. Inside, storage chests divided individual family areas. Beds lined the walls, covered by mattresses made of cedar bark. Hereditary designs were used for decoration on posts and beams. The Nootka painted their faces for sunburn protection.

Like other Northwest coastal groups, the Nootka hunted seal and sea otters or fished for salmon and other fish. Like the *Makah*, they hunted whales, as well.

A British trading post was established on Nootka Sound in 1788. During the 1790 *Nootka Convention [IV]*, Spain ceded its interests in the Pacific Northwest to England. The Nootka obtained several small reserves in the 1880s.

Currently, there are 18 small village reserves on Vancouver Island. They have adopted a new tribal name, Nuu-Chah-Nulth, which means "all along the mountains." Canada's provincial and federal governments recognize most Nootka bands.

Ojibwa (See Anishinabe)

Okanagon

The Okanagon, meaning "our people," were the largest tribe within a related cultural group that included the *Colville*, *Sanpoil*, and Senijextee. They are sometimes referred to by different names in the United States (Sinkaietk) and Canada (Northern Okanagon). Their lands were artificially divided when the international boundary between Canada and the United States was established in 1846. They spoke a dialect of Interior *Salish*.

Their traditional lands were in Washington State and British Columbia. Today, most Okanagon live on the Colville Reservation in Washington State and on reserves in British Columbia, Canada. Their population was estimated by anthropologists to be 2,500 in the late 18th century. In 1990, the majority of the approximately 2,000 Okanagon lived in Canada.

They wrapped their dead in robes or mats, then buried them under rocks or earth. Canoes or carvings were also placed over graves. Those in mourning cut their hair and clothing. A pleasant afterlife was thought to exist to the West or South. Okanagon men could have more than one wife. They frequently intermarried with *Spokan*, Thompson, and other Interior Salish people.

The Okanagon lived in partly below ground earth lodges as large as 16 feet in diameter, with an entrance in the roof. They also built mat-covered lodges. Salmon was a staple of their diet. When the *horse [I]* was introduced in the 1700s, the Okanagon also began to hunt *buffalo [I]*. Women wove baskets tight enough to hold water. The Okanagon traditionally fought with the *Nez Perce* and *Yakama* and were allies of the Colville.

A *gold [IV]* strike in their region in 1858 brought an onslaught of white miners onto their lands. The Colville Reservation was established in 1872, and most Okanagon in the United States were resettled there. The Okanagon in Canada were given small reserves near their traditional lands. The Okanagon today are provincially and federally recognized in Canada, and they are federally recognized in the United States.

Omaha

The Omaha (O-muh-haw), who referred to themselves as *Umon'hon*, are part of the Dhegiha division of the Siouan language group. The Omaha belonged to a Siouan-speaking group of people that lived along the Ohio River in the 15th century before their westward migration, when the group split into five separate tribes. The other four are the *Kaw, Osage, Ponca*, and *Quapaw*. While the Quapaw migrated southward, the Omaha and Ponca migrated farther north than the others. They settled briefly near the Pipestone Quarry in the area that is now southern Minnesota.

By the 18th century, the Omaha had settled downriver from the Ponca in the area of what is now northeastern Nebraska. Historians estimated their population to be 2,800 by the late 18th century. In 1990, there were approximately 6,000 enrolled members.

The Omaha were farmers who lived in earth lodges. Once they acquired the *horse [I]* in the 1700s, they adopted some traits of the Western Plains Indian culture, including hunting *buffalo [I]* and using hide tipis when hunting. Some of the tribe's most sacred relics are two pipes that have mallard duck heads attached to the stems.

The Omaha built earth lodges as large as 40 feet in diameter, similar to those of the *Arikira*. The staples of their diet were corn, beans, and squash, which were raised by women. They used hairbrushes made of stiff grass. The Omaha experienced conflict with the *Dakota, Lakota*, and *Nakota.*

In 1802, a smallpox epidemic caught from traders reduced their numbers to just 300. In 1854, they ceded their lands east of the Missouri River in exchange for a reservation in Nebraska. In 1865, the federal government assigned the northern part of their reservation to the Ho-Chunk (Winnebago). In 1882, the U.S. government allotted Omaha Reservation lands with the surplus lands sold to whites. This act, known as the 1882 Omaha Allotment Act, was a precursor of the General Allotment/*Dawes Act [IV]* of 1887.

Some of the most prominent Omaha individuals came from the La Flesche family. Joseph LaFlesche, a principal chief in the late 19th century, encouraged the adoption of some aspects of European American culture. Three of his ten children became famous: Susette LaFlesche became a writer and lecturer on Indian issues; Susan LaFlesche was the first western-trained

American Indian female physician; and Francis LaFlesche was an anthropologist and writer.

The Omaha Reservation was established in 1854 on the border of Iowa and Nebraska. Only 8,500 acres of the 26,792 acres of the reservation are tribally owned. Approximately 2,000 American Indian residents live on the reservation. The tribal council consists of seven members and a chair. Omaha children learn the tribal language in school.

One of the most commonly performed male dances at powwows around the country, the Grass Dance, was formerly called the Omaha Dance, which originated with the tribe. In 1989, the nation obtained the return of their sacred pole, Umon'hon'ri, or the "Real Omaha," a symbol of tribal unity, from Harvard's Peabody Museum. Two years later, in 1991, the Omaha also achieved the return of their sacred White Buffalo Hide from the Museum of the American Indian in New York.

Oneida

The Oneida (oh-NI-duh) were one of the five original tribes of the *Iroquois League [IV]*. Their name is derived from the Iroquoian word *Onayotekoana,* meaning "people of the upright stone," which referred to a large rock in their territory. They spoke a northern dialect of Iroquoian and used porcupine quills and wampum belts to record historic events.

Their traditional lands were in central New York. According to historians, there were approximately 1,000 Oneida in the mid-17th century. In 1990, there were 11,000 enrolled members of the Wisconsin Oneida tribe, 4,600 Oneidas in Ontario, and 700 in New York.

The Oneida lived as farmers in New York since at least the year 800. Huron Prophet *Deganawida [II]* and *Mohawk* shaman *Hiawatha [II]* founded the Iroquois League some time before 1450.

Important Oneida rituals included the Green Corn, Maple Sap, and Strawberry ceremonies. They also held an eight-day New Year's festival in midwinter as a time to give thanks. Oneida healers used more than 200 plant medicines. Divorce was possible in their society but frowned upon. They often adopted captives to replace lost family members.

Some Iroquois villages had more than 150 longhouses and populations of more than 1,000. Longhouses held maternally related families and were up to 100 feet long.

In the early 19th century, many Iroquois followed the teachings of *Handsome Lake [II]*, a *Seneca* prophet who led a religious revival that blended Christianity and traditional spirituality. Within a few years, however, more Oneida had returned to traditional religious practices, and the influence of Handsome Lake receded.

Fifty chiefs appointed by women ruled the Iroquois League, to which the Oneida sent nine representatives.

In the American Revolution of 1775–1783, the *Tuscarora* supported the American rebels, but other Iroquois nations such as the *Cayuga*, Mohawk, *Onondaga*, and *Seneca* supported the British. That split in loyalties divided and ended their 300-year-old confederacy. In the winter of 1777, the Oneida and Tuscarora provided bags of corn to the starving army of George Washington at Valley Forge, even though they themselves were short of food supplies.

The 1784 Treaty of Fort Stanwix guaranteed the Oneida and Tuscarora their lands in New York in recognition of their help during the Revolutionary War. However, the state of New York ignored that treaty and worked to remove the Indian population from its boundaries. Some Oneida moved across the border to Ontario to join the Mohawk, who had been British supporters. When *missionaries [IV]* attacked traditional spiritual and political practices, some Iroquois joined in the attack, seeing it as a way to wrestle power away from clan mothers and traditional chiefs.

Half the Oneida bought land from the *Menominee* tribe in the 1820s and settled near Green Bay, Wisconsin. When the Treaty of Buffalo Creek in 1838 demanded the removal of all Iroquois from the state of New York, additional Oneida moved to the Six Nations Reserve in Ontario, Canada. The Oneida are currently federally recognized in Canada and in the United States.

Onondaga

The Onondaga (au-nun-DAG-uh), meaning "people of the hills," were one of the five original tribes of the *Iroquois League [IV]*. They spoke a northern dialect of Iroquoian.

Their traditional lands were in upstate New York near present-day Syracuse. They have resided on these lands for more than 10,000 years. Records indicate there were approximately 1,000 Onondaga in the mid-

1600s. In 1990, approximately 1,600 Onondaga lived in the United States and 3,000 resided in Canada.

Their main village, Onondaga, was the meeting place of the annual Iroquois Confederacy Great Council, and the Onondaga tribe was responsible for keeping written records of the meetings, which were recorded on wampum belts. They sent 14 chiefs, chosen by Onondaga women, as tribal representatives to the Great Council of 50 members.

The Onondaga lived in villages having as many as 140 longhouses. Several maternally related families lived in each longhouse, which were as long as 100 feet. The Onondaga experienced conflict with *Algonquin*, Montagnais (see *Naskapi-Montagnais*), Ojibwa (see *Anishinabe*), and *Cree*.

Beginning in 1799, Seneca Prophet *Handsome Lake [II]* began teaching a blend of Christianity and traditional spirituality that was very popular among the Iroquois.

Handsome Lake, spiritual founder of the Longhouse Religion, died in 1815 and is buried next to the Onondaga Longhouse near Nedrow, New York. In the 1990s, the Onondaga successfully recovered some wampum belts of the Iroquois League from the New York State Museum, which had held them since 1898.

IN THEIR OWN *Words*

We know our lands are now become more valuable. The white people think we do not know their value; but we are sensible that the land is everlasting, and the few goods we receive for it are soon worn out and gone . . . with respect to the lands still unsold by us. Your people daily settle on these lands, and spoil our hunting. We must insist on your removing them . . . It is customary with us to make a present of skins whenever we renew our treaties. We are ashamed to offer our brethren so few, but your horses and cows have eaten the grass our deer used to feed on. This has made them scarce, and will, we hope, plead an excuse for our not bringing a larger quantity. If we could have spared more, we would have given more; but we are really poor; and desire you'll not consider the quantity, but few as they are, accept them in testimony of our regard.

—CANASATEGO (CANASSATEGO), ONONDAGA GRAND SACHEM (c. 1690–1750).
STATED IN 1742 TREATY NEGOTIATION DISCUSSIONS.

The Onondaga rejected a representative style of government in the 1940s and are one of very few Indian nations in the United States to retain their traditional system of leadership. In other words, their chiefs continue to be elected by clan mothers. The Onondaga in Canada have both a traditional and representative system.

Osage

The Osage refer to themselves as *Ni-U-Ko'n-Ska*, meaning "people of the mid-waters." Osage (OH-saje) is the French pronunciation of the name of their largest band, Wazhazhe. The Osage believed they were the children of the middle waters between the sky, earth, and water. They referred to whites as *I'n-Shta-Heh*, meaning "heavy eyebrow," referring to their view of whites as hairy. The Osage language is part of the Dhegiha division of the Siouan language.

The Osage originally lived with other Siouan-speaking groups, including the **Kaw, Omaha, Ponca,** and **Quapaw,** on the Ohio River before migrating onto the eastern plains. They then lived in Missouri, northern Arkansas, southeastern Kansas, and northeastern Oklahoma.

In the early 19th century, white traders caused a split in the tribe; half the Osage under Chief Claremore moved to the Three Forks area in Arkansas, where they became known as the Arkansas Osage. The entire tribe's population, as estimated by historians, was about 1,000 by the early 18th century. In 1870, there were 3,679 full-bloods and only 280 mixed bloods. By 1890, their population was almost equally half mixed-bloods and half full-bloods. In 1990, they had approximately 11,000 enrolled members, of whom the majority are of mixed blood.

Osage homes were oval or rectangular pole frames, as large as 100 feet long and 10 feet high. Poled framed houses were covered with woven mats or bark. Women raised corn, beans, squash, and pumpkins. The Osage acquired the *horse [I]* in the 1700s and began hunting *buffalo [I]*.

The Osage ceded to the American government huge tracts of land in several treaties signed in 1808, 1818, 1825, 1839, and 1865. An 1870 treaty established the Osage Reservation in what was northeastern *Indian Territory [IV]*, now near the town of Pawhuska, Oklahoma, a site of former Osage hunting grounds. The Osage adopted a written constitution in 1881. Oil was discovered on the Osage Reservation in 1896; oil and gas production has provided $1 billion to the tribe since then.

Land allotments to 2,229 Osage followed with the 1906 Osage Allotment Act. However, through several decades of encroachments—both legal and illicit—Osage land gradually passed out of tribal members' control into the hands of whites. White guardians were appointed for those judged to be legally incompetent and often cheated their wards of their wealth. Osage who were born after 1907 were not included on the allotment roll, so they were landless. By the 1960s, more than half the allotted parcels had passed from ownership by tribal members. Some Osage were able to keep their lands and gained wealth through oil and natural gas leases. One of the most famous Osage in the 20th century was prima ballerina Maria Tallchief, born in 1925.

The Osage capitol is in Pawhuska, Oklahoma, where traditional dances are held every June. Only those who own land from the original 1906 allottees can vote in tribal elections. That policy disenfranchises more than 11,000 tribally enrolled Osage who have no land holdings. By the 1990s, only one-third of the original allotments were still owned by tribal members. Only about 200 Osage speak the tribal language today.

Otoe

Otoe (OH-tow) means "lovers" or "lechers" and reportedly relates to the behavior of a chief's son who tried to seduce the daughter of another, causing the tribe to split off from the *Missouria*. The Otoe-Ioway-Missouri language is part of the Chiwere division of the Siouan language. The Otoe are often classified as Prairie Indian but eventually adopted the lifestyle of Plains Indians.

The Otoe originally lived in the Great Lakes region along with other Siouan-speaking groups, including the Ho-Chunk (Winnebago), *Ioway*, and Missouria. By the 16th century, however, they had migrated to southeastern Nebraska. Historians estimate that their population in 1780 was 900. By 1990, there were 1,550 enrolled members.

Otoe homes were earth lodges as large as 40 feet in diameter. Otoe women traditionally raised corn, beans, and squash for sustenance. Once they moved to the plains, however, the Otoe people came to rely more on buffalo hunting than on crops. Their burial ceremony involved placing their dead in the ground or in trees, followed by a four-day mourning period. Their enemies included the *Pawnee*, Sauk, Fox, *Omaha*, and *Lakota*.

In 1829, the Otoe absorbed the Missouria after they suffered a small-pox epidemic. In 1854, they ceded most of their lands in Nebraska to the federal government. When whites discovered timber resources in 1881 on the small land parcel the Otoe had managed to keep, the Otoe were moved to *Indian Territory [IV]* in present-day Kansas. They were moved again in 1882 to north central Oklahoma. In 1899, their reservation was divided into 514 individual allotments and surplus lands were sold to whites. In 1912, oil was discovered on Otoe land and many Indians were forced to give up their allotments to the federal government. More than 90 percent of those lands passed from tribal ownership.

The Otoe and Missouria, now known as the Otoe-Missouri tribe, adopted a constitution in 1984. They hold an annual powwow in July.

IN THEIR OWN Words

Before the palefaces came among us, we enjoyed the happiness of unbounded freedom and were acquainted with neither riches, wants, nor oppression. How is it now? Wants and oppression are our lot; for are we not controlled in everything, and dare we move without asking, by your leave? Are we not being stripped day by day of the little that remains of our ancient liberty? Do they not even kick and strike us as they do their black faces? How long will it be before they will tie us to a post and whip us and make us work for them in their cornfields as they do them? Shall we wait for that moment or shall we die fighting before submitting to such ignominy?

Have we not for years had before our eyes a sample of their designs, and are they not sufficient harbingers of their future determinations? Will we not soon be driven from our respective countries and the graves of our ancestors? Will not the bones of our dead be plowed up and their graves be turned into fields? Shall we calmly wait until they become so numerous that we will no longer be able to resist oppression? Will we wait to be destroyed in our turn without making an effort worthy of our race? Shall we give up our homes, our country, bequeathed to us by the Great Spirit, the graves of our dead, and everything that is dear and sacred to us, without a struggle? I know you will cry with me: Never! Never!

—TECUMSEH, SHAWNEE (C. 1768–1813). 1811 WABASH RIVER DEBATES AMONG INDIAN NATIONS ABOUT FORMING A SOUTHERN CONFEDERATION.

Ottawa

Ottawa is the anglicized version of the tribal name of Adawa or Adawu, which means "to trade." The name was also given to the capital city of Canada as well as the river that separates Quebec from Ontario. The Ottawa spoke a dialect of the *Anishinabe* and *Algonquian* languages.

The Ottawa, *Potawatomi*, and Chippewa (Ojibwa) were one people in the past. Those three Algonquin tribes formed the Council of Three Fires. At contact, the Ottawa were living on the northern part of Lake Huron, which they had controlled since before the 15th century. Historians record the estimated Ottawa population as 8,000 in 1600. In 1990, there were 10,000 enrolled members, 4,000 of whom lived in Canada.

Like other Algonquin tribes, the Ottawa believed in a creator called Manitou. Their creation stories differed from those of other Algonquin, however. They traced their descent from three different creatures: Michabou, the Great Hare; Namepich, the Carp; and the Bear's Paw. At puberty, both genders sought guardian spirits in dreams or on vision quests. Men in Ottawa society could have more than one wife. Memorial feasts for the dead were held every year or as close to each year as possible.

The Ottawa lived in fir or cedar-bark longhouses that were built on pole frames and housed extended families. Ottawa women raised corn, beans, squash, and collected maple sap. They decorated birchbark items

Depiction of an 1825 treaty council held at Prairie du Chien, Wisconsin, between U.S. commissioners and several Great Lakes–area tribes, including the Chipewayan, Potawatomi, Menominee, Ioway, and Ottawa. *Library of Congress.*

using templates with zigzag bands and floral designs. The Ottawa experienced conflict with the *Iroquois* and *Dakota*.

One of the first Europeans the Ottawa encountered was Samuel de Champlain in 1615. From that time on, the Ottawa were allies of the French. In 1763, an Ottawa chief named Pontiac led an uprising called *Pontiac's Rebellion [IV]*, in which many Old Northwest tribes tried to retain their lands. Pontiac wanted to drive the British from the Great Lakes area after they defeated the French in the *French and Indian Wars [IV]* (1689–1763). Pontiac negotiated peace in 1766, but was killed three years later by an Illinois Indian thought to be in the employ of the British.

In 1831, the Ottawa ceded their traditional lands to the federal government and were moved to a reservation in Kansas. They were relocated again in 1867 to Oklahoma, where their lands were allotted in the 1890s. The tribe was terminated in 1956 but was reinstated in 1978. The annual powwow in Oklahoma is held on Labor Day weekend. The Ottawa in

IN THEIR OWN Words

The white man's God cannot love our people or He would protect them. They seem to be orphans who can look nowhere for help. How then can we be brothers? How can your God become our God and renew our prosperity and awaken in us dreams of returning greatness. If we have a common heavenly father, He must be partial—for He came to His paleface children. We never saw Him. He gave you laws but had no word for his red children whose teeming multitudes once filled this vast continent as stars fill the firmament. No; we are two distinct races with separate origins and separate destinies. There is little in common between us.

To us the ashes of our ancestors are sacred and their resting-place is hallowed ground. You wander far from the graves of your ancestors and seemingly without regret. Your religion was written upon tables of stone by the iron finger of your god so that you could not forget. The Red Man could never comprehend nor remember it. Our religion is the traditions of our ancestors—the dreams of our old men, given them in the solemn hours of night by the Great Spirit—and the visions of our sachems and is written in the hearts of our people.

Your dead cease to love you and the land of their nativity as soon as they pass the portals of the tomb and wander way beyond the stars. They are soon forgotten and never return. Our dead never forget the beautiful world that gave them being.

—SEATH'TL (NOAH; SEALTH, SEATHL, SEATTLE, SEE-YAT), DUWAMISH-SUQUAMISH CHIEF (C. 1786–1866). STATEMENT TO GOVERNOR STEVENS, 1855.

Ontario have several small reserves. Some bands in the United States who live outside the group in Oklahoma are still seeking federal recognition.

Paiute

Paiute (PIE-oot) translates as "water Ute," indicating the tribe's ancestral relationship with the *Ute*. The Northern Paiute traditionally lived in areas of Nevada, Oregon, Idaho, and California; the Southern Paiute lived in parts of Utah, Nevada, Arizona, and California. Both Northern and Southern dialects of Paiute are related to the Shoshone dialect and belong to the Uto-Aztecan language group. The Paiute are classified in the Great Basin Indian cultural group.

Their diet included ground seeds of rice, grass, and pine nuts. Whites referred to them as "Digger Indians" because they dug for many of their foods.

Northern Paiute were involved in many conflicts after gold was discovered in California in 1848. They were allies of the *Coeur D'Alene* in the Coeur d'Alene Conflict of 1858–1859. They were also involved in the *Bannock Conflict [IV]* of 1878. The Paiute Conflict started in 1860, just before the *Civil War [IV]*, when white traders in California kidnapped and raped two Northern Paiute girls. Warriors from the tribe attacked the traders' post, killing five whites and rescuing the girls.

In the late 1880s, Northern Paiute prophet Wovoka (Jack Wilson) founded the *Ghost Dance [IV]* religion. Wovoka experienced a vision during a sun eclipse and soon began preaching that Paiute ancestors and the buffalo would return and that whites would be removed from the earth. To bring this new existence into being, Indians had to refrain from alcohol. Indians could glimpse this paradise by participating in the prayer and dancing of the Ghost Dance. Some even claimed that wearing Ghost Shirts would protect them from bullets. The Ghost Dance religion spread to nations throughout the West including the Shoshone, *Arapaho*, *Lakota*, *Dakota*, and *Nakota*. Whites were threatened by these practices and moved to repress them at every opportunity, including the 1890 massacre of Lakota at *Wounded Knee [IV]*.

Several Paiute activists have risen to national prominence. Sarah *Winnemucca [II]* lectured nationally on behalf of Indian issues and authored the book *Life Among the Paiute, Their Wrongs and Claims,* in

1883. In the 20th century, Nevada Paiute Mel Thom was a founder of the *National Indian Youth Council [IV]* (NIYC) in 1961.

Passamaquoddy

Passamaquoddy (pah-suh-muh-KWOD-ee) translates as "those who fish the pollock." The Passamaquoddy farmed but relied on fishing more than many other tribes in the northeastern area. They spoke *Algonquin*, a dialect closest to the *Maliseet* language. Passamaquoddy Bay in Maine bears their name.

The Passamaquoddy of northern Maine were part of the *Abenaki* Confederacy. Today, the two Passamaquoddy reservations at Pleasant Point and Indian Township near Calais, Maine, are the easternmost land held by American Indians in the United States. Historians record that the Passamaquoddy population was 1,000 in the 17th century. In 1990, however, there were around 25 enrolled members.

In Passamaquoddy marriages, men served the bride's parents for a year before the marriage itself, which was marked with a feast. Attitudes towards sexual relations were restricted; divorce was rare.

Log walls surrounded their villages. Within these walls, families lived in rectangular, log-framed wigwams that were covered with birch bark. Council houses held as many as 100 people. Corn was a staple of the diet, as was maple sap. Dishes and containers were made from birch bark.

They were one of the earliest tribes to have contact with Europeans and, as a result, one of the earliest to suffer from exposure to European diseases: a smallpox epidemic in 1617 killed 75 percent of the population. In the years that followed, many Passamaquoddy intermarried with the French, and they were part of the pro-French Abenaki Confederacy in the mid-18th century. The last hereditary chief of the Passmaquoddy died in the 1870s. During World War II, a Passamaquoddy township served as a German prisoner of war camp; the land was then sold to whites after the war. Maine was one of the last states in the United States to allow Indians the right to vote in 1954. However, in 1965, Maine was one of the first states to create a Department of Indian Affairs. Reflecting their long association and intermarriage with the French, many Passamaquoddy today are Catholic.

The Pleasant Point State Reservation in Sipayik, Maine, has been the main Passamaquoddy village since 1770. A six-member council governs each reservation. Since 1842, each reservation has alternated selecting a representative to the Maine state legislature. Unemployment for members runs around 30 percent.

Pawnee

Pawnee (PAW-nee) comes from the Caddoan word for "horn" or "hunter." They referred to themselves as *Chahiksichahiks,* meaning "men of men." They continued to exhibit aspects of the early Mound Builders culture of the Southeast, but unlike their relatives the *Caddo*, they are not generally classified among the Southeast Indians. They exhibited traits of the Prairie culture that included farming in settled villages, and aspects of the Great Plains Indian culture such as *buffalo [I]* hunting. Both dialects of Skidi and Southern Pawnee are Caddoan languages.

The Pawnee originated near Texas, then migrated north to southern Kansas, away from other Caddoan-speaking people, around the 13th century. Their Caddo relatives include the Caddo, *Wichita*, and *Arikira.* By the 16th century, the Pawnee were living in eastcentral Nebraska. Their population was estimated at 10,000 in the 18th century. By 1906, their numbers had declined by 94 percent to just 600 members. In 1990, there were 2,500 enrolled members.

Tirawa, the sun, was their creator spirit, while the morning and evening stars represented male and female spirits, respectively. The position of chief was inherited matrilineally.

Although their Caddo and Wichita relations lived in grass houses, the Pawnee lived in round earth lodges as large as 60 feet in diameter. Lodges were constructed to last about 10 years. Tipis were used as shelters when the Pawnee hunted buffalo. Pawnee women raised corn, beans, pumpkins, and sunflowers. Over the years, they came into conflict with a number of tribes, including the *Lakota, Dakota, Nakota, Cheyenne, Arapaho, Kiowa*, and *Comanche.*

The 1805 Treaty of Table Rock called for the relocation of the Pawnee to a reservation in Genoa, Nebraska. Presbyterian missionaries arrived in 1834, and the Pawnee suffered a devastating smallpox epidemic three years later. Cholera reduced their numbers further in 1850. They held their last tribal hunt in 1873 and ceded their Nebraska reservation to the federal government in 1876, moving to northcentral *Indian Territory [IV]*, where many continue to live near the city of Pawnee, Oklahoma. Half the reservation of more than 170,000 acres was allotted to whites in 1892. Today, only a few hundred acres are tribally owned.

In the 1970s, the Pawnee successfully reobtained tribal lands that had been confiscated by the federal government and given to the city of Pawnee. They hold a four-day homecoming every July. The Pawnee are federally recognized.

Pee Posh

Pee Posh, or Pipatsje in their language, translates as "the people." Also known as the Maricopa, they speak River Yuman, a Hokan-Siouan language.

The Pee Posh lived near the Gila River region since before the 1600s. Today, most Pee Posh live with the *Pima* on the Gila River and Salt River reservations in Arizona. Their population was estimated at 2,500 in the 1800s. By 1900, their numbers had been cut in half because of European *diseases [IV]*. In 1990, there were approximately 800 enrolled members.

Dreams held significant spiritual value to the Pee Posh. Following a death in the tribe, villages were sometimes moved to a different location. The dead and their possessions, including their residences, were usually burned. Puberty ceremonies were held for girls, after which girls were tattooed. They lived in flattened dome houses with walls of packed earth. Men planted and cultivated corn and mesquite bean crops; women harvested them.

The Pee Posh provided their surplus wheat to whites en route to the California gold rush of 1848. Around the same time, the Pee Posh population was reduced due to several epidemics. In 1863, the U.S. government established a reservation for the Pee Posh and Pima on the Gila River. Soon afterward, however, whites diverted the water upstream from the reservation, so reservation residents had to relocate to the Salt River, where the Salt River Reservation was established in 1879. Continued diversion of the Gila River by whites caused the Pee Posh to suffer crop failure and famine in that area throughout the 1880s. The *Bureau of Indian Affairs [IV]* didn't challenge the whites but forced the Indians to use contaminated well water that could not be used on edible crops. Both reservations were allotted in 1914 into parcels too small to be farmed. Tribal members who opposed allotment were jailed, while those who supported allotment were given the best lands.

The Pee Posh share a tribal government with the Pima. Cremation and mourning observances remain an important part of their culture today.

Penobscot

Penobscot (puh-NOB-scot), from the word *Panawahpskek,* referred to "rocky falls in the river," and is the name of a tribe who gave their name to a river and bay in Maine. The Penobscot belonged to the Abenaki Confederacy in the mid-18th century, an alliance that united them with the *Abenaki, Maliseet, Micmac*, and *Passamaquoddy*. The Penobscot are culturally similar to the Micmac and Passamaquoddy and speak an eastern Algonquian language.

They continue to live on their traditional lands at Indian Island on the Penobscot River in Maine. Their population, estimated at 1,000 around 1600, was reduced to a mere 389 members by 1910. In 1990, there were approximately 2,000 enrolled members.

The Penobscot traditionally lived in square houses about 12 feet by 12 feet with pyramid roofs, but they also dwelled in cone-shaped wigwams. Log walls surrounded their villages. Corn was a staple of the diet, as was maple sap. Their marriages were marked by gifts given to the bride's family; some men could have more than one wife. Their traditional enemies were the *Mohawk*.

The British decision to place bounties on Penobscot scalps pushed them to side with the French in the *French and Indian Wars [IV]*. Later they sided with the rebels in the *American Revolution [IV]*. Nevertheless, the new American government confiscated most of their lands. They signed a treaty with Massachusetts in 1796, but the United States Congress, as mandated by the 1790 Trade and Intercourse Act, never ratified it. Their last hereditary chief died in 1870. Indians in Maine did not gain voting rights until 1954.

The 4,400-acre Penobscot Reservation, situated on 200 islands in the Penobscot River, was established in 1820. The only island that is regularly inhabited is Indian Island, where the main village of Old Town is located. They gained federal recognition in 1979. A 12-member tribal council governs the tribe, and sends a nonvoting delegate to the Maine legislature. The population on the reservation is approximately 400. Most Penobscot are Catholic, a consequence of their old alliance and affiliation with the French. They run a Penobscot Nation Museum at Indian Island.

Pequot

The Pequot (PEE-kwot), meaning "destroyers," lived in Connecticut and Rhode Island in the early 17th century. Today, most members live in southern Connecticut. Their population, estimated at 4,000 in 1600, today consists of 1,000 members. The Pequot spoke an eastern dialect of the Algonquian language.

One of the most important Pequot ceremonies was the Green Corn. They wrapped their dead in skins or woven mats and buried them with their possessions and some food. Houses belonging to the dead were abandoned.

They lived in villages surrounded by log walls. Individual homes were covered with bark or woven mats. They also had longhouses, which could be as large as 100 feet by 30 feet and could house as many as 50 people. The Pequot experienced conflict with the Long Island Montauk, the *Narragansett*, and the Niantic.

In 1636–1637, in what became known as the Pequot War, colonists from the Plymouth Colony and Massachusetts Bay Colony attacked the Pequot in retaliation for the Pequot killing of a dishonest English trader. Following attacks on both sides and the burning of a Pequot village, an English military force attacked a Pequot village near New Haven, Connecticut, killing almost 600 Indians. The few who did not escape to live with other tribes were sold into slavery in the Caribbean. This devastating conflict ended the Pequots as a presence and a power in southern New England, and colonists forbade the very mention of the tribe.

The Pequot today have four small reservations in Connecticut. The Western Pequot (Mashantucket) own 1,800 acres, an ownership that was acknowledged in 1667. They adopted a constitution in 1974. The Eastern Pequot (Paucatuck) have a 226-acre reservation in Connecticut that was established in 1623. The 400-acre Schaghticoke State Reservation was established in 1792, and the 700-acre Golden Hill Reservation in 1886. Some Pequot reside with the Brotherton tribe headquartered in Fond du Lac, Wisconsin. The Golden

Hill Paugussett tribe has been denied federal recognition. The Mashantucket and Mohegan Pequot are federally recognized, and the Paucatuck and Schaghticoke Pequot are awaiting a decision on their status.

Pima

Pima (PEE-mah) is derived from their phrase *pi-nyi-match*, which meant "I don't know," and was a common response to Spanish questions. They refer to themselves as *Akimel O'Odham* (AH-kee-mul-oh-OH-tum), meaning "river people." Piman is part of the Uto-Aztecan language.

Their traditional lands were in Arizona and Sonora, Mexico, and they were descended from Indians of the *Hohokam culture [I]*, who constructed advanced irrigation systems. Their numbers were estimated at 50,000 in 1500 and 3,000 by 1700. In 1990, the combined Pima-Maricopa Reservation population was approximately 12,000.

Their most powerful spiritual guides were the Earth Maker and Elder Brother. The man-on-the-maze pattern on their baskets represents Elder Brother preparing to journey through the maze of life. The Pima used a lunar calendar and marked time on calendar sticks. In general, men farmed, fished, hunted, built houses, and wove cotton; women gathered food, made baskets, pottery, and clothing, and carried firewood. They raised corn, squash, pumpkins, beans, and cotton. They irrigated crops by diverting water from rivers through the use of dams made of logs and branches. They also built canals and feeder ditches. Pima homes were small, round pole-framed structures covered with grass and mud. The dead were buried in stone huts with their tools and some food. The houses of the dead were burned. The Pima experienced conflict with the *Apache* and Yavapais. Their main allies were the *Pee Posh*.

The Pima provided food for some of the people traveling to the 1848 California gold rush. In spite of their friendship, whites took the best farmland in the area and diverted water for their own use. In 1879, Pima wheat production exceeded that of their nearby neighbors, but the water diversion created by the whites soon left the Pima without water for their crops. A Pima-Maricopa Reservation was established in 1879 but was allotted in 1914. Each tribal member received 10 acres of land.

One of the best-known Pima was Ira Hayes (1923–1955), a World War II Marine who helped raise the American flag on Iwo Jima. The Pima have one of the highest rates of diabetes in the world, resulting from dietary changes in modern times. It is surmised that their eating styles resulted partially from the need to store calories against periodic famines, so they sometimes resorted to binge eating.

The 370,000-acre Gila River Reservation was established in 1859; the 52,600-acre Salt River Reservation was established in 1879. Water rights remain a pressing issue for the Pima today. The water table in their area has gone down more than 300 feet since whites arrived in the area.

Pomo

The name Pomo (PO-mo) probably means "village" or "those who live at red earth hole" in their language. The Pomoan language is of the Hokaan group.

For more than 10,000 years, traditional Pomo lands were on the Pacific coast, 50 miles north of San Francisco. Today, 20 Pomo rancherias exist in northern California. Their population was estimated at 15,000 in the early 19th century. In 1990, there were approximately 4,700 enrolled members.

The Pomo lived in single-family, cone-shaped dwellings. Their council lodges, however, were partially below ground structures. The Pomo were talented mathematicians who used strings and beads to count to as high as 40,000. Pomo basket makers were able to weave so tightly that a microscope is needed to count the stitches. Basket making was a female craft in most tribes, but among the Pomo, men also made baskets. There were many different types of doctors in Pomo culture. Bear doctors, for example, who could be male or female, had the power to cure. The Pomo also practiced birth control and abortion. After four days of mourning, they cremated their dead. Sometimes gifts or the homes of the dead ancestor were also burned. They experienced conflict with the Patwin, Wapp, *Wintun*, and Yuki.

The Pomo had contact with both Spanish and Russian explorers over the centuries, with disastrous results in each case. Beginning in the 18th century, Russian fur traders kidnapped women and children as hostages in order to compel the men to work for them. They forced them to hunt animals—particularly the sea otter—and clean hides. In 1812, the Russians established a permanent base, Fort Ross, on Bodega Bay on Pomo lands but abandoned the area in 1841.

Pomo chief Marin led an uprising against the Spanish in the early 1800s. (Marin County, California, is named after him.) Thousands died of cholera and smallpox in the 1830s, and more were sold into slavery by the Mexican army.

Americans arrived after 1849 as a result of the California gold rush. The California state legislature passed laws that sanctioned the kidnapping and enslavement of Indians in the state. In 1856, the Pomo were forced onto a reservation at Mendocino. Eleven years later, they were dispossessed of land altogether and left without legal rights. By 1900, through foreclosure and debt, they had lost 99 percent of the lands they had once inhabited. A 1907 Supreme Court decision, however, recognized the rancherias in California as Indian land to be held in trust.

At the same time, the Pomo attended segregated schools and were barred from white churches. Local businesses even displayed signs that read "No dogs or Indians allowed." In 1923, Pomo member Stephen Knight in Mendocino County won a suit against the state public school segregation laws. Mr. Knight later sued a local movie theater that would not admit Indians.

In 1958, the California termination bill passed by the United States Congress terminated 41 California rancherias, including several Pomo rancherias. Federal recognition was restored to 17 rancherias in the 1970s, although some Pomo are still seeking federal recognition today.

Ponca

Ponca (Popgun) is thought to mean "sacred head." The Ponca are related to the *Kaw*, *Omaha*, *Osage*, and *Quapaw*. They speak a Dhegiha dialect of the Siouan language and combine cultural traits of the Prairie and Plains Indians.

They probably originated in the Ohio Valley. Around 1200, they were living near Pipestone quarry in southern Minnesota with the Omaha but eventually split off and migrated to the border between Nebraska and South Dakota, where they were living by the late 17th century. At that time, their population was estimated to be 100; in 1990, there were around 3,200 enrolled members.

The Ponca possessed a sacred pipe, used in the Pipe Dance, which had been carved of calamite when the Ponca still lived in Minnesota. They also practiced a version of the Sun Dance that included self-mutilation. They traditionally wrapped their dead in buffalo robes with their possessions and food and buried them in graves. After moving onto the Plains, they adopted the practice of placing the dead on platforms.

By the time they encountered the Lewis and Clark expedition in 1804, epidemics had already reduced their numbers by more than 90 percent. Beginning in 1817, they ceded more than 2 million acres of land to the United States. In 1858, they accepted a 100,000-acre reservation, but in 1877, they were forced to relocate to *Indian Territory [IV]*. Within a year, the hunger and disease that accompanied the move killed one-quarter of the remaining tribe.

Chief *Standing Bear [II]* attempted a 500-mile journey to return to Ponca traditional lands in order to bury his son. He and his companions were arrested and held on the Omaha Reservation in Nebraska. In 1879, a judge ruled that the government could not forcibly restrain Indians in restricted areas or prevent them from returning to their traditional lands.

The roughly 30 Ponca who returned to Nebraska were called the Northern Ponca; those who remained in Oklahoma, the larger group, were called the Southern Ponca. In 1879, Standing Bear went on a lecture tour of eastern cities with Omaha reformer Susette LaFlesche. In 1880, the federal government granted the Ponca a reservation near their traditional lands. In 1908, their lands in Oklahoma were allotted. Today, Ponca continue to live in both Oklahoma and Nebraska.

The Northern Ponca were terminated in the 1950s, and by the mid-1960s, they had lost all their remaining land. In 1961, Ponca Clyde Warrior helped found the *National Indian Youth Council [IV]* (NIYC).

The Northern Ponca regained federal recognition in 1990 and have reobtained 413 acres of their former reservation. The Southern Ponca, located in north-central Oklahoma, adopted a constitution in 1950 and are governed by a seven-member tribal council.

Potawatomi

Potawatomi (pot-uh-WOT-uh-mee) in the Algonquian language means "people of the place of fire." They referred to themselves, however, as *Weshnabek,* meaning "the people." They are classified in the Northeast Indian cultural group and spoke Potawatomi, an Algonquian language. We know a good deal about their history because they kept records on birchbark scrolls using pictographs.

They originated in the Northeast, where they were once united with the *Anishinabe* and *Ottawa*. However, since at least the early 17th century, they had lived in southwest Michigan, before migrating southward toward the present-day Chicago area. Today, most Potawatomi live in Kansas and Oklahoma. Their population was estimated at 8,000 in the early 17th century, and grew to approximately 10,000 members in the early 19th century. By 1990, there were an estimated 22,000 Potawatomi in the United States and in Canada.

The Potawatomi believed they could obtain guardian spirits through fasting and practiced a number of ceremonies including the Peace Pipe, Midewiwin Dance, and the Sacred Bundle Ceremony. Their afterworld was located in the west. Women sometimes served as village chiefs. Their marriages were marked by a gift exchange, and newlyweds lived with the bride's family for a year. Babies were named only after they were a year old.

Potawatomi homes were rectangular, bark-covered structures or smaller wigwams covered with mats. Women raised corn, beans, and squash, and gathered wild rice and maple sap. The Potawatomi were allies

IN THEIR OWN *Words*

*M*y Father: a long time has passed since first we came upon our lands; and our people have all sunk into their graves. They had sense. We are all young and do not wish to do anything that they would not approve, were they living. We are fearful we shall offend their spirits if we sell our lands; and we are fearful we shall offend you if we do not sell them. This has caused us great perplexity of thought, because we have counseled among ourselves, and do not know how we can part with our lands.

My Father: we have sold you a great tract of land already; but it is not enough. We sold it to you for the benefit of your children, to farm and to live upon. We have but a little left. We shall want it all for ourselves. We know not how long we will live, and we wish to leave some lands for our children to hunt upon. You are gradually taking away our hunting grounds. Your children are driving us before them. We are growing uneasy. What lands you have you may retain. But we shall sell no more.

—METEA [KISS ME], POTAWATOMI CHIEF OF THE ILLINOIS NATION (C. 1775–1827). SPOKEN AT 1821 TREATY SIGNING.

of the Ottawa and Anishinabe and sporadically fought with the *Iroquois* and *Dakota.*

They were trading partners of the French and intermarried with them. They fought against the British in *Pontiac's Rebellion [IV]* of 1763, which united several tribes who attempted to retain their lands in the Old Northwest. They participated in three further united Indian rebellions to try to keep their traditional lands: *Little Turtle's War [IV]* of 1790–1794, *Tecumseh's [II]* Rebellion of 1809–1811, and the *Black Hawk War [IV]* of 1832. In all, they signed 53 treaties with the United States.

Their forced migration to *Indian Territory [IV]* in Kansas in 1838 is called the "Trail of Death" because of the immense loss of life it caused. Most of the Potawatomi lands in Kansas were allotted by 1890. During the Depression, many Potawatomi fled to California along with displaced whites and mixed-raced groups known as "Okies." Several bands today have federal recognition (Prairie, Citizen, Hannaville, Nottawaseppi-Huron, Pokagon, and Forest County). Their annual powwow is held in June.

Powhatan

Powhatan (pow-uh-TAN) means "at the falls." The Powhatan, classified as part of the Northeast cultural area, are an Algonquian-speaking group.

Their traditional lands centered around Virginia but ranged from North Carolina to New Jersey. Powhatan was the main village of the 30-tribe Powhatan Confederacy. At the time of contact, Powhatan villages had a population around 600, while the confederacy as a whole consisted of approximately 14,000 members. By 1705, that number had declined to 500. Today, the Powhatan have about 600 members.

Their homes, unique because of rounded roofs, were otherwise similar to Iroquoian longhouses and could be as long as 100 feet. The Powhatan had a chief deity and temples in every village. They believed that an afterlife existed in a western paradise. Chiefs were chosen through matrilineal descent. The dead were wrapped in mats and buried in the ground. Marriages occurred with an exchange of gifts, and men could have multiple wives. Fish was a staple of their diet, as were three varieties of corn, beans, and squash, which Powhatan women raised.

Following the establishment of the Jamestown settlement in 1607, the Powhatan led assaults over land conflicts on the Virginia colonies in

1622 and 1624. Powhatan Indians taught the settlers how to plant tobacco and they began large-scale cultivation of the crop. Tobacco, however, rapidly depleted the soil and required increasing amounts of land. The Powhatan were attacked by whites on several occasions because of land conflicts and by 1675 they had nearly disappeared. Most Powhatan fought on the side of the Union in the *Civil War [IV]*.

Many English immigrants, including Captain John Smith, wrote about the Powhatan, including about *Pocahontas [II]*, one of the most famous American Indian women in history. It is difficult to separate myth from reality in the well-known story of how she reportedly saved Captain John Smith from execution. Pocahontas died in 1617 while waiting in Gravesend, England, to board a ship returning to Virginia. Her father, Powhatan, died the following year. Some descendants of the Powhatan and of Pocahontas continue to reside in the northeastern part of the United States.

Pueblo

All Pueblo people are probably descended from the ancient *Anasazi [I]* or the *Mogollon culture [I]*, whose distinctive style of architecture the Pueblo adopted. They farmed and made pottery and baskets. In the 1200s, the Anasazi abandoned their traditional canyon settlements around the time that Acoma Pueblo was founded. The reason for this movement remains unclear, but it may have been precipitated by climate or social change.

The Pueblo recognized sacred mountains in four directions. Many of their spiritual ceremonies were centered on the attainment of rain. Katsinas, which represented sacred beings who lived in the mountains, were used in rituals. Each pueblo contained at least one kiva, a religious chamber that evoked the original emergence into this world from the world below. Pueblo Indians observed a four-day vigil after death.

Housing was constructed of adobe bricks in three-story apartment dwellings. The ground level, used mainly for storage, had no doors or windows and served as both a refuge and defensible position at times of attack. The dwelling had entryways in the roof.

The Acoma grew corn, beans, and squash as their primary crops, and built dams and terraces for irrigation. Sunflowers and tobacco were also cultivated. A thin corn bread, Mut-tze-nee, was a favorite food. Domesticated turkeys supplemented their diets, and the Pueblo also hunted small game and gathered seeds, nuts, and berries. Women made fine pottery; men were weavers and silversmiths. Women wore cotton dresses and either sandals or moccasins; men wore cotton kilts and leather sandals.

In 1598, Juan de Oñate and settlers from New Mexico founded the first Spanish colony among the Pueblos. In 1620, a royal decree created civil offices at each pueblo. As part of the royal decree, governors of each pueblo were given silver-headed canes to symbolize their authority. The canes are still used today by Pueblo Indians. In 1680, the Pueblo united in a revolt against the Spanish, led by Pope from San Juan Pueblo. The Pueblos' list of grievances was long, and included forced labor, enslavement, persecution of traditional religious practices, torture, and famine caused by the overgrazing of Indian land. To coordinate the uprising, runners were sent to each pueblo with knots in a cord to signify the number of days left until the rebellion. On August 10, 1680, they succeeded in driving the Spanish from the region. They allowed the Spanish to escape Santa Fe and flee to El Paso. The Spanish eventually reconquered Santa Fe and the region in 1692, but the practice of forced labor ceased and the Church allowed them to continue practicing their traditional religion in "secret."

The 18th century was marked by smallpox epidemics and raiding parties of *Apache, Comanche*, and *Ute*. Railroads brought tourists to the Pueblo by the 1880s. Selling traditional crafts to tourists provided some income.

The All-Indian Pueblo Council began meeting again in the 1920s, a tradition that had been halted 300 years earlier. The council was successful in slowing the loss of lands and addressing religious persecution. The 1924 Pueblo Lands Act recognized Pueblo lands. Although these Indians are collectively referred to as "Pueblo Indians," there are in fact 18 separate Pueblo groups throughout New Mexico, each occupying a distinct region and having a distinct history.

Acoma Pueblo

Acoma (A-ko-ma) is derived from the Acoma language meaning "the place that always was home for many ages," or "people of the white rock." Acoma (Sky City) is thought to be the oldest consistently inhabited site in the United States. Like the Laguna, **Zuni**, and **Hopi**, the Acoma are part of the Western Pueblo group. They were divided into twenty matrilineal clans and speak a Western Keresan dialect.

Acoma is 60 miles west of Albuquerque, New Mexico. The reservation is composed of approximately 10 percent of the original traditional lands of 5 million acres. The Acoma Pueblo population, estimated between 5,000 to 10,000 in 1550, dropped below 500 in 1900. However, current tribal enrollment is around 4,000, with just over half the members living at the Acoma Pueblo.

The cacique, or Sun chief, symbolizes the Acoma tribe. His primary duties are to watch the sun and determine the solstices and planting calendars. The Acoma believe that the Sun is the highest of spirits, and he is prayed to with offerings of cornmeal or pollen. Eight days before the solstice, the people in the village perform various rituals to cleanse the body and purify the soul, such as abstaining from sex and certain foods. Many dances are performed, with masked men impersonating spirits such as Cloud People, who are thought to provide rain.

The first European visitors to the Acoma Pueblo probably accompanied the explorer Estevan in 1539 as scouts for the Coronado expedition. The following year another member of Coronado's group, Hernando de Alvarado, arrived. The Pueblo faced Spanish aggression in 1599 when 800 Acoma were murdered; others were tortured and enslaved and the pueblo was destroyed.

The Spanish used the surviving Acoma for forced labor and renamed the pueblo after Catholic saints. In 1629 Franciscans founded a mission at Acoma.

Today, the Acoma Pueblo consists of 500,000 acres. Only tribal members can own Pueblo property. A religious leader, or cacique, from the Antelope clan, appoints members of the tribal council as well as the governor. The Acoma Pueblo has several mineral resources, including *gold [IV]* and natural gas. Uranium mines, which employed some tribal members until their closure in the 1980s, caused high levels of radiation pollution. Unemployment remains high at 60 percent. However, the religion and language remain intact.

Cochiti Pueblo

The Cochiti speak an eastern dialect of the Keresan language. Descent was matrilineal.

The Cochiti Pueblo has been in its current location, 25 miles southwest of Santa Fe, for several centuries. It is estimated that approximately 500 tribal members lived at Cochiti in 1700. By 1980, there were 900 members, and today the population is approximately 1,300, with about half living at the pueblo and about the same number off the reservation.

The Cochiti Pueblo had two circular kivas and two accompanying societies, the Squash and Turquoise. All Cochiti males participated in Katsina societies. Kiva groups were based on patrilineal descent.

The 50,000-acre Cochiti Pueblo did not adopt a constitution; they are governed by tradition. Unemployment runs at an average of 20 percent. Most Cochiti are Catholics. A few still speak Keresan or Spanish. Clan ceremonies are still held and two of the three traditional medicine societies remain intact. The major feast day is San Buenaventuras Day.

Isleta Pueblo

Isleta comes from the Spanish word meaning "little island." The Isleta Pueblo speak Southern Tiwa, a dialect of the Kiowa-Tanoan language.

Isleta lands are located several miles south of Albuquerque. Their population, estimated at 410 in 1790, was 2,200 members in 1966. Today, the Isleta Pueblo have about 3,900 enrolled members, of whom 2,900 live on the reservation.

There are two tribal factions and each one is responsible for ceremonies for half of the year and the planning of one major dance: the Red Eyes supervise summer activities, and the Black Eyes supervise winter activities. The Isleta Pueblo were further divided into seven corn groups that offered support for members during times of crisis and social ceremonies. The Isleta have

A Hohokam culture ball court in modern-day Arizona, dating from A.D. 950 to 1200. *Pueblo Grande Museum and Archaeological Park, Phoenix, Arizona.*

one kiva, a partially underground chamber that symbolizes their original ascent from beneath the earth.

The Isleta did not participate in the All Pueblo Alliance that revolted against the Spanish in 1680. Despite their neutrality, however, the Spanish attacked the Isleta in 1681 and took hundreds of prisoners to El Paso. Further contact occurred when trade along the Santa Fe Trail began in 1821. When the nearby Laguna Pueblo divided over political differences in 1880, the Isleta accepted some Lagunas into their village. Lagunas returned to their village a few years later, but the masks and rituals of the Laguna remained. The Isleta continued traditional spiritual practices and, as late as 1963, the Isleta evicted a priest who was intolerant of their traditions. They adopted a constitution in 1947 that permits each male at age 21 to vote for governor of the pueblo in elections held during the first 10 days of December.

Some Isleta still speak the language and maintain the ritual corn groups and the winter/summer ceremonial divisions.

Jemez Pueblo

Jemez (He-mish) is the Spanish translation of the name they called themselves, *Walatowa*, meaning "this is the place." Descent was matrilineal. Like the Isleta, they speak Tiwa, from the Kiowa-Tanoan language group.

The Jemez Pueblo is 1 of 18 Pueblo groups located in New Mexico. They have lived on their traditional lands in New Mexico for at least the last 2,000 years. Historians estimate the population to have been 30,000 in 1530. The Jemez were one of the largest of the Pueblo cultures. Those numbers were reduced to 100 by 1744. Today, the Jemez Pueblo have approximately 3,000 enrolled members. Their pueblo is located 55 miles northwest of Albuquerque and 70 miles southwest of Santa Fe.

There were two patrilineal kiva groups, Squash and Turquoise, who organized spiritual practices.

Twenty-nine Jemez leaders were hanged in 1645 for joining a *Navajo* rebellion. They participated in the Great Pueblo Revolt of 1680. Despite these defeats, they continued their spiritual practices in secret. In 1858, Congress acknowledged the previous Spanish land grant of 17,000 acres to the Jemez Pueblo. The Jemez and Pecos Pueblos consolidated in 1936.

Walatowa is the main village in Jemez Pueblo. The traditional forms of government, which include a cacique or spiritual leader, are still practiced. A Spanish style of civil government with a governor and staff is also still in place. Governing positions are lifetime offices. The Pueblo own natural gas, oil, and uranium resources. In the 1980s, they successfully stopped a geothermal development that would have threatened their holy places in the Jemez Mountains. Their ceremonies and language are intact, although traditional laws forbid translating the language into writing. Most ceremonies are closed to outsiders, but some dances with Catholic elements are open to tourists. Some of the dances that are open to the public include the Nuestra Senora de Los Angeles Feast Day on August 2, the San Diego Feast Day on November 12, and the Nuestra Senora de Guadeloupe

Feast Day on December 12. English has replaced Spanish as a second language.

Laguna Pueblo

The Laguna speak a Kersan dialect, similar to their Pueblo neighbors at Acoma. Laguna, Spanish for lake, referred to a pond near the pueblo. Descent was matrilineal.

The Laguna and Acoma Pueblo have lived on their traditional lands since 3000 B.C. and, according to tradition, may have been united in prehistory. The Laguna Pueblo is located 32 miles west of Albuquerque, New Mexico, and is comprised of six villages. Laguna population, estimated at 480 in 1700, today includes about 7,000 members, half of whom live on the reservation.

Many important ceremonies were held in two kivas. There were seven clans. Women used white clay to make pottery.

The Laguna participated in the Pueblo revolt against the Spanish in 1680. In the 1870s, the American territorial governor destroyed two big kivas. A uranium mine was operated at Laguna from 1953 until 1982, at the time the largest open-pit uranium mine in the world. Yellow radioactive clouds drifted over the reservation during those years. Roads and houses were built using radioactive ore and crushed rock. The groundwater is still contaminated and cancer rates are high.

The 528,079-acre Laguna Reservation in central New Mexico is divided by Interstate-40. A 21-member council governs the Laguna. The Laguna Pueblo own coal, natural gas, oil, and uranium resources. Each village has a Catholic mission and celebrates an annual feast for their patron saints. The feast of St. Joseph, the largest feast, is celebrated at old Laguna on September 19.

Nambe Pueblo

Nambe is a Spanish translation of a Tewa word meaning, "rounded earth." The Nambe speak a dialect of Tewa, from the Kiowa-Tanoan language group.

Nambe Pueblo is located 15 miles north of Santa Fe, New Mexico, and has been continuously occupied for more than six centuries. Its population was estimated at 350 in 1600. Today, there are 630 enrolled members, of whom nearly 500 reside at the pueblo.

The Nambe have one kiva today, a round partly underground structure that is used for ceremonies symbolizing their emergence from the underworld. There were two divisions: the summer squash kiva and the winter turquoise kiva. More than other Pueblos they intermarried with their Spanish neighbors. Currently, 63 percent of the residents at Nambe are Latino. The United States granted their pueblo grant in 1864 and the reservation was established in 1902. In 1905, Nambe lands were confiscated as part of the national forests.

The 19,000-acre Nambe Pueblo has no written constitution. Women who marry outside the pueblo cannot have their children enrolled unless they successfully petition the male pueblo council, although males who marry outside the pueblo can enroll their children. Some Nambe speak Tewa and the language is still used in council meetings, though Spanish and English are more commonly spoken. They hold a ceremony for tourists each July at Nambe Falls and a festival of Saint Francis in October.

Picuris Pueblo

Picuris comes from the Spanish word for "at the mountain gap." Picuris Pueblo Indians refer to their pueblos as *Pignut,* which means "mountain pass place." They speak a dialect of Northern Tina, a Tanoan language.

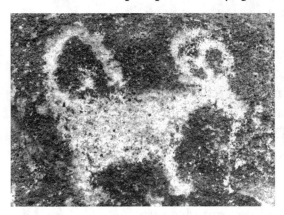

A Hohokam culture bighorn sheep petroglyph.
Pueblo Grande Museum and Archaeological Park,
Phoenix, Arizona.

Picuris is 18 miles south of the Taos Pueblo, between Santa Fe and Taos, New Mexico. It is the second smallest of the Rio Grande pueblos. Their population was estimated at 3,000 in the 1630s. However, their numbers declined by 90 percent in the years between 1680 and 1716. By 1744, there were just 400 members, and only 91 members by 1890. In 1990, there were 1,880 enrolled members, 147 of whom lived on the reservation.

In Picuris Pueblo tradition, the dead were buried after a four-day vigil, with a prayer feather in each hand and a food bag.

The Picuris joined the Pueblo rebellion of 1680, which was a response to religious persecution, torture, forced labor, and enslavement by the Spanish. When the Northern Pueblo revolted again in 1696, the Picuris went to live on the plains for 20 years with the *Apache.* A 600-year land grant was recognized for the Picuris in 1858. Their first civic elections to replace traditional leadership were held in 1950.

A council headed by a governor presides over the 15,000-acre Picuris Pueblo. Only 250 acres of the reservation are arable. Four kivas have been restored and are now in use. The main feast day is San Lorenzo's Day on August 10. Picuris Pueblo are federally recognized.

Pojoaque Pueblo

Pojoaque is an adaptation of the Tewa word *Posuwaegeh,* meaning "drink water place." The Pojoaque speak Tewa, a Kiowa-Tanoan language.

The Pojoaque Pueblo is located 16 miles north of Santa Fe and has been occupied since before A.D. 900. It is the smallest of the six Tewa villages. In 1500, their population was estimated at 500. In 1870, there were 32 members recorded. In 1990, there were approximately 2,500 enrolled members, although only 177 resided at the pueblo.

The Pojoaque participated in the 1680 pueblo revolt against Spanish religious persecution, torture, forced labor, and enslavement. Spanish reprisals caused many of them to flee to other pueblos. The last cacique died in 1900, and today a tribal council governs the 11,600-acre Pojoaque Pueblo. In 1974, the Pojoaque became the first pueblo to elect a woman as governor. Since then, they have elected other women to serve as governors and on the tribal council. They no longer have a kiva society, and few speak Tewa.

San Felipe Pueblo

The name San Felipe was assigned to this group of Indians by the Spanish from the name of a patron saint, although they referred to themselves as *Katishtya.* The people of the pueblo are Keresan-speaking. San Felipe is located in Sandoval County, New Mexico, which has a more than 20 percent Native American population.

The San Felipe Pueblo people were recognized in a Spanish land grant in 1689 and registered in 1864. They are located 25 miles north of Albuquerque. Their population, estimated at 600 in 1680, today averages about 2,500.

The San Felipe Pueblo comprises 4,900 acres. Many residents still speak Keresan and live in traditional adobe houses.

San Ildefonso Pueblo

San Ildefonso is the Spanish name of a mission established at the pueblo in 1617. They refer to themselves as *Powhoge,* which means "water runs through." They speak a dialect of Tewa.

The San Ildefonso Pueblo is located 22 miles northwest of Santa Fe. Their population, estimated at 800 people in 1680, today has about 1,500 members, with approximately 350 living at the pueblo.

The San Ildefonso had two religious societies: the Squash and Turquoise kivas. Membership in both was patrilineal. The San Ildefonso Indians gave their dead food to assist them in the spirit land; the deceased's possessions were broken and placed on their graves. A mourning period of four days followed.

The San Ildefonso Pueblo today consists of 26,000 acres and is ruled by a 12-member council. Many people still speak Tewa.

San Juan Pueblo

The people of San Juan Pueblo referred to themselves as *Ohke,* the meaning of which is unknown. Like other Pueblo Indians, they speak a dialect of Tewa.

San Juan is located 25 miles north of Santa Fe. The San Juan Pueblo is the northernmost of the six Tewa-speaking communities in north central New Mexico, and is called the Mother Village of the Tewa in creation stories.

Their population was estimated at 422 in 1920 and today averages about 2,300 people. The San Juan Pueblo today comprises 12,000 acres.

Sandia Pueblo

Sandia is Spanish for watermelon, which may refer to the size, shape, and color of the nearby mountains. The people of the Sandia Pueblo refer to themselves as *Nafiat,* meaning "sandy place." The Sandia speak a Southern dialect of the Tewa language.

Sandia is located about 13 miles north of Albuquerque, New Mexico, and was founded around 1300. The total reservation acreage is 22,884. The Sandia had a population of about 3,000 in 1680 and 350 in 1748. Today their total tribal enrollment is 481.

The pueblo celebrates one of its major feasts, the annual Feast of San Antonio, on June 13, with a Corn Dance. Each year, a new pueblo government is installed on January 6, when an Eagle Dance and Buffalo Dance are performed.

Santa Ana Pueblo

The Santa Ana refer to themselves as *Tamaya,* the meaning of which is unclear. They speak a dialect of Keresan and are located 27 miles northwest of Albuquerque. Their population was estimated at 340 in 1700 and is 480 today.

Santa Clara Pueblo

The Santa Clara refer to themselves by the Tewa name *Capo*, the translation of which is uncertain. Santa Clara is the second largest Tewa pueblo. They speak a dialect of Tewa.

Santa Clara is located 25 miles northwest of Santa Fe. Its population was estimated at several thousand in 1500 and around 650 in 1780. Today, tribal enrollment runs around 2,000, though the pueblo's population is greater than that. The reservation contains 46,00 acres.

Santa Clara was the first tribe to adopt a written constitution during the Indian Reorganization Act of 1934. Many members still speak a dialect of Tewa.

Santa Domingo Pueblo

The Spanish renamed the Pueblo Santo Domingo in 1691. The people refer to themselves as *Kiuw*, the meaning of which is unknown. They speak a Keresan language.

The Santo Domingo Pueblo is located in north central New Mexico, about 35 miles southwest of Santa Fe. The population was estimated at 150 in 1680. It's currently 2,857.

The reservation comprises 71,000 acres. There is no written constitution, so common law is used to govern. There are about 3,500 acres of irrigated farmland and about 65,000 acres of open grazing lands. There is an annual arts fair and museum. Many still speak Keresan and some Spanish.

Taos Pueblo

The Taos Pueblo is also known as San Geronimo, from a Tewa word meaning "in the village." The Taos Pueblo, located in north central New Mexico, is three miles from the town of Taos and seventy miles north of Santa Fe. The reservation has 95,000 acres ruled by a 60-member council. Electricity and running water are not permitted inside the old village. Each year, more than 1 million tourists visit the Taos Pueblo. The pueblo has been nominated as a world heritage site since it has been continuously inhabited since at least A.D. 1350. The population was estimated at 2,000 in the late 17th century. Today, tribal enrollment is around 1,800. Some believe that the Anasazi Pueblo of Chaco in northwest New Mexico is the ancestral home of the Taos.

In 1906, the federal government confiscated the tribe's holiest site, the Blue Lake region, and 48,000 surrounding acres and incorporated them into the Carson National Forest. The Taos won restoration of the lake and their land in 1970. This marked the first time that land rather than monetary compensation was offered to a tribe. A pilgrimage is made to Blue Lake each August. San Geronimo Day (September 29–30) is a major feast day.

Tesuque Pueblo

Tesuque is a Spanish pronunciation of the Tewa word *tecuge*, which means "structure at narrow place." The Tesuque speak Tewa.

The pueblo is located nine miles north of Santa Fe. Their population was estimated at 200 in 1680. Today, they have 480 enrolled members.

The Tesuque Pueblo contains approximately 17,000 acres. Tesuque was one of the first pueblos to have electricity and modern housing. Many people still speak Tewa. An annual Katsina Dance each October is closed to outsiders. Their annual feast day is November 12.

Zia Pueblo

Zia is from the Spanish spelling of a Keresan name. The Zia speak a dialect of Keresan. The Zia Pueblo is located 30 miles north of Albuquerque, New Mexico. Their population was estimated at 20,000 in 1540, 300 in 1690, and 100 in 1890. Today, there are about 650 enrolled members. They own 121,000 acres. Many Zia still speak Keresan.

Quapaw

Quapaw (KWAW-paw) comes from the Siouan word *ugaakhpa* meaning "downstream people." Their name may have referred to their southern migration along the Mississippi. The *Algonquin* and French called the Quapaw "Arkansas." They are usually classified as part of the Great Plains culture, and their language is of the Siouan group.

The Quapaw once lived with other Siouan groups, the *Kaw*, *Omaha*, *Osage*, and *Ponca*, in the Ohio Valley. By the 17th century, they had migrated westward down the Mississippi to territory in southeastern Arkansas. Their population was estimated around 20,000 at the beginning of the 18th century. Today, most of the approximately 2,000

Quapaw live near a tribal center in Miami, Oklahoma, where an annual powwow is held.

They lived in palisaded villages in bark-covered, rectangular houses with domed roofs. Woven mats, hides, and grass were also used to cover their houses. They built mounds that contained temples and graves and subsisted primarily on farming. They had 22 patriarchal clans and celebrated the Green Corn Dance. Women planted three crops of corn per year as well as beans, squash, and tobacco. They acquired the *horse [I]* by the early 1700s and hunted *buffalo [I],* as did other Plains tribes.

Two of the first Europeans they had contact with were French explorers Jacques Marquette in 1673 and René Robert La Salle in 1682. At the time, the Quapaw occupied four villages near the confluence of the Mississippi and Arkansas rivers and were the only Dhegiha Siouxspeakers in the lower Mississippi valley. The Quapaw were forced to cede all their Arkansas lands in 1818 and 1824 treaties and to relocate to northeast Oklahoma. In 1824, they agreed to relocate to Texas and live among the *Caddo*, but most of the tribe drifted back to the Arkansas River region.

In 1833, white settlers complained about the Indian presence in Arkansas. Consequently, the federal government forced the Quapaw to relocate and live with the Osage in *Indian Territory [IV]*. The Quapaw rejected the Indian Reorganization Act of 1934. Some older women still give Quapaw names for infants.

The Quapaw currently have small land holdings in northeastern Oklahoma.

Quechan (see Yuma)

Quileute

Quileute is taken from the name of a village located at the current site of La Push on the Olympic Peninsula in Washington State. The tribe's population was estimated at 500 in the 18th century. Today, the Quileute have approximately 875 enrolled members, and they continue to live on their traditional lands on the Pacific coastline of the western Olympic Peninsula in Washington. They are part of the Chimakuan language family.

They lived in plank houses as large as 60 feet by 40 feet that had sleeping platforms built on the sides. Potlatches—gift-giving ceremonies—accompanied important life events. They believed that guardian spirits could be obtained through nature, ancestors, or special visions. Quileute adolescents sought spiritual powers by fasting and visiting remote places. Divorce was not uncommon in their society. They wrapped their dead in mats or blankets and buried them in canoes or hollow logs. Mourners cut their hair and painted their faces.

An 1855 treaty was negotiated that removed the Quileute to a reservation near the town of Forks, Washington. In 1889, a fire set by a local white destroyed 26 Quileute homes and almost all pre-contact artifacts held by the tribe.

The Quileute Reservation, comprised of 594 acres, was established in 1889. A Quileute dictionary exists but only a few can speak the language. Annual Quileute days are usually held on the first weekend in August. Elders Week celebrations are held in May, and they still practice the potlatch gift-giving ceremony.

Salish

The central, northern, and southern Salish consist of many distinct tribes. They referred to themselves as *Se'lic,* meaning "people," and speak the Salishan language.

Their traditional lands were located on the coast in Canada and the United States, although many today reside in western Montana. Their population was estimated at 20,000 in the mid-1800s. Today, there are around 16,000 members.

The Salish sought luck or skills from a guardian spirit, whose power could be accessed through songs. Men and women practiced medicine. They observed First Salmon ceremonies. They also practiced the potlatch tradition. Usually, several families in the village held the potlatch together to mark a special occasion. Fish was a staple of their diet. They used shredded bark for towels and mattresses and tule mats to line interior walls of houses. Body paint was applied as protection against insects.

Around 1592 they had first contact with the Spanish, including Juan de Fuca. Smallpox epidemics began to strike villages by the 1790s. The *Hudson's Bay Company [IV]* built Fort Langley on the Fraser River in 1827 and Fort Victoria in 1843.

The Treaty of Washington in 1846 split the central-coast Salish country between the United States and Canada. On the Canadian side, the British created small reserves for every village; the United States created a few regional *reservations [IV]*, but many groups were left landless. When *gold [IV]* was discovered on the Fraser River in 1858, a flood of whites arrived. The Salish lost more than one-third of their population in the 1950s during the government's policy of relocation. Many tribes struggled for legal enforcement of their treaty rights, a struggle that was partially successful in 1974, when Judge George Boldt ruled in *United States v. Washington* that half the harvestable salmon and steelhead in Washington were to be reserved for federally recognized tribes.

Sanpoil

The Sanpoil are culturally similar to the Nespelem, and speak a dialect of Interior Salish.

Their traditional lands were semi-arid areas of north central Washington. Their population was estimated at 1,600 in 1775. Today the tribe comprises several hundred members.

The Sanpoil believed that guardian spirits could be sought through singing, fasting, and praying. Spiritual quests of this sort were mandatory for men and optional for women. Some Sanpoil had as many as six spirit helpers. The five-day First Salmon ritual was their most important ceremony.

Only men could be Salish chiefs, unlike in other Plateau groups. Some villages had as many as 100 people, who lived in partly below ground, wood-frame homes from 10 to 16 feet in diameter. The interior was covered with a layer of grass. Fish was a staple of their diet.

The Sanpoil were decimated by severe epidemics in the late 18th century and again in the late 1840s and 1850s. They were moved to the Colville Reservation in 1872, where they still live today and hold an annual pow-wow and Circle Celebration.

Seminole

Seminole (SEM-in-ole) is derived from the Spanish word *Cimarron*, meaning "runaway." During the 18th century, the Seminole split off from the *Creek* in the states of Georgia and Alabama and migrated southward. They had a matrilineal clan structure and spoke the Muskogean language.

Seminole chief Osceola, a leader in the Second Seminole War (1835–1842). *National Archives.*

Their homes were made with pole foundations and had thatched roofs. They wore a distinctive style of clothing that used patchwork and rickrack in bright colors. They observed the Green Corn ceremony in early May or June. They farmed, and the women raised corn, beans, squash, and tobacco.

In the early 1800s, the Seminole befriended African Americans who had escaped slavery and welcomed them into their communities. General Andrew Jackson used the runaway slaves as an excuse to attack the Seminole in Florida, at the time a Spanish territory. Once Jackson became president, he forced the relocation of 3,000 Seminole, as well as thousands of members of other tribes, to Oklahoma, in what became known as the Trail of Tears. The term *Trail of Tears [IV]* is the name the *Cherokee* gave to their experience of forced marches to Oklahoma, but other tribes were also removed in this manner. The term is used to refer specifically to the experience of the five major southeastern tribes (Cherokee, *Chickasaw*, *Choctaw*, Creek, and Seminole). Many Seminole fought to resist removal from their lands in Florida in three separate guerrilla wars against the United States. Osceola, a leader in the Second Seminole War of 1835–1842, was captured through promise of a peace council and died three months later in captivity. A third Seminole War was fought in 1855–1858. Today, the Seminole retain less than 10 percent of their original treaty-protected territory. There are now around 10,000 Seminole in Oklahoma, including about 1,000 African American members. In Florida, the 1920s land boom led to further land loss and to the impoverishment for Seminoles in the area.

In the 1950s, the Seminole tribal status was scheduled for termination during the Eisenhower administration. However, in 1957 the Seminole incorporated as a tribe in Florida. Today they have five reservation tracts in the southern part of the state. A branch of the tribe, the Miccosuke, incorporated in 1962.

The Seminole who relocated to Oklahoma were recognized as the Seminole Nation of Oklahoma and hold trust lands in Seminole County.

Seneca

The Seneca (SEN-uh-kuh) refer to themselves as *Ononondowagah,* meaning "people of the great hill." They were the westernmost nation in the *Iroquois League [IV]*, which also included the *Cayuga, Mohawk, Oneida, Onondaga,* and *Tuscarora.* They spoke a Northern Iroquois dialect.

Today they have five reservations: three in New York; one in Brantford, Ontario; and one in northeastern Oklahoma. The largest group, with 6,240 members, lives on the Allegany Reservation in New York. The Tonawanda group, also in New York, numbers about 1,050. There are approximately 260 Seneca in Canada, the descendants of those who followed Mohawk Chief Joseph *Brandt [II]* into Canada after the *American Revolution [IV]*. The Seneca population was estimated at 5,000 in the mid-17th century. Today, there are approximately 8,000 members in the United States and 1,000 in Canada.

Like their fellow Iroquois, the Seneca celebrated Maple Sap, Strawberry, and Corn ceremonies. Their society also included eight matrilineal animal-named clans. They buried their dead in a sitting position with food and tools. Entire villages were moved about twice a generation when firewood and soil were exhausted in a particular area. They lived in elm-bark longhouses 50 to 100 feet long. Raised bed platforms lined the side walls.

Seneca Jesse Cornplanter, a descendant of Chief Cornplanter, making a ceremonial mask at Tonawanda Community House in Tonawanda, New York, 1940. *National Archives.*

285

The Seneca had many prominent leaders. Cornplanter Gayentwahga was an ally of the British during the American Revolution. Cornplanter's half-brother, *Handsome Lake [II]*, founded the Longhouse religion in 1799, which combined elements of Christianity and the traditional Haudenosaunee religion. In 1869, Seneca Ely Samuel *Parker [II]* became the first American Indian commissioner of the *Bureau of Indian Affairs [IV]*. Parker had served with distinction under General Ulysses Grant. In 1848, the Seneca adopted a written constitution with a tripartite system of government.

The Seneca in Oklahoma are actually part of the Seneca-Cayuga tribe, and live on trust lands in Ottawa County in that state. In the late 1950s and early 1960s, tribal members protested having their lands flooded by the building of a dam on the Allegany Reservation. Despite their objections, they lost 10,500 acres to the Kinzua Dam, which covers sacred land, including the original grave site of Cornplanter.

IN THEIR OWN Words

Brother, listen to what we say. There was a time when our forefathers owned this great island. Their seats extended from the rising to the setting sun. The Great Spirit had made it for the use of Indians. He had created the buffalo, the deer, and other animals for food. He had made the bear and the beaver. Their skins served us for clothing. He had caused the earth to produce corn for bread. All this he had done for his red children because he loved them. If we had some disputes . . . they were generally settled without shedding much blood.

But an evil day came upon us. Your forefathers crossed the great water and landed on this island. Their numbers were small. They found friends and not enemies. They told us they had fled from their own country for fear of wicked men . . . They asked us for a small seat. We took pity on them, granted their request, and they sat down among us. We gave them corn and meat, they gave us poison in return . . .

They wanted more land, they wanted our country . . . Wars took place . . . You have got our country, but you are not satisfied. You want to force your religion upon us . . . But we also have a religion which has been given to our forefathers and handed down to us; their children . . . Brother, we do not wish to destroy your religion or take it from you. We only want to enjoy our own.

—RED JACKET (SAGOYEWATHA [HE KEEPS THEM AWAKE]), SENECA (c. 1755–1830). LETTER SENT TO GOVERNOR DEWITT CLINTON OF NEW YORK IN 1821.

Shasta

They referred to themselves as *Kahusariyeki,* which means "among those who talk right." They lived on both sides of the modern California and Oregon border and spoke a Hokan language.

Today the Shasta are still located in northern California and Southern Oregon. Their population was estimated at 3,000 in the 18th century. Today there are approximately 600 enrolled members.

They lived in rectangular homes with wooden walls. Each home held one to four families. Shasta religious leaders were usually women, who acquired their powers through dream trances. Among the Shasta, the possessions of the dead were burned or buried. Widows cut their hair and covered their faces with charcoal as a sign of mourning.

A treaty signed with the United States in November 1851 near Fort Jones, California, called for a Shasta Reservation in Scott Valley, but the state of California refused to ratify the treaty. After signing the treaty, the Shasta were served poisoned meat and bread that had been laced with strychnine by the locals. Thousands died. Thousands more died while being hunted by white vigilantes. No one was ever prosecuted for these murders since no white could be convicted of any offense, even murder, on the testimony of an Indian.

The Shasta Nation is currently petitioning for federal recognition of its 1,300 members.

Shawnee

Shawnee (shaw-NEE) comes from the Algonquian word *chawunagi,* which meant "southerners." The Shawnee lived south of other Algonquin groups in parts of Tennessee, Kentucky, and West Virginia. In the 1800s, the Shawnee relocated to Kansas, Missouri, Arkansas, Texas, and Oklahoma. They are closely related to the *Kickapoo,* Sauk, and Fox.

Their population, estimated at 50,000 in the 16th century, dropped to 3,000 by 1650. Today there are about 12,000 members, most of whom live in Oklahoma.

Female leaders were important in Shawnee culture, and included female war and civil chiefs. Their creator was called Waashaa Monetoo; Earth Mother, Corn Woman, and Pumpkin Woman were also important spiritual figures. The Shawnee held Bread Dances in October and men-versus-women football matches in May. As part of their burial customs, tobacco was sprinkled over the bodies of the dead and their possessions divided among relatives. They lived in bark-covered lodges in towns of as many as a thousand people. Shawnee women raised several varieties of corn. They allied with the *Lenape* and later the *Creek* and *Cherokee*. They experienced conflict with the *Chickasaw, Cherokee, Catawba,* and *Iroquois*.

With other Algonquin, they sided with the French during the *French and Indian Wars [IV]* from 1689 to 1763. The majority joined *Pontiac's Rebellion [IV]* of 1763 against the English. The Shawnee sided with the British against American rebels in the *American Revolution [IV]*, primarily because the British offered some recognition of Indian lands while American rebels ignored proclamations regarding Indian land rights. Shawnee leaders Cornstalk and Blue Jacket defended the Ohio region against white intruders from the 1740s to the 1770s. In the 1795 Treaty of Greenville, they were compelled to cede southern and central Ohio. In 1811, *Tecumseh [II]*, a Shawnee, led an intertribal rebellion against white encroachment.

A group known as Absentee Shawnee divided from the main body of the tribe in Kansas in the 1800s and lived in Arkansas and Texas before further relocation to *Indian Territory [IV]*. About 6,000 Shawnee now live in Oklahoma, and few speak the language.

Shoshone

The Shoshone (sho-SHO-nee) speak a dialect of the Uto-Aztecan language. They were once united with the *Comanche*, with whom they lived in western Wyoming. Around 1700 or so, the Comanche broke away from the Shoshone and moved to Texas, while the Shoshone continued to live in Wyoming. Their precontact population was estimated at 30,000 but was cut by 90 percent by the mid-19th century. Today there are about 3,000 members.

The Shoshone believed they could gain spiritual power through dances or by sleeping in sacred places, usually marked with a vision. With the introduction of the *horse [I]* in the early 18th century, *buffalo [I]* hunting became a part of Shoshone culture, as did Plains-style tipis.

One of the most famous American Indian women in history was a Shoshone: Sacajawea. She is known to history for having assisted Lewis and Clark on their expedition to the West Coast in 1803 through 1806. She had been captured by the *Hidatsa* and sold to a Frenchman, Toussaint Charbonneau. On the expedition, she was able to serve as guide and translator, contributing significantly to its survival and success.

The Shoshone today have reservations in California and Nevada.

Shuswap

Shuswap means "to know" or "recognize." Their language is of the Salishan group.

The Shuswap's original lands were in British Columbia, where they have resided for at least 9,000 years. Their population was estimated at 7,000 in the early 19th century. Today, their population is around 5,000.

Young Shuswap boys sought guardian spirits through fasting, praying, and vision quests. Masked dances reenacted a person's vision quest. The Shuswap buried their dead in sand banks or rock slides with their possessions; sometimes small mourning houses were built by the grave. In winter they lived in circular lodges of cedar bark on wood frames. Their homes, which housed multiple families, could be as much as six feet below ground level, and were twenty to thirty-five feet in diameter, with floors covered with spruce boughs. Shuswap homes also featured the clan totem, which was carved on the home's center pole or outside. Fish was a staple of their diet. Their traditional enemies were the *Okanagon, Thompson, Cree, Chilcotin,* and *Carrier.*

The *Hudson's Bay Company [IV]* established company posts near Shuswap lands for the fur trade. A Shuswap Reserve sixteen miles square was created in 1865 but was quickly reduced to one square mile; it is where many Shuswap continue to reside today.

A statue of Sacagawea, in Bismarck, North Dakota. *State Historical Society of North Dakota.*

Sinkiuse

Sinkiuse, meaning "between people," is the name of the tribe that has traditionally lived on the east bank of the Columbia River in Washington. The Sinkiuse continue to reside in areas around the central part of the state. Their population was estimated at 800 in the late 18th century. Today, they number around 300. They speak a dialect of Interior *Salish*.

Guardian spirits were an important element of Sinkiuse culture and were sought through the traditional means of singing, fasting, and praying. They shared a number of cultural traditions with other Northwest Coast groups: the First Salmon ritual, midwinter Spirit Dances, and First Fruits rites were important occasions. They built plateau-style, semi-excavated, wood-framed houses, which could range from 24 to 60 feet in length and were 14 feet high. Fish was a staple of their diet.

The Columbia Reservation was established in 1879 but abolished several years later. Four Sinkiuse bands followed their leader, Chief Moses, to the Colville Reservation, where they live today.

Spokan

The Spokan (spo-KAN), meaning "people of the sun," live in the northeastern part of Washington (along the Spokane River) and northern Idaho. They spoke a Salishan language with a dialect similar to the *Coeur d'Alene*, *Kalispel*, and Flathead. Spokan society had three divisions: upper, lower, and southern.

They lived in partly below ground wood-framed houses constructed of pole frames covered with woven mats. Later, some built skin tipis for housing. They were allied with the Kalispel and experienced conflict with the *Crow* and *Blackfeet*.

Salmon and wild roots, such as camas, were traditionally staples of their diet; they also hunted *buffalo [I]*.

Among the first Europeans they encountered were Lewis and Clark in 1805. Smallpox epidemics followed in 1846. They joined the Coeur d'Alene, *Palouse*, *Paiute*, and *Yakama* in an 1858 rebellion, which was quickly put down. In the 20h century, the Grand Coulee Dam, built on the Columbia River in 1941, blocked much of their fish runs. They successfully fought against termination in 1955.

Today, the Spokan Reservation in Washington (established in 1881) comprises 133,302 acres. There are some language preservation programs, and an annual festival is held over Labor Day weekend. There are currently 2,100 enrolled Spokan Indians, slightly more than their population in the early 19th century.

Tillamook

Tillamook is a *Chinook* word meaning "land of many waters." The Tillamook Indians speak a Salishan language and live along a coastal strip in present-day Oregon. Their population was estimated at 2,200 in 1805 but had dropped to less than 250 by 1950. Today there are only around 50 members.

They lived in rectangular, cedar-plank houses occupied by as many as four families each. In Tillamook culture, spirits were thought to be closer to humans in winter than during the rest of the year. The dead were painted, wrapped in a blanket, bound in cedar bark, then buried in canoes. There were five types of shamans in their society, including one kind known as "baby diplomats." Baby diplomats foretold events by talking with babies.

The Tillamook suffered from exposure to smallpox as early as 1788. Lewis and Clark encountered them on their expedition in 1811, although by the 1830s, epidemics of malaria, syphilis, and smallpox had reduced the Tillamook population by approximately 90 percent. In 1850, the Donation Land Act opened Tillamook lands for white settlement. The Indians ceded their remaining lands in an unratified 1851 treaty and became landless. Congress terminated the Tillamook in 1956.

Tipai-Ipai

The Tipai-Ipai (also known as the Diegueno Mission Indians) speak a Yuman dialect of the Hokan language family. They lived in southern California and on the Baja Peninsula for at least 20,000 years, although today they live on 13 reservations in San Diego County, California. Their population was estimated at 9,000 in the 18th century. Currently, however, there are approximately 2,000 enrolled members.

The Tipai-Ipai lived in pole-framed domes covered with bark and subsisted in part on acorns, a staple of their diet. Parents arranged marriages for their adolescent children, and divorce in their society was easy to obtain. They cremated their dead along with their possessions, then held mourning ceremonies that lasted four days, during which mourners cut their hair and blackened their faces. They blended aspects of their traditional spiritual practices with Christian religion. A major feast is the Fiesta de las Cruces on November 14.

Tlingit

The Tlingit (TLING-kit) tribe speak an Athapascan language and were comprised of four divisions: the Coastal, Gulf Coast, Northern, and Southern Tlingit. Tlingit in their language means "people."

For at least 10,000 years, humans have lived in Tlingit country, which incorporated southeastern Alaska and northern British Columbia along the Pacific coast. Their northern neighbors were the *Inuit* and *Aleut*, their southern neighbors, the *Haida* and *Tsimshian*. Their numbers have been estimated at 15,000 at first contact. That number was reduced by more than 50 percent after the smallpox epidemics of 1835–1840.

They traditionally lived in large houses constructed of beams and planks of wood and displayed several aspects of Northwest Coastal culture, including the use of totem poles, wooden ceremonial masks, dugout canoes, and the potlatch gift-giving ceremony. A distinctive clothing item is the Chilkat blanket, named after one of their bands. Women weave these blankets from cedar-bark fiber and mountain-goat wool. The colors used are white, black, blue-green, and yellow. The completed blanket is about six feet long, with a straight edge at the top and a slight wedge at the bottom. The blankets have attached fringe and employ abstract designs and animal forms.

Tlingit society was divided into clans. Each clan owned its own crest, which depicted its origin and history. The crests adorned ceremonial objects, jewelry, totems, house posts, and house fronts. In most villages, there were two matrilineal clans: the Raven and Eagle. Babies were believed to be reincarnations of maternal relatives.

Their houses, rectangular-planked structures that could hold 40 to 50 people, were lined with wooden sleeping platforms. Fish was a dietary staple.

The Tlingit resisted Russian colonialism in the early 19th century. Following Russia's sale of Alaska to the United States in 1867, a *gold [IV]* rush in 1880 brought unprecedented numbers of white immigrants to the area. The Tlingit participated in the Alaska Native Brotherhood, one of the earliest intertribal organizations. (It was founded in 1912.)

In 1971, a land settlement was reached in the *Alaska Native Claims Settlement Act [IV]*. As a result of the 1971 act, Alaskan villages had to form corporations, of which tribal members were shareholders. The Tlingit formed the Sea of Alaska Corporation with the Haida.

Tohono O'odham

Tohono O'odham (TO-ho-no oh-OH-tum) means "desert people" in their language. They have also been known as the Papago, a name given to them by their neighbors the Akimel O'odham (*Pima*), which means "bean people." They speak a dialect of the Uto-Aztecan language and may be descendants of the ancient *Hohokam culture [I]*.

Their lands were traditionally in the Sonoran Desert along what is now the international border between southwest Arizona and northwest Sonora, Mexico. While they did not have to relocate from traditional lands, their land holdings were significantly reduced, and today they live in four reservations in southern Arizona. Their numbers were estimated at 50,000 in 1500 but had shrunk to 3,000 by 1700. The current enrolled membership is approximately 17,500. Their origin story states that Elder Brother, known as *I'toi*, led them into their lands from the underworld.

They were farmers who practiced desert irrigation, raising corn, beans, and squash. They also collected wild plant food such as the mescal plant and beans from the mesquite tree. One of their most important ceremonies, known as the *Vigida*, centered around bringing rain. In late summer, the fermented saguaro fruit is turned into a wine called *nawait*. Drinking nawait is believed to bring annual rain and marks the beginning of the Tohono O'odham New Year.

One of the first Europeans they encountered was Father Eusebio Kino, who established missions among them beginning in 1687. Some of their tribe participated in the Pima Uprising of 1751. Following the Mexican War, their territory was claimed as part of the Gadsden Purchase in 1853, thus falling under United States jurisdiction. The Gadsden purchase gave the United States the northern Mexican territory, what is today the Southwest region and the state of California. The purchase was advocated by business interests of a southern transcontinental railroad. The United States government paid $10 million in exchange for the vast area of land. The railroad came to the area in the 1880s and brought with it an influx of settlers. In 1916, President Woodrow Wilson issued an executive order establishing the Papago Reservation. The Tohono O'odham have the second largest reservation in the United States, which comprises 2,774,370 acres.

The Tohono O'odham ratfied a tribal constitution in 1937. A 1986 constitutional revision created a tripartite form of government. Unemployment remains around 30 percent. They hold an annual rodeo and fair in October.

Tonkawa

The Tonkawa (THAN-kuh-wh), whose name comes from the Waco word *tonkaweya*, meaning "they all stay together," speak an Athapascan language.

Their original lands were in central Texas, although they currently live in Texas, eastern New Mexico, and southern Oklahoma. Their precontact population was around 2,400. They were one of the more warlike tribes in the Southwest, fighting not only enemy tribes but the Spanish and, later, American settlers in Texas. Among the first Europeans they had contact with were Spanish explorers Alvar Núñez Cabeza de Vaca in the 1530s and Francisco Vásquez de Coronado in the 1540s. In 1542, Luis de Moscoso, a member of Hernando de Soto's expedition, visited the Tonkawa on the Trinity River in Texas. In 1719, French explorer Jean Baptiste Benard de la Harpe mentioned the Tonkawa as one of the "roving nations" he encountered in the upper Red River region. Beginning around 1800, the Tonkawa were allies of the Lipan Apache and were friendly to the Texans. By 1837, they had for the most part drifted toward the southwestern frontier of Texas; some had crossed over into Mexican territory. Around the same time, however, their numbers declined because of epidemics of cholera, measles, and diphtheria. In 1855, the Tonkawa and other Texas tribes were relocated to two small *reservations [IV]* in Texas. Because of white vigilantism in Texas, they were relocated again in 1859, this time to Indian Territory in Oklahoma. However, during the *Civil War [IV]*, their long-standing ties to Texans made them generally loyal to the Confederacy. Early on the morning of October 24, 1862, a party of *Delaware* and *Shawnee*, armed by federal forces in Kansas, attacked an encampment of Tonkawa, kiilling 167 of them. By the turn of the century, their population was reduced by 95 percent due to measles and cholera, to only 200 people. Today, there are approximately 500 members.

They lived in redwood-planked houses. Religious leaders were mostly women or cross-dressing men. Bride prices were paid at marriage. Wealthy men might have several wives. They wrapped their dead in tule mats and buried thcm with their possessions. Like other Plains tribes, they practiced a number of ceremonial dances, including the Buffalo Dance, the Notched Stick Dance, and a religious ceremony known as the Water-Drum Dance, or *Tome-ka*. Perhaps their most sacred dance, however, was the Wolf Dance, which commemorated the creation story of the Tonkawa and was generally kept secrct from outsiders. The Tonkawa language today is extinct. A powwow is held every June in the town of Tonkawa.

Tsimshian

Tsimshian (CHIM-shee-un) means "people of the Skeena River." Their ancestral lands are in northwestern British Columbia and southern Alaska. They speak a dialect of the Penutian language group, which makes them the northernmost Penutian speakers. (Other tribes who speak dialects of Penutian live in Washington, Oregon, and California.) They were culturally similar to the *Haida* and *Tlingit*.

Their population was estimated at 10,000 in 1800. Today, there are about 2,400 in the United States and 4,500 in Canada.

Tsimshian homes contained extended maternal families and were built of red-cedar timbers with as much as 2,500 square feet of living space with side platforms for beds. Beds were generally cedar-bark mats. House fronts were painted with crest designs. There were four matrilineal clans: Wolf, Eagle, Raven, and Blackfish or Killer Whale.

Fish, salmon, and sea mammals are important to their diet, although they do not hunt whales as some other Northwest Coastal groups do. They still practice potlatch gift ceremonies and participate in secret shaman societies. Women make distinct Chilkat fringed blankets from cedar bark and goat's hair decorated with abstract and animal designs. After the introduction of European trade goods, they began making a blue blanket with a red border and animal shapes made from mother-of-pearl buttons.

Tubatulabal

The traditional lands of the Tubatulabal (meaning "pine nut eaters") are in the Kern River Valley and southern Sierra Nevada. Tubatulabal is one of three Uto-Aztecan language groups.

Today, many Tubatulabal live on reservations in Tulare County, California. Their population was estimated at 1,000 in the early 19th century. Today there are around 500 members.

Their homes were circular structures of brush and mud, between 30 to 50 feet in diameter. Acorns and fish were staples of their diet. Religious leaders were both male and female, although shamanism was an inborn quality that could not be acquired. Marriages were formalized by gift exchanges, or the grooms performed services to their new in-laws. The dead were wrapped in tule mats and buried.

Spanish missionaries arrived in the area in 1776, and miners arrived in the 1850s. Many Tubatulabal worked for local ranchers. Their numbers were reduced by severe measles and influenza epidemics in 1902 and 1918. Their last hereditary leader died in 1955.

The Tule River Reservation was established in 1873 in Tulare County. It comprises 55,356 acres and has a population of approximately 750.

Tunica

Tunica (YOON-uh-chu), meaning "those who are the people," are classified as of the Southeast cultural area. They were culturally similar to the Yazoo, and are descendants of the Southern *Hopewell culture [I]*.

The Tunica traditionally lived along the lower Mississippi River valley and in territory that is now eastern Arkansas and eastern Louisiana. Their population was estimated at 2,000 in the late 17th century but had been reduced to fewer than 30 members by 1800. Today there are about 430 members.

They lived in thatched houses and built their temples on mounds. Clothing was woven from mulberry plant cloth. They lived in villages and women raised corn, beans, squash, sunflowers, and melons. They worshiped the sun and celebrated the Green Corn Dance. (Corn, in fact, was such a central part of their culture and diet that the Tunica made 42 different dishes from it.)

One of the first Europeans they encountered was Hernando de Soto in 1541, although they allied themselves with the French. Jesuit *missionaries [IV]* established a presence in the area around 1700. One of their chiefs was murdered in 1841 because he resisted the theft of Tunica land. Their last chief died in 1976.

Federal recognition was granted in 1981 to the Tunica-Biloxi tribe. Their traditional New Corn ceremony is still celebrated but is not open to the public. The Tunica language is no longer spoken.

Tuscarora

The Tuscarora (tusk-uh-ROAR-uh), meaning "shirt-wearing people," were part of the *Iroquois League [IV]* of Six Nations, as were the *Cayuga*, *Mohawk*, *Oneida*, *Onondaga*, and *Seneca*. Their society was matrilineal, and the Tuscarora Council of Chiefs is still chosen by a council of clan mothers. They speak an Iroquoian language, which probably indicates a northern origin.

Their numbers in Virginia and North Carolina were estimated at 5,000 in 1500. Today, there are about 1,400 members in New York and 1,200 in Canada.

The Tuscarora painted the faces of the dead black and wrapped their bodies in blankets for burial. A small house was then built over the grave. Villages had hundreds of homes and were palisaded. Houses were pole lodges covered with cedar or pine bark. Corn, beans, and squash were staples of their diet. They were allies with the **Cree**, Pamlico, and Machapunga. They experienced conflict with the **Catawba, Creek**, and some **Cherokee** early on.

Their original lands were in northeastern North Carolina and southeastern Virginia, but they migrated to the New York area in the early 1700s and were recognized as a sixth nation of the Iroquois in 1722. The Tuscarora had been friendly with the English, but a history of treachery that included stolen lands, kidnapping, and enslavement prompted many Tuscarora to flee north. The **Tuscarora Conflict [IV]** of 1711–1713 was fought over the issue of enslavement against the North and South Carolina militia and provided the English with an opportunity to exterminate the Tuscarora and drive them from the Carolinas.

They settled with the Oneida, who represented them at the Iroquois League Great Council. Later, during the **American Revolution [IV]**, most Tuscarora and Oneida sided with the American rebels. That split in allegiance caused a permanent division in the Iroquois League. Afterward, despite their support of the American cause, their villages were burned and looted. A few practiced the **Handsome Lake [II]** religion until Christians burned their longhouse. In 1784, they gained a state reservation in the northwestern corner of New York near Niagara Falls.

In 1957, the Tuscarora lost a United States Supreme Court case to prevent the sale of their lands for a dam. Over their protests, a reservoir flooded hundreds of acres of their reserve during the next three years.

A Tuscarora picnic and field day is held each July. In addition to the 5,700-acre reservation in Niagara County, New York, about 200 Tuscarora also live on the Six Nations Reserve in Ontario, Canada.

Umatilla

The Umatilla (um-uh-TIL-uh), whose name means "many rocks," had ancestral lands in northern Oregon and southern Washington State. They are culturally similar to the **Klikitat**, **Nez Perce**, Walla Walla, and **Yakama**. Their language is of the Sahaptian language group, and they are classified with the Plateau cultural area.

Today they live in northeastern Oregon, near their traditional lands. Their population in 1780 was estimated at 1,500, but it is approximately 2,000 today.

They lived in A-frame mat lodges that could be up to 60 feet long, although some adopted the use of hide tipis in the 18th century. They believed that guardian spirits could be found in nature by fasting and visiting remote places. Like other tribes in their region, they practiced the First Salmon and First Fruits ceremonies. Unmarried men slept in sweat lodges, but most Umatilla married by age 14. A bride price tradition was practiced, as was polygamy. They painted the faces of their dead, who were then wrapped in deerskin and buried with their possessions. Boulders and cedar stakes marked grave sites. Those in mourning cut their hair and wore tattered clothing. Salmon and wild plant foods, such as the camas plant, were staples of their diet.

Around 1805, they encountered the expedition of Lewis and Clark, whose journey paved the way for numerous Americans moving west across their lands on the Oregon Trail in the following decades. The Umatilla, along with the *Cayuse* and Walla Walla, gained a reservation in 1855 near Pendleton, Oregon. They adopted a constitution in 1949.

The Umatilla Reservation in Oregon is comprised of 172 acres and was established in 1855; it is governed by a nine-member council. They hold an annual powwow, a festival of Indian arts, and a rodeo called the Pendleton Roundup.

Upper Umpaqua

The Upper Umpaqua were an Athapascan-speaking group whose traditional lands were in southwest Oregon. They referred to themselves as *Etnemitane*. Today, there are only a few hundred Umpaqua left.

Their houses were made of planks, were as large as 20 by 30 feet, and were decorated with fern and grass wall mats. They required that the family of anyone killed in battle be compensated for the death, a practice that helped to lower casualty rates. Healers, who were generally women, derived their powers from guardian spirits.

The fur trade began in their region around 1818 and was expanded when the *Hudson's Bay Company [IV]* established Fort Umpaqua in 1836 on their lands. Whites flooded in after the 1840s gold rush. In 1854, the tribe signed a land cession treaty and agreed to move to the Grand Ronde Reservation. Moving to the new reservation involved a forced journey over mountains in winter, during which several hundred died from exposure and starvation. Some members moved instead to live with the Cow Creek Band, terminated in 1956 but formally restored in 1982. Others joined the nearby Siletz, who finally obtained tribal status in 1977 and a reservation in 1980. The Cow Creek Band hosts a weeklong powwow each July.

Ute

The Ute (YOOT) referred to themselves as *nunt'z*, meaning "the people." They speak a dialect of the Uto-Aztecan language family like their neighbors the *Paiute* and *Shoshone*.

They occupied most of Utah and Colorado as well as parts of southern Wyoming and northern New Mexico. By 1879, their population dropped to 800, less than 20 percent of its estimated precontact size. Today there are about 7,000 members. Traditionally, the Utes were divided into seven loosely confederated bands. There were the Mouache and Capote Utes, who now live on a reservation in Ignacio, Colorado, and are known as the Southern Utes. There were the Weeminuches, whose traditional lands were in the valley of the San Juan River and its tributaries in Colorado and New Mexico, and who are now known as the Ute Mountain Utes, headquartered in Towaoc, Colorado. And there were the Tabeguache, Grand, Yampa, and Uintah, who are now known as the Northern Utes and who inhabit the Uintah-Ouray Reservation, with headquarters in the town of Fort Duchesne, Utah.

In Ute tradition, both men and women could acquire spiritual power from dreams, and some undertook vision quests. Bears symbolized leadership, wisdom, and strength, and the 10-day Bear Dance was used to welcome spring. The Sun Dance was held in midsummer. Divorce was easy to obtain in their society, and men could have multiple wives. They lived in domed willow houses as large as 10 to 15 feet in diameter. Later, they also built tipis, used during *buffalo [I]* hunts.

One of the first Europeans they encountered was Franciscan Fray Escalante in 1776. Mormon settlers came to their lands in 1847 and expanded their presence in 1855. *Gold [IV]* was discovered near their lands in Colorado in 1858. The growth of mining interests in western Colorado and eastern Utah led to calls for displacement of the Ute from their lands, leading to the political slogan, "The Utes must go." Governor Pitkin of Colorado even called for the extermination of the Ute. By 1934, the Ute controlled less than 1 percent of their original lands.

In 1990, Ute families earned half the average income of most American families. They have three reservations in Colorado and Utah and hold three annual Bear Dances and Sun Dances in the summer.

Wailaki

Wailaki is a *Wintun* word that means "north language." The Wailaki are a southern Athapascan-speaking people who resided in northwestern California. Today most live near Mendocino County. Their population was estimated at 2,700 in the 1850s, although the current enrolled membership is 1,090.

The Wailaki lived in domes made of redwood or bark with conical roofs. They practiced a form of herbal abortion. They traditionally burned or buried the house and possessions of the dead and marked graves with a pile of stones.

Local whites persecuted them nearly to the point of extinction in the 1860s; those who survived hid in the hills, working as ranchers. In the 1900s, because the young were frequently kidnapped and indentured to whites, parents often tattooed their children, so they would always know their ancestry. The work of Indian reformers called for the establishment of small reservations for homeless Indians in California.

Their reservation, gained in 1864, consists of 35,522 acres in Mendocino County. They adopted an Indian Reorganization Act in 1936 and are currently seeking federal recognition.

Wampanoag

The Wampanoag (meaning "the eastern people") speak an Algonquian dialect and originally lived in Massachusetts and Rhode Island. Their population estimates show a rapid decline in population, from 24,000 precontact, to 3,000 by 1602 and 2,500 in 1674. Today they have nearly 1,000 members and reside mainly in the Northeast.

Their village chiefs were known as sachems, a position that both men and women could hold. Sachems, chosen by the Wampanoag community from among leading families, relied on a council of elders for support and decision making. Occasionally, a particularly respected or charismatic sachem such as Massassoit (see *King Philip's War [IV]*) could unite other Wampanoag groups for wars or other cooperative efforts. Wampanoag men could have more than one wife. They wrapped their dead in mats and buried them with their possessions. They blackened their faces for mourning and believed that the dead traveled to a land in the West. They lived in palisaded villages, in wigwams up to 100 feet long that were covered with birch or hickory bark. Women raised corn, beans, and squash. Their allies included the Massachusett; their enemies were the *Penobscot* and *Narragansett.*

They had lived in their traditional lands for at least 8,000 years. It was Wampanoags who greeted the Pilgrims on their arrival on Cape Cod in 1620. They also fought in King Philip's War from 1675 to 1676, an attempt to drive the British from their territory. The two main tribes participating, the Wampanoag and Narragansett, were nearly exterminated, and most Wampanoag were either enslaved or killed.

The Wampanoag celebrate Cranberry Day on the second Tuesday of October. Although it no longer lasts three or four days, it is still their most important holiday. They also hold a powwow on the Fourth of July.

Wichita

Wichita (WITCH-uh-taw) is believed to derive from the *Choctaw* word *wia-chitoah,* meaning "big arbor." They refer to themselves as *Kitikitish,* meaning "raccoon-eyed," most likely referring to their practice of face painting. They speak a Caddoan language.

The Wichita migrated southward in the 17th century, separating from other Caddoan groups, the *Caddo, Arikira,* and *Pawnee.* After a period of migration, they settled in areas of Kansas, Oklahoma, and Texas. Their current population is about 1,700.

Their homes were cone-shaped grass houses constructed of branches covered with thatch. Sleeping platforms lined the walls. They acquired horses *[I]* in the 1700s and began hunting *buffalo [I]* and using skin tipis similar to other Plains groups. They also farmed and raised corn, beans, squash, and tobacco. A Deer Dance was held three times a year. They were allies of the *Comanche* and experienced some conflict with the *Osage* and *Apache.*

Among the first Europeans they encountered was Spanish explorer Francisco Vásquez de Coronado in 1541. At the time of contact, the Wichita were living in central Kansas.

They signed their first treaty with the United States in 1835. By 1850, they moved near Fort Sill in *Indian Territory [IV]* and were assigned a reservation with the Caddo in 1859. During the *Civil War [IV]*, many returned to Kansas, near Wichita. In 1872 they returned to their lands in Oklahoma and ceded other lands to the United States. In 1960 the Wichita united with the Waco, Tawakonie, and Keechi and organized their membership into one governmental entity under the name Wichita and Affiliated Tribes. Today they hold one small tract of land in Oklahoma that they share with the Caddo and Delaware (see *Lenape*). A seven-member tribal council governs them, although only 20 members speak the Wichita language. A dance is held near Anadarko each August.

Wintun

Wintun (WIN-tun) (meaning "people") speak a Penutian dialect, as do other California Indian groups, such as the *Maidu* and Miwok.

Their lands were in northern California but they did not incorporate attributes from Northwest Coastal area groups, as other tribes to their north did, or become targets of missionary zeal by the Spanish, like groups to their south. Their precontact population was estimated at 2,244. Their eighteenth-century population was estimated at 15,000. Today there are 2,200 enrolled Wintun.

Some of their homes were made of brush and grass; others were bark-covered and were built partly below ground. The Wintun had secret societies, which impersonated spirit beings in order to acquire some of their power. The girls' puberty ritual involved seclusion for up to seven months in a special hut. Boys' adolescence was marked by their first hunt. Wealthy men could have more than one wife. The dead were buried with acorn meal, water, and personal items. The Wintun experienced conflict with the *Shasta*, *Klamath*, *Modoc*, and *Yana*.

The Wintun had contact with the Spanish as early as 1808 but managed to stay outside the mission system. Malaria epidemics, however, killed 75 percent of their population in the early 1830s. Their numbers were further reduced by a massacre led by Captain John Fremont in 1846 that killed 1,705 Wintun. White settlers poisoned 100 Wintun at a friendship feast in 1850, and 300 more died when miners attacked and burned their village. Wintun children were excluded from schools until 1928. Dam construction begun in the 1930s flooded the remaining Wintun lands.

The Wintun today hold several small rancherias. They are involved in current struggles to protect Mount Shasta and other sacred sites.

Wishram

The Wishram were a Plateau group with many cultural attributes of the Northwest Coast Indians. They were culturally similar to the Wasco and spoke a Penutian language.

Today, many live on the *Yakama* Reservation in Washington State. Their population, estimated at 1,500 in the 18th century, had only 10 members in 1962.

The Wishram built plank-style homes with bed platforms along the walls. Fish was a staple of their diet, and they participated in both the First Salmon ritual and midwinter Guardian Spirit Dances. They wrapped their dead in buckskin and buried them in plank containers.

In 1855, the Wishram were forced to sign treaties ceding their land of 1 million acres. By the turn of the century, many had been moved onto the Yakama or Warm Springs Reservation, but non-Indians owned 80 percent of those reservation lands. Fishing was destroyed by the construction of several dams, including the Bonneville in 1938, Grand Coulee in 1941, and Dalles in 1956. During the dam constructions, salmon and steelhead that returned to the Yakama River to spawn declined by 99 percent. A 1974 ruling by Judge George Boldt recognized Indian fishing rights guaranteed in treaties and mandated that 50 percent of fish be harvested by federally recognized tribes, including the Wishram.

The Yakama Reservation in Washington comprises 1.4 million acres and was established in 1859; the Warm Springs Reservation, established in

1855, comprises 643,507 acres. Unemployment among the Wishram runs between 30 and 60 percent, and at least 755 reservation residents live in poverty. The Wishram also host an annual All-Indian Rodeo and Huckleberry Festival.

Wiyot

The Wiyot live in northwestern California on three rancherias. They are Algonquian-speakers and are culturally similar to the *Yurok*.

Their traditional lands were in Humboldt County, California, where many continue to reside. Their population was estimated at 3,500 in the early 19th century; today there are approximately 400 members.

The Wiyot lived in rectangular redwood-plank houses. Unlike many other Indian cultures, both men and women hunted for food; acorn and salmon were staples of their diet. Female cross-dressers played a role in Wiyot ceremonies. Married couples lived with the groom's family. The dead were buried in plank-lined graves with their valuables.

Every February, the Wiyot conducted a multiday annual ritual known as the world renewal ceremony on Indian Island in Humboldt Bay. After the California gold rush in 1848, many Wiyot died of disease and murder by white vigilantes. In 1860, during the week of the ceremony, citizens of Eureka attacked the tribe in the early morning hours, killing all but a few. Additional attacks took place that night. In all, at least 250 Wiyot were killed. Their current population is about 450 and they are not federally recognized. They hold an annual vigil in memory of the victims of the 1860 massacre.

Wyandotte/Huron

Most Wyandotte today live in Oklahoma, Kansas, and Quebec. They refer to themselves as *Wendat*, meaning "island people." They are a successor tribe to the Huron Confederacy, which was destroyed in 1650.

In the 16th century, the Huron lived in the St. Lawrence River Valley, in what is now Canada, inhabiting a region called Huronia by European explorers. At that time (the early 17th century), the Huron population was estimated between 16,000 and 30,000. Their population declined to 10,000 by the 1650s, and by the early 19th century there were only 200 left. Today there are about 2,000 members in Oklahoma and Kansas and about 2,700 in Quebec, Canada.

The Wyandotte recognized several deities, including the sun and sky. The position of chief was inherited matrilineally but was also determined by merit and required a confirmation process. Clan mothers held positions of political authority among the Wyandotte. Divorce was unusual after children had been born, but in such cases women retained custody of their children. The dead were placed on a scaffold with a small hut built over it and gifts placed near the body. They built pole-framed homes covered with elm or cedar that could be up to 30 feet wide. Women raised corn, beans, squash, and sunflowers. The Wyandotte were allies with other Algonquin groups, such as the *Ottawa*, but experienced conflict with the *Iroquois*—especially the *Seneca*.

In 1843, the Wyandotte were forced from the St. Lawrence River to lands in Kansas. By 1857, they were moved from Kansas to northeastern Oklahoma. The Oklahoma reservation was divided into allotments in 1893. The Wyandotte Tribe of Oklahoma was established in 1937 but faced termination by the Eisenhower administration in 1956. After a 20-year struggle, they were able to regain federal recognition in 1978. Today they own 192 acres, and tribal enrollment is around 3,600.

Yakama

Yakama (YAK-uhmuh) means "a growing family." (The tribe officially changed the spelling of their name from Yakima to Yakama in 1994.) They speak a Sahaptian Penutian language and are classified in the Plateau cultural area.

The Yakama traditionally occupied an area in south central Washington. Their population was estimated at 7,000 in the late 18th century, a number that had been reduced by half by 1805. The population was just 1,362 in the 1910 census. Today there are 6,000 enrolled members.

They lived in partly underground, pole-framed earth lodges. Some, during the 18th century, built skin tipis. Fish was a staple of their diet. They believed in a creator and animal spirits and marked their graves with a ring of stones. When they acquired the *horse [I]* around 1730, they began hunting *buffalo [I]*.

In 1855, the governor of the Washington territory, Isaac Steven, called on Indian nations in the region to cede their lands for reservations. Those he addressed included the Yakama, *Cayuse, Umatilla*, Walla Walla, and *Nez Perce*. They became the Consolidated Tribes and Bands of the Yakama Indian Nation after a treaty on June 9, 1855.

The tribe was involved in many fishing rights cases. One of the first was *Taylor v. Yakama Tribe* in 1887. It was brought when a white settler's fence blocked access to a Yakama fishery. In that case, the Supreme Court ruled in favor of the Indians. In a 1905 decision, the Supreme Court, in *United States v. Winans,* upheld their rights again. By 1942, courts were allowing more state regulation of fishing as reflected in the *Tulee v. Washington State* decision. The Yakama refused participation in the 1934 Indian Reorganization Act and instead organized the Confederated Tribes of the Yakama Nation.

Fishing was hampered by the construction of the Bonneville Dam in 1938, the Grand Coulee dam in 1941, and the Dalles Dam in 1951. In addition, state officials routinely arrested Indians when they exercised their treaty-guaranteed rights to fish. Fishing and hunting rights were often retained by Indians in the region when land was ceded, since that was an important source of protein in their otherwise meager diet. In *United States v. State of Washington* in 1974, Judge George Boldt upheld the tribes' treaty rights to 50 percent of the harvestable fish.

The Yakama Reservation is located in Washington and comprises 1.4 million acres. It was established in 1859 and is ruled by a 14-member tribal council. Non-Indians, however, lease 80 percent of the irrigated land, which is an important source of timber. Unemployment remains high and 75 percent of the people on the reservation live at the poverty level. The Yakama have a cultural center, museum, four-year liberal arts college, tribal newspaper, and radio station. They hold an annual All-Indian Rodeo, pow-wow, and a Huckleberry Festival.

Yaqui

The Yaqui (YAH-kee) (meaning "chief river") actually refer to themselves as *Yoeme*. Like many tribes, they are known by the names others have given them, in this case Jesuit *missionaries [IV]* in the early 17th century. They spoke a dialect of the Uto-Aztecan language family and are classified in the Southwest cultural area.

Their original lands were in the northwestern Mexican state of Sonora but they have lived in southern and southwest Arizona since the late 19th century. Their population was estimated at 30,000 in 1533; tribal enrollment is about 10,000 today.

One of the first Europeans they encountered was Nuno de Guzman in 1533. By 1610, the Yaqui signed a treaty with Spain and found Jesuits establishing eight missions among them. The Yaqui staged a revolt in 1740 over land transgressions and missionary abuses by the Spanish, which was eventually put down.

At Easter, the Mexican and American Yaqui often celebrate a week-long Pascola Ceremony, which blends Catholic and native rituals and involves dancers in masks and deer costumes. One of the most important ceremonies of the year is the Waehma, or the reenactment of the Holy Week of Christ's final days. Today there are eight rancherias. The Yaqui have a constitution, established in 1988, and a tribal council. They received official government recognition in 1978.

Yokuts

The Yokuts (meaning "person") speak a California Penutian language. Their traditional lands were in the San Joaquin Valley and Sierra Nevada foothills. Today they live on two rancherias in Tulare and King counties in California. Their population was estimated at 50,000 in the early 18th century; today it has dwindled to 1,150 members.

They lived in pole-framed homes that were covered with tule mats and had raised beds of pine needles along the walls. Acorns were staples of the Yokuts diet. Cross-dressing men usually served as undertakers for the dead, who were generally cremated with their possessions. In Yokuts society, religious leaders derived power from animal spirits gained in dreams or vision quests.

Cholera and malaria epidemics in the 1830s killed three-fourths of the Yokuts in the region. After the United States annexed California in 1848, a campaign began to exterminate all Indians in the state. Tribes signed treaties with the federal government to cede their lands in exchange for reservations, but the state of California refused to ratify treaties and continued to pursue Indians. Some Yokuts ended up working on local ranches, others in forced-labor situations.

Yuchi

Yuchi (YOO-chee) means "those far away." They are classified as part of the Southeast cultural group and were culturally similar to the *Catawba*. Their language was a linguistic isolate but possibly related to the Siouan language.

Their ancestral lands were in eastern Tennessee, but today they live in Georgia, Florida, and South Carolina. Many Yuchi who stayed in Tennessee and North Carolina merged with the *Cherokee*. Others in Georgia joined the *Creek*, and some migrated to Florida with the *Seminole*.

One of the Yuchi's most important ceremonies was a three-day Corn Harvest Festival, since corn was a staple of their diet. They also traditionally named their babies on the fourth day of life.

One of their earliest contacts with Europeans was with Hernando de Soto in 1539. By the 19th century, however, the Yuchi no longer existed as a tribe since so many had combined with other groups. Their population has increased from 500 at the turn of the 20th century to about 1,500 today, although only 50 or so still speak the native language. In Oklahoma they have remained formally united with the Creeks but maintain their own stomping grounds and churches.

Yuma

The Yuma (YOO-muh) speak the Yuman language common to tribes in western Arizona and southeastern California. Their name comes from a *Tohono O'odham* word that means "people of the river." There are two tribal divisions: the Upland Yuman and the River Yuman. The Upland Yuman include the *Havasupai*, *Hualapai*, and Yavapai. The River Yuman include the *Mojave* and *Quechan*.

Their ancestral lands were in desert country near the Gila River, close to the present border between the United States and Mexico. There were an estimated 4,000 Yuma in the 16th century. Today they have about 3,000 members.

They lived in rectangular earth pit houses or domed brush huts. They fished and raised corn, beans, pumpkins, mesquite, beans, and tobacco. Both genders farmed. Sandals were their preferred footwear and clothing consisted of aprons or breechcloths. They still cremate their dead and burn their belongings and mark a four-day period of mourning. The Yuma believed it was possible to visit ancestors in dreams, and powerful dreamers often served as religious and political leaders. Dreams could also bestow healing and other powers on the dreamer. Song cycles, consisting of dreams and tribal mythology accompanied with shaking rattles and sticks, were used for curing, funerals, and celebrations. Girls had a four-day puberty rite, and boys had their noses pierced in a ceremony at age seven. Their allies were the Mojave, and they fought sporadically with the *Cocopah*, *Pee Posh*, and *Pima*.

Among the first Europeans they encountered was Hernando de Alarcón in 1540. The Jesuit priest Eusebio Francisco Kino visited them in 1698, and two missions were established in their territory by 1780. Until then, they had resisted Spanish power, and only ceded their control of a key river crossing in 1781. Later, the California gold rush brought an influx of whites passing through their territory. To control this passage, in 1852 the U.S. army built Fort Yuma and ended Indian resistance in the area. The Fort Yuma Reservation was established in 1883. Mandated allotments and lack of water rights left families with small lots they were unable to farm.

The Fort Yuma Reservation consists of 4,300 acres. Many Yuma also live on the 6,000-acre Cocopah Reservation, established in 1917 in Arizona. They adopted an Indian Reorganization Act Constitution in 1936.

The tribe has not yet won a single court case against powerful agricultural businesses and urban areas, including Los Angeles and Phoenix. Few people speak Yuma today.

Yurok

Yurok (YOUR-ock) is a Karuk word meaning "downstream." The Yurok speak the *Karuk* language, which is part of the Algonquian language group. With ancestral lands in northern California, the Yurok are the westernmost Algonquian speakers. Today, many live in Humboldt County. Their precontact population, estimated at 2,500, declined by 73 percent to 668 around 1910 before reaching the current number of 3,500. They exhibited many aspects of the Northwest cultural group, including eating salmon as a staple of their diet and dwelling in rectangular, cedar-planked homes.

Unlike some other tribes that didn't recognize private property, the Yurok owned land individually and recognized social status. Family wealth could be increased by limiting family size, which was limited by the practice of sexual abstinence.

The Yurok had some contact with the Spanish around 1775, but in 1826 British and American trappers began arriving in Yurok territory. The California gold rush in 1848 brought a further influx of white immigrants and miners, whose presence led to the virtual extermination of the Yurok and other California Indians. An 1851 treaty that promised a Yurok reservation was never ratified.

Today the tribe holds several small rancherias. In 1983, the Yurok won a ten-year legal battle over a sacred site in the Six Rivers National Forest of northern California.

Zuni

Zuni (ZOON-yee) is the name of both a pueblo and a people. They refer to themselves as *Ashiwi,* which means "the flesh." Zunian is part of the Penutian language group, unlike that of other *Pueblo* groups. They might be descendants of the *Mogollon [I]* and *Anasazi [I]* cultures.

Zuni territory is in the western region of New Mexico near the Arizona border, and is much diminished from what it once was. Zuni lands today occupy less than 3 percent of their original territories. Zuni pre-contact population was estimated as high as 20,000. Currently there are approximately 7,000 tribal members.

The Zuni lived in multistoried apartments connected by ladders. Unlike other pueblos, they were built of stone and plaster, not adobe

Zuni Pueblo, New Mexico. *National Archives.*

bricks like those used in pueblos to the east. Using dams and ditch irrigation, men raised six types of corn as well as beans, squash, and tobacco. The Zuni New Year began at the winter solstice, during which time they held a 20-day cleansing period known as *Itiwana.* Prayer sticks and cornmeal accompanied the four-day mourning ceremony.

One of the first Spanish missions north of the Rio Grande was established at Zuni in 1629. In 1680, they were drawn into a major revolt against the Spanish that united the Pueblo. The Spanish were driven from the area for years. In 1877, four tracts of federal trust lands were established in New Mexico and Arizona by executive order. In the 1890s, the United States undermined the Zuni traditional political system by jailing all Zuni Bow Priests and the Priestly Council.

Most Zuni today live in the old pueblo, which has been rebuilt as single-story houses. They adopted the Indian Reorganization Act in 1934 and ratified a constitution in 1970. Most Zuni speak English as a second language and continue to practice their tribal religion.

PART IV

Politics and Post-Contact History

Although this section is titled "Politics and Post-Contact History," the very words "post-contact" denote a European worldview. From a European point of view the arrival of Columbus may have been a turning point in global history, but archaeological and other research suggests that there had in fact been many previous migrations and ocean crossings—in both directions—between the Americas and other continents. The last 500 years in the Americas are a history of death and displacement but not of conquest and defeat. American Indians experienced a genocide, both physical and cultural, and loss of traditional sacred lands. Indians were not conquered and defeated, however; they did more than survive. Their culture and spiritual practices continue to thrive—to grow, evolve, and sustain future generations.

The colonial powers adopted different styles of occupation and control over the Indian peoples they encountered. The Spanish, for example, the earliest European colonizers, implemented the *encomienda* system in 1512, giving Spanish landowners the legal right to enslave Indians on their lands. By 1769, the Spanish had established a mission system in California that practiced forced labor, kidnappings, torture, sexual assault, and starvation.

Elsewhere on the North American continent, the French colonial economy at first revolved around the fur trade, rather than agriculture or mining. This type of economy depended on friendly relations with Indians who were relied upon as hunters, guides, and interpreters. French trappers often lived within tribes and intermarried at higher rates than groups such as the English who came over in family units. The fur trade also meant fewer French settlers, with a slower rate of population spillover from France, and fewer permanent settlements. These somewhat friendly relations led many tribes to side with the French against the British in conflicts, though most alliances were based on trading partnerships and geographical proximity.

Unlike the French and Spanish, the English came over as families early on and so had more interest in owning family farms. The English colonists generally wanted to live separately from Indian nations, rather than among them, and discouraged intermarriage. In the early years of the Virginia colony, the son of Pocahontas and John Rolfe even had trouble gaining permission from white authorities to visit his Indian relatives. There were fears that some colonists would flee to live in Indian tribes if they fraternized with them. In the South, Indians were kidnapped for enslavement on English plantations, and often rebelled against their oppressors. In an attempt to separate the two populations, an English proclamation in 1763 banned white settlements west of the Appalachians but was generally ignored by settlers.

With the coming of the American Revolution, Indian groups sometimes found their loyalties divided between Great Britain and her rebellious colonies. Most notably, divided loyalties caused the Six Nations of the Iroquois League to separate in 1777. From the beginning, Indians had been involved in fighting in colonial wars, for one European side or the other, though these actions rarely led to better treatment from their white allies. In 1778, the fledgling United States signed its first treaty with an Indian tribe, the Delaware. In it, the Delaware were promised state status and representation in Congress, although this promise never materialized. In the following decades, as the population of the newly independent nation began to expand, pressure for white settlement onto Indian lands began to grow. To clear up land for American settlers, the 1787 Northwest Ordinance called for the establishment of reservations for Indian tribes. For the first 60 years of U.S. history, from 1789 to 1850, the sale of appropriated Indian land accounted for 80 percent of federal revenues.

In 1803, the Louisiana Purchase, which extended United States land claims far beyond the Mississippi River, opened up the continent to white settlement and prompted some of the most tragic forced removals of Indians in American history. The federal government had begun plans to move eastern tribes west of the Mississippi as early as 1803. In 1817, Cherokee lands in Georgia were exchanged for lands in Arkansas Territory. By 1820, several thousand Cherokee had immigrated west into Arkansas.

Debates during the 1830s Indian removals set boundaries for Indians west of the Mississippi River. In 1830, Congress passed the Indian Removal Act, which mandated the removal of eastern tribes to Indian Territory west of the Mississippi. The Cherokee fought their case against removal successfully in the Supreme Court, but President Andrew Jackson ignored the Supreme Court and enforced the removal. The Five "Civilized" Tribes (Cherokee, Choctaw, Chickasaw, Creek, and Seminole) in the Southeast had adopted many aspects of European-American culture, including housing, legal codes, and educational systems. This did not stop the view that they were unassimilated when whites coveted their lands. The Five Civilized Tribes and others were force marched to what was supposed to be Indian territory forever—today, we know it as the states of Arkansas, Kansas, Nebraska, Colorado, Wyoming, and Oklahoma. As many as one in four died on what became known as the "Trail of Tears." (Some tribes were forcibly removed a second time in the 1870s to Oklahoma.)

Even farther west, the quest for gold led to reduced Indian populations, beginning with the 1848 California gold rush. Removals continued with Kit Carson leading one against the Navajo from 1860 to 1864. Carson burned all Navajo villages and force marched the Navajo to Bosque Redondo on what became known as the "Long Walk." Uprisings against this kind of forced removal continued in the Southwest with the Apache uprisings led by Mangas Coloradas and Cochise from 1861 to 1863.

During the Civil War, most Indian nations attempted to remain neutral. Many were divided in their loyalties, as they had been during the American Revolution. The Confederates, for example, held out the promise of statehood to those tribes that would support them. Just as after the American Revolution, regardless of which side they had supported, tribes were punished at the conclusion of the war by land confiscations and the destruction of villages.

After the Civil War, the U.S. military turned its full attention to the incarceration of all Indians on reservations. Battles over removal, trespassing, and further land reductions ensued. After a number of massacres such as the Sand Creek in 1864, white progressives joined prosettlement and expansionist advocates in calling for removal and reduced contact between whites and Indians. Most whites wanted access to land and resources regardless of treaty promises, although some white progressives were also concerned with the continuing atrocities inflicted largely by whites. In 1866–1868, the Lakota, led by chief Red Cloud, were successful in their battle to control construction of the Bozeman Trail through their lands. They were able to negotiate favorable terms in the 1868 Fort Laramie Treaty. The 1867 Treaty of Medicine Lodge resulted in the removal of the Cheyenne and Arapaho to reservations in Oklahoma on lands taken from the Five Civilized Tribes. The Fourteenth Amendment to the United States Constitution in 1868 gave African-American males the right to vote but excluded American Indians. In 1869, President Ulysses Grant implemented a peace policy aimed at preventing the violence whites inflicted on Indians by removing Indians to separate and remote lands.

In 1871, after 372 ratified treaties, Congress formally abolished the treaty process altogether. Later agreements did not recognize tribes as sovereign nations. During this time, Indians were forbidden to leave reservations without written permission from the local Indian agent. By 1881, white hunters also began eradicating the buffalo, a major food source for Plains tribes. By the late 1880s, fewer than 1,000 buffalo remained. The Cheyenne, Arapaho, Comanche, and Kiowa fought a war in an attempt to save the remaining buffalo herds from destruction in Oklahoma and Texas but were ultimately unsuccessful against the buffalo hunters, who were backed by the U.S. Army.

During this period of incarceration on reservations, some nations attempted to escape their disease- and starvation-ridden conditions. The Nez Perce, for example, led by Chief Joseph, fled more than 1,000 miles toward the Canadian border after refusing relocation; they were captured by the United States military within sight of the border and relocated to Oklahoma.

Like the Nez Perce, the once wide-ranging Lakota faced increased attempts to reduce their land holdings and confine them to land least desirable to whites. The 1868 Fort Laramie Treaty had guaranteed the Black Hills to the Lakota as part of their territory. After whites trespassed and discovered gold in the area, a war ensued that united the Lakota, Cheyenne, and Arapaho under Chiefs Crazy Horse and Sitting Bull. After winning a brief victory at the battle of the Little Big Horn against Custer's Seventh Cavalry in 1876, Sitting Bull fled to Canada and Crazy Horse was finally incarcerated on a reservation. Sitting Bull was eventually assassinated in 1890 while in police custody.

It was during this period of confinement on reservations that white reform groups began to organize. Groups such as the Indian Rights Association, the Women's National Indian Association, and the National Indian Defense Association were all formed around this time. Many of these groups supported the goals of assimilation and the allotment of tribal lands, since the prevailing view at the time was that traditional cultures and the possession of tribal lands were keeping Indians from progressing. To assimilate young Indians into white culture, Indian boarding schools were created. One of the first, Carlisle, opened in 1879 and became a model for others. In order to speed the process of assimilation, Carlisle forcibly removed young Indian children from their families. In 1887, Congress passed the General Allotment Act, which divided tribal lands among individual owners and sold the surplus land to whites. Tribes lost two-thirds of their lands under this act. The Great Sioux Reservation, for example, was divided into six smaller reservations, with the surplus lands sold to whites, and the establishment of the states of North and South Dakota followed.

During this time of disillusionment, assassination of leaders, incarceration on reservations, starvation, and further loss of lands, the Ghost Dance movement arose. The movement promised that ritual dancing would bring the return of the buffalo and ancestors. Fearing a general uprising, white authorities suppressed the movement and in 1890 soldiers at Pine Ridge Reservation killed more than 200 Ghost Dance followers in what became known as the Wounded Knee Massacre. For some, Wounded Knee became a potent symbol of the end of the "Indian wars" in the West. Eighty-three years later, American Indian activists returned to this site in a takeover and drew on its symbolic significance in American history to bolster their cause.

American Indians won the right to vote in 1924 when Congress passed the Citizenship Act. With Franklin Roosevelt's election, the policy of allotment ended and the 1934 Indian Reorganization Act endorsed the right to tribal self-government.

The decades after World War II saw the creation of a number of American Indian civil rights and other political organizations, a trend that had begun with the founding of the National Congress of American Indians in 1944. For the first time, too, these political movements and organizations were being founded by Indian leaders, activists, and intellectuals themselves, rather than by well-meaning white reformers. However, even as these new organizations were formed to defend and promote Indian causes and interests, American Indians were facing a new threat. In 1946, Congress established the United States Indian Claims Commission to settle all land claims, a first step in a tribe termination program. In 1950, the Bureau of Indian Affairs designed a program to relocate Indians from reservations to urban areas and then terminate the status of their tribes. In 1953, Congress passed the termination resolution, a plan to end the status of all tribes. Opposition by Indian groups to the planned termination mounted.

The American Indian Movement (AIM) was founded in Minneapolis, Minnesota, with an initial focus on urban Indian problems such as police harassment. AIM spread its reach to reservations when it responded in 1972 to the murder of Raymond Yellow Thunder by local whites in Gordon, Nebraska; and in 1975 AIM activists occupied Wounded Knee, South Dakota, for 71 days to draw attention to the corrupt activities of tribal chair Dick Wilson on the Pine Ridge Reservation. Numerous tribes struggled to regain their status throughout the 1980s and 1990s. When federal funding was cut in the 1980s, tribes turned to gaming, opening casinos on their tribal lands in attempts to create new sources for infrastructure financing and uphold tribal sovereignty.

At the beginning of the 20th century, the majority of whites had assumed that American Indians were a vanquished and vanishing race. When these predictions were made, American Indian population numbers were at their lowest point ever. Photographers and collectors hoped to establish exhibits in museums to remember a race that once existed on the continent. Their predictions were proven wrong. American Indian nations survived the 20th century, growing from under one-quarter million at the beginning of the century to nearly 2 million at its end. American Indian civil rights groups sparked a cultural renewal for thousands.

Many of the struggles Indians face today are connected to the heavy toll of poverty, such as high academic dropout rates and high incidence of substance abuse. But their struggles are also connected to the less tangible yet equally insidious role that covert and overt racism has played in their history and in their lives. As each generation continues to build upon the enormous sacrifices that elders made to bring us to the ground we are able to stand on, we share in a retelling of the past, significant struggles in our present, and an enduring hope in our future centered on our young people.

1894 *The United States Army imprisons Hopi leaders on Alcatraz Island.*

1896–1898 *The Klondike gold rush in Alaska and the Yukon Territory.*

1898 *The Curtis Act abolishes the tribal governments of the Five Civilized Tribes and extends allotment of tribal lands to Indian Territory (Oklahoma).*

1901 *Creek Indians, under the leadership of Chitto Harjo, resist allotment in the Snake Uprising.*

1902 *Typhus eliminates the Inuit population in Hudson Bay; the Reclamation Act helps whites gain land in the West by subsidizing water development.*

1904 *The federal government outlaws the Sun Dance.*

1906 *To create a national park, the federal government confiscates 50,000 acres of land in northern New Mexico, including the Blue Lake, which is sacred to Taos Pueblo Indians.*

1907 *Oklahoma is admitted as the 46th state.*

1909 *Two days before leaving office, President Theodore Roosevelt issues executive orders confiscating 2.5 million acres of Indian lands for national forests.*

1910 *The Bureau of Indian Affairs (BIA) establishes the first Indian Health Services facilities.*

1912 *Sauk and Fox tribal member Jim Thorpe wins the pentathlon and decathlon at the*

Olympic Games in Stockholm, Sweden. His medals are rescinded the next year because he played semiprofessional baseball one summer, but are reinstated in 1984 after intensive lobbying by his family and supporters.

1915 *The Bureau of Indian Affairs (BIA) is authorized by Congress to buy land for landless tribes in California.*

1917 *Federal subsidies for Indian education to religious groups are stopped; the Tohono O'odham (Papago) Indian Reservation in Arizona is the last reservation to be established by executive order.*

1918 *The Native American Church is incorporated in Oklahoma.*

1922 *The All-Pueblo Council forms to lobby on land issues. It is reunited after Spanish authorities squelched its existence in 1680; Cayuga Chief Deskaheh travels to Europe seeking recognition for his tribe at the international level from the League of Nations.*

1924 *Congress grants American citizenship to American Indians.*

1926 *The National Council of American Indians is founded.*

1928 *Kansas tribal member and U.S. Senator Charles Curtis is elected vice president of the United States under President Herbert Hoover; the Meriam Report issues a stinging critique of federal Indian policy, including allotment.*

Politics and Post-Contact History (continued)

1930 *The Northern Cheyenne Reservation is the last land to fall victim to allotment.*

1934 *The Indian Reorganization Act (IRA) ceases the policy of allotment and promotes the right to tribal self-government. The IRA constitution is adopted by 181 tribes; 77 tribes reject the IRA proposals in favor of traditional governance.*

1941–1945 *More than 25,000 American Indians serve in the armed forces during World War II. Navajo code talkers use their native language as a code that opposing forces are never able to break. More than 900,000 acres of Indian lands are taken for use as air bases, gunnery ranges, nuclear test sites, or internment camps for Japanese Americans.*

1944 *The National Congress of American Indians is organized in Denver, Colorado.*

1946 *The United States Indian Claims Commission is established by Congress to settle land claims.*

1948 *Courts order the state of Arizona to give Indians the right to vote.*

1950 *Dillon Meyer, former director of the Japanese-American relocation camp program during World War II, becomes head of the Bureau of Indian Affairs (BIA). He supports a program designed to relocate reservation Indians to urban areas and supports termination of tribes.*

1951 *The Canadian Indian Act gives indigenous people the right to vote.*

1953 *Congress repeals laws prohibiting the sale of alcohol to Indians; Congress passes the Termination Resolution, a plan to end the federal status of all tribes.*

1954 *The Menominee Termination Act is passed. The land claims settlement payment is withheld unless the Indians agree to termination; the state of Maine allows Indians to vote, one of the last to do so.*

1957 *The Seneca oppose construction of the Kinzua Dam and the proposed flooding of their lands.*

1958 *The Miccosukee of Florida resist the Everglades Reclamation Project, for which their lands would be confiscated.*

1961 *The American Indian Charter Convention in Chicago and subsequent National Indian Youth Conference (NIYC) usher in a period of increased activism; the Keeler Commission on Rights, Liberties and Responsibilities, headed by Cherokee Chief William Keeler, recommends support of tribal self-determination.*

1962 *The federal government forces New Mexico to allow Indians to vote in state elections; the Institute of American Indian Art is founded in Santa Fe, New Mexico.*

1964 *The National Indian Youth Council (NIYC) participates in the fish-in movement in Washington State to support the fishing rights of Indian tribes.*

1965 *Approximately 33,000 California Indians are compensated for the two-thirds of the state of California that they ceded. Each person receives approximately $900, or 47 cents an acre.*

1966 *The Alaska Federation of Natives is founded.*

1968 *The first tribally controlled college, the Navajo Community College, is established in Arizona.*

1968 *The American Indian Civil Rights Act restricts states from assuming jurisdiction on reservations and extends the Bill of Rights to reservation residents; the American Indian Movement (AIM) is founded in Minneapolis, Minnesota, with a focus on urban problems. It is modeled on the Black Panthers and first addresses the issue of police harassment; Mohawks in St. Regis, Ontario, protest to restore border crossing rights guaranteed in the Jay Treaty of 1795 by blocking the International Bridge between the United States and Canada.*

1969 *Vine Deloria, Jr., publishes* Custer Died for Your Sins.

1969–1971 *American Indian activists occupy Alcatraz Island to draw attention to the status of Indians.*

1970 *A sit-in takes place at the Bureau of Indian Affairs office in Washington, D.C., following a cross-country march.*

1970 *President Richard Nixon formally ends the termination policy that had been in effect for nearly 20 years.*

1970 *The sacred Blue Lake is returned to the Taos Pueblo in New Mexico.*

1971 *Kiowa tribal member N. Scott Momaday is awarded the Pulitzer Prize for his novel* The House Made of Dawn.

1971 *The Five Civilized Tribes lobby to regain the right to elect their own chiefs and government systems, a right that was suspended in 1902.*

1972 *The Alaska Native Claims Settlement Act reaches a financial settlement with Alaskan tribes.*

1972 *Raymond Yellow Thunder is beaten to death by local whites in Gordon, Nebraska. His death is ruled a suicide until the American Indian Movement (AIM) organizes more than 1,000 protesters to demand justice from local officials. Two of the killers are eventually convicted of manslaughter.*

1973 *The Menominee Restoration Act restores the tribe's federal status after intensive organization of the tribe led by Ada Deer.*

1974 *The Trail of Broken Treaties caravan travels cross-country from Alcatraz to Washington, D.C., just before federal elections to publicize Indian issues, then occupies the Bureau of Indian Affairs (BIA) office.*

1974 *The Navajo-Hopi Land Settlement Act seeks to resolve land disputes between the tribes by forcibly moving people onto separate land areas. This forces the relocation of more than 12,000 Navajo.*

1974 *Women of All Red Nations (WARN) founded by American Indian women activists, many of whom had also been members of the American Indian Movement (AIM).*

1974 *The International Treaty Council is founded to gain United Nations representation for indigenous people.*

1975 *The American Indian Movement (AIM) occupies Wounded Knee, South Dakota. AIM members undertake a 71-day siege to draw attention to corrupt tribal chair Dick Wilson and the murders occurring on the reservation in an atmosphere of civil war. A shootout on the Pine Ridge Reservation between AIM members and FBI agents results in the deaths of an Indian activist and two federal agents. Leonard Peltier is later convicted, but many view him as a political prisoner.*

1976 *One hundred eighty-five American Indian Movement members are indicted after the occupation of Wounded Knee. Dennis Banks and Russell Means are convicted on assault and riot charges. Banks goes into hiding.*

1978 *The Longest Walk is another cross-country walk from Alcatraz to Washington, D.C., to protest a new termination law under debate and the sterilization abuse of American Indian women; the American Indian Freedom of Religion Act offers First Amendment protection of Indian religious practices; the Indian Claims Commission ends. Tribes win awards in 60 percent of their claims. Future cases are handled in the Court of Claims; four Oklahoma tribes, the Ottawa, Modoc, Wyandotte, and Peoria regain their federal status. More tribes regain federal recognition throughout the 1980s and 1990s.*

1979 *The Council of Energy Resources Tribes is founded in Denver, Colorado, to protect tribal mineral rights.*

1984 *Jim Thorpe's Olympic medals are returned 29 years after his death in 1953.*

1985 *Wilma Mankiller becomes Principal Chief of the Cherokee Nation, the first woman to lead the largest tribe in the United States.*

1988 *The Indian Gaming Regulatory Act requires tribes that want to open casinos to negotiate with the states.*

1988 *The Termination Resolution passed by Congress in 1953 is officially repealed.*

1990 *The Native American Graves Protection and Repatriation Act protects American Indian grave sites and calls for the return of Indian remains and cultural objects to the tribes.*

1992 *Planned Columbus Quincentennial events are protested.*

1996 *The Native American Rights Fund files a class action lawsuit for mismanagement of tribal trust funds and 2.4 billion dollars*

Politics and Post-Contact History (continued)

unaccounted for by the Bureau of Indian Affairs.

1990 *The Centennial of the Wounded Knee Massacre is observed at Pine Ridge Reservation.*

1994 *The National Museum of the American Indian opens in New York.*

2001 *President George W. Bush awards the Navajo code talkers of World War II the gold Congressional Medal of Honor. Five code talkers appear to accept their medals, and twenty-four are awarded the medal posthumously.*

Alaska Federation of Natives

The Alaska Federation of Natives (AFN), a statewide native organization that represents regional corporations, was founded in October 1966 during a three-day meeting in Anchorage held to discuss Alaska Native Aboriginal land-rights issues. The AFN's original goal was to lobby for settlement of native land claims. This goal was achieved in 1971 when Congress passed the *Alaska Native Claims Settlement Act* (ANCSA). The AFN then focused on assisting indigenous people in their efforts to implement the ANCSA, and now continues to lobby on health, education, and environment issues.

Alaska Native Claims Settlement Act

Passed in 1971, the Alaska Native Claims Settlement Act (ANCSA) extinguished Indian land claims to most of Alaska in exchange for approximately one-ninth of the state's land plus nearly a billion dollars in compensation. Alaska, purchased by the United States from Russia in 1867, became the 49th state in 1959. Its valuable natural resources include large oil reserves.

ANCSA changed the relationship between Indians and the land from one of co-ownership of shared lands to one of corporate shareholding. In addition, the secretary of the Interior was authorized to withdraw unreserved lands from these corporations if he believed they might be suitable for inclusion in the national park, forest, wildlife refuge, or the wild and scenic river systems.

Passed by Congress and signed by President Nixon in 1971, the ANCSA accomplished three major goals. First, it provided native people with written title to nearly 44 million acres of land. Second, natives were compensated $962,500,000 to satisfy their claim to the rest of Alaska. The United States government paid $400 million over 11 years, while oil revenues contributed the remaining $562 million. Finally, the ANCSA established 13 regional corporations and 211 village corporations to manage the land and money. Nearly 80,000 natives were enrolled in ANCSA corporations, each receiving 100 shares of stock in regional corporations and another 100 shares of stock in village corporations. Critics of the act expressed concern that traditional tribal authority was supplanted with money-oriented corporations. In addition, the legislation resulted in the loss of millions of acres of land as well as hunting and fishing rights, although it did partially recognize the rights to land and to self-determination demanded by Alaskan groups.

Alcatraz Island occupation

On November 20, 1969, hundreds of American Indians began a 19-month occupation of Alcatraz Island, marking a critical shift in the activist movement. Before this event, Indian activism was tribal in nature, centered in small geographic areas, and focused on specific issues. The occupation strategy drew national and international media attention to the struggles of American Indians in the late 20th century.

The core group of original occupiers was composed of Indian students from throughout the state of California who called themselves Indians of All Tribes. They were supported by the Bay Area Indian community and were

---

IN THEIR OWN Words

Proclamation to the Great White Father and all his People:

We, the native Americans, re-claim the land known as Alcatraz Island in the name of all American Indians by right of discovery. . . . We will give to the inhabitants of this island a portion of the land for their own to be held in trust by the American Indian Affairs and by the Bureau of Caucasian Affairs to hold in perpetuity—for as long as the sun shall rise and the rivers go down to the sea. We will further guide the inhabitants in the proper way of living. We will offer them our religion, our education, our life-ways, in order to help them achieve our level of civilization and thus raise them and all their white brothers up from their savage and unhappy state. We offer this treaty in good faith and wish to be fair and honorable in our dealings with all white men.

We feel that this so-called Alcatraz Island is more than suitable for an Indian Reservation, as determined by the white man's own standards. By this we mean that this place resembles most Indian reservations in that: . . . it has no fresh running water . . . sanitation facilities are inadequate . . . no industry . . . no health care facilities . . . soil is rocky and unproductive . . . no educational facilities . . . the population has always been held as prisoners.

—PROCLAMATION OF ALCATRAZ INDIANS TO THE UNITED STATES, NOVEMBER 20, 1969.

soon joined by thousands of American Indians from across the country. Alcatraz, a maximum-security federal prison until 1963, had no electricity or running water—conditions that the occupiers pointed out existed on many *reservations*. The occupiers operated a school, newspaper, radio station, health clinic, and security force named the Bureau of Caucasian Affairs.

Alcatraz inspired 74 other occupations of federal facilities such as the *Bureau of Indian Affairs* (BIA) headquarters takeover in 1972, and the *Wounded Knee Occupation* in 1973.

After the Alcatraz occupation, the official United States government *termination policy* for Indian tribes was replaced by a policy of Indian self-determination. The occupation of Alcatraz was—and still is—seen as the start of the Red Power movement and remains a potent symbol of increased racial pride and consciousness for Indians today.

All-Indian Pueblo Council

In the 1500s, *Pueblo [III]* leaders formed an intertribal council soon after the Spanish invaded their lands. In 1922, the organization was revived as the All-Indian Pueblo Council (AIPC), an important Indian interest group. During the 1950s, the AIPC protested the federal government's termination and relocation policies.

The mission of the AIPC is "to promote justice and encourage the common welfare, to foster the social and economic advancement of all the Pueblo Indians, and to preserve and protect our common interest." The AIPC, headquartered in Albuquerque, is a consortium of the 19 Pueblo Indian tribes of New Mexico: Acoma, Cochiti, Isleta, Jemez, Laguna, Nambe, Picuris, Pojoaque, San Felipe, San Ildefonso, San Juan, Sandia, Santa Ana, Santa Clara, Santo Domingo, Taos, Tesuque, Zia, and *Zuni [III]*.

allotment (see Dawes Act)

American Indian Charter Convention

Founded on the premise that a group of people informed of their alternatives to action is able to choose what is best more wisely than outside expert advisors, the American Indian Charter Convention (renamed the American Indian Chicago Conference) formed to share information among the culturally and geographically diverse Indian peoples.

From June 13 through 20, 1961, more than 500 Indians representing 90 tribes and bands from across North America assembled on the Chicago University campus to combat the lack of public awareness of their status and the lack of opportunities for improving their condition. Many members of the group were younger students, frustrated with the pace of change pursued by older American Indian civil rights organizations such as the *National Congress of American Indians*. The Chicago group held a subsequent meeting in New Mexico that led to the founding of the *National Indian Youth Council*, a prominent Red Power group in the 1960s and 1970s.

American Indian Defense Association

The American Indian Defense Association (AIDA) was founded in 1923 by white reformers in order to lobby on issues such as Indian poverty rates and the lack of religious freedom for Indians. John Collier served as executive secretary of the group from 1923 until 1933.

AIDA was formed in response to the *Bureau of Indian Affairs'* (BIA) decisions in 1921 and 1923 to outlaw native dances and spiritual practices. Specifically, it grew out of the merging of a new group called the New Mexico Association on Indian Affairs with the older Indian Rights Association. Expanding their scope to form a national organization, the groups renamed themselves the American Indian Defense Association. AIDA supported freedom of Indian religion and culture, citizenship, and an end to allotment. Partly as a result of AIDA's advocacy, United States citizenship was granted in 1924 to American Indians (see *Citizenship Act*). Collier became the commissioner of Indian affairs under the administration of President Franklin Roosevelt in 1933. The following year he drafted the Indian Reorganization Act of 1934, which included constitutional guarantees of religious freedom for American Indians and the right to establish formal tribal governments. In 1936, it merged with the National Association of Indian Affairs to form the Association of American Indian Affairs.

American Indian Movement

The American Indian Movement (AIM) is a prominent Red Power group. It was founded in Minneapolis, Minnesota, in 1968 by a group of urban Indians, who modeled themselves after another power group of the 1960s, the Black Panther Party. A primary focus of AIM at the time was the issue of police harassment.

A spiritual and cultural movement, AIM requires no formal membership. Community activists George Mitchell, Dennis *Banks [II]*, and Clyde Bellecourt founded the AIM to discuss such critical issues as slum housing conditions, high unemployment rates, police brutality, lack of public education, and the welfare system. AIM now develops partnerships to focus on the fulfillment of treaties made with the United States government.

AIM grew rapidly, with branches in cities throughout the nation, and excelled at taking symbolic actions to draw media attention to various issues. In 1971, AIM occupied the *Mayflower* on Thanksgiving Day and buried Plymouth Rock under sand. In 1972, they briefly occupied *Bureau of Indian Affairs* headquarters in Washington, D.C. Around the same time, AIM began answering calls from families on *reservations*. Murders of American Indians by white people in border towns near reservations were often not prosecuted. AIM arrived en masse in small towns and demanded routine prosecution for these murders. AIM also responded to elders on the Pine Ridge Reservation who called for protection during a period of civil unrest on the reservation. Their response led to the 71-day Wounded Knee Occupation in 1973. By 1974, AIM began to promote the *International Indian Treaty Council* and continued to support local struggles regarding land and resources.

American Indian Policy Review Committee

Congress established the American Indian Policy Review Committee in 1975 in the wake of the 1973 *Wounded Knee Occupation*. The goal was to offer recommendations for the reform of existing Indian policy. A final 923-page report was submitted to Congress in 1977, in which the commission argued that tribal treaties should be enforced and relations should be based on international law, given their sovereign status. In all, 206 legislative and policy recommendations were offered. The *Indian Self-Deter-*

mination Act of 1975, the *American Indian Religious Freedom Act* of 1978, and the *Indian Child Welfare Act* of 1978 were based on the commission's recommendations. Issues presented made it clear that an ongoing legislative committee should be reestablished in the Senate. On April 28, 1983, Senator Mark Andrews, chair of the Select Committee on Indian Affairs, introduced Senate Resolution 127 to establish permanent status for the committee.

American Indian Religious Freedom Act

The American Indian Religious Freedom Act, originally passed in 1978, preserves the inherent right of American Indians to believe, express, and exercise the traditional religions of the American Indian, Eskimo, Aleut, and Native Hawaiians, including—but not limited to—access to sites, use and possession of sacred objects, and the freedom to worship through ceremonials and traditional rites.

American Indian religious ceremonies, dances, and the practices of medicine were routinely suppressed until the administration of President Franklin Roosevelt in 1934 reevaluated these policies. Access to sacred sites and state laws that prohibited the possession of peyote, used in some *Native American Church [I]* rituals, however, continue to present points of struggle.

In 1964, the California Supreme Court ruled in *People v. Woody* that constitutional freedom of religion should be extended to American Indians, a ruling that affected only those Indians living in California. The 1978 American Indian Religious Freedom Act did allow an expansion of religious freedom to American Indians. These rights continue to face court challenges. Notwithstanding these legal protections, many Indian communities continue to struggle to protect sacred sites from development.

American Revolution

Indian tribes were divided during the American Revolution among those who supported the British, those who supported the rebels, and those who attempted to remain neutral. After the revolution, even those who had been allies of the Continental army were treated unfairly by the new United

States government. Many argue that if the British had made full use of their Indian allies, they might have won the war.

At the time of the American Revolution, the British had established American boundaries through the Royal Proclamation of 1763 in order to prevent further European expansion and hopefully avoid conflict with Indian nations. Despite this, Americans frequently trespassed on Indian land.

The British formed an Indian Department in 1764. Just three months after the battle of Lexington in 1775, Americans organized their own Indian department, called the Committee on Indian Affairs. Both sides in the revolution originally encouraged neutrality among Indians, so they played a very minor role during the first year of fighting. But the following year, tribes were pressured to take part in military maneuvers on both sides.

Mohawk [III] Chief Thayendanega, known as *Joseph Brandt [II]*, was the most visible British ally during the revolution. Brandt had been schooled in colonial institutions, including Moor's Charity School, which later became Dartmouth College. Brandt had an audience with King George when

IN THEIR OWN Words

F riends! Listen to what I have to say to you! You see a great and powerful nation divided! You see the father fighting against the son, and the son against the father. The father has called on his Indian children to assist him in punishing his children, the Americans, who have become refractory. I took time to consider what I should do—whether or not I should receive the hatchet of the father to assist him. At first I looked upon it as a family quarrel, in which I was not interested. At length it ap-

peared to me that the father was right, that his children deserved to be punished a little. That this must be the case, I concluded, from the many cruel acts his offspring has committed from time to time against his Indian children, by encroaching on their lands, stealing their property, shooting at and even murdering, without cause, men, women, and children. Yes, even murdering those who, at all times, had been friendly to them. Look back at the murders committed by the Long Knives on many of our relations, who lived peaceably as neighbors to them on the Ohio. Did not they kill them without the least provocation? Are they now, do you think, better men than they were?

BUCKONGAHELAS (BUCKANGEHELA [BREAKER IN PIECES]), DELAWARE (LENAPĖ) CHIEF (?–C. 1804).
STATED AT MEETING WITH COMMISSIONER AT FORT PITT IN 1775.

he traveled abroad and was accepted into the Masons. Brandt's pro-British feelings stemmed from the fact that the royal court recognized *Iroquois [III]* land rights. Brandt was instrumental in convincing some Iroquois to support the British. Four of the six Iroquois nations sided with the British: the Mohawk, *Onondaga [III]*, *Cayuga [III]*, and *Seneca [III]*. The *Oneida [III]* and *Tuscarora [III]* sided with the Americans.

Mohawk, *Shawnee [III]*, and Leni *Lenape [III]* (Delaware) representatives traveled to the Southeast in 1776 to help the British win the support of southeastern tribes like the *Cherokee [III]*, *Creek [III]* (Muskogee), *Choctaw [III]*, and *Chickasaw [III]*. The Cherokee participation was limited to rare and isolated attacks, but in 1780, North Carolina used that as an excuse to invade Cherokee lands, destroy villages, and demand more land.

When the Treaty of Paris ended the American Revolution in 1783, the British made no arrangement for the tribes who had supported them. Some Indians moved to Canada. Others, including Joseph Brandt and his followers, were granted lands by the Canadian government on which to settle. The tribes who supported the Americans received no better treatment than those who sided with the British.

The American Revolution was a watershed for American Indians because it marked a change in white public policy toward Indian lands. After the war, Indians were no longer dealing with distant British rulers who were more supportive of limiting the expansion of settlers. From then on they would be confronted with the American government and its policy of Manifest Destiny.

Articles of Confederation

Until 1754, each of the 13 British colonies implemented its own Indian policy. A majority of tribes at the time supported the French, who were viewed as being more accepting of Indian cultures. The French were also considered to be primarily interested in acquiring furs while the British were interested in acquiring land. In 1754, the British government established northern and southern Indian departments under the direct supervision of the royal government, rather than under the authority of individual colonies. That move was meant to establish better relationships with Indian tribes. A superintendent was appointed for each of the two regions.

When the *American Revolution* began in 1775, the Continental Congress established a Committee on Indian Affairs modeled after the British system, except it had three departments: the northern, central, and southern. The northern department oversaw policy with the *Iroquois [III]* and all tribes to their north; the southern division was assigned the *Cherokee [III]* and all tribes to their south; and the central division covered all the tribes in between.

The English, French, and Dutch had all recognized Indian tribes as sovereign nations and entered into treaties with them to verify land purchases and gain favorable trade agreements. These treaties, however, were repeatedly broken by Europeans. The sovereign status of tribes was also challenged repeatedly by settlers and by state and federal governments, despite the British Royal Proclamation of 1763, which upheld the property rights of Indians to all lands west of the Appalachian Divide.

The Articles of Confederation implemented in 1781 affirmed that the federal government, rather than individual states, should regulate Indian affairs, and that their land should not be taken. The Office of Indian Affairs was established under the secretary of war in 1786 with superintendents of Indian Affairs serving under him.

The 1787 Northwest Ordinance reaffirmed the previous proclamation by the British. The federal Constitution, enacted in 1789, adopted the same principles regarding Indian policy. Indian policy was further codified in subsequent trade and intercourse acts passed by Congress from 1790 through 1834. Nevertheless, forcible removals of Indians from their lands continued and would culminate in the Indian *Removal Policy* of 1836 that would force march thousands of eastern Indian tribe members west of the Mississippi to what was supposed to be *Indian Territory* forever. Today, that territory is the state of Oklahoma.

Assimilative Crimes Act

The Assimilative Crimes Act passed by Congress in 1948 was one of the first termination laws designed to end the legal status of tribes. Specifically, it challenged traditional judicial processes within tribes.

The Assimilative Crimes Act makes state law applicable on Indian *reservations* within that state. However, violations of state law are put on trial in federal court, not state court. In addition to minor violations, the statute has been invoked to cover several serious criminal offenses defined by state law, such as burglary and embezzlement. Nevertheless, the Assimilative Crimes Act cannot be used to override other federal policies as expressed by acts of Congress or by valid administrative orders.

Bacon's Rebellion

In 1675, conflict arose when English settlers refused to pay a debt owed to the *Nanticoke [III]*. As reparation, the Nanticoke took some hogs from whites and were killed for doing so. Violence escalated as colonists murdered another 11 Nanticoke. The Virginia and Maryland militias also murdered 14 Susquehannock who were not involved in the original incident. The militias surrounded a Susquehannock village, and when five chiefs came forward under a flag of truce, soldiers killed them. An investigation into the massacre of the Indians led to only one fine imposed on one major.

Nathaniel Bacon, cousin of the governor of Virginia, joined a group of vigilantes who attacked the peaceful Occaneechi and Monacan communities as well as the Susquehannock. The governor excused Bacon with a warning. Bacon continued his rampage, however. In fact, he led an army of settlers to Jamestown and threatened to unleash violence there unless he was commissioned as commander in chief of the Indian war. As a side issue, he also demanded reforms on behalf of small farmers. The Virginia House of Burgesses was coerced into commissioning him as a commander in chief and they promised some small agricultural reforms on behalf of small farmers.

Bacon led his band of vigilantes in an attack against the Pamunkey band of *Powhatan [III]*. The Pamunkey fled to a swamp and offered no resistance but were massacred anyway.

The governor in Jamestown removed Bacon's commission, since it had only been granted under threat of violence. Bacon responded by bringing his group to Jamestown again. Bacon captured the city and put it to the torch. He died of tuberculosis a few months later. He left a grim legacy to colonial Virginia, as conflicts between the settlers and Indian tribes continued to serve as a convenient excuse for the massacre of Indians and confiscation of their lands.

Bannock Conflict

The Bannock Conflict was fought in Oregon and Idaho in 1878. It united the Bannock, *Cayuse [III]*, *Northern Paiute [III]*, and *Umatilla [III]* in a struggle against the United States. The war was sparked when the tribes' right to hunt and gather, guaranteed in a treaty, was challenged. Since the Indians were given inadequate government rations, the right to supplement their diet through hunting and gathering was crucial to their survival. Some foods, such as the camas root, were also central to cultural or spiritual practices, but pigs that belonged to the white ranchers in the area were drastically reducing the availability of camas root.

A group of 200 Bannock and Paiute rose up under the leadership of chief Buffalo Horn. When Buffalo Horn was killed in a clash with volunteer forces, the group was then led by a Paiute medicine man, Oytes, who had been preaching against whites. The group was pursued by the military throughout mountainous regions in southeastern Oregon and southern Idaho. Once the resisters were captured, the federal government punished them by terminating the Paiute reservation at Malheur. The prisoners were resettled at the *Yakama [III]* Reservation in Washington. The Bannock were eventually released and allowed to return to their reservation in Idaho.

Bascom Affair

After the Treaty of Guadelupe Hidalgo ended the Mexican War in 1848, American troops began arriving in *Apache [III]* territory. Relations remained largely peaceful until the army mishandled an incident in 1861 that sparked 35 years of Apache resistance. A white rancher wrongfully accused Apache leader *Cochise [II]* of theft and kidnapping. Lieutenant George Bascom took a force of 54 soldiers to Apache Pass and called Cochise to a meeting. Cochise arrived with his brother and two nephews. Bascom attempted to arrest the chief, but Cochise escaped. Bascom held the family members of Cochise as hostages. As a bargaining chip, Cochise took white hostages. When talks broke down, both sides killed their hostages, and a period of hostilities ensued. The Chiricahua, led by Cochise, soon joined the White Mountain and Mimbreno Apache headed by *Mangas Coloradas [II]*, Cochise's father-in-law.

The *Civil War* took priority for several years and reduced the number of troops stationed in the Southwest. After the Civil War ended, troops returned to the Southwest and turned their attention to the total suppression of the Apache.

Black Hawk Conflict (Black Hawk War)

The Black Hawk Conflict was the last white-Indian war fought in the Old Northwest. Problems began when Governor William Henry Harrison of Indiana negotiated unfairly with the Sac and *Mesquakie [III]* for their lands in 1804. A delegation of five chiefs, who had been inebriated with liquor and given gifts, signed a treaty that gave away all their lands east of the Mississippi, including large sections of Illinois and Wisconsin, for just $2,000 and an annuity in goods worth $1,000. In addition, the delegation that met with Harrison had lacked the tribal authority to negotiate.

Ma-ka-tai-me-she-kia-kiak, or Black Sparrow Hawk, called Black Hawk, was a Sac chief who had fought with *Tecumseh [II]* on the side of Canadians in the War of 1812. Like many Sac and Mesquakie, Black Hawk considered the 1804 treaty to be fraudulent.

In 1827, the federal government set about removing all Indians from Illinois. Black Hawk and his followers refused to leave their lands. Another Sac chief, Keokuk, and followers agreed to the removal.

Black Hawk. *Library of Congress.*

Governor John Reynolds gathered state militia and federal troops to remove Black Hawk, but when the troops arrived, the village was empty. The band had slipped across the Mississippi during the night. Support for Black Hawk grew among other bands.

During this time, White Cloud, a Ho-Chunk (Winnebago) prophet, preached against whites and garnered support for Black Hawk among the Ho-Chunk, *Potawatomi [III]*, and *Kickapoo [III]*. A series of skirmishes and battles followed over the next several months. Black Hawk was finally defeated and sent to Washington, D.C., at the request of President Jackson. He was imprisoned in Virginia for several months and released only on the condition that he recognize Keokuk as the sole chief of the Sac. Keokuk became wealthy by selling all tribal holdings except for 40 acres. Having

IN THEIR OWN Words

Had our fathers the desire, they could have crushed the intruders out of existence with the same as we kill the blood-sucking mosquitoes. Little did our fathers then think they were taking to their bosoms, and warming them to life, a lot of torpid, half-frozen and starving vipers, which in a few winters would fix their deadly fangs upon the very bosoms that had nursed and cared for them when they needed help.

From the day when the palefaces landed upon our shores, they have been robbing us of our inheritance, and slowly, but surely, driving us back, back, back towards the setting sun, burning our villages, destroying our growing crops, ravishing our wives and daughters, beating our papooses with cruel sticks, and brutally murdering our people upon the most flimsy pretenses and trivial causes.

You know the cause of our making war. It is known to all white men. They ought to be ashamed of it. The white men despise the Indians and drive them back from their homes. But the Indians are not deceitful. The white men speak bad of the Indian, and look at him spitefully. But the Indian does not tell lies. Indians do not steal. An Indian who is as bad as a white man could not live in our nation. He would be put to death and eaten by the wolves.

The white men are bad schoolmasters. They carry false looks and deal in false actions. They smile in the face of the poor Indian, to cheat him; they shake him by the hand to gain his confidence, to make him drunk, and to deceive him, to ruin his wife. We told them to let us alone, and keep away from us; but they followed on, and beset our paths, and they coiled themselves among us, like the snake. They poisoned us by their touch. We are not safe; we live in danger. We are becoming like them, hypocrites and liars; all talkers and no workers.

—BLACK HAWK (BLACK SPARROW HAWK; MA-KA-TAI-ME-SHE-KIA-KIAK; MAKATAIMESHIEKIAKIAK), SAUK (C. 1770–1838). IN *AUTOBIOGRAPHY OF BLACK HAWK AS DICTATED BY HIMSELF TO ANTOINE CLAIR*, WISCONSIN HISTORICAL SOCIETY, 1833.

lived long enough to see his tribe removed and their traditional lands overrun by whites, Black Hawk dictated his autobiography in 1833. He died in 1838. Vandals robbed his grave and used his head in a touring sideshow.

buffalo head nickel

Employing three different Indians as models, James E. Fraser designed the five-cent coin known as the buffalo head nickel, which debuted in 1913. Until that time, except for Bella Lyon Pratt's quarter and half eagle of 1908, Indians portrayed on U.S. coins were primarily Caucasians wearing Indian headdresses, epitomized by Augustus Saint-Gaudens's Greek Nike head on the 1907 Indian eagle. Fraser's design was considered an accurate portrayal of Indians as they looked. Fraser's portrait was a composite of three chiefs who posed for him. The bison was modeled after a buffalo named Black Diamond in the New York Zoological Gardens. Coins from the first bag to go into circulation were presented to outgoing President Taft and 33 Indian chiefs at the groundbreaking ceremonies for the National Memorial to the North American Indian at Fort Wadsworth, New York.

Bureau of Indian Affairs

The Bureau of Indian Affairs (BIA) oversees the federal government's relationship with more than 500 tribes and Alaskan communities. In various historical periods, the BIA has been referred to as the Indian Bureau, the Indian Office, the Indian Service, and the Indian Desk. For many American Indians, the history of the BIA has been one of forced acculturation, fraud, and mistrust.

In 1824, Secretary of War John Calhoun created a branch within the War Department called the Bureau of Indian Affairs. The bureau was to oversee treaty negotiations, Indian schools, and Indian trade. By 1840, the bureau and the United States military had removed more than 30 tribes to lands west of the Mississippi. There was widespread corruption at the time among the white Indian agents of the BIA. The BIA agents were supposed to distribute annuities to tribes, but often pocketed most of the income.

In 1849, Congress moved the Indian Office from the Department of War to the newly formed Department of the Interior. From 1850 to 1857, the bureau created the reservation system, in the process imposing white values and lifestyles upon the tribes.

Beginning in 1865, the bureau moved to dismantle tribal governments. *Seneca [III]* Ely *Parker [II]* was the first Indian to serve as commissioner of the bureau. In 1869, President Ulysses S. Grant turned over many administrative functions, such as running Indian schools, to religious organizations. Federal regulations in the 1870s demanded that the Indians perform manual labor in exchange for rations promised to them in treaties.

The 1887, the General Allotment, or *Dawes Act*, eradicated communal ownership of tribal lands. Lands were divided into individual parcels, with the "surplus" land open to white settlers. This policy reduced tribal landholdings by two-thirds. In the face of starvation, many individual allotments were sold. In 1900, the Office of Indian Affairs employed more than 4,000 people, of whom one-half were teachers. The BIA played an active role in suppressing any signs of Indian culture, such as their spiritual practices, dances, and music.

IN THEIR OWN *Words*

The white man has been the chief obstacle in the way of Indian civilization. The benevolent measures attempted by the government for their advancement has been almost uniformly thwarted by the agencies employed to carry them out. The soldiers, sent for their protection, too often carried demoralization and disease into their midst. The agent appointed to be their friend and counselor, business manager, and the almoner of government bounties, frequently went among them only to enrich himself in the shortest possible time, at the cost of the Indians, and spend the largest available sum of the government money with the least ostensible beneficial result.

—COLONEL ELY SAMUEL PARKER (DEIONINHOGAWEN, DONEHOGAWA; HA-SA-NO-AN-DA), MIXED SENECA CHIEF AND FIRST INDIAN COMMISSIONER OF INDIAN AFFAIRS (1828–C. 1895). 1864 MEMORANDUM ON INDIAN PROBLEMS TO PRESIDENT GRANT.

In 1928, the Meriam Report highlighted the dire situation of American Indians. (The report was named after one of the social scientists who headed the study, Lewis Meriam.) During the Roosevelt administration, John Collier headed the BIA. Under Collier's administration, the allotment of Indian lands was stopped, and Indian education programs were strengthened. The United States passed the 1933 Indian Reorganization Act (IRA) with the aim of restoring political decision making to tribes.

Some nations chose to retain their traditional ways of exercising authority but many tribes felt pressured to adopt the IRA system of government, a model that closely followed that of the United States government. In 1934, the BIA implemented a policy of preference for hiring Indians within its own ranks.

In the 1950s, the federal government decided to end its relationship with the tribes. More than 100 tribes were forcibly disbanded when the federal government formally ended their status. Thousands of people were relocated from reservations to urban areas in order to speed the termination process. Dillon Meyer, who had implemented the Japanese internment camps during World War II, served as head of the BIA during this time.

The BIA's policies and its support for some tribal chairs who were dictatorial in their governing became a focus of protest among Red Power groups in the 1960s and 1970s. By 1980, American Indians constituted 78 percent of BIA employees.

Today, more than 30 tribes have total control over their complete agenda of programs due to the Tribal Self-Governance Demonstration Project Act, passed in 1991. If this trend continues, the role of the BIA may be greatly reduced in the future.

Bureau of Indian Affairs Adult Vocational Training Program

The Division of Job Placement and Training is responsible for the bureau's Job Placement Program (adult vocational training and direct employment programs). Public Law 102-477, the Indian Employment, Training, and Related Services Demonstration Act passed in 1972, is designed to reduce joblessness in Indian communities.

Public Law 102-477 is intended to assist adult American Indian and Alaska Native people to obtain job skills and to find and retain jobs leading to self-sufficiency. Tribes are encouraged to provide services directly. The secretary of the Interior, in cooperation with the secretaries of labor and health and human services, can allow a tribal government to consolidate certain federally funded employment, training, and related services into a single fully integrated program. Integration provides greater flexibility in the delivery of services.

burial grounds

The Native American Graves Protection and Repatriation Act (NAGPRA) of 1990 is the primary federal legislation pertaining to Indian graves and their human remains in archaeological contexts. In the 1970s and 1980s, American Indian activists pushed for the return of Indian cultural artifacts and the remains of dead Indians. Hundreds of thousands of Indian skeletons had been collected by whites over the centuries, many at a time when the purpose of their study was to prove Indians' racial inferiority.

As many as 600,000 American Indian remains are still held in universities, museums, historical societies, and private collections in the United States, and another 2 million are held worldwide. Many more artifacts are uncovered each year, and many of these Indian finds are obtained illegally. Nearly all cultures attach a spiritual quality to their ancestors, and American Indians are no exception.

Drawing of an Indian burial ground. *National Archives.*

In 1868, the surgeon general of the United States ordered a study of American Indian crania in order to document Indians' racial inferiority. More than 4,000 crania were collected and eventually transferred to the Smithsonian National Museum of American History. This collection comprises the largest single collection of American Indian remains in the United States. Eleven thousand bodies are also held at the University of California.

NAGPRA provides priorities concerning the ownership or control of Native American cultural items that are excavated or discovered on federal or tribal lands after the date NAGPRA was enacted. NAGPRA further requires all museums to make an inventory of such items, stipulating that geographical and cultural affiliation be identified, if possible. In addition, upon request from a tribe, museum, or federal agency, the museum should provide documentation and repatriate materials, if appropriate.

Native American human remains, graves, and ritual objects located on federal and tribal land are protected. In cases where in-place preservation is not possible, or if archaeological excavation is necessary for planning or research, or if the remains are inadvertently discovered, consultation is necessary prior to excavation under Archaeological Resources Protection Act permits. If remains covered by the law are discovered, the project is stopped for 30 days while a review and consultation process take place.

Burke Act

The *Dawes Act* of 1887 allotted Indian land, divided tribal holdings among individual Indians, and sold the surplus to whites. The act offered a limited safeguard in the form of a 25-year trust period over allotted lands, which meant that individual Indian landholders could not sell their lands or use the lands as collateral for loans for the duration of the trust. Less than 20 years later, South Dakota Congressman Charles Burke sponsored the 1906 Burke Act, a modification of the Dawes Act, which declared American Indians competent to dispose of their own property, with approval of the Department of the Interior. The result was that the act accelerated the pace of the loss of Indian lands.

IN THEIR OWN Words

The white man does not understand the Indian for the reason that he does not understand America. He is too far removed from its formative processes. The roots of the tree of his life have not yet grasped the rock and soil. The white man is still troubled with primitive fears; he still has in his consciousness the perils of this frontier continent. . . . He shudders still with the memory of the loss of his forefathers upon its scorching deserts and forbidding mountaintops. The man from Europe is still a foreigner and an alien. And he still hates the man who questioned his path across the continent.

—LUTHER STANDING BEAR, OGLALA LAKOTA CHIEF (1868–1939).
IN *MY PEOPLE, THE SIOUX* BY CHIEF STANDING BEAR, HOUGHTON MIFFLIN, 1933.

Canada's Office of Native Claims

The Supreme Court of Canada, in 1973, established the Office of Native Claims to negotiate the validity of land claims. Comprehensive land claims are based on the assertion of continuing aboriginal title to lands and natural resources, and settlements are negotiated to clarify the rights of ab-original groups to lands and resources in a manner that will facilitate their economic growth and self-sufficiency. Settlements are intended to ensure that the interests of aboriginal groups in resource management and environmental protection are recognized and that claimants share in the benefits of development. These rights and benefits usually include: full ownership of certain lands in the area covered by the settlement; guaranteed wildlife harvesting rights; guaranteed participation in land, water, wildlife, and environmental management throughout the settlement area; financial compensation; resource revenue sharing; specific measures to stimulate economic development; and a role in the management of heritage resources and parks in the settlement area.

Canadian Indian Act

Both Canadian and United States Indian policy was modeled on that of the British, but Canadian policy remained closer to the original model. The British Royal Proclamation of 1763 demanded tribal consent for land acquisitions. The terms *aboriginal* and *native* or *First Nations* are more commonly used in Canada than the term *Indian*.

Canada's Indian Act of 1868 gave individuals or bands of natives the right to gain enfranchisement as Canadian citizens in exchange for giving up their tribal status. Status women who married nonstatus men automatically lost their tribal status. Status men, however, did not lose their tribal status upon marriage to nonstatus women. Many Canadian Indians did choose to become citizens and thus forfeited their tribal membership. The effect of the act was a further disruption of tribal life and diminished tribal population numbers.

Canadian White Paper

Members of Canada's parliament Jean Chretien and Pierre Trudeau delivered the infamous 1969 White Paper that shocked Indians out of a political sleep. In the White Paper, Trudeau insisted that the Indian Affairs Department and special status for Indians should be abolished in the name of a just society. The Red and Brown Papers produced by Indians in response to the White Paper, along with an absence of government policy after the failure of the White Paper (shelved in 1970), solidified the framework of the system controlling Indian lives in Canada today.

Carlisle Indian School

The Carlisle Indian School was opened in 1879 on an abandoned military base in Carlisle, Pennsylvania. By 1900, more than 1,200 students had enrolled from 79 tribes. Carlisle was the first nonreservation boarding school established by the federal government. Before the establishment of federal Indian schools such as Carlisle, Congress had provided funds to religious schools for Indian education.

The first director of Carlisle, Richard Henry Pratt, was an army officer who had previously run an Indian prisoner-of-war camp in St. Augustine, Florida. Many Indian reformers believed that education would "civilize" and assimilate the Indians. As Pratt stated, the goal of Carlisle was to "kill the Indian and save the man." Students were taken to boarding schools by force or under the threat of having their annuities withheld. Young children were shipped to other states in order to remove them from the "bad" influences of their families and traditional Indian ways. Many

Students in a metalworking shop at the Carlisle Indian School, circa 1904. *Library of Congress.*

children attempted to run away from those institutions; some died in the attempt.

Boys were taught mechanical and agricultural skills; girls were taught sewing, cooking, and laundry. Some boys also learned vocational training in trades such as blacksmithing, carpentry, and masonry. Students were not allowed to return home during the summers but were placed in white homes, where they performed manual labor.

At Carlisle, students dressed in military uniforms and were not permitted to speak native languages. Other schools modeled on Carlisle opened in the 1880s, and included Haskell, Chilocco, and Chemawa. By the end of the decade, 153 federal Indian schools were in operation. Students who were trained in the industrial schools, however, were usually unable to find employment in white society, so many returned to their reservations, where there were few job opportunities.

The Carlisle school was closed in 1918 and the facilities were returned to the army. Reliance on schools operated directly by the Bureau of Indian Affairs (BIA) diminished in subsequent decades following the 1928 publication of the Meriam Report on the status of Indians and reform initiatives following President Franklin Roosevelt's New Deal Administration.

Cheyenne Arapaho War (see Sand Creek Massacre)

Citizenship Act

On June 2, 1924, Congress authorized the secretary of the Interior to issue, under the Snyder Act, certificates of citizenship to all Native Americans born in the United States. Some supporters viewed the granting of citizenship as a first step in legally terminating tribal status. However, it did not provide full protection under the Bill of Rights to Indians living under tribal governments. Assuming guardianship over Native American reservations within their borders, states could still suppress Indian rights. Several Indian Nations, including the *Hopi [III]* and the *Iroquois [III]*, declined citizenship in favor of retaining sovereign nationhood. Chief Clinton Rickard of the *Tuscarora [III]* Nation Territories expressed the feeling of many Indians at the time, when he asked, "How can you be a sovereign nation and be forced to be a citizen in a foreign government?" For some Indians, citizenship implied the loss of tribal status as sovereign nations; for others it implied the long-overdue right of U.S. citizenship to America's first inhabitants and the veterans of every war since the *American Revolution.* According to the latest estimates by the U.S. Census Bureau, there are approximately 2,448,000 American Indians, Aleuts, and Eskimos living in the United States today, the majority of whom are U.S. citizens.

Civil Rights Act of 1964

The 1964 Civil Rights Act was a landmark legislative attempt to improve the quality of life for African Americans and other minority groups. Although civil rights had a long history as a political and legislative issue in the United States, the 1960s marked a period of intense activity by the federal government to protect minority rights. The act did not resolve all problems of discrimination but did open the door to further progress by lessening racial restrictions on the use of public facilities, providing more job opportunities, strengthening voting laws, and limiting federal funding of discriminatory aid programs. An exemption was given to American Indian tribes so that preferential employment might be extended to Indians in the *Bureau of Indian Affairs.*

Title IV of the Civil Rights Act of 1964 called for a survey "concerning the lack of availability of equal educational opportunity by reason of race, color, religion, or national origin in public educational institutions at all levels." Following this act, sociologists James S. Coleman of Johns Hopkins University and Ernest Q. Campbell of Vanderbilt University studied 600,000 children at 4,000 schools. The results, known as the Coleman Report, were released in 1966. The report found most children attended schools where they were the majority race. It also found that minority children were academically a few years behind the whites and that the gap widened by the high school years. Most provocative, however, were the findings that poor minority children did better academically in integrated middle-class schools.

Coleman's work had a far-reaching impact on government education policy. The following year, another study conducted by the Civil Rights Commission, *Racial Isolation in the Public Schools,* confirmed Coleman's findings. The government introduced a policy of affirmative action to racially integrate schools and to end de facto segregation produced by income level and neighborhood ethnic composition. A result of the policy was busing school children to schools outside their neighborhoods. The objective was to achieve racial balance among schools by preventing black and minority enrollment from exceeding 60 percent.

Title I of the act barred unequal application of voter registration requirements but did not abolish literacy tests. Title II outlawed discrimination in hotels, motels, restaurants, theaters, and all other public accommodations engaged in interstate commerce; private clubs were excluded. Title III encouraged the desegregation of public schools and authorized the United States attorney general to file suits to force desegregation. Title IV authorized, but did not require, that federal funds be withdrawn from programs that practiced discrimination. Title V outlawed discrimination in employment in any business exceeding 25 people and created an Equal Employment Opportunities Commission to review complaints.

Civil War

Approximately 20,000 Native Americans served in the Union and Confederate armies during the Civil War. By supporting the war effort, Native

An 1871 Thomas Nast cartoon satirizing contemporary attitudes about Indians' political rights within the United States. *Library of Congress.*

Americans hoped to gain favor with the prevailing government in whose territory they found themselves. They also saw war service as a means to end discrimination and relocation from ancestral lands to western territories. Instead, while the war raged and African Americans were proclaimed free, the United States government continued its policies of pacification and removal of Native Americans.

The *Cherokee [III]* Nation was one of the most negatively affected of the American Indian tribes during the Civil War. Its population declined from 21,000 to just 15,000 between 1861 and 1865. In 1861, the Cherokee Nation was divided, with one side led by Principal Chief John Ross and the other by renegade Stand Watie. Although Ross vowed to remain neutral, the federal government abandoned *Indian Territory* early in the war, leaving the area vulnerable to Confederate occupation. In their place, Confederate troops arrived and promised protection for the Indians and tribal representation in the Confederate Congress, something denied them by the United States federal government. Although the majority of the full bloods among the Cherokee, *Creek [III]*, and *Seminole [III]* initially favored neutrality, on October 7, 1861, Ross reluctantly signed a treaty with the Confederate States with the understanding that no Indian regiment would be called to fight outside Indian Territory. The same year, the *Chickasaw [III]*, *Choctaw [III]*, Creek, *Osage [III]*, *Quapaw [III]*, Seminole, *Seneca [III]*, *Shawnee [III]*, and *Wichita [III]* also signed treaties of alliance with the Confederacy.

(In addition to the promise of tribal representation, the Confederacy may have held another appeal for Southern Indian tribes: with the exception of the Seminole, many of those tribes had slave owning traditions.)

Three Indian regiments fought for the Confederacy: the Choctaw-Chickasaw, Creek-Seminole, and Cherokee regiments. Two regiments fought with the Union, including a Cherokee regiment. In all, more than 10,000 Indian troops participated in the Civil War.

The defeat of Confederate troops at the Battle of Pea Ridge in Arkansas on March 7–8, 1862, opened the way for Union troops to move back into Indian Territory. Following the battle, Ross defected to the Union forces in Kansas. In the summer of 1862, federal troops captured Ross and paroled him. In his absence, Colonel Stand Watie was chosen principal chief of the Cherokee Nation, and he immediately drafted all Cherokee males aged 18 to 50 into Confederate military service. Watie was considered a genius in guerrilla tactics and the most successful field commander in the Trans-Mississippi West.

In Virginia and North Carolina, the Pamunkey and *Lumbee [III]* chose to serve the Union; the Lumbee, in particular, fought against being drafted by the Confederates. The Pamunkey served as civilian and naval pilots for Union warships and transports, while the Lumbee acted as guerrillas. In 1864, a Lumbee teenager named Henry Berry Lowry formed a guerrilla band of Lumbee and African Americans who raided plantations and distributed goods to the poor. Members of the *Iroquois [III]* nations joined Company K, 5th Pennsylvania Volunteer Infantry, while the *Powhatan [III]* served as land guides, river pilots, and spies for the Army of the Potomac.

The most famous Native American unit in the Union army in the East was Company K of the First Michigan Sharpshooters. They were assigned to the Army of the Potomac just as General Ulysses S. Grant assumed command.

With military units fighting in the East, some tribes in the West revolted in attempts to repossess lands. With the absence of federal troops, some state governments organized local militia units to deal with American Indians. These units were often less disciplined and more violent than the army, resulting in events like the Sand Creek Massacre of 1864.

At the end of the war, Seneca tribe member General Ely S. *Parker [II]* drew up the articles of surrender that General Robert E. Lee signed at the Appomattox Court House on April 9, 1865. Parker, a trained lawyer who was once rejected for army service because of his race, served as General Ulysses S. Grant's military secretary. At Appomattox, Lee allegedly remarked to Parker, "I am glad to see one real American here," to which Parker replied, "We are all Americans."

At the end of the war, outlaw gangs roamed throughout Indian Territory, killing, burning, and looting, decimating one-fourth of tribal populations in Indian Territory and devastating local economy. However, the federal government voided its treaties with the tribes and demanded that western land be ceded to the United States.

Coeur d'Alene Conflict (Coeur d'Alene War)

The Coeur d'Alene Conflict of 1858 occurred in the Washington and Idaho territories and can be viewed as a continuation of the *Yakama [III]* "War" fought in 1855 that involved a number of Plateau tribes, including the Yakama, *Cayuse [III]*, Columbia, Palouse, *Umatilla [III]*, and Walla Walla. Since the 1855 conflict, Chief Kamiakin of the Yakama had been calling for an alliance of Plateau tribes because of the repeated pattern of trespassing, forced treaties, and land cessions to whites. The encroachment of miners was a particular grievance. The Northern *Paiute [III]* and *Spokan [III]* joined the *Coeur d'Alene [III]* in the 1858 rebellion, sometimes referred to as the Spokan war because of that tribe's heavy involvement.

The so-called war consisted of three battles between the united Indians and the United States military. The first battle took place when 164 federal soldiers from Fort Walla Walla marched into *Indian Territory*. They were met by 1,000 Coeur d'Alene, Spokan, and Palouse, who were able to repel the troops. Another force of 600 soldiers was sent with instructions to capture chief Kamiakin and his family. In the subsequent two battles fought on open fields, the tribes suffered high casualties and retreated to their villages. The army made its way through Indian land and rounded up any dissidents it could find. Fifteen Indians were hanged and others were jailed. The son of Kamiakin was shot while in captivity, although Kamiakin himself managed to escape into Canada. Rebellions in the area would continue, culminating in the *Nez Perce [III]* uprising in 1877.

Commission on Indian Reservation Economies

On January 17, 1983, President Ronald Reagan formed a Commission on Indian Reservation Economies, which recommended shifting away from tribal goals and waiving tribal immunity in certain lawsuits. The committee's nine members came from the private sector, reservation tribal governments, economic academicians, and federal employees. Reagan also designated both a non-Indian representative and an Indian representative to serve as co-chairs.

The commission's purpose was to advise the president on developing a stronger private sector on federally recognized Indian reservations, lessening tribal dependence on federal monies and programs, and reducing the federal presence in Indian affairs. In carrying out its responsibilities, the commission was authorized to conduct hearings, interviews, and reviews at field sites and to confer with Indian tribal government officials and members, as well as private sector business officials and managers.

The commission focused on defining and removing the existing local, state, and federal legislation and obstacles that interfered with the creation of positive economic environments on Indian reservations. It also
recommended ways for the private sector, both Indian and non-Indian, to
participate in the development and growth of reservation economies, including capital formation.

Committee of One Hundred

The first eruption in public opinion of government schools, which set the
Bureau of Indian Affairs (BIA) reform in motion, was the report from the
Committee of One Hundred. One hundred people concerned about Indian affairs met in Washington, D.C., in 1923 and issued a report the following year.

The report covered the whole field of Indian affairs but gave particular attention to educational needs. It recommended increased federal appropriations for the appointment of competent personnel, provision of
adequate school facilities, increased Indian enrollment in public schools,
and scholarships to high schools and colleges for Indian individuals.

The immediate reaction of the bureau was to increase Indian public
school enrollment and revise its course of study to parallel more closely
the public school curriculum. Day schools on reservations were extended
to include six grades, boarding schools to include eight grades, and
nonreservation boarding schools through high school. At the time of the
report, the Haskell Institute was the only government school offering work
above the eighth grade; by 1925, three other schools were offering high
school courses and by 1929, the number grew to six.

As some educators pointed out, the extension of grades did not raise
school standards; vocational training was mediocre; and the course of study
still was not related to Indian needs.

Constitution

American Indians are the only ethnic group specifically mentioned in the
United States Constitution. The Constitution acknowledged the jurisdic-

tion of the federal government over state and local governments in the area of Indian affairs in Article 1, Section 8.

During the years that the Articles of Confederation were in effect, from 1781 to 1789, state governments tried to implement their authority over Indian populations and lands within their boundaries. The framers of the Constitution reverted to a version of the British philosophy, namely that a consistent federal policy, not different state policies, was the best approach to dealing with Indian nations. States could not enter into treaties with foreign governments or pass taxes on other states, nor could they do so with Indian nations.

The Constitution went into effect in 1789, although Indians were not considered citizens of the United States until 1924. In addition, under Article 1, Section 2, of the Constitution, Indians living under tribal authority could not be counted in population numbers that determined the number of representatives in the House of Representatives.

Council of Energy Resource Tribes

The Council of Energy Resource Tribes (CERT) was founded in 1976 by the leaders of 25 tribes to chart a new course of informed resource development that would include tribal priorities and values.

Historically, the federal government had dominated resource management of Indian lands. While these lands contained some of the continent's richest natural resource regions, their Indian populations remained impoverished due to federal mismanagement of leases. CERT's leaders restructured the federal-Indian relationship regarding mineral development on Indian lands and forged alliances and partnerships with industry. Up to 40 percent of uranium, 33 percent of coal, and 5 percent of oil and natural gas resources in the United States are located on American Indian reservations.

The resources of most Indian nations are developed under long-term leases negotiated by the *Bureau of Indian Affairs* at below market prices. CERT has tried to keep nations informed of the true value of their resources. CERT has also been involved in researching federal mismanagement of federal trust responsibility to Indian tribes and federal energy and environmental policy.

Dawes Act

The Dawes Act of 1887, also known as the General Allotment Act, caused tribes to lose two-thirds of their lands in less than 50 years. The act was named after its sponsor, Massachusetts Senator Henry Dawes. Ironically, the act was intended by white reformers to prevent violence against Indians. As long as tribes held land, the argument went, whites would continue to commit acts of violence against the Indians. Instead, through allotment, Indian tribal lands would be broken into individual small farm allotments to enrolled members. Essentially, the act permitted whites to gain Indian lands through "legal" means rather than violence. Allotment was imposed on tribes; many resisted but were eventually forced to comply.

Settlers, land speculators, and white reform Indian rights organizations all supported the act. The goal of the act was to eliminate tribal government and tribal cultures and to push full assimilation onto Indian communities and individuals. The "surplus" lands could then be opened to white settlement. More than half the tribal lands, over 60 million acres, was sold as "surplus" land.

Allotment was supposed to encourage Indian farming but it actually had the opposite effect. In 1910, there were more than 3.1 million acres of Indian farms in Oklahoma and the 10 other states in which most allotments were issued. By 1930, those lands had declined to less than 2.4 million acres.

Initially, the act called for 160 acres to be allotted to heads of families and 80 acres to be allotted to single adults. Since reformers felt that Indians could not handle their own affairs, they placed restrictions on the use and disposal of the lands. Specifically, the allotted land was to be held in trust by the government for 25 years. In other words, during the 25-year period, allottees could not lease, sell, or will their lands. At the end of that time, allottees would hold title and be free to sell their lands. As a result, they could not get bank loans and Indian farmers had no access to credit for necessary improvements or new machinery. In poverty, two-thirds of the Indians ended up selling their lands at the end of the 25 years.

An 1891 amendment passed by Congress reduced allotments to 80 acres for each adult and allowed the commissioner of Indian affairs to lease allotments to white farmers. Later amendments allowed tribal members to lease their 80 individual acres to white farmers or mining, ranching, and timber companies, although these leases seldom reflected their fair market values.

The *Burke Act* of 1906 allowed the commissioner of Indian affairs to declare allottees competent to manage their own affairs before the 25-year time period; however, it also allowed the commissioner to extend the period of guardianship beyond 25 years.

The *Five Civilized Tribes* had lobbied to gain an exemption from the original Dawes Act. However, the Curtis Act, passed in 1898, abolished their tribal governments and began allotment of their lands. They resisted that by every possible avenue, including taking their case to federal court, but were ultimately defeated.

Many tribes tried to retain "surplus" lands not allotted to individuals. In 1903, Lone Wolf, a *Kiowa [III]*, filed a lawsuit to block the sale of surplus lands on the reservation without tribal consent. The courts ruled that the federal government did not need tribal consent, no matter what previous treaties had mandated.

IN THEIR OWN *Words*

*S*uppose the federal government should send a survey company into the midst of some of your central counties of Kansas or Colorado or Connecticut and run off the surface of the earth into sections and quarter sections and quarter sections and set apart to each one of the inhabitants of that country 60 acres. Rescinding and annulling all title to every inch of the earth's surface which was not included in that 60 acres, would the State of Connecticut submit to it?

Under our old Cherokee regime I spent the early days of my life on the farm up here of 300 acres, and arranged to be comfortable in my old age; but the allotment scheme came along and struck me during the crop season, while my corn was ripening in full ear. I was looking forward to the crop of corn hopefully for some comforts to be derived from it during the months of the winter. When I was assigned to that 60 acres, and I could take no more under the inexorable law of allotment enforced upon us Cherokees, I had to relinquish every inch of my premises outside of that little 60 acres. And I am here today, a poor man upon the verge of starvation— my muscular energy gone, hope gone. I have nothing to charge my calamity to but the unwise legislation of Congress in reference to my Cherokee people.

—DeWitt Clinton Duncan, Cherokee, 1906 testimony before a Senate committee about allotment.

The Alaska Allotment Act of 1906 extended the Dawes Act to Alaska, but land in Alaska was so poor that 160-acre farms were too small to support agriculture. As a result, whites in Alaska had little interest in acquiring the land.

Some reservations were able to avoid allotment, including lands in New York that were subject to state law and densely populated reservations in Arizona and New Mexico, where little surplus land was left for whites after allotments to individual tribal members. Reservations were abolished entirely, however, in what became the state of Oklahoma.

Once a tribe was designated for allotment, there was little they could do to stop the process. The Dawes Act remained in effect until 1934, when Congress passed the Indian Reorganization Act, promoted by President Franklin Roosevelt's administration.

diseases

It is estimated that contagious diseases have killed up to 90 percent of indigenous populations in most areas after just 100 years of that population's contact with Europeans. Some tribes became extinct as a result. Others, such as the *Mandan [III]*, were brought to the verge of extinction (in the Mandans' case, an 1837 smallpox epidemic left just over 100 members alive). On average, disease claimed the lives of 25 to 50 percent of tribes, whereas battles with whites caused only a 10 percent decline. Europeans and Africans, ravaged by periodic epidemics throughout history, had built up immunity to the various illnesses they brought with them to the Western Hemisphere. Because of their millennia of relative isolation from other humans, American Indians had no resistance to many diseases, including measles, scarlet fever, typhoid, influenza, tuberculosis, cholera, diphtheria, smallpox, bubonic plague, pneumonia, and venereal infections. Historians have surmised that some ancient temple mound cultures might have come to an end through such epidemics. In order to motivate conversions to Christianity, Europeans would tell Indians that they faced death from the diseases because they were not Christians. Diseases contributed to the defeat of tribes in battle. Whites practiced a type of germ warfare by distributing smallpox-infected blankets and handkerchiefs to Indians.

Scientists who have analyzed blood groups argue that most American Indians are descended from a few original ancestors. They were less diverse genetically than Old World populations. Therefore, because pathogens increase in virulence as they reproduce in people of the same genotypes, Indians were much more susceptible to disastrous epidemics.

An influenza epidemic was spread by the domestic animals *Columbus [II]* brought on his second voyage to Hispaniola (Haiti and the Dominican Republic) in 1493. Smallpox made its appearance on that island in 1518. Spanish invaders added to the spread of European diseases with their invasion of Mesoamerica in 1520. During Cortés's invasion of the Aztec empire, there were so many dead bodies from an epidemic in Mexico City that Cortés and his men had to walk over them when they captured the city. As Cortés recalled, "God saw fit to send the Indians smallpox, and there was a great pestilence in the city." Measles led to high mortality rates between 1531 and 1533 in Mesoamerica and then spread northward. Spanish military expeditions into the American Southeast in 1539 to 1543 spread diseases further. A disease that may have been typhus killed millions of Mesoamericans from 1545 to 1548.

Those who developed some immunity had no protection for subsequent epidemics of measles, plague, and influenza. When whole villages were struck by an epidemic, there was often no one left to farm, and mass starvation often followed. Indian deaths led to a labor shortage and increased slavery in some areas. Some medical practices among tribes included sweat lodges followed by plunges in cold water. This proved ineffective with the European diseases and may have aggravated some high fevers. European medical practices were equally ineffective, since resistance in populations is built up over time.

Between 1613 and 1617, a bubonic plague killed half of Florida's indigenous population. By 1618, the disease had reached New England. *Squanto [II]*, who would later help the Plymouth settlers survive, was fortunate enough to be in England for several years after 1614. On his return home, he found that he was the sole survivor of his tribe, wiped out in the pestilence of 1618. So many Indians died that in 1620 the Pilgrims took it as a sign from God that He wanted them to settle the area. John Winthrop wrote "God hath consumed the natives with such a great plagues in these parts, so as there be few inhabitants left."

In 1633, measles and smallpox struck New England and the Great Lakes region, followed a few years later by scarlet fever. Smallpox recurred in 1649, 1662, 1669, and 1687; measles struck in 1658 and 1692; influenza in 1647 and 1675; and diphtheria in 1659. Malaria had also reached southern North America by the 1690s.

Thirteen major epidemics occurred during the 17th century, and 16 in the 18th century. Lethal epidemics continued in the 19th century with each new wave of westward invasion by Europeans. From 1837 to 1870 alone four different epidemics struck on the Plains.

When vaccinations were invented, few were allocated to tribes. While fatality rates from smallpox in 19th-century Europe could run as high as 30 percent in some areas, in Indian populations in the Americas, death rates of 75 percent or more were common.

After World War II, a noncontagious disease, diabetes, emerged as a major health crisis among American Indians, killing and maiming many. It seemed to be caused by abandoning traditional diets and adopting low-nutrition, high-fat American diets.

Dutch West Indian Company

The Dutch of New Netherlands (which included Pennsylvania and New York) recognized Indian tribes as sovereign nations and made treaties with them in an attempt to demonstrate the legitimacy of their land claims and to gain more favorable trading terms. When attaining tribal lands became more important than trading with tribes, the Dutch began to use force and trickery to gain lands.

The Dutch West Indian Company was chartered in 1621 and conducted commercial activity until 1664. During that time, the Dutch simply negotiated with tribes for small tracts of lands on which to establish trading posts and villages. Starting in the 1630s, however, the Dutch began a campaign of encouraging agricultural colonization, which required more land. This change was in part due to the depletion of fur-bearing animals and the threat of British expansion. The company deeded land titles to those who purchased tracts of land and sent at least 50 Europeans to settle on them. With the growth of independent traders, however, the company lost its trade monopoly.

Unlike the English, the Dutch were more willing to accept living near Indian cultures without forcing assimilation on them. The Dutch Reform church established some missions to convert Indians but not on the scale that the Spanish, French, and British did.

educational funding

Historically, education has been the primary vehicle by which Europeans worked to convince tribes to abandon their way of life and to adopt European ways. They viewed children as more open to influence and so removed them from their communities for schooling. Before the *American Revolution*, a small number of Indian students attended eastern colleges such as Harvard and what later became Dartmouth.

Despite the Constitution's provision that separated church and state, the federal government offered church organizations funding to provide education to Indians. The Indian "Civilization" Fund established in 1819 provided federal funding to religious groups to instruct Indians in western agricultural practices and ways. More than one-fourth of the treaties

IN THEIR OWN Words

We know you highly esteem the kind of learning taught in these colleges and the maintenance of our young men, while with you, would be very expensive to you. We are convinced, therefore, that you mean to do us good by your proposal; and we thank you heartily. But you who are so wise must know that different nations have different conceptions of things; and you will not therefore take it amiss, if our ideas of this kind of education happens not to be the same with yours. We have had some experience of it. Several of our young people were formerly brought up in the colleges of the northern provinces; they were instructed in all your sciences; but, when they came back to us, they were bad runners, ignorant of every means of living in the woods, unable to bear either cold or hunger, knew neither how to build a cabin, take a deer, or kill an enemy, spoke our language imperfectly, were therefore neither fit for hunters, warriors, nor counselors; they were totally good for nothing. We are however not the less obliged for your kind offer, though we decline accepting it; and to show our grateful sense of it, if the gentlemen of Virginia shall send us a dozen of their sons, we will take great care of their education, instruct them in all we know, and make men of them.

—CANASATEGO (CANASSATEGO), ONONDAGA GRAND SACHEM (C. 1690–1750). RESPONSE TO VIRGINIA LEGISLATURE AT THE TREATY OF LANCASTER, 1744 .

357

signed between tribes and the United States government included promises of schooling.

Schools were especially prevalent among the *Five Civilized Tribes* in the Southeast. After the forced removal from their lands to *Indian Territory* (Oklahoma), the southeastern tribes established their own schools, including institutions of higher education. When Congress passed the Curtis Act in 1898, all Indian governmental institutions were disbanded, including the schools.

Starting in the 1870s, boarding schools, which removed Indian children from their families, became more prevalent. *Carlisle Indian School* in Pennsylvania, opened by former army officer Richard Henry Pratt in 1879, served as a model to many schools that followed. By 1900, 24 similar schools had opened. Carlisle closed in 1918.

Federal schools offered limited and substandard food and relied on the forced labor of their students. Military discipline and punishments were meted out to students caught not speaking English or running away. Despite the harsh environment, students from divergent tribes often united in a pan-Indian identity.

During the 1930s, John Collier, Commissioner of Indian Affairs under Franklin Roosevelt, modified the policy of forced assimilation in education. The government began reimbursing public schools for enrolled

IN THEIR OWN *Words*

Today there are Indians who are ashamed they are Indians. Believe me, this is so . . .

We would like to be proud we are Indians, but . . . many schools for Indian children make them ashamed they are Indians . . . the schools forget these are Indian children. They don't

recognize them as Indians, but treat them as though they were white children. . . . This made for failure, because it makes for confusion. And when the Indian history and the Indian culture is ignored, it makes our children ashamed they are Indians.

I started to school when I was seven years old. I couldn't speak a word of English. I had long hair that hung to my waist, and it was in four braids. When I made progress in school a braid was cut off to mark my progress.

—BEN BLACK ELK, OGLALA LAKOTA (1898–1972). FROM *BLACK ELK SPEAKS, BEING THE LIFE STORY OF A HOLY MAN OF THE OGLALA SIOUX* AS TOLD TO JOHN G. NIEHARDT, MORROW, 1932.

Indian students, allowing children to stay in or near their communities. Congressional battles over Indian schooling continued, culminating in a number of legislative changes in the 1970s, including the *Indian Education Act* of 1972, the Indian Self-Determination and Education Assistance Act of 1975, and the Tribally Controlled Community College Assistance Act of 1978.

Today there are two dozen tribally controlled community colleges. Eighty-five percent of Indian children attend public schools.

Elementary and Secondary Education Act

The Elementary and Secondary Education Act was passed in 1965 in order to provide a better education for elementary and secondary school students. Some educational reformers of this time argued that poorly funded school systems perpetuated poverty, since school funding is tied to property tax bases. Originally authorized for five years of resources, it has been reauthorized every five years since.

The act's objectives are to reduce class sizes, provide more technology to students, start charter schools, fund initiatives to help disadvantaged children, make schools safe and drug free, place more focus on helping Native American and other minority children achieve high academic standards, and provide bilingual education. Funds go directly to local schools to meet the unique academic and cultural needs of Indian students. These funds may be used to support local educational agencies in their efforts to reform elementary and secondary school programs. The act's standards are to be used for all students and are designed to assist Indian students meet those standards in reaching the national education goals.

Everglades Reclamation Policy

In the early 1900s, politicians thought the Everglades wetlands in Florida should be removed to make room for new housing and agriculture. To do this, they proposed to straighten the river running through the Everglades. More than 56 miles of canals were dug 30 feet deep, and huge levees, dikes, and pumping stations were built.

During the drainage era of 1906 to 1927, a canal was built connecting Lake Okeechobee to the Caloosahatchee River to lower water levels in the lake and to aid in draining the northern Everglades to reclaim land for farming. Dredging of the Miami, New River, Hillsboro, West Palm Beach and St. Lucie canals provided additional drainage for the agricultural area south of the lake. An eight-foot muck dike was built along the lake's south shore to protect residents, but during the hurricanes of 1926 and 1928, massive damage occurred and many lives were lost.

The drainage, dikes, and levees altered the natural watershed and brought about severe environmental consequences for the fragile ecosystem of the Everglades. From the 1930s to mid-1940s, south Florida was subject to alternating periods of drought and severe flooding, as the natural water cycle of the Kissimmee-Okeechobee-Everglades watershed was being changed dramatically. Many species of bird, animals, and plant life are nearing extinction. The reclamation of the Everglades also forced many *Seminole [III]* Indians from their homes. Water and land rights are still being disputed.

Factory System

Early in its history, the United States government became involved in the fur trade by establishing a system of trading houses called the Factory System. The American Congress passed four Trade and Intercourse Acts from 1790 to 1799. These acts established the Department of Indian Agents and the licensing of federal traders. In 1806, an Office of Indian Trade was created within the War Department to oversee trading practices with the tribes. In 1822, the Factory System of federal trading houses was abolished and independent traders were licensed.

By the 1840s, the international fur market was in decline due in part to the beaver hat going out of style and the depletion of fur-bearing animals due to overhunting, and advances in European farming. In place of the abolished Office of Indian Trade, in 1824 the secretary of war created an Office of Indian Affairs. In 1832 the new system was formally recognized by an act of Congress that gave the president the right to appoint a commissioner of Indian Affairs. Within a decade, this institution evolved into the *Bureau of Indian Affairs*.

fishing rights

In 1855, the United States government signed treaties with several Indian tribes, guaranteeing their right to take fish at their usual fishing sites in return for 40 million acres of land. Retention of hunting and fishing rights was important to tribes, given their need to feed families under impoverished conditions. However, those rights were challenged in 1937, when construction of the Bonneville Dam on the Columbia River began. The damming of the river caused dramatic declines in salmon runs, and the tribes were unable to harvest the salmon as they had before. The government then decided to create hatcheries along the river, promising that fish lost due to dams would be replaced. However, the location of the hatcheries did not help the areas where the tribes were fishing. Therefore, the tribes started fishing at locations off their reservations, a right they had been guaranteed in treaties. Fish and Game officers confiscated tribal fishing boats and arrested Indians who continued to fish in these areas.

> ## IN THEIR OWN *Words*
>
> *M*y strength is from the fish; my blood is from the fish, from the roots and the berries. The fish and the game are the essence of my life. I was not brought from a foreign country and did not come here. I was put here by the Creator. We had no cattle, no hogs, no grain, only berries and roots and game and fish. We never thought we would be troubled about these things, and I tell my people, and I believe it, it is not wrong for us to get this food.
>
> —CHIEF MENINOCK, YAKAMA, TESTIMONY IN 1915 TRIAL IN A CASE WHERE INDIANS HAD BEEN ARRESTED FOR VIOLATING A STATE LAW BANNING THEIR FISHING, A RIGHT GUARANTEED IN A TREATY.

The tribes won a major court victory in 1974 with the *Boldt* decision in Washington State, which upheld the right of tribes to fish off their reservation lands as granted in treaties. Several federal cases have since upheld fishing rights, including *Puyallup Tribe v. Department of Game* in Washington; *Lac Courte Oreille Band of Lake Superior Chippewa Indians v. Lester P. Voigt* in Wisconsin; and the *United States v. Michigan* in Michigan.

Five Civilized Tribes

Whites referred to the five major tribes of the Southeast—the *Cherokee [III]*, *Chickasaw [III]*, *Choctaw [III]*, *Creek [III]*, and *Seminole [III]*—as the Five "Civilized" Tribes because, in their view, they had successfully adopted many white ways. These tribes had early contact with Europeans and developed constitutions, judicial systems, legal codes, and other white standards of "civilization."

Cherokee Phoenix newspaper, circa 1828. *Library of Congress.*

By 1808, the Cherokee had codified their laws. *Sequoyah [II]* developed a Cherokee written language, which allowed publication of newspapers and books. In 1828, the first Indian newspaper, the *Cherokee Phoenix*, was published. The five tribes also established national governments following the American model of executive, judicial, and legislative branches.

The Creek adopted written laws in 1817 and organized a tribal government in 1839. The Cherokee printed their law code in 1821; the Chickasaw published theirs in 1844. By 1835, the Creek were publishing books in their language. The Choctaw and Chickasaw also developed constitutions, in 1838 and 1848, respectively. Despite all of this, the *Indian Removal Act* of 1830 mandated the forced removal of these tribes, along with all other tribes east of the Mississippi, to live west of the Mississippi River. Once they were resettled in *Indian Territory* (Oklahoma), all the tribes established schools, including institutions of higher education.

forced patent period

Trust assets are property in which Indians hold and maintain legal interests, but which are held in trust by the United States for tribes and individuals. They include, but are not limited to, land, water, fish, wildlife, plants, and minerals.

In 1887, Congress passed the *Dawes Act*. Under this act, the president could, whenever he saw fit, divide a reservation and give each member of the tribe on that reservation a certain number of acres. Upon selecting a parcel of land for himself, the individual was to receive a fee patent that stipulated in part that the land would be held in trust by the United States government for 25 years. Congress believed 25 years was all that was necessary for Indians to learn how to live more like whites, to adopt white customs, and thus to become responsible citizens.

French and Indian War

In the late 17th and 18th centuries, a series of battles for colonial control of North America took place. That series of conflicts is generally referred to as the French and Indian War. It consisted of *King William's War* from 1689 to 1697; *Queen Anne's War* from 1702 to 1713; *King George's War* from 1744 to 1748; and the French and Indian War itself, also known as the Seven Years' War, from 1754 to 1763. After the ultimate defeat of France in North America in 1763, a number of tribes who had allied with the French rebelled against the new dominant colonial power of England.

There were several rebellions by Indians during the French and Indian War. Rebellions against the English included the *Tuscarora [III]* War in 1711, the Yamasee War in 1715, and the *Cherokee [III]* War in 1759. Rebellions against the French included the *Mesquakie [III]* Resistance in the 1720s, the *Natchez [III]* Revolt in 1729, and the *Chickasaw [III]* Resistance in 1734.

The first battle in the series known as the French and Indian War, King William's War, grew from economic and territorial conflicts. At the time, the *Iroquois League* dominated the fur trade. Once the Dutch colonial government fell out of power, the British became the preferred trading partner of the *Iroquois [III]*. The British had cheaper and higher quality goods than their French adversaries. In response, the French began a campaign to gain an alliance with the Iroquois or at least their neutrality. The French were already allied with the Abenaki Confederacy (*Abenaki [III]*, *Maliseet [III]*, *Micmac [III]*, *Passamaquoddy [III]*, *Penobscot [III]*, and Pennacok). Conflicts between Abenaki and

A copy of the *American Magazine*, founded during the French and Indian War, distributed in the colonies and England, showing a Frenchman and an Englishman competing for trade with an American Indian. *Library of Congress.*

British colonists increased, as did conflicts between the Iroquois Confederacy and French settlers. In 1690, the French launched an assault into New York, New Hampshire, and Maine. By gaining a military advantage over the British, they hoped to convince the Iroquois to become their allies. The Iroquois remained allied with the British, however, and in 1697, England and France ended the inconclusive, expensive war by signing the Treaty of Ryswick.

By 1702, the French had gained the neutrality of the Iroquois Confederacy and of the Spanish in Florida. When a new war erupted in Europe (known there as the War for the Spanish Succession), fighting broke out in New England again. The French made an unsuccessful attempt to gain military support from southeastern tribes such as the Cherokee and Chickasaw, who had been trading with the English. They were, however, able to gain some military support from the *Choctaw [III]* and some bands of *Creek [III]*. A state of war continued until Queen Anne sent reinforcements to the English colonies in 1710. In 1713, various European nations signed the Treaty of Utrecht, in which France ceded Hudson Bay and surrounding areas to the English.

King George's War was a relatively small-scale conflict. Its roots lay in the continual trespassing by the French and their Indian allies through Iroquois territories on their way to English settlements. The English built more northern forts in response, which the French claimed sat on their territorial lands near Lake Ontario. The French raided New York and New

IN THEIR OWN *Words*

O n this side of the river and on the other side is our country. If you do not know anything about it, I will tell you about it, for I was raised here. You mark all our country, the streams and mountains, and I would like to tell you about it; and what I say I want you to take to heart.

Those mountains are full of mines. The whites think we don't know about the mines, but we do. We will sell you a big country; all the mountains. Now tell us what you are going to give for our mountains. We want plenty for them. Am I talking right? The young men think I am talking right. Every one here is trying to get plenty. The railroad is coming. I want to see what you will give for the mountains; then we will talk about the rest of our land.

—BLACKFOOT, CROW, SPEECH AT COUNCIL AT CROW AGENCY, MONTANA, ON AUGUST 11, 1873.

England frontier settlements. Under threat from French incursions, the *Mohawk [III]* ended their neutrality and allied with the English. Battles between the English allies, the Cherokee and Chickasaw, and the French allies, the Choctaw and Creek, broke out. A peace accord was reached in 1748 at Aix-la-Chapelle. Peace was, once again, only temporary.

The French and Indian War was the final and greatest conflict of the colonial era. After a brief period of peace, an undeclared war began again in North America in 1754, fought over lands in the Ohio Valley. In the Treaty of Paris, signed at the end of the European Seven Years' War, France ceded New France and all the territories it had claimed east of the Mississippi to England. Florida was passed from Spain to England and Spain took Louisiana from the French in exchange.

gold

Beginning with the voyage of *Columbus [II]* to the Americas, Europeans sought valuable resources such as gold from Indian tribes and their land, resulting in the widespread abuse of Indians and the decimation of entire cultures. The Arawak, under Columbus, were ordered to find a certain quota of gold on a monthly basis or they would have their limbs amputated. Likewise, Cortés invaded Mexico City on hearing reports that it was a city rich in gold. Gold was stolen from Indian nations and their labor used to mine gold under inhumane conditions.

More than two centuries later, one of the reasons that the *Cherokee [III]* were forcibly removed from their lands in Georgia in the 1830s was that gold had been discovered there. The discovery of gold in places such as Pikes Peak, Colorado, (1858) and northern California (1848) brought a flood of white invaders to those areas. Land dispossession and massacres of local Indians

THE WAY THEY GO TO CALIFORNIA.

A cartoon from 1849 satirizing the influx of white Americans into California during the gold rush. *Library of Congress.*

often accompanied the discovery of gold and other valuable resources on Indian land.

Similarly, when gold was discovered in the Black Hills in 1874, the government confiscated the sacred lands of the *Lakota [III]*. (The Black Hills, which are sacred land to the Lakota and guaranteed in treaty, still have not been returned.) One-tenth of all gold mined in the United States has come from the Homestake Mine in the Black Hills of South Dakota. Another gold rush in South Dakota and Wyoming ensued, followed by violent attacks on Indians. In some areas, such as California, Indians were hunted by white vigilantes almost to extinction.

Grant's Peace Policy

Following the *Civil War,* President Ulysses Grant adopted a policy that aimed to avoid the massacring of Indians by whites that occurred as whites trespassed on Indian lands searching for *gold* and other resources. Known as Grant's Peace Policy, it consisted largely of removing Indians from living in close contact with whites. As a result, Indians were forced onto *reservations*. The alternative policy, favored by some whites at the time, was that of total extermination of Indians.

IN THEIR OWN

Words

hen the great father at Washington sent us his chief soldier to ask for a path through our hunting grounds, a way for his iron horse to the mountains and the western sea, we were told they merely wished to pass through our country, not to tarry among us, but to seek for gold in the far west. Our old chiefs thought to show their friendship and good will, when they allowed this dangerous snake in our midst. They promised to protect the wayfarers.

Yet before the ashes of the council fire are cold, the Great Father is building his forts among us. You have heard the sound of the white soldier's ax upon the Little Piney. His presence here is an insult and a threat. It is an insult to the spirits of my ancestors. Are we then to give up their sacred graves to be plowed for corn?

—RED CLOUD (MAHPIUA LUTA, MAKHPIA-SHA, MAKHPIYA-LUTA, MAKHPYIA-LUTA [SCARLET CLOUD]), OGLALA LAKOTA CHIEF (C. 1820–1909). SPEECH AT COOPER UNION, NEW YORK CITY, 1870.

Gratten Affair

The Treaty of Fort Laramie of 1851 was supposed to ensure safe passage for settlers on the Oregon Trail. The settlers, however, broke the peace in 1854. A Mormon party in Wyoming let a cow escape and wander into a Brule *Lakota [III]* camp. Frightened by the Indians, the Mormons fled to Fort Laramie, where they reported that a cow had been stolen. In the meantime, a visiting Lakota from another band killed the cow. When the Brule learned what had happened, they offered to make payment for more than the cow was worth.

However, Lieutenant John Gratten led a force of 30 soldiers and two cannons to the Brule village and gave orders to fire. Chief Conquering Bear was killed in the round of howitzer fire that rained on the camp. The Brule defended themselves successfully and managed to kill nearly all the troops. Whites called the incident the Gratten Massacre and retaliated by sending 600 troops from Fort Keany, in Nebraska, to attack a Brule village. There they killed nearly 100 Indians and took another 70 women and children as prisoners.

Conflict with the Lakota would continue. One of those who witnessed the murder of chief Conquering Bear was a youth named *Crazy Horse [II]*. He would later become a leader of the Lakota in subsequent wars on the Plains.

Hancock Campaign

In 1865, at the end of the *Civil War*, the U.S. Army undertook an aggressive campaign, known as the Hancock Campaign, against the Indians of the central plains. Business interests such as the backers of the transcontinental railroad and mining companies were anxious to have western lands cleared of Indian occupants. They also had significant lobbying power in the federal government. General Winfield Scott Hancock set up a command at Fort Larned along the Santa Fe Trail in western Kansas. From there he launched attacks against tribes including the Southern *Cheyenne [III]*. Hancock's chief commander in the fields was George Armstrong Custer, who pursued the Cheyenne and *Lakota [III]* throughout Kansas, Colorado, and Nebraska over the next several years. The heavy-handed military policies of the Hancock Campaign only served to increase conflict in the region.

The army suffered setbacks in their battles with the Southern Cheyenne, Southern *Arapaho [III]*, and some Lakota, so the Hancock Campaign was abandoned. A peace commission of the government resulted in the *Treaty of Medicine Lodge* of 1867 in Kansas and the Fort Laramie Treaty of 1868 in Wyoming.

Hollywood

The film industry has had an enormous impact on public perception of American Indians (as well as Indians' perceptions about themselves). Films have often served as a form of propaganda in presenting particular views of history or stereotypes of Indians. But despite his presence on the big screen over the decades, the Hollywood Indian (sometimes called a "Reel" Indian) is a fictional creation.

The feathered war bonnet, which came to symbolize Indians, was worn among a minority of individuals in a minority of Indian nations. Films, of course, didn't reflect that reality. Feathered war bonnets were photogenic and became a mainstay of visual images of Indians. A particular "Indian" talk was also common, presenting Indians as speaking a kind of pidgin English. The screen was filled with silent, grunting braves with artificial dialects. Facial and body immobility were standard. While Indian men were often portrayed as savage and animal-like in behavior, Indian women have been largely invisible, other than the occasional Indian princess or squaw in film.

Early silent films replayed themes that were popular in the Wild West shows of the time, a tradition that continued in the American art form of the western. Many argue that these themes demeaned American Indians, showed them as an vanishing race of people who lived in the past, and popularized the mythology of virtuous whites winning the West. Until the early 1970s, white actors almost always played American Indians in film; ironically, real Indians were not thought to look Indian enough. During times of war, westerns were a particularly popular genre, since they tended to show a noble image of the United States military spreading civilization around the world.

Two recurring portrayals of American Indians—the brutal savage and the noble savage—have appeared throughout the history of films as well as in literature, painting, and photography. For example, in the 1950 Jimmy Stewart film *Broken Arrow*, *Cochise [II]* appears as a noble savage willing to make friends with whites, while *Geronimo [II]* is portrayed as a brutal savage who can't be reasoned with. John Ford's 1956 film *The Searchers,* starring John Wayne, showed the *Comanche [III]* as brutal savages. This trend has continued in recent movies like 1992's *The Last of the Mohicans*, in which the noble savages are represented by the last two surviving Mohicans, and the brutal savages are the Huron (see *Wyandotte/Huron [III]*) who are the enemies of the Mohicans and their white friends.

Revisionist westerns began appearing in the 1970s, when antiwar sentiment in the wake of the Vietnam War was at its height, and American Indian activism had made mainstream society more aware of Indian issues and grievances. One of the first revisionist westerns of note was *Little Big Man* in 1970, starring Dustin Hoffman. This film, based on the 1964 novel by Thomas Berger, covered many of the themes that some Americans saw in the evening news coverage of Vietnam: crazed generals, a military that condoned the slaughter of women and children, and soldiers blindly obeying orders. Also around this time, American Indian actors began to play minor and some major roles. Two of the earliest American Indian actors to gain prominence in the 1970s were Chief Dan George and Will Sampson. The late 1980s saw movies with Indians as the primary characters for the first time, such as *Powwow Highway* in 1989 with actors Gary Farmer and A Martinez. One of the first films directed and written by American Indians was *Smoke Signals* in 1998, based on the short-story collection *Tonto and the Lone Ranger Fistfight in Heaven* by author Sherman Alexie, a *Coeur d'Alene [III]* Indian. These occasional breakthrough movies, however, continue to be overshadowed at the box office by white-produced and -directed Hollywood blockbusters like *Dances with Wolves* in 1990 and *Black Robe* in 1992.

Homestead Act

The reduction of *Indian Territory*—which now encompasses the states of Kansas, Nebraska, and Oklahoma—began in the 1850s. Railroads at the time were lobbying for additional lands for their transcontinental routes and the growing U.S. population was pressing to continue its westward expansion. In 1854, Congress changed the northern part of Indian Territory into the Kansas and Nebraska territories and opened them to white settlement.

In 1862, the Homestead Act further encouraged white settlement by opening Indian lands in the remaining Indian territories to homesteaders. Those white inhabitants were deeded 160-acre plots of land after they had lived on that land for five years. Tribes in Kansas and Nebraska were relocated to the southern portion of Indian Territory (Oklahoma), which itself would be opened to white settlement in the 1880s.

Hudson's Bay Company

Chartered in 1670 to take advantage of Canadian areas that were rich in fur-bearing animals, the Hudson's Bay Company quickly set up a series of trading posts on Indian lands. Furs that Indians procured were purchased by traders, often below market value. Among the most sought-after furs was beaver, used for making hats. Gradually, Indian communities became dependent on the fur trade and European goods. When traditional hunting areas were depleted of fur-bearing animals, tribes began to hunt in their neighbors' territories, which caused intertribal conflicts. Their European trading partners armed some tribes with guns, giving those tribes an advantage in expanding their hunting territories.

Hunting territory conflicts were further complicated by European disputes over land. The eastern Canadian and American boundary, for example, remained unsettled until the 1842 Webster-Ashburton Treaty. British and American claims to territory farther west were not settled until 1846 when the 49th parallel was accepted as the dividing line.

In the 18th century, the Hudson's Bay Company expanded its contacts with Indian tribes farther west. The company faced competition from the North West Company, which was chartered in 1784 by the Scots and dominated the Montreal-based fur trade until it merged with the Hudson's Bay Company in 1821. Their presence was part of the European disruption of Native American cultures, creating new imbalances in arms, depleting resources, and introducing *diseases*.

Indian Appropriations Act

Since Europeans first came to the Americas, tribes were viewed as sovereign nations with whom treaties were to be made. Treaty making with tribes formally ended in 1871 with passage of the Indian Appropriations Act. The act was not supposed to nullify previously ratified treaties. Instead, it allowed Congress to simply pass legislation regarding tribes rather than enter into treaty negotiations and agreements with them.

Language in the act barred the president and the Senate from making any new treaties with tribes. The last treaty was made with the *Nez Perce [III]* in 1867. Henceforth, presidents issued executive orders to establish *reservations* or recognize certain groups as tribes, until Congress barred those measures by statute in 1919. Congress then relied on recommendations from the secretary of the Interior to grant federal recognition to petitioning tribes. The act took away the status of tribes as sovereign nations but did not give American citizenship to Indians until 1924.

Indian Arts and Crafts Board

The Indian Arts and Crafts Board, a separate agency of the United States Department of the Interior, was created by Congress to promote the economic development of American Indians and Alaska Natives through the expansion of the Indian arts and crafts market. The Indian Arts and Crafts Board Act became law in 1935 when President Franklin Roosevelt signed it as part of his Indian New Deal program.

A top priority of the board today is the implementation and enforcement of the Indian Arts and Crafts Act of 1990, an enhanced version of the original act that provides criminal and civil penalties for marketing products as "Indian-made" when such products are not made by tribally enrolled Indians.

The board's other activities include providing professional business and marketing advice, fund-raising assistance, and promotional opportunities to Native American artists, craftspeople, and cultural organizations. As an integral part of its mission to promote contemporary Indian arts and crafts, the board operates three regional museums: the Sioux Indian Museum, the Museum of the Plains Indian, and the Southern Plains Indian

Museum. The board also produces a consumer directory of approximately 190 Native American–owned and –operated arts and crafts businesses.

Indian Child Welfare Act

Due to the cultural differences between Native Americans and whites, it was discovered through *Bureau of Indian Affairs* documents that by the 1970s, 25 to 35 percent of Indian children were being removed from their homes by nontribal agencies. In order to preserve Indian families and, therefore, Indian cultures, the Indian Child Welfare Act (ICWA) was passed in 1978. This act gave authority back to the tribes concerning the protection, adoption, and guardianship of Native American children, while limiting state intrusion in this area. With the exception of divorce, placement cases are required to be heard in tribal courts if possible. Otherwise, the tribe could be involved in state court proceedings. If it is thought a child should be removed from his or her home, expert witnesses familiar with Indian culture must testify. Should the child be eventually removed for foster care or adoption, the child must be placed with his or her extended family, other tribal members, or other Indian families. If the child is not living on the reservation, but is still under 18 and is taken into custody, the tribe must be notified.

Indian Civil Rights Act of 1968

The Indian Civil Rights Act of 1968 (ICRA), signed by President Lyndon Johnson, effectively reversed the 1896 Supreme Court decision that declared that individuals living under tribal governments were not protected by the Bill of Rights. The ICRA prohibits Indian tribal governments from enacting or enforcing laws that violate certain individual rights. Being similar to the Bill of Rights in the United States *Constitution* and the Fourteenth Amendment to the Constitution, the ICRA guarantees personal freedoms against actions of the federal government and extends those protections to actions of state governments. Since these constitutional limitations do not apply to tribal governments, Congress adopted the ICRA to ensure that tribal governments respected the basic rights of Indians and non-Indians. These rights included: the right to freedom of religion and free speech; freedom from unreasonable search and seizures and from prosecution more than once for the same offense; freedom not to testify against oneself in a criminal case; freedom not to have private property taken for public use without just compensation; a speedy and public trial, the right to be informed of charges, to confront witnesses, and to subpoena witnesses; and freedom from excessive bail, excessive fines, and cruel and unusual punishment.

The Indian Civil Rights Act does differ from the Constitution's Bill of Rights in several ways; however, the ICRA guarantee of free exercise of religion does not prohibit a tribe from establishing a religion, in recognition of the fact that, to many tribes, religion is inseparable from government and other areas of life. Although the ICRA guarantees a criminal defendant the right to have a lawyer at his or her own expense, there is no requirement that a tribe provide a lawyer for a defendant who cannot afford to hire one. The ICRA does not require a tribe to provide the right to jury trial in civil cases.

A person alleging a violation of the ICRA by a tribal government may pursue any avenue of appeal available through tribal government. However, money damages cannot be recovered from the tribe unless the tribe consents to being sued. The ICRA provides only one federal court remedy for its violation: a person may seek a writ of habeas corpus to test the legality of his or her detention when he or she is being held in jail or otherwise detained by an order of an Indian tribe. A person must first exhaust all remedies available through the tribal court, including tribal court appeals, unless the effort would be futile or irreparable injury would result from the delay.

Indian Claims Commission

Before the creation of the Indian Claims Commission in 1946, tribes were barred from pursuing claims against the United States. With the creation of the Indian Claims Commission, tribes were given five years to file their cases and the commission had ten years to settle. Any compensation for land was supposed to reflect the market prices at the time land was taken from the tribe. Three hundred seventy treaties had been negotiated with Indian nations by the federal government between 1784 and 1871, but when payments to tribes were agreed to, they were often below market value for the land and its resources. Even then, full payments were rarely made. Tribes sought legal redress in United States courts but seldom achieved any measure of success. Even when the Supreme Court ruled in their favor, such as the 1832 *Worcester v. Georgia* case involving the removal of the *Cherokee [III]* nation, other branches of the federal government ignored the rulings.

Inundated with requests by members of various tribes to have their cases heard by United States courts, Congress created the commission in 1946. Between its creation and its expiration in 1978, it awarded more than $500 million to tribal members whose land had been taken by the United States government. Claims made prior to August 13, 1951 were heard by the commission; claims made after that date fell under the jurisdiction of the United States Court of Federal Claims. When the commission ceased operations, only 285 claims of 850 on file had been awarded money.

Indian Country

The idea of an Indian Country and a boundary between the Indians and the whites originated with the 1763 British royal proclamation that prevented white settlement west of the Appalachian Mountains. The United States government reaffirmed that policy in the Northwest Ordinance in

President Harry Truman with Indian tribal representatives after signing the Indian Claims Commission Act in 1946. *Library of Congress.*

1787. In practice, however, federal troops were used to keep Indians partitioned in certain areas but not to keep white settlers from Indian lands.

In 1825, Secretary of War John Calhoun, with the support of Congress and the Monroe administration, set aside lands that were to comprise a new Indian Country west of the Mississippi. The Trade and Intercourse Act of 1834 gave the federal government the right to quarantine Indians in that area; that same year, Congress passed legislation that defined Indian Country as that portion of the western United States that was not part of any state or territory.

Today, Indian Country generally refers to lands within the boundaries of Indian reservations. In legal terms, Indian Country is still a definition of American Indian political and legal jurisdictions. Among American Indian activists, Indian Country has been used to refer to all the American continents. In spiritual terms, Indian Country can include lands appropriated unjustly from tribes but having sacred meaning, like the Black Hills of South Dakota.

Some nations such as the *Navajo [III]* were able to remain on parts of their traditional lands. Other tribes, especially eastern tribes, were forcibly relocated to distant locations. For tribes like the *Creek [III]* and *Cherokee [III]*, Indian Country may be viewed as both the lands in Oklahoma where they were forcibly relocated and their traditional lands in Georgia.

One of the first cases to test the boundaries of Indian Country was brought by the Cherokee Nation against the state of Georgia. When *gold* was discovered on Cherokee lands, the state of Georgia argued that those lands were under the control of the state government and not the Cherokee government. Georgia then held a lottery to open the inhabited lands to white settlement. In *Worcester v. Georgia* (1832), the United States Supreme Court ruled that the state laws of Georgia were not valid in Indian Country. President Andrew Jackson nevertheless refused to enforce the Supreme Court decision, famously (or infamously) declaring, "The Supreme court has made its decision. Now let it enforce it."

In 1948, Congress revised the federal criminal code, giving the federal government jurisdiction over criminal cases in Indian Country. In the 1975 Supreme Court ruling in *DeCoteau v. District County Court*, federal government was expanded to include jurisdiction over civil cases in Indian Country as well.

The sovereignty of Indian Country and Indian nations continues to be challenged. Public Law 280 in 1953 permitted the states of California,

Oregon, Minnesota, Wisconsin, and Nebraska to assume jurisdiction over *reservations* within their borders. More recent Supreme Court decisions have continued to erode the principle of tribal sovereignty. In *Oliphant v. Susquamish Indian Tribe* (1979), the Court ruled that even on reservation lands, tribal courts had no criminal jurisdiction over non-Indians. The debate over the roles of tribal, state, and federal governments in Indian Country continues.

Indian Education Act

The Indian Education Act of 1972 has allowed public schools to hire more Indian teachers and administrators and to let them develop local curriculums. The act followed the 1969 Kennedy Report, *Indian Education: A National Tragedy—A National Challenge,* which found that some of the highest dropout rates in the nation were among American Indians. The report urged extension of federal education services to Indians who were not members of federally recognized tribes. As a result, some schools now provide initial reading instruction in tribal languages, teach English as a second language, and even teach some tribal history and culture. Under this act, schoolteachers wishing to teach Indian students must have approval from the secretary of the Interior stating that their programs adequately address the educational needs of Indian students. When non-Indian students participate in these programs, monies expended for the programs are prorated to cover the participation of only the Indian students.

Indian Gaming Act

The Indian gaming regulatory act of 1988 allowed tribes the opportunity to build casinos and expand employment opportunities on reservations. Congress passed the act and established a National Indian Gaming Commission to enforce regulations. Controversy over the casinos continues within Indian nations and the rest of American society. Some tribal members object to gambling on moral grounds, while others view casinos as the new *buffalo [I]*, the new food source for Indian people. The *Oneida [III]* in Wisconsin, for example, use 90 percent of their gaming funds to pay for improvements in roads, schools, and health services. Revenues from tribal casinos are almost at the level of Atlantic City casinos. A common misperception is that many Indians are now rich from casino profits. In fact, most tribes do not have casinos, and most Indians are not collecting direct benefits from casino revenues because some of those casinos are not making profits. Like any other business, the secret to a casino's success is its location. Casinos in rural areas have experienced far less success than those within driving distance of urban areas. While state lottery revenues are not taxed, many non-Indians would like to see Indian casinos taxed. The economic benefits have been good for the few tribes who have done well. Most states that run gaming enterprises like lotteries have positive, though indirect, benefits for residents. Similarly, reservations with profitable gaming businesses are benefiting residents indirectly. Most patrons and employees of Indian casinos are white and so there is a good deal of benefit to the surrounding local white economy as well.

Indian Health Services

The Indian Health Service (IHS), an agency within the Department of Health and Human Services, has responsibility to provide federal health services to American Indians and Alaska Natives. The provision of health services to members of federally recognized tribes grew from the special government-to-government relationship between the federal government and Indian tribes. That relationship, established in 1787 and based on Article I, Section 8 of the Constitution, has been given form and substance by numerous treaties, laws, Supreme Court decisions, and executive orders.

One of the first legal commitments to provide health services to an Indian nation was elaborated in an 1832 treaty with the Ho-Chunk, which offered a physician as partial payment for ceded lands. Congress terminated the policy of treaty making in 1871, but by that time, more than 24 treaties promised medical services. Indian health services have remained inadequate. By the mid-1950s, only 16 Indian hospitals existed. Bills that elaborated the federal responsibility to provide health care were reiterated through congressional acts in 1976 and 1980.

The IHS is the principal federal health care provider and health advocate for Indian people, with the goal of raising Indian health care to the highest possible level. The IHS currently provides health services to approximately 1.5 million American Indians and Alaska Natives who belong to more than 557 federally recognized tribes in 34 states. Its annual appropriation is approximately $2.2 billion. Since 1960, nearly 200,000 Indian homes have benefited from IHS funding for water and sewage facilities. As a result, the death rate from gastrointestinal disease for American Indians and Alaska Natives has decreased by 91 percent in the past 40 years.

Indian Removal Act

After the *Louisana Purchase,* Americans—including President Thomas Jefferson—viewed the newly acquired region as a potential area to move all tribes west of the Mississippi River. Reports from surveyors classified the Great Plains as a desert unfit for farming but fit enough for Indians.

Jefferson was one of the first advocates of removal, though he viewed it as voluntary. Encouraged "voluntary"removals were followed by forced removals. In 1825, the federal government set aside all land from Missouri and Arkansas westward for the planned resettlement of Indians. Voluntary removal ended with the election of President Andrew Jackson in 1828. Jackson promised to force all eastern tribes across the Mississippi, a promise he kept once the Indian Removal Act was passed in 1830. Soon after, the forced marches began, including the infamous "*Trail of Tears*" where as many as one-quarter of all Indians died on their way to western lands. Many more died of starvation and disease once they reached the new lands when the promised government provisions did not arrive.

The removal began with the *Choctaw [III]* in 1830. The *Chickasaw [III]* had ceded lands to the United States in western Kentucky and Tennessee in 1818 but were pressured again in the 1830s to give up their remaining lands in northwestern Arkansas. The *Cherokee [III]* were next. When Cherokee newspapers published editorials against the forced removal, they were destroyed by white mobs. Most Cherokee were removed in 1838. Several rebellions against removal occurred, including the *Black Hawk War,* the *Creek [III]* War from 1835 to 1836, and the *Seminole [III]* War.

After the *Civil War,* a second removal occurred as Plains tribes were forced onto reservations in Indian territories. Many of the tribes rebelled, including the *Apache [III], Modoc [III],* and *Nez Perce [III].* Tribes living in the northern areas of *Indian Territory* were pushed out of Kansas and Nebraska into Oklahoma. By the end of the 19th century, more than 100 tribes had been moved to Oklahoma, making it home to more tribes than any other state. Twenty-five tribes still have their headquarters in Oklahoma.

Removal policies were followed by a policy of *reservations* after the Civil War that sought to segregate Indians onto small parcels of land rather than removal to one large Indian territory.

IN THEIR OWN Words

Indian Removal Act, May 28, 1830

An Act to provide for an exchange of lands with the Indians residing in any of the states or territories and for their removal west of the river Mississippi.

Be it enacted by the Senate and House of Representatives of the United States of America, in Congress assembled, that it shall and may be lawful for the President of the United States to cause so much of any territory belonging to the United States, west of the river Mississippi, not included in any state or organized territory, and to which the Indian title has been extinguished, as he may judge necessary, to be divided into a suitable number of districts, for the reception of such tribes or nations of Indians as may choose to exchange the lands where they now reside, and remove there; and to cause each of said districts to be so described by natural or artificial marks, as to be easily distinguished from every other.

And be it further enacted, that it shall and may be lawful for the President to exchange any or all of such districts, so to be laid off and described, with any tribe or nation of Indians now residing within the limits of any of the states or territories, and with which the United States have existing treaties, for the whole or any part or portion of the territory claimed and occupied by such tribe or nation, within the bounds of any one or more of the states or territories, where the land claimed and occupied by the Indians, is owned by the United States, or the United States are bound to the state within which is lies to extinguish the Indian claim thereto.

And be it further enacted, that in the making of any such exchange or exchanges, it shall and may be lawful for the President solemnly to assure the tribe or nation with which the exchange is made, that the United States will forever secure and guarantee to them, and their heirs or successors, the country so exchanged with them; and if they prefer it, that the United States will cause a patent or grant to be made and executed to them for the same: Provided always, that such lands shall revert to the United States, if the Indians become extinct, or abandon the same.

Indian Reorganization Act (see Wheeler Howard Act)

Indian Resources Development Act

The purpose of the Indian Resources Development Act of 1978 is to create statewide Indian resource development institutes. In this manner, the states participate with the federal government and Indian tribes to assist the tribes in developing agriculture, minerals, energy, forestry, wildlife, recreation and business resources, associated technical and managerial resources, and other areas deemed necessary to promote Indian economic self-sufficiency.

Indian Self-Determination Act

In the 1970s, Congress passed a series of laws—including the Indian Self-Determination Act, the *Indian Child Welfare Act*, and the Health Care Improvement Act—all of which aimed to improve the quality of reservation life without destroying tribal government. The Indian Self-Determination Act and the Education Assistance Act of 1975 recognized the obligation of the United States government to provide maximum participation by Native Americans in federal programs and services to Indian communities, including education.

The secretary of the Interior is directed, upon the request of any Indian tribe, to enter into self-determination contracts with tribal organizations to plan, conduct, and administer programs, including those that the Department of the Interior is authorized to administer for the benefit of Indians.

The new policy of self-determination reversed the federal government's *termination policy* and was aimed at reversing decades of mismanagement by the Bureau of Indian Affairs. With the new policy came greater acceptance of Indian culture and tribal governments.

Indian Territory

Indian Territory was created because of the *Indian Removal Act* of 1830, which forced the relocation of eastern tribes west of the Mississippi River to what was supposed to be a permanent territory for the tribes.

Indian Territory included Oklahoma, Kansas, southern Nebraska, and eastern Colorado. Reduction of the land began in the 1850s due to pressure from railroad companies seeking transcontinental routes. In 1854, by an act of Congress, the northern part of Indian Territory became the Kansas and Nebraska Territories. In 1862, the *Homestead Act* opened up Indian lands to white settlers.

In the 15 years following passage of the Indian Removal Act, more than 100,000 Indians were force marched to Indian Territory. Indian Territory was never afforded the status or structure of other territories by the federal government, such as a territorial government or appointed governor. Instead, individual tribes governed themselves.

The Indian population was not evenly distributed within the territory. The largest tribes, the *Cherokee [III], Chickasaw [III], Choctaw [III], Creek [III],* and *Seminole [III],* were located in the southern part. Many small midwestern and Plains tribes populated the northern part of the territory in Kansas.

A second removal occurred in 1854 when 12 treaties were negotiated with tribes living in the northern part of Indian Territory. They ceded their newly resettled land and moved southward. That area became Kansas and Nebraska Territory.

A third removal took place when the federal government moved Indian tribes from Texas, Nebraska, Kansas, and elsewhere into the eastern part of the territory. Between 1866 and 1885 the *Apache [III], Cheyenne [III], Arapaho [III], Comanche [III], Ioway [III], Kaw [III], Kickapoo [III], Kiowa [III], Modoc [III], Otoe [III], Missouria [III], Osage [III], Pawnee [III], Ponca [III],* Sauk, and *Mesquakie [III]* were forced to move to Oklahoma. Indian Territory eventually came to contain more than 100 different tribes.

Inevitably, what was supposed to be Indian Territory forever was reallocated to whites. In 1887, Congress passed the General Indian Allotment Act (see *Dawes Act*), which divided tribal property and dissolved tribal governments. Reservations with good agricultural land were allotted first. Tribes lost more than two-thirds of their lands, and of the lands they managed to retain, half were either desert or semidesert. In 1890, Indian Territory was split again, into Oklahoma Territory and Indian Territory. By 1893, Indian Territory had been reduced to just the *reservations* of the *Five Civilized Tribes* and small reservations in the northeast corner of Oklahoma. In 1893, the Dawes Commission negotiated agreements with the

Five Civilized Tribes to allot their lands. Leaders of the Five Civilized Tribes drew up a constitution and petitioned to be admitted to the Union as the state of Sequoyah, but Congress rejected the plan. In 1907, all that remained of Indian Territory was incorporated into the new state of Oklahoma.

Inter-American Conference on Indian Life

In the late 1930s, while Mexico was still suffering from the worldwide depression, Mexico's President Lazaro Cardenas promised to return to the Indian people of Mexico the lands and rights they had fought for in the recently ended civil war. The United States government provided initiative to establish cooperation with Mexico on such matters. In 1938, when the Eighth International Conference of the American Nations was held, a resolution was adopted to start an Inter-American Indian Congress. Two years later, the first Inter-American Congress was held in Patzcuaro, Mexico. At that meeting, a treaty was signed stating that national Indian institutes would be developed. The congress also passed a resolution to create the Inter-American Indian Institute. In 1941, the treaty was ratified, and contributions to the institute from the United States government were included in the budget of the State Department. The convention's purpose was to promote the development of education, health, and agricultural projects and to revitalize Indian arts and crafts throughout the Western Hemisphere.

International Indian Treaty Council

The International Indian Treaty Council (IITC) is an organization of indigenous peoples from North, Central, and South America, and the Pacific working for their sovereignty and self-determination and the recognition and protection of indigenous people's rights, traditional cultures, and sacred lands.

American Indians founded the IITC in 1974 at a gathering at Standing Rock, South Dakota attended by several thousand representatives of 98 indigenous Indian nations. The *American Indian Movement* (AIM) had organized the meeting.

In 1977, the IITC became the first organization of indigenous people to be reorganized as a nongovernmental organization (NGO) with consultative status to the United Nations Economic and Social Council. The United Nations declared 1993 the Year of the World's Indigenous Peoples.

The IITC focuses on building indigenous people's participation in key UN forums such as the Commission on Human Rights, the Working Group on Indigenous Populations, the Sub-Commission on Prevention of Discrimination and Protection of Minorities, the Conference of the Parties to the Convention on Biological Diversity, UNESCO, and the Commission on Sustainable Development.

Iroquois League

The Iroquois League, a major intertribal political organization in what is now the northeastern United States, may have been established as early as the 1100s. According to tradition, *Deganawida [II]*, a *Wyandotte/Huron [III]*, had a vision of a tree with three branches. He preached a message of unity among the *Mohawk [III]*, *Oneida [III]*, *Onondaga [III]*, *Cayuga [III]*, *and Seneca [III]*, assisted by *Hiawatha [II]*, a Mohawk. The five tribes, united in a confederacy, were collectively known as the *Iroquois [III]*.

Their idea for a confederacy was based on democratic and representative principles recorded in the Great Law. The Great Law was written on wampum, a beaded system of written language. They included the formation of a tripartite system of government and a representative body of 50 Iroquois representatives from various villages. An oral recitation of the Great Law could take several days. Excerpted versions of it have been translated into English for more than a hundred years. Many who participated in the

IN THEIR OWN

Words

The Haudenosaunee, or Six Nations Iroquois Confederacy, is among the most ancient continuously operating governments in the world. Long before the arrival of the European peoples in North America, our people met in council to enact the principles of peaceful coexistence among nations and in recognition of the right of peoples to a continued and uninterrupted existence. European people left our council fires and journeyed forth in the world to spread principles of justice and democracy which they learned from us and have had profound effects upon the evolution of the Modern World.

—HAUDENOSAUNEE STATEMENT TO THE WORLD. APRIL 17, 1979.

383

American Revolution cited that law as their model for the new nation. Benjamin *Franklin [II]*, for example, followed the Great Law in his 1754 draft of the Albany Plan of Union. The Great Law called for a complex system of checks and balances. The United States also borrowed the symbol of the eagle with a bunch of arrows in its talons. The bundle of arrows indicated that a group of arrows was more difficult to break than a single arrow, symbolizing the strength that could be found by uniting with other groups.

The Grand Council was composed of 50 sachems, or chiefs, from the Five Nations: 10 Cayuga, 9 Mohawk, 9 Oneida, 14 Onondaga, and 8 Seneca. Clan mothers gathered in their own council and selected the men who would serve in the Grand Council. The leader of the women's council, known as the Mother of Nations, or Peace Queen, would seize the horns of authority (a symbolic headdress of the chief) and place them on the heads of representatives. The Iroquois League was further divided into houses or brotherhoods: the elder brothers were the Mohawk and Seneca; the younger brothers were the Oneida and Cayuga. The Onondaga were known as the firekeepers and the Grand Council was held in their centrally located land. When consensus could not be achieved, a vote was taken. In the 18th century, another tribe, the *Tuscarora [III]*, driven from their traditional lands in Virginia and North Carolina following conflicts with English settlers there, moved north to what is now New York State and were accepted into the League as its sixth member.

Clan mothers could impeach a representative for any abuse of office, a power that was similar to judicial review in the United States court system; objections could be raised to proposed measures if they were inconsistent with the Great Law. By emphasizing debate and parliamentary procedure, the alliance was able to prevent intertribal warfare and strengthen the members through mutual support.

The alliance was finally torn apart by the American Revolution, when the Iroquois became divided in their support of the warring parties. Four of the six Iroquois Nations supported the British: the Mohawk, Cayuga, Onondaga, and Seneca. The Oneida and Tuscarora lent their support to the American rebels.

The six tribes, still organized as a league, continue to recite the Great Law today and issue their own passports. They convene on an intertribal basis and remain an enduring model of participatory democracy on this continent.

Josephy Report

In a 1969 report to the White House, sociologist Alvin Josephy examined the *Bureau of Indian Affairs* (BIA), specifically, its failures. On *reservations*, where Indians were trying to participate constructively to help frame, design, and execute programs to meet their needs, they were frustrated daily by the endless round of delays created by the internal workings of the bureau. As a result, Indians could not participate in making their own decisions, for in meaningful things, the decisions could not be made at the local level. According to the report, "One thing does seem certain: the present structure not only serves to reward unassertive behavior and docility but punishes, usually by transfer, those who persist in behaving like leaders. The reward system of BIA discourages leadership on purpose. It is, therefore, not possible to conceive of change and improvement within the present structure." The report was an indicator (not the only one) to officials that the Bureau of Indian Affairs needed restructuring in order to better serve Indian populations.

King George's War

King George's War (1744–1748) was the North American phase of the European War of Austrian Succession, the underlying cause of which was the economic rivalry between England and Spain. Inevitably, its effects were felt by several Indian nations, particularly those, like the *Iroquois [III]*, whose lands lay between English- and French-held territories. The Iroquois had attempted to remain neutral in many of the colonial wars, but the French and their Indian allies often overran Iroquois lands on their way to attacking English settlements. In response, the English built Fort Oswego to block invasion routes. The French claimed that the northern forts were on their territory.

In 1746 and 1747, the French launched major inland offensives against English settlements in New York and Massachusetts. At that time, the northern Indian superintendent for the English colonies, William Johnson, began actively seeking Iroquois support. Some *Mohawk [III]* ended their neutrality and joined Johnson's colonial forces. His friendship with the Mohawk, in particular with his brother-in-law *Joseph Brandt [II]*, proved critical to the ultimate success of the English.

The English had other allies in the South, including some *Chickasaw [III]* and *Cherokee [III]*. The *Choctaw [III]* and *Creek [III]* (Muskogee) fought with the French. The final victories in King George's War took place further north, in Nova Scotia. Peace was finally negotiated in 1748 at Aix-la-Chapelle.

King Philip's War

King Philip's War was fought between the Algonquin nations and the New England colonists who constantly trespassed onto Indian lands. Since Chief Massassoit had first welcomed the *Pilgrims* in 1620, relations between English colonists in Massachusetts and the Algonquin had become increasingly strained. There were numerous areas of conflict. Many tribes believed they had granted permission to the English for the use of their land, much like a lease, whereas English colonists understood their transactions with Indians as granting them permanent possession of Indian lands. *Missionaries* aggressively sought to convert Indians to Christianity, a source of contention for many Algonquin. English traders saddled the Indians with debts and many became more dependent on European goods as the resources on their traditional lands eroded due to European settlement. In addition, when Indians committed an offense according to colonial values, they were dragged into colonial courts and punished by English law and not by their own tribal rules. European *diseases* also devastated entire villages.

An 1810 engraving of a conflict from King Philip's War. *Library of Congress.*

A leader among the Algonquin arose in this conflict-ridden environment. A *Wampanoag [III]* tribal member, Metacom (or Metcomet), had seen his father, Chief Massasoit, repeatedly offer assistance to the colonists. When he was 24, Metacom's brother had died at the hands of the colonists, reputedly poisoned when they brought him in for questioning. When Metacom became sachem, or chief, the Europeans dubbed him King Philip.

Metacom was forced to sign two treaties and to surrender all the tribe's guns. While he complied outwardly, he simultaneously held secret meetings with neighboring tribes for the purposes of forming an alliance. War broke out in 1675 when colonists hanged three Wampanoag for the alleged murder of a Christianized Indian. Colonial settlements throughout New England were attacked as the Nipmuc, *Narrangansett [III]*, and tribes from as far away as Maine joined the cause. In reaction, the New England Confederation of Massachusetts Bay, Plymouth, Rhode Island, and Connecticut formed several armies. Not only did the colonists have larger numbers and superior firepower, but they also enlisted Indian allies from among the Mohegan, *Pequot [III]*, Niantic, Sakonnet, and Massachuset for their battle. The *Iroquois* also served as a northern barrier so that Metacom's allies who engaged in battle could not retreat. The decisive battle was fought a few months later, in December 1675, at the Great Swamp, near Narrangansett Bay in Rhode Island. Skirmishes continued for several months afterward.

In May 1676, Metacom was ambushed and killed. His body was dismembered and his killers took his body parts as trophies. Soon afterward, the colonists wiped out the remaining rebel bands. Metacom's wife and son were sold into slavery in the West Indies along with hundreds of other Indians. Indians in New England had suffered a disastrous defeat, and King Philip's War was one of the last armed uprisings by Algonquin in colonial New England.

King William's War

In the late 17th and early 18th centuries, the colonial powers fought a series of wars for control of North America, referred to collectively as the French and Indian War. King William's War, sometimes referred to as the *Abenaki [III]* Wars, was the first in the series and lasted from 1689 to 1697.

It was fought by England and France over territory in North America. At the time, the *Iroquois League* dominated the eastern fur trade. Once the Dutch relinquished power in the area to the British, the English became trading partners and allies of the *Iroquois [III]*. This trading relationship led the Iroquois to side with the British against the French in most conflicts, including this one.

Tensions mounted as British traders and colonists moved onto lands west of the Appalachians that the French had recently claimed as theirs. The French were aided by Indian allies in the Abenaki Confederacy and they pressured the Iroquois League to support them or at least to remain neutral. A series of battles ensued. In 1697, England and France ended the inconclusive and costly war by signing the Treaty of Ryswick.

Lake Mohonk Conference

After the *Civil War* ended, many white reformers turned their attention to the plight of American Indians and formed Friends of Indians groups. In seeming contradiction, they worked toward the end of Indian culture, language, and civil rights in order to achieve Indians' full assimilation into white American society.

In 1883, the wife of Albert Smiley, a member of the Board of Indian Commissioners, suggested that a conference for reformers should be held annually. Every fall between 1883 and 1916, more than 100 people gathered for the Lake Mohonk Conference of the Friends of the Indian. It was named for Lake Mohonk, located 100 miles upstate of New York City, where the conference was held. The four-day conference included educators, *missionaries*, congressional representatives, and representatives of groups such as the Board of Indian Commissioners, the Indian Rights Association, the Women's National Indian Association, the Ladies National Indian League, and the Boston Indian Citizenship Committee.

Their 1895 platform stated their goal of pushing Indians toward assimilation. They agreed about the need for a set of policies that would end *reservations*, support individual ownership of land, and establish boarding school education of Indian children. They also advocated reforms in the *Bureau of Indian Affairs* to address abuses in the system. They lobbied for and won passage of the *Dawes Act* or General Allotment Act of 1887. That act eliminated tribal governments and eventually led to the loss of two-thirds of tribal lands. With their Christian, ethnocentric, and individualist biases, the Mohonk Conference organizers pushed well-intentioned but ultimately destructive "reforms" for Indians. Many of their proposals reflected white arrogance toward Indian traditions. It was a disaster for Indian people.

Little Turtle's War

The *Miami [III]* War, also known as Little Turtle's War, took place from 1790 to 1794. In 1790, after a minor conflict between Indians and white settlers, U.S. Army General Josiah Harmar was sent to make an attack on those Indians near Fort Wayne, Indiana. Under Harmar's command were 1,100 Pennsylvania, Virginia, and Kentucky militia and 300 federal troops. They were met by a confederacy of tribes led by Miami chief Little Turtle (Michikinikwa). The confederacy included Miami, *Anishinabe [III]*, Leni *Lenape [III]*, *Ottawa [III]*, *Potawatomi [III]*, and *Shawnee [III]*. The soldiers burned the Indian villages, but when a battle ensued, many of the troops fled. After General Harmar's defeat, President Washington ordered General St. Clair to attack with 1,400 men in 1791. When St. Clair's troops arrived, Little Turtle led 1,200 warriors into battle just before sunrise, surprising the American army, which had encountered many problems en route, including too little food and tents that did not keep out the rain. The soldiers were defeated, and those surviving abandoned their equipment, weapons, and horses.

Following those embarrassing defeats, Washington appointed Revolutionary War hero General "Mad" Anthony Wayne as the new commander. Wayne arrived with an army of 3,000 well-trained and well- equipped men. Although efforts at peace talks were made, government representatives refused to uphold an agreement the British made in 1768 that recognized the colonies' eastern boundaries at the Ohio River. Correctly assessing the strength of the troops under Wayne, Little Turtle counseled his people to accept peace. Little Turtle signed the Treaty of Greenville, establishing the dividing line between the Indians and whites in the Old Northwest.

Long Walk

At the beginning of the *Civil War*, General James Carleton established Fort Sumner in east central New Mexico as a place to deposit Indian prisoners. This was part of the federal government's plan to subdue Indians through resettlement. First he rounded up the Mescalero *Apache [III]* in 1862, and then, in 1863, he pursued the *Navajo [III]*. The army campaign against the Navajo was led by Colonel Christopher "Kit" Carson. In his campaign, Carson destroyed Navajo homes and fields and in 1864 forced on them the choice of starvation or surrender. Their surrender of more than 8,000 people was the largest in all the Indian wars. In 1864, they began a forced march to Fort Sumner, 400 miles away. One in ten died along the way in what became known as the Long Walk. Soldiers shot any Indians who could not continue, and their bodies were left on the trail.

On the Bosque Redondo Reservation near Fort Sumner, the Navajo were left without food, clothing, or fuel on overcrowded and infertile land. Many died under those conditions. The Navajo petitioned for a return to their homelands, sending *Manuelito [II]* and other Navajo leaders to Washington, D.C., to plead their case. In 1868, they gained a reservation on their original lands and returned home.

Longest Walk to Washington, D.C.

In 1978, more than 30,000 members of tribes across the United States marched from San Francisco to Washington, D.C. Trying to gather support to halt proposed legislation to abrogate Indian treaties with the federal government, the Indians walked more than 3,600 miles. The group of marchers proposed legislation that would have affected Indian lands, resources such as fishing and timber, sacred sites, and water. A tipi was erected and maintained on the grounds of the White House. Shortly afterward, the United States House of Representatives passed a resolution stating: "Henceforth it shall be the policy of the United States to protect and preserve for American Indians their inherent right to freedom to believe, express, and exercise the traditional religions of the American Indian, Eskimo, Aleut, and Native Hawaiians, including but not limited to access to sites, use and possession of sacred objects, and the freedom to worship through ceremonial and traditional rites."

Louisiana Purchase

Colonial claims to "possession" of lands in North America were often in name only: in other words, they would declare their ownership by proclamation but not occupy the land or undertake any significant economic development. Spain, for example, had claimed the Trans-Mississippi province of Louisiana and ceded it to France in 1762. In 1803, those lands were in turn "bought" from France by the United States with the Louisiana Purchase. The purchase allowed the United States to claim a huge tract of Indian land west of the Mississippi River, extending from New Orleans to Canada. This began a new era of western exploration, starting with the Lewis and Clark expedition. In 1818, the border between the United States and Canada was formed at the 49th parallel. The alleged ownership of territory west of the Mississippi would continue to be contested for decades as Indians resisted the trespassing and appropriating of their lands.

Maine Indian Claims Settlement Act

In 1980, President Jimmy Carter signed legislation known as the Maine Indian Claims Settlement Act, which ended a long legal battle concerning American Indian claims to nearly two-thirds of the land in the state of Maine. Applauded at the time as a fair resolution of a difficult case, the $81.5 million settlement does not seem to have led to improved relations between Indians and non-Indians in Maine.

The settlement was supposed to resolve claims by the *Passamaquoddy [III]* and *Penobscot [III]* tribes to more than 12.5 million acres in northern and eastern Maine. The tribes contended the land belonged to them because Congress never ratified the treaties under which the Indians lost their land. A federal appeals court ruled that Maine tribes were subject to a 1790 law requiring such approval, giving weight to the Indian claims and leaving the federal government with the duty of helping the tribes regain their lands.

In return for rescinding their claims to the land and as much as $25 billion dollars in damages, the Penobscot and Passamaquoddy each received a $13.5 million trust fund and $26.6 million for the purchase of 150,000 acres in other areas of the state. The Houlton band of *Maliseet [III]* received $900,000 to buy 5,000 acres.

In retrospect, some tribal leaders claim it was a mistake to accept a settlement that did not include ironclad assurances regarding sovereignty. Despite the settlement, the lands are subject to the same state and federal laws as the rest of the state. The settlement also left many unanswered questions regarding jurisdictional issues that Indians view as essential to their cultural survival. The gray areas paved the way for disagreements with the state on matters ranging from fishing rights to enforcement of water quality standards.

Most problematic to Indians was the state's success in blocking a Passamaquoddy bid to develop a high-stakes bingo parlor on land acquired by the tribe in Albany Township.

Mariposa Conflict

The discovery of *gold* in California in 1848 brought a flood of settlers and led to the near extermination of California Indians. The accompanying mining camps brought European *diseases*, and many miners shot Indians on sight, so that within a few years the Indian population had been reduced by two-thirds. Because many California Indians had been missionized by the Spanish, they did not put up much resistance to new hostilities. One of the exceptions to this was what became known as the Mariposa Indian War.

In 1850, the Miwok and *Yokut [III]* of the Sierra Nevada foothills and San Joaquin Valley rebelled against the gold miners. A Miwok chief, Tenaya, led attacks on prospectors and trading posts that moved onto their lands. In response, a state militia called the Mariposa Battalion was sent to the Sierra Nevadas in 1851 to repress the Indians. The conflict gradually faded because of the increased military presence. A larger rebellion involving the *Modoc [III]* would occur 20 years later in northern California (see *Modoc Conflict*).

Meriam Report

In 1926, researchers were assembled to study conditions on Indian *reservations*. By 1928, with the data collected, they issued *The Problem of Indian Administration*, a study that became known as the Meriam Report. That report, named after the director of the project, showed that living conditions on reservations were deplorable and offered a stinging criticism of allotment policies that led to lower standards of living for American Indians.

The report stated that governmental emphasis had always been on the property of the Indians rather than on their welfare. Many children taken from their parents were placed in boarding schools on the assumption that they would adopt white culture. The students in the boarding schools were malnourished, overworked, lethargic, and consequently not able to learn. Measles, pneumonia, trachoma, and tuberculosis were at epidemic levels among many Indian Nations. Many children had tuberculosis, and no efforts were made to prevent the disease's spread among the students. Many reservations had no hospitals on or near them, no plumbing, and very little food. After the report was published, an outraged public started a movement to improve conditions on the reservations.

Mexican Kickapoo Uprising

In the early 1850s, Mexico granted land to some *Kickapoo [III]* in order to create a barrier between Mexican settlements and *Apache [III]* and *Comanche [III]* raiders. During the American *Civil War,* Confederate and Union armies pressured the Kickapoo in Kansas to join their armed forces. To escape the tensions of war, some Indians decided to join their relatives in Mexico.

In 1865, the Mexican Kickapoo were attacked by Texas rangers. The Kickapoo responded with attacks on Texas border settlements. In 1873 the federal government sent the Fourth Cavalry across the Rio Grande to attack the Mexican Kickapoo while most of the males were away on a hunt. The soldiers returned to Texas with more than 50 women and children, who were transported as hostages to Fort Gibson in *Indian Territory* (Oklahoma). Mexico protested to the United States government about the border violation, with little effect. In the ensuing years, more than 300 Kickapoo, relatives of the hostages, and almost half the Mexican Kickapoo population moved to Indian Territory.

missionaries

Over the course of several centuries, Europeans waged a religious war against American Indian culture and spiritual practices. European countries sent missionaries along with armies and traders to convert Indians to Christianity. In the beginning, there was even considerable debate about whether Indians could be classified as human beings altogether. In 1512, Pope Julius II issued a bull that stated that the Indians were human, after all, but until they became Christianized, they were to be considered pagan savages. Many Indian cultures valued openness to the spiritual practices of others, and so some tribes adopted Christianity, hoping it was the key to the resistance Europeans exhibited to epidemics that decimated Indian populations.

The Protestant English pursued a policy of assimilation through measures such as boarding schools that removed Indian children at young ages from the cultural influences of their families. The Catholic French and Spanish, however, went into communities and rounded up Indians for forced conversions. Spanish missions established throughout the West and Southwest had a devastating impact on local populations. The Indians were often enslaved, died in large numbers, and were buried in mass graves.

In the early years of the Spanish conquest, the *requerimiento* (requirement) was a royal decree read by Spanish conquistadors to native populations that told them to submit or be enslaved. Back in Spain, the Inquisition had declared a holy war on non-Christians; this war was continued in the Americas. In 1512, the Law of Burgos established the *encomienda* system. Under this system, Spanish settlers who were granted lands by the crown also owned the labor of the people on the land, a form of legal enslavement. Unlike the English colonies, New Spain needed labor, so Indians were not driven from the land, but rounded up.

The French economy in the new world revolved around the fur trade, rather than agriculture or mining. French success depended on friendly relations with the Indians on whom they relied as hunters, guides, and interpreters. French trappers were more likely to live among the tribes and to intermarry with Indian women. There were also fewer French colonists, meaning a slower rate of population spillover from France.

The English colonials usually came as families and farmers with a desire for privately held land in areas separate from the Indians. A proclamation in 1763 was supposed to limit English settlement to east of the Appalachian Mountains as a way to prevent hostilities with Indians.

California had one of the most densely populated areas at contact. The Spanish mission system there was especially harsh on Indian populations. Since their labor was needed, soldiers rounded up Indians to work at the missions. On these plantations they experienced forced labor, forced conversions, hunger, disease, whipping, torture, and sexual assault. The average lifespan of an Indian in the missions was around six years. When the missions were secularized and closed by the Mexican government in 1834, many Indians found themselves homeless. Not long after that, however, came the 1848 gold rush, with California Anglo Americans flooding the area. Indians were again enslaved, kidnapped, and hunted down by vigilantes.

Following the *Civil War*, President Ulysses *Grant's Peace Policy* turned the administration of Indian programs and *reservations* over to Christian organizations. This period, from 1869 to 1887, represented a high point in the Christianization of Indians.

Beginning around that time, various Protestant and Catholic denominations ran boarding schools for Indian children, not only to ensure their conversion to Christianity, but to educate them and, in the long run, force them to assimilate white ways.

Attempts to missionize Indian cultures sometimes met resistance. The *Pueblo (III)* Rebellion of 1680, led by the prophet Popé, arose because of religious persecution. The Pueblo Indians were successful in driving the Spanish from New Mexico for several years, and when the Spanish did return they exhibited more tolerance toward traditional spiritual practices. Spiritual prophets inspired other intertribal resistance movements. *Pontiac's Rebellion*, the Rebellion of *Tecumseh [II]*, and the *Black Hawk Conflict* in the late 18th and early 19th centuries were motivated by the teachings of Delaware prophet Neolin, *Shawnee [III]* prophet Tenskwatawa, and Winnebago prophet White Cloud. Those leaders preached resistance to white culture and religion and a return to traditional Indian ways.

Some religious practices among Indians combined Christianity with traditional elements. In 1799, *Seneca [III] Handsome Lake [II]* (Skaniadariio) founded a movement among the *Iroquois [III]* that taught the "good word" as recorded in the Code of Handsome Lake. Handsome Lake was raised traditionally but later studied the Quaker religion and combined the two philosophies in his code. The Indian Shaker Religion was founded in 1881 by Squaxin tribal member John Slocum and is still practiced today. (The Squaxin were a southern Salish tribe based on the coast of what is now Washington State. Reduced to only 30 members by 1874, they eventually merged with the related Twana community.) Slocum's wife, Mary Thompson Slocum, introduced a ritual involving shaking motions that brushed off sins while practitioners were in a meditative state. The Indian Shaker followers were repeatedly imprisoned for fomenting resistance to federal programs.

Some religious movements arose among the tribes following a series of military defeats and the establishment of reservations. The Seven Drum Religion among the Columbia Plateau Indians, for example, followed on the heels of 19th-century epidemics. The Drum Religion began among the Santee *Lakota [III]* in the Dakota Territory around 1880 and spread to tribes in the western Great Lakes region, including the *Anishinabe [III]*, *Mesquakie [III]*, Ho-Chunk (Winnebago), *Kickapoo [III]*, *Menominee [III]*, and *Potawatomi [III]*.

A *Paiute [III]* prophet, Wodziqod, founded the *Ghost Dance Movement [I]* in 1870. In its revival from 1889 to 1890 it is referred to as the Ghost Dance religion. The Ghost Dance called for a return to spiritual and cultural traditions that would bring about the resurrection of ancestors and buffalo. The Indians believed that Ghost Dance shirts could stop bullets. Whites felt threatened by the spiritual gatherings of Indians, so the Ghost Dance was repressed, leading to the massacre of Lakota by soldiers at Wounded Knee in 1890 (see *Wounded Knee Massacre*).

Modoc Conflict

California Indians carried out few rebellions against the United States, making the Modoc Conflict one of the few U.S.–Indian conflicts to occur within the state of California. The *Modoc [III]* had limited contact with whites until the California *gold* rush in 1848. In 1864, a Modoc chief signed away most of the Modoc lands and moved the entire tribe to the *Klamath [III]* Reservation in Oregon. On the reservation, food was scarce, disease rampant, and tension high between the Modoc and Klamath. The Modoc asked for their own reservation in California north of Tule Lake, a request the state and federal government denied.

Frustrated, a Modoc chief, Kintpuash, nicknamed Captain Jack by whites because he wore a uniform with brass buttons, left the Klamath Reservation with approximately 200 followers in 1865 to return to California. Kintpuash (meaning "having indigestion") was born about 1840 at Wa'chamshwash Village in California near the Oregon border. In an attack known as the Ben Wright Massacre of 1846 whites killed Kintpuash's father, a Modoc chief. Consequently, Kintpuash became leader of his band at a young age. The federal government sent troops to gather Kintpuash and his Modoc followers in California in 1872. Gunfire was exchanged in the Battle of Lost River that November. Two soldiers and one Modoc died.

Reinforcing the federal troops, 309 California and Oregon troops and volunteers joined the attack on the Modoc. In the Battle of the Stronghold in January 1873, the troops suffered 11 dead; no Modoc were wounded.

A massive force of 1,000 troops was brought into the conflict and peace negotiations were arranged. About 50 Modoc men fought the 1,000-member force in a series of guerrilla battles. The white loss of life totaled 64; Modoc losses totaled 18. During the negotiations in April 1873, Captain Jack allegedly drew a gun and killed General Edward Sprig Canby. Outraged whites called for the extermination of the tribe. Another Modoc leader, Hooker Jim, was caught and bargained for his life by offering to lead the troops to Captain Jack's hideout, where he was captured.

Captain Jack and three of his warriors were sentenced to hang in October 1873. Two other Modoc males were imprisoned for life. The day after the hanging, grave robbers dug up Captain Jack's body and embalmed it in order to display it in a carnival tour. The 155 Modoc survivors were exiled to *Indian Territory* (Oklahoma). In 1909, 51 Modoc were allowed to return to the Klamath Reservation from their exile in Oklahoma.

Mohawk blockade

One of the first Red Power protests was the 1968 *Mohawk [III]* blockade of the international border between the United States and Canada. Under the 1794 Jay Treaty, the Mohawk were given the right to cross the border between the United States and Canada. During the 1950s and 1960s, Canadian authorities began blocking the free movement of the Mohawk across the border. Mohawk activists drew attention to their situation by blocking traffic on the Cornwall Bridge, which crossed the St. Lawrence River. The Canadian government acknowledged Mohawk rights in resulting negotiations. Soon afterwards, the Mohawk began publishing the journal *Akwesasne Notes* to draw attention to the rising Indian militancy across the nation and its borders.

Mormons

The Mormons considered Indians to be one of the ten lost tribes of Israel, the Lamanites of *The Book of Mormon*. Those lost Hebrews had become "idle" and "full of mischief" because of their loss of belief. Other whites besides the Mormons also believed that Indians may have originally been Israelites and credited any signs of "civilization" to this past heritage. Beginning in the 1950s, Brigham Young University enrolled approximately 500 Indian students annually. The university also ran an Indian Placement Program, which placed more than 60,000 Indian children with Mormon families. This program was phased out during the 1970s when the removal of Indian children from their families and culture came under criticism.

National Congress of American Indians

Eighty Indians from 50 tribes founded the National Congress of American Indians (NCAI) in 1944 in Denver, Colorado. The NCAI remains the oldest intertribal American Indian civil rights organization in America. Early leaders in the organization included D'Arcy McNicle and Ruth Muskrat Bronson.

The NCAI supported the expansion of federal recognition of Indian nations. Some federally recognized tribes, concerned that limited federal funds might be divided even further, opposed this stance, as did the National Tribal Chairmen's Association (NTCA). The NCAI lobbied in support of the Indian claims commission and against the federal government's policy of termination, which finally ended in 1970. During the 1970s, they took a controversial stand in their defense of Pine Ridge Oglala tribal chair Dick Wilson, who was viewed as dictatorial by many.

Younger, more militant groups of American Indians emerged in the 1960s and 1970s, somewhat supplanting the NCAI's role. The NCAI was most effective in its early efforts in the legislative arena. It was less successful when political tactics on the national level shifted to courtrooms and lawsuits in the 1980s. By then, organizations such as the Native American Rights Fund (NARF) had risen to greater prominence. However, even in the 1990s, the NCAI could still boast of 1,500 tribally enrolled members from more than 200 tribes.

National Council of American Indians

The National Council of American Indians (NCAI) was founded in 1926. Gertrude Bonnin served as president, and other leaders included Dr. Charles Eastman, Dr. Carlos Montezuma, and Arthur Parker. The group composition reflected a "talented tenth" of American Indians who had been educated through white systems that emphasized integration as a solution to Indian problems. That stance was viewed as a form of Red Progressivism, as opposed to traditionalists who often argued for the separation of cultures. The council supported voting and passage of the Indian Reorganization Act of 1934.

National Indian Youth Council

In the 1960s, whenever tribal members fished for salmon and steelhead trout off their *reservations*, state law enforcement officials, despite treaty rights that protected such fishing, arrested them. State regulations prohib-

IN THEIR OWN

Words

The white people, who are trying to make us over into their image, they want us to be what they call "assimilate," bringing the Indians into the mainstream and destroying our own way of life and our own cultural matters. They believe we should be contented like those whose concept of happiness is materialistic and greedy, which is very different from our way.

We want freedom from the white man rather than to be integrated. We don't want any part of the establishment, we want to be free to raise our children in our religion, in our ways, to be able to hunt and fish and live in peace. We don't want power, we don't want to be congressmen, or bankers . . . we want to be ourselves. We want to have our heritage, because we are the owners of this land and because we belong here.

The white man says, there is freedom and justice for all. We have had "freedom and justice," and that is why we have been almost exterminated. We shall not forget this.

—GRAND COUNCIL OF AMERICAN INDIANS, 1927.

ited the use of nets and traps even though those were traditional native methods for taking fish from rivers and streams. Native Americans, insisting on rights guaranteed by treaties signed by Territorial Governor Isaac Stevens (1818–1862), were subjected to arrest and prosecution. The right to fish became a unifying cause among the diverse tribes of Puget Sound who traditionally were tied to natural resources rather than to real estate concerns.

Consequently, the National Indian Youth Council (NIYC), a Native American civil rights organization formed in Gallup, New Mexico, in 1961, joined local groups in the fish-in movement. NIYC members applied their knowledge of activism and civil disobedience to tribal issues. The NIYC protested denial of treaty rights by fishing in defiance of state law. Fish-ins were used throughout the 1960s to highlight racial discrimination, violations of treaty rights, and the plight of Native Americans.

IN THEIR OWN *Words*

The protection of our land and water and other natural resources are of utmost importance to us. Our culture not only exists in time but in space as well. If we lose our land we are adrift like a leaf on a lake, which will float aimlessly and then dissolve and disappear.

Our land is more than the ground on which we stand and sleep, and in which we bury our dead. The land is our spiritual mother who we can no easier sell than our physical mother.

We are products of the poverty, despair, and discrimination pushed on our people from the outside. We are the products of chaos. Chaos in our tribes. Chaos in our personal lives.

We are also products of a rich and ancient culture which supersedes and makes bearable any oppressions we are forced to bear. We believe that one's basic identity should be with his tribe. We believe in tribalism, we believe that tribalism is what has caused us to endure.

—NATIONAL INDIAN YOUTH CONFERENCE POLICY STATEMENT, 1961.

Native American Women's Health Education Resource Center

The Native American Women's Health Education Resource Center is a reservation-based, woman-operated, nonprofit organization in South Dakota that serves Native American women and their families. At the local level, it provides a variety of public health promotion projects, covering such issues as reproductive health, AIDS and HIV education, diabetes, and drug and alcohol abuse. The Native American Women's Health Education Resource Center is the first resource center located on a reservation in the United States. It runs a food pantry for the community and the elderly, offers adult education classes, and gives early childhood Dakota culture/language programs. The women have also led community protests against environmental racism. They run a domestic violence shelter and provide emergency services for women and children affected by domestic violence. They also provide community workshops on domestic violence and school workshops on healthy relationships, dating violence, drug and alcohol abuse, and self-esteem.

IN THEIR OWN

Words

We, the members of the Indian tribes of the United States of America invoking the Divine guidance of Almighty God in order to secure to ourselves—the Indians of the United States and the Natives of Alaska—and our descendants the rights and benefits to which we are entitled under the laws of the United States, and the several states thereof, to enlighten the public toward the better understanding of the Indian people, to preserve rights under Indian treaties or agreements with the United States, to promote the common welfare of the American Indian, to foster the loyalty and allegiance of American Indians to the flag of the United States do establish this organization and adopt the following Constitution and By-laws.

—PREAMBLE TO NATIONAL CONGRESS OF AMERICAN INDIANS CONSTITUTION.

Navajo Community College

Navajo Community College (NCC), also known as Diné College, was established in 1968, and is the first tribally controlled community college in the United States. The *Navajo [III]* created an institution of higher education to encourage Navajo youth to become contributing members of Indian communities. Under the direction of a 10-member Board of Regents confirmed by the Government Services Committee of the Navajo Nation Council, Diné College serves residents of the 26,000-square-mile Navajo Nation, spanning the states of Arizona, New Mexico, and Utah. As a post-secondary educational institution, NCC awards associate degrees and technical certificates in areas important to the economic and social development of the Navajo Nation.

Navajo Hopi Land Settlement Act

The Navajo Hopi Land Settlement Act was implemented in 1974 to resolve a dispute over land belonging to the *Hopi [III]* tribe located in northeastern Arizona. The history of the dispute spans more than 100 years and involves numerous pieces of congressional legislation and several court cases. The *Navajo [III]* have lived in peaceful coexistence with the Hopi on the Hopi's traditional land base for a longer period than recent conflicts would indicate. Post-contact displacement created greater territorial stress between the two tribes. Spanish livestock, for example, required large tracts of grazing lands. Displaced Navajos began settling on Hopi and Zuni lands.

Starting in the 1880s, the federal government set aside approximately 2.4 million acres (roughly 3,750 square miles) for the Hopi Indians. At that time, the Navajo Reservation was located many miles east of the Hopi Reservation. Over the years, the Navajo Reservation was enlarged several times until it surrounded the Hopi Reservation and encompassed more than 15 million acres (23,500 square miles).

The Navajo began to live on large portions of the Hopi land set aside in the 1880s, almost to the total exclusion of the Hopi tribe. In 1958, the Hopi tribe sued the Navajo tribe in order to establish its right to the land. Determining that the best solution was to divide the land between the two tribes, the courts established the Navajo Hopi Land Settlement Act in 1974, which called for the relocation of members of the Navajo tribe who resided on lands the act had partitioned to the Hopi tribe. The bill was meant to reverse centuries of Navajo encroachment on Hopi land. Instead, the land dispute has continued, with more than a thousand Navajos still refusing to leave Hopi land.

Nootka Convention

The Nootka Convention was an agreement reached between Britain and Spain over their land claims in British Columbia, Canada, on the Nootka Sound, an inlet of the Pacific Ocean and a natural harbor on the west coast of Vancouver Island. The Spanish were the first nonnatives to discover the sound. In 1774, Juan Josef Perez Hernandez and his crew visited Nootka Sound in his ship, *Santiago*. Although they visited the harbor, they never went ashore. They did, however, have contact with the Mowachaht, or *Nootka [III]*, people. The Spaniards made a second voyage in 1775. Although both ships never touched land, Spain claimed to have discovered the sound. It was British captain James Cook and his men who first anchored on the mainland in the sound. Their arrival started the maritime fur trade in the Pacific Northwest.

The Nootka Sound quickly became one of the main ports of the world fur trade, attracting hunters from everywhere due to the abundance of sea otter. The furs were considered more valuable than a human's weight in gold and were traded to many foreign countries.

In response to the British popularity of Nootka's sea otter pelts, the Spanish established a settlement to protect their interests. At that site the Spanish seized many British ships, including those of Captain John Meares. After the confiscation, Meares returned to London, where he described the incident. Great Britain responded immediately to this Nootka controversy. The British believed their territory had been seized; in response, they gathered the greatest number of war vessels to that date.

The dispute, which escalated quickly, was resolved with the Nootka Convention of 1790. That treaty gave both parties the right to trade in the areas of the Pacific Northwest, with the Nootka Sound remaining open to both. However, in 1794, the convention was amended and the Spanish agreed to rescind all claims to the area.

Northwest Ordinance

The Northwest Ordinance of 1787, considered one of the most significant achievements of the Congress of the Confederation, indicated that the land north of the Ohio River and east of the Mississippi would be settled, eventually becoming part of the United States. Until then, that area had been temporarily forbidden to development. However, increasing numbers of settlers and land speculators had been attracted to what are now the states of Ohio, Indiana, Illinois, Michigan, and Wisconsin. That pressure, as well as demands from the Ohio Land Company, who would soon obtain vast holdings in the Old Northwest, prompted Congress to pass the ordinance.

The area opened by the ordinance was based on lines originally laid out in 1784 by Thomas Jefferson in his Report of Government for Western Lands. The ordinance provided for the creation of not less than three but no more than five states. In addition, it contained provisions for the advancement of education, the maintenance of civil liberties, and the exclusion of slavery. Above all, the Northwest Ordinance accelerated the westward expansion of the United States.

Oklahoma Indian Welfare Act

When the 1934 Indian Reorganization Act was passed, Oklahoma tribes were omitted. However, in 1936 the Oklahoma Indian Welfare Act (OIWA) was passed. The bill applied some of the provisions of the Indian Reorganization Act of the Franklin Roosevelt administration to tribes in Oklahoma. Tribes in Oklahoma had been banned and lost their lands. The act allowed tribes to own land in common and to form tribal constitutions and governments. Section III of the Oklahoma Indian Welfare Act provides that "any recognized tribe or band of Indians residing in Oklahoma shall have the right to organize for its common welfare and to adopt a constitution and by-laws." Section XVI of the Indian Reorganization Act provides that "any Indian tribe, or tribes, residing on the same reservation, shall have the right to organize for its common welfare, etc."

Robert Latham Owen was the second Indian elected to the U.S. Senate. He served from 1907 to 1925. *Library of Congress.*

Paxton Riots

In the midst of *Pontiac's Rebellion* on December 14, 1763, a mob of Presbyterians from Paxton, Pennsylvania, raided a tribe of peaceful Conestoga Indians, setting fire to their village and killing six. The mob's purpose was to seek revenge against all Indians, whether or not they were allied with Pontiac, the leader of an Indian rebellion.

Fourteen Indian survivors fled to Lancaster, where they were placed in protective custody. On December 27, the Paxton mob stormed the jail and massacred the rest. Benjamin *Franklin [II]* condemned the act and, fearing genocide, brought several hundred Moravian Indians to safety in Philadelphia. The Paxton mob descended on the city, only to be turned back by thousands of Philadelphians waiting for them at the courthouse. The mob returned to Paxton, and no charges were ever brought against any perpetrators.

Pequot Conflict

The first of many wars between whites and Indians was fought in 1637 between the *Pequot [III]* and New England settlers. The Pequot, centered along the Thames River in southeastern Connecticut, had numerous quarrels with the colonists, culminating in the murder of slave trader John Oldham in July of 1636.

In August, Governor John Endicott of the Massachusetts Bay Colony organized a military force to punish the Indians. On May 26, 1637, the first battle of the Pequot War occurred when the New Englanders, under John Mason and John Underhill, attacked the Pequot stronghold near present-day New Haven, Connecticut. The Indians' forts were burned and about 500 men, women, and children were killed. Survivors fled in small groups. One group, led by a Pequot named Sassacus, was trapped two days later near present-day Fairfield, and nearly all the Indians were killed or captured. The captives were made slaves by the colonists or were sold in the West Indies.

The few Pequot able to escape the English fled to surrounding Indian tribes and were assimilated. The war ended up destroying the Pequot, once a powerful Indian nation. Even the mention of their name was forbidden by colonial authorities. That conflict set the stage for the ultimate domination of all northeastern native tribes by English colonists and set the tone for the treatment of other tribes throughout the country over the next three centuries.

Pilgrims

The story of the Pilgrims began with a congregation of religious dissidents in Nottinghamshire, England, who separated from the Church of England and established a church of their own in 1606. Persecuted by government authorities, the congregation fled to Leiden, the Netherlands, where they could worship as they chose. However, poor economic conditions and cultural competition caused them much hardship. They decided to emigrate to the English colonies in North America, then known collectively as *Virginia*. After receiving financial backing from a consortium of London merchants, almost 50 members of the Leiden group, accompanied by a similar number of other English emigrants, started across the Atlantic on September 6, 1620, aboard the *Mayflower*.

A 19th-century painting showing the arrival of the Pilgrims at Plymouth Rock, along with an Indian watching their arrival. *Library of Congress.*

The *Mayflower* arrived at Cape Cod in southeastern Massachusetts on November 9, 1620, after a 66-day voyage. The Pilgrims remained in New England, since it was too late in the season to go to the northern part of Virginia, where they had permission to settle. They signed an agreement on November 11 (now known as the *Mayflower* Compact) to guarantee cooperation within their uncharted community. On December 11, 1620, an exploring party found the site of the future town of Plymouth. This is celebrated in legend as the landing on Plymouth Rock, a solitary boulder at the foot of the hill on which Plymouth is built. Construction of the new settlement began on Christmas Day, 1620.

IN THEIR OWN *Words*

O ne day at a conference we were singing "My Country Tis of Thee" and we came across the part that goes: "Land where our fathers died, Land of the Pilgrims' pride . . . " Some of us broke out laughing when we realized that our fathers undoubtedly died trying to keep those Pilgrims from stealing our country.

—VINE DELORIA, JR., STANDING ROCK LAKOTA (1933–). FROM *CUSTER DIED FOR YOUR SINS*, MACMILLAN, 1969.

Winter weather and poor diet caused half the small company to sicken and die that winter. In the spring of 1621, the survivors planted their crops and made friendly contact with the neighboring *Wampanoag [III]* Indians. An English-speaking Wampanoag named *Squanto [II]* taught the colonists how to plant corn, and a peace treaty that lasted 50 years was signed between Sachem Massasoit and Plymouth's first governor, John Carver. The Wampanoags remained neutral in the *Pequot Conflict* of 1636 and most were Christianized. Relations with the settlers became strained due to Pilgrim encroachments on Wampanoag land and the Pilgrims' introduction of alcohol to the tribe. In an attempt to drive the British out of their territory, the Wampanoag participated in *King Philip's War* from 1675 to 1676 and were nearly exterminated. Most surviving Wampanoags were enslaved or killed; a few survivors fled into the interior of Cape Cod.

Pontiac's Rebellion

After the *French and Indian War*, Ottawa Chief Pontiac led a coalition of Indian nations in resistance to white settlements west of the Appalachians. Pontiac sent his battle messages on wampum belts to other tribes in the region. The *Ottawa [III]*, Chippewa, *Kickapoo [III]*, *Illinois [III]*, *Miami [III]*, *Potawatomi [III]*, *Seneca [III]*, and *Shawnee [III]* participated in the uprising. The British sent smallpox-infected blankets and handkerchiefs to the Indians as a form of biological warfare. Even though the French never delivered the assistance they had promised the Indian forces, the Ottawa, Shawnee, Delaware, Miami, and Kickapoo were successful in capturing several English forts. The English conceded by passing the Proclamation of 1763, prohibiting further white settlement in the area. White immigrants ignored the proclamation and continued to trespass on Indian lands.

Major William Campbell arguing with Ottawa chief Pontiac. *Library of Congress.*

407

Public Law 280

Public Law 280 (PL-280), passed in 1953, was an attempt to compromise between transferrring control over Indians to the states and maintaining them as federally protected wards. The statute mandated state legal jurisdiction over Indian residents in six states (Alaska, California, Minnesota, Nebraska, Oregon, and Washington) and allowed other states to assume jurisdiction over their Indians without the Indians' consent. It did not, however, terminate the protected status of reservation lands. As a compromise measure, PL-280 left both the Indians and the states dissatisfied. The Indians did not want state jurisdiction imposed on them against their will, and the states resented the reservations' remaining federal protections.

Queen Anne's War

Queen Anne's War, fought between 1702 and 1713, was part of a larger European power struggle known as the War of Spanish Succession. England, Austria, the Netherlands, and Portugal joined forces in an attempt to prevent France from becoming too powerful, specifically because Louis XIV's grandson was in line to become the King of Spain.

The major battlefield in the New World was the New England frontier. The French and their Indian allies traveled south from Canada to raid English settlements. The English countered with raids of their own. In the winter of 1705, an English force captured the Indian stronghold of St. John's; five years later, British and colonial forces attacked and captured Port Royal and Acadia. Following a series of French defeats, the war ended with the Peace of Utrecht in 1713, and France lost its claims to Acadia (Nova Scotia) and Newfoundland.

Reclamation Act

The Reclamation Act of 1902 designated the proceeds from the sale of public land in 16 western states as a fund for the development of irrigation projects. The settlers were to repay the cost of the projects, creating a permanent revolving fund. The Reclamation Act committed the federal government to support and, ultimately, control the large-scale irrigation that transformed the landscape, economy, and social and political structure of much of the West.

The history of the act began when settlers in the western United States were forced to use irrigation for agriculture due to insufficient rainfall. At first, settlers simply diverted water from streams, but in many areas, demand outstripped supply. As demand for water increased, settlers wanted to store the wasted runoff from rain and snow for later use, thus making more water available in drier seasons. At that time, private and state-sponsored storage and irrigation ventures were pursued but often failed due to lack of money and/or lack of engineering skill.

Pressure mounted for the federal government to undertake storage and irrigation projects. Congress had already invested in America's infrastructure through subsidies to roads, river navigation, harbors, canals, and railroads. The irrigation movement demonstrated its strength in 1900 when proirrigation proposals found their way into both Democratic and Republican platforms. Eastern and midwestern opposition in the Congress quieted when westerners filibustered and killed a bill containing river and harbor projects favored by opponents of western irrigation. On June 17, 1902, Congress passed the act.

Lt. Woody J. Cochran, a Cherokee from Oklahoma, holding up a captured Japanese flag in New Guinea. Cochran, a bomber pilot, earned the Silver Star, the Purple Heart, the Distinguished Flying Cross, and the Air Medal during World War II. *National Archives.*

relocation program

Beginning in 1952, the *Bureau of Indian Affairs* (BIA) conducted the Voluntary Relocation Program for American Indians. The program offered temporary housing and some employment counseling for as much as a year. The BIA offered limited assistance to Indians for "permanent removal from the reservation." Relocation offices were located in Chicago, Denver, Los Angeles, San Francisco, San Jose, and St. Louis. The relocation program was part of the termination policy enacted by the United States government in the 1950s. Moving Indians from reservation areas also offered the future possibility of opening reservation land to white ownership.

The relocation program led to large increases in the urban Indian population. Some Indians who relocated found urban living difficult, employment opportunities limited to minimum-wage jobs, and substandard housing and later returned to reservations.

removal policy

After the *Louisiana Purchase*, debates began about removing all Indians to a separate territory.

Between 1790 and 1830, for example, the population of Georgia increased six fold. The western push of the settlers created a problem. Georgians continued to take Indian lands and force them into the frontier. By 1825, the Lower

---

IN THEIR OWN

Words

*W*hole Indian Nations have melted away like snowballs in the sun before the white man's advance. They leave scarcely a name of our people except those wrongly recorded by their destroyers. Where are the Delaware? They have been reduced to a mere shadow of their former greatness. We had hoped that the white men would not be willing to travel beyond the mountains. Now that hope is gone. They have passed the mountains, and have settled upon Tsalagi (Cherokee) land.

They wish to have that usurpation sanctioned by treaty. When that is gained, the same encroaching spirit will lead them upon other land of the Tsalagi. New cessions will be asked. Finally the whole country, which the Tsalagi and their fathers have so long occupied, will be demanded, and the remnant of the Ani Yvwiya, The Real People, once so great and formidable, will be compelled to seek refuge in some distant wilderness. There they will be permitted to stay only a short while, until they again behold the advancing banners of the same greedy host. Not being able to point out any further retreat for the miserable Tsalagi (Cherokees), the extinction of the whole race will be proclaimed.

—DRAGGING CANOE (CHEUCUNSENE; KUNMESEE; TSIYU-GUNSINI; TSUNGUNSINI), CHEROKEE CHIEF OF THE CHICKAMAUGA BAND (C. 1730–1792). 1775 TREATY DISCUSSION.

Creek [III] had been completely removed from Georgia under provisions of the Treaty of Indian Springs. By 1827, all the Creek were gone.

The *Cherokee [III]* had long called western Georgia home. In 1828, the rumored gold, for which de Soto relentlessly searched, was discovered in the northern part of the state. In 1830, the Congress of the United States passed the *Indian Removal Act,* later informally called the termination policy. Many Americans opposed the act, most notably Tennessee Congressman Davy Crockett. But President Andrew Jackson, who had promised in 1828 to remove all eastern tribes to land west of the Mississippi, quickly signed the bill into law. Congress mandated the removal of all Indians from east of the Mississippi River to the newly established *Indian Territory* located in what is present-day Oklahoma. Tribes subjected to removal included the *Shawnee [III]*, *Potawatomi [III]*, Sac, Fox, *Kickapoo [III]*, Winnebago, *Choctaw [III]*, Creek, *Chickasaw [III]*, Cherokee, and *Seminole [III]*.

The Cherokee attempted to fight removal legally by challenging the law in the Supreme Court and by establishing an independent Cherokee nation. In *Cherokee Nation v. Georgia,* the court refused to hear a case extending Georgia's laws to the Cherokee because they did not represent a sovereign nation. In 1832, the United States Supreme Court ruled in favor of the Cherokee on the same issue in *Worcester v. Georgia.* In that case, Chief Justice John Marshall ruled the Cherokee nation was sovereign, making the removal laws invalid. The Cherokee would have to agree to removal in a treaty, which then would have to be ratified by the Senate.

The Treaty of New Echota, signed by a faction of the Cherokee, gave Jackson the legal document he needed to remove them from their lands. Ratification of the treaty by the United States Senate, which passed by a single vote, sealed the fate of the Cherokee.

In 1838, the United States began the Cherokee removal to Oklahoma on what would be called the *Trail of Tears,* when thousands of Cherokee died. By the close of the 19th century, more than 100 tribes had been removed to Oklahoma.

reservations

Contrary to popular belief, the majority of American Indians today live in urban areas and cities, not on reservations. In fact, only 22.3 percent of the American Indian population resides on reservations and 10.2 percent on trust lands in Oklahoma. On reservations themselves, only 54 percent of the population are Indians. (There have always been non-Indians on Indian land. The rise of Indian casinos in recent years has brought droves of non-Indians as temporary visitors onto reservations, a development that, while popular with local white businesses, is not always appreciated by Indian residents.)

Forty-one percent of those living on reservations live below the poverty level, primarily because reservations have borne the brunt of economic underdevelopment, and partly because they are often geographically isolated from economic centers where employment and other opportunities can be found. Unemployment on reservations averages 49 percent. People were first placed on land that could not be farmed to sustain life. Constant shortages of promised government rations led to starvation, and the poor quality of life continues to contribute to malnutrition and diseases like diabetes.

Reservations were first created by 17th-century English colonizers to establish borders and separate the whites and Indians. Reservation lands were continually diminished through subsequent treaties, allotment policies, the building of dams, and confiscation of lands for national parks. The largest national reservation is the 16-million acre *Navajo [III]* Reservation. In the 19th century, many Indians died from starvation and disease after their removal to reservation land that was unwanted by whites. When resources were later discovered on reservation lands, some tribes went through removal and dispossession again.

A painting on muslin, done between 1900 and 1915, depicting Sitting Bull's arrest and murder. *State Historical Society of North Dakota.*

There are 310 reservations in 33 states, the majority of which are located west of the Mississippi. With more than 500 tribes, it is obvious that not every tribe owns reservation lands. California has the highest number of reservations at around 100, but most are under a few hundred acres. One of the smallest, for example, is Ranch Rancheria, with an area of only 80 square yards. Many young people leave reservations to seek jobs or educations but return later in life to participate in the culture and contribute to their nation. Some Indian families move back and forth between cities and reservations trying to seek the right balance in their lives.

IN THEIR OWN
Words

It gives me pleasure to announce to Congress that the benevolent policy of the government, steadily pursued for nearly thirty years, in relation to the removal of the Indians beyond the white settlements is approaching to a happy consummation. Two important tribes have accepted the provision made for their removal at the last session of Congress, and it is believed that their example will induce the remaining tribes also to seek the same obvious advantages.

The consequences of a speedy removal will be important to the United States, to individual states, and to the Indians themselves. The pecuniary advantages which it promises to the Government are the least of its recommendations. It puts an end to all possible danger of collision between the authorities of the general and state Governments on account of the Indians. It will place a dense and civilized population in large tracts of country now occupied by a few savage hunters. By opening the whole territory between Tennessee on the north and Louisiana on the south to the settlement of the whites it will incalculably strengthen the southwestern frontier and render the adjacent states strong enough to repel future invasions without remote aid. It will relieve the whole state of Mississippi and the western part of Alabama of Indian occupancy, and enable those States to advance rapidly in population, wealth, and power. It will separate the Indians from immediate contact with settlements of whites; free them from the power of the States; enable them to pursue happiness in their own way and under their own rude institutions; will retard the progress of decay, which is lessening their numbers, and perhaps cause them gradually, under the protection of the government and through the influence of good counsels, to cast off their savage habits and become an interesting, civilized, and Christian community.

What good man would prefer a country covered with forests and ranged by a few thousand savages to our extensive Republic, studded with cities, towns, and prosperous farms embellished with all the improvements which art can devise or industry execute, occupied by more than 12,000,000 happy people, and filled with all the blessings of liberty, civilization and religion?

—ANDREW JACKSON'S SECOND ANNUAL MESSAGE TO THE NATION, 1830.

Riel rebellion

In 1885, in Prince Albert, Canada, Chief Poundmaker, also known as Louis Riel, and the Metis (of mixed Indian and French Canadian blood) rebelled against the Canadian dominion authorities. For a year Riel had been asking the Canadian government to respond to a petition that served as a Bill of Rights for the Metis. The petition asked for confirmation of lands; formation of provinces, schools, and hospitals; and provision of aid for the mixed-blood Indians. The bill was sent to Ottawa and ignored. Meanwhile, a plan was being made to build a coast-to-coast railroad, and Riel wanted to prevent that invasion.

Riel formed his own government, seized trading posts, and took prisoners. The bitterest fighting occurred in May 1885. The rebellion ended in June that year when Riel allowed a surrounded group of Canadian troops to withdraw. Riel and his small army were defeated, Riel was captured, his followers dispersed, and the refugees were sent to Montana. Riel was hanged for high treason on November 16, 1885. The Riel rebellion was one of the few conflicts between the government of Canada and the Indian population.

In 1982, almost 100 years after Riel's death, the Metis were finally included as an aboriginal group in the Canadian constitution.

Russian American Fur Company

During the early period of Russian exploration of North America, the imperial government was initially content to leave further development of Alaska in the hands of private traders. Attracted by the fur-bearing animals of the Aleutian Islands, Russians did not settle in the new territory but only hunted seasonally.

In 1784, however, Grigorii Shelikhov established the first permanent Russian outpost on Kodiak Island at Three Saints Bay. Eager to eliminate rival Russian companies and gain control of the entire North Pacific fur trade, Shelikhov expanded the sphere of Russian influence along the Alaskan coast and petitioned Empress Catherine the Great to grant him a monopoly. Shelikhov did not live to see his plans implemented, but in December 1799, Catherine's successor, Paul I, issued a charter to the Russian-American Company. Many colonists were known for their brutal and coercive methods, including kidnapping women and children to be held as hostages until the men of the villages delivered their quota of furs.

The company failed, however, in its intention to create a large, settled Russian population. The inhospitable climate, persistent shortages of food and supplies, and the unwillingness of the czar to send serfs to North America kept the colony small. In the 1840s, as profits from the fur trade began to decline, the czarist government took control of the Russian-American Company. The company was officially dissolved in 1867 when Alaska was sold to the United States.

Sand Creek Massacre (Cheyenne-Arapaho War)

The Sand Creek Massacre ended a series of conflicts with a massacre of two hundred peaceful *Cheyenne [III]* and *Arapaho [III]* who had surrendered to whites. The label "Cheyenne-Arapaho War" is a bit of a misnomer as the conflict was waged upon both the Cheyenne and Arapaho by whites, rather than being fought between the two tribes.

The Cheyenne-Arapaho War, also referred to as the Colorado War of 1864–1865, united many Plains tribes. It consisted of a series of conflicts that occurred as whites trespassed on Indian lands and forced removal of the Cheyenne and Arapaho from their tribal lands.

After *gold* was discovered at Pikes Peak in Colorado in 1858, there was pressure from miners to open Cheyenne and Arapaho lands to white settlement. The territorial military commander, Colonel John Chivington, was a notorious Indian-hater

IN THEIR OWN *Words*

Black Kettle had a large American flag up on a long lodge pole as a signal to the troop that the camp was friendly. Part of the people were rushing about the camp in great fear. All the time Black Kettle kept calling out not to be frightened, that the camp was under protection and there was no danger. Then suddenly the troops opened fire.

—GEORGE BENT, MIXED SOUTHERN CHEYENNE (1843–1918). FROM "FORTY YEARS WITH THE CHEYENNES," *THE FRONTIER*, 4, NO. 6 (DECEMBER 1905).

who believed in a policy of extermination. In 1864, his troops began attacking all Indians in the region and burning their villages. Several tribes united to respond to the attacks, including the Cheyenne, Arapaho, *Lakota [III]*, *Comanche [III]*, and *Kiowa [III]*. Chivington reinforced his troops by forming a militia of short-term volunteers. Clashes continued for months. After a meeting outside Denver, the tribes understood that they could receive sanctuary by declaring peace and camping near army posts. Cheyenne chief Black Kettle led a group of 600 Cheyenne and Arapaho to a camp 40 miles from Fort Lyon near Sand Creek and informed the military commanders of their surrender and peaceful intentions.

Upon hearing of Black Kettle's presence, Colonel Chivington gathered 700 soldiers, including the short-term volunteers. Chivington informed the fort of his plans to attack. He led the troops, with four howitzers, to the Indian camp. Black Kettle had raised an American flag and a white flag of truce, when the soldiers opened fire. Two hundred Indians were slaughtered, many of them women and children, although Black Kettle and others managed to escape. Word of the massacre spread among tribes and served to unite many of them in their mistrust of whites. Chivington was later forced to resign. In the aftermath of the Sand Creek Massacre, President Grant implemented a "peace policy," which force marched Indians to remote reservations so they would not live near, nor be exposed to, the violence of whites (see *Grant's Peace Policy*).

Seminole uprisings

The *Seminole [III]* Indians, one of the *Five Civilized Tribes* living in northern Florida, were composed of *Creek [III]* Indians (Muskogee) originally from Georgia. They were made of many smaller groups of mixed-blood Indians and some runaway African American slaves.

General (and future president) Andrew Jackson went to Florida in 1817 to capture those runaways. What transpired was looting, burning, and killing. After Florida was purchased from Spain by the United States, more raiders came searching for runaway slaves and often killed or captured many Seminole. In 1829, Jackson, as president, conducted even stronger attacks against the Indians east of the Mississippi.

Federal troops forced many tribes to head westward, but the Seminole retaliated and held ground against forced migration until 1842. During this standoff, the Seminole were led by a Georgia-born Seminole chief named Osceola. He became famous by his symbolic act of rebellion when he slashed the removal treaty with a knife. From 1835 to 1837, Osceola led 5,000 warriors on raids from the Everglades. In

1837, he was tricked by the government and captured. He was killed the following year while in captivity.

Eventually, many Seminole gave up and headed west with the other tribes. Some Seminole, however, remained and journeyed even deeper into the Florida Everglades to fight the soldiers who came to capture them. Eventually, the federal troops tired of guerrilla-style warfare and left the remaining diehards to inhabit the Everglades.

Senate Investigating Committee on Indian Affairs

The Senate has had a standing committee on American Indian policy for more than a hundred years. The current committee on Indian affairs was established in 1977 and made permanent in 1984.

A special investigating committee began a series of hearings in 1928, focusing on the poor administration of Indian affairs. The focus of the committee inspired news articles and editorials on a national level. Led by Senator William H. King of Utah, the committee investigated the *Bureau of Indian Affairs* (BIA) and discovered that the Indians had lost 90 million acres of land since 1887, that $5.5 billion of tribal trust funds had been spent during the same period, and that the money had been diverted to federal uses. The committee also revealed that Congress had authorized and appropriated that spending.

Today the committee continues to hold hearings on possible corruption within the Bureau of Indian Affairs or within other tribal entities. One recent debacle concerned the disappearance of billions of dollars in tribal profits through leased lands through the bureau. The committee provides a public hearing on issues of concern to Indian communities.

Sheepeater conflict

During the late 1870s, the so-called Bannock and Sheepeater Wars took place. They were not so much wars as attempts by Indians to escape a series of mistreatments. The Bannock War broke out in 1878, due in part to excitement generated by the flight of the *Nez Perce [III]* the previous years and tensions mounting on the reservation since its establishment.

417

Inadequate supplies, religious disagreements, and restrictions on movement ranked high among problems with reservation life. White settlers objected to Indians leaving the reservation during their annual journey to gather camas bulbs on Camas Prairie. In the summer of 1878, the Indians mostly encountered cattlemen who were grazing their cattle on the prairie, which had been opened to settlement since 1872. Since livestock were destroying an important source of food for frustrated and hungry Indians, fighting flared that summer but was quickly extinguished. The Indians who were involved in the fighting retreated to their reservation.

In 1879, the infamous Sheepeater War followed a similar course. The Sheepeater Indians lived in the mountainous regions of western Montana, Wyoming, and central Idaho, and were expert hunters of mountain sheep, elk, deer, and antelope.

Like other disputes with Indians, trouble started when *gold* was discovered in the Boise Basin in 1862 and in the Yankee Fork of the Salmon River. Those places and another gold camp on Panther Creek were in the middle of Sheepeater winter camps. By 1870, Leesburg on Panther Creek had 7,000 prospectors mining for gold.

The Sheepeater tried to avoid the inevitable conflict. Early in 1879, five Chinese laborers were killed in northern Idaho. The Sheepeater were blamed for the incident, though later proof showed the Indians had nothing to do with the attack. Nevertheless, General O. O. Howard dispatched troops from Boise to Challis to investigate the matter.

On October 1, about 60 Indians surrendered. The prisoners were taken to the Vancouver Barracks in Washington State. Although the Indians denied killing the five Chinese, they were taken to the Fort Hall Reservation in Idaho.

Snake Conflict

The Mormon experience introduced a new chapter marked by violence into Indian-white relations in the Snake River in Utah during the mid-19th century. Numerous minor clashes occurred between whites and Indians, the result of increased emigrant travel and settlement. As their grasslands and game disappeared, members of the *Shoshone [III]* and

Bannock tribes grew resentful and retaliated in an effort to protect their ancestral rights. In 1863, army volunteers were sent to protect the newly settled, largely Mormon community of Franklin in the Bear River Valley. The volunteers slaughtered nearly an entire band of Shoshone in one encounter, the majority of whom were women and children. Some historians believe the severity of the conflict made the Shoshone and Bannock more willing to negotiate a treaty with the federal government.

In 1867, the Fort Hall Reservation was established. In 1868, the Fort Bridger Treaty brought both Fort Hall Shoshone and Bannock together to live on the Fort Hall Reservation.

Snyder Act (see Citizenship Act)

termination policy

In the 1950s, the United States government implemented a termination policy as a way to phase out the government's obligations to Indian tribes and to end tribal governments. Between 1953 and 1962, 60 separate termination bills were pursued in Congress.

Termination policy was originally called liquidation, since it was supposed to dispose of all tribal lands, thus ending all tribal governments as well as federal responsibilities toward Indian nations. The *Bureau of Indian Affairs* (BIA) developed a 50-year termination plan for Indian tribes. One of the earliest steps in that direction occurred in 1946 when Congress passed the *Indian Claims Commission Act*, which allowed tribes to push for final settlements on their past land claims. In 1947, the acting commissioner of Indian affairs was directed to identify and clarify tribes on a list indicating their readiness for termination. In 1949, the Hoover Commission recommended ending all federal Indian programs. Dillon Meyer, who had supervised the Japanese-American relocation camps during World War II, was then appointed head of the BIA by President Harry Truman. He aggressively sought termination of all tribal status.

In 1953, under the administration of President Dwight Eisenhower, *Public Law 280* passed into law. California, Minnesota, Nebraska, Oregon, and Wisconsin were ordered to terminate tribal jurisdictions within their states. By 1962, Congress had passed termination bills affecting 99 tribes and bands: 38 in California and 61 in Oregon. Among tribes facing termination in 1954 were the *Menominee [III]*, *Klamath [III]*, western Oregon Indians, *Alabama-Coushatta [III]*, and the *Ute [III]*. In 1956, the Peoria and *Ottawa [III]* were also terminated. Most terminated groups faced increased poverty and loss of land.

The growth of the civil rights movement led to a reversal of the termination policy in 1970. Some groups, such as the Menominee, Klamath, Oregon Siletze, and the Alabama-Coushatta successfully reversed the termination in subsequent decades. Federal recognition was returned to the Menominee in 1973; the *Modoc [III]*, *Wyandotte/Huron [III]*, and Peoria in 1978; the *Paiute [III]* of Utah in 1980; the Grande Ronde in western Oregon in 1983; the Klamath in 1986; the Alabama-Coushatta in 1987; and the *Ponca [III]* of Nebraska in 1990. In 1988, Congress passed the Repeal of Termination Act, which prohibited Congress from ever terminating the federal recognition of a tribe.

Tippecanoe

Tippecanoe, a wooded area seven miles north of modern-day Lafayette, Indiana, played a major role in American history. The trading post of *Keth-tip-pe-can-nunk* was established by whites in the 18th century. The village, known as Tippecanoe, was razed in 1791 in an attempt to scatter Indian residents in the area and open the land to new white immigrants.

Seventeen years later, in 1808, two *Shawnee [III]* brothers, *Tecumseh [II]* and Tenskwatawa (the Prophet), founded a new Indian village. Tecumseh and the Prophet planned to unite many tribes into an organized defense against white intrusions. Whites were disturbed by the activities of Tecumseh and his followers.

William Henry Harrison and his army built a stockade in October 1811, christening it Fort Harrison. In November, Harrison met with representatives of the Prophet. A battle ensued and the Indians left Tippecanoe, which the army then burned. Tecumseh's disastrous defeat at Tippecanoe ended his uprising as well as the dream of a united Indian front against white encroachment.

Trail of Broken Treaties Caravan

The Trial of Broken Treaties Caravan was a 1972 cross-country march of American Indian activists. Protesters marched in a caravan from San Francisco to Washington, D.C., to present a proposal regarding federal Indian policy. The proposal was designed to bring attention to the political, economic, and cultural struggles faced by Indian nations. Eight Indian organizations planned the event, including the *American Indian Movement* (AIM), the National Indian Brother-hood, the Native American Rights Fund, the *National Indian Youth Council*, the National American Indian Council, and the National Council on Indian Work. The National Tribal Chairmen's Association (NTCA), funded by the Nixon administration, opposed the Trail of Broken Treaties.

The protesters stopped in Minneapolis and developed the document entitled "Twenty Points," which supported tribal sovereignty. Once the caravan reached Washington, D.C., the organizers occupied the *Bureau of Indian Affairs* (BIA) building for six days. On departure, Indian activists confiscated numerous BIA files, some of which revealed the widespread practice of sterilization abuse.

Trail of Tears

In 1838, the United States began the *Cherokee [III]* removal to Oklahoma on what would later be called the Trail of Tears. The term also refers to the general forced relocation of dozens of American Indian tribes from the East into Oklahoma during the 1830s and 1840s. The *Indian Removal Act* of 1830 had legislated this forced removal.

The Cherokee fought their removal through the courts, going all the way to the Supreme Court. They won their case in *Worcester v. Georgia* in 1832, but President Andrew Jackson insisted on executing their removal anyway.

IN THEIR OWN

Words

Although it is so crucial for us to focus on the good things—our tenacity, our language and culture, the revitalization of our tribal communities—it is also important that we never forget what happened to our people on the Trail of Tears. It was indeed our holocaust.

—WILMA PEARL MANKILLER, WESTERN CHEROKEE CHIEF (1945–). *MANKILLER: A CHIEF AND HER PEOPLE*, ST. MARTIN'S PRESS, 1993.

Ordered to move, Cherokee general John Wool resigned his command in protest, delaying the action. His replacement, General Winfield Scott, arrived at New Echota on May 17, 1838, with 7,000 men. Early that summer, General Scott and the United States Army began the invasion of the Cherokee Nation.

Cherokee men, women, and children were taken from their land, herded into makeshift forts with minimal facilities and food, then forced to march 1,000 miles. (Some made part of the trip by boat in equally dismal conditions.) Under the generally indifferent army commanders, human losses for the first groups of Cherokee removed were extremely high. Chief John Ross made an urgent appeal to Scott, requesting that the general let his people lead the tribe west. General Scott agreed. Ross organized

IN THEIR OWN Words

The removal of the Cherokee Indians from their life-long homes in the year of 1838 found me a young man in the prime of life, and a Private soldier in the American Army. Being acquainted with many of the Indians and able to fluently speak their language, I was sent as interpreter into the Smoky Mountain Country in May, 1838, and witnessed the execution of the most brutal order in the history of American warfare. I saw the helpless Cherokees arrested and dragged from their homes, and driven at the bayonet point into the stockades. And in the chill of a drizzling rain on an October morning, I saw them loaded like cattle or sheep into six hundred and forty-five wagons and started toward the west.

One can never forget the sadness and solemnity of that morning. Chief John Ross led in prayer, and when the bugle sounded and the wagons started rolling, many of the children rose to their feet and waved their little hands good-bye to their mountain homes, knowing they were leaving them forever. Many of these helpless people did not have blankets, and many of them had been driven from home barefooted.

On the morning of November the 17th we encountered a terrific sleet and snow storm with freezing temperatures, and from that day until we reached the end of the fateful journey on March the 26th, 1839, the sufferings of the Cherokees were awful. The trail of the exiles was a trail of death. They had to sleep in the wagons and on the ground without fire. And I have known as many as twenty-two of them to die in one night of pneumonia due to ill treatment, cold, and exposure.

—PRIVATE JOHN G. BURNETT, CAPTAIN ABRAHAM MCCLELLAN'S COMPANY, 2ND REGIMENT, 2ND BRIGADE,
GIVING HIS EYEWITNESS ACCOUNT IN 1890 OF THE TRAIL OF TEARS.

the Cherokee into smaller groups and let them move separately through the wilderness so they could forage for food. Although the parties under Ross left in early fall and arrived in Oklahoma during the brutal winter of 1838–1839, his reorganization significantly reduced the loss of life among his people.

Approximately 4,000 Cherokee died because of the removal. The route they traversed and the journey itself became known as the Trail of Tears or, as a direct translation from Cherokee, "the trail where they cried" (*Nunna daul Tsuny*).

Treaty of Medicine Lodge

In the fall of 1867, 5,000 Indians from the *Cheyenne [III]*, *Arapaho [III]*, *Kiowa [III]*, *Apache [III]*, and *Comanche [III]* tribes gathered at Medicine Lodge, Kansas, to meet with commissioners of the federal government to negotiate a peace agreement. The area of Medicine Lodge was considered sacred and the rivers were believed to have healing properties. The Southern Plains tribes were hostile to inroads the whites were making into their lands, and the settlers wanted the government to move the tribes to reservations to eliminate danger.

While waiting for the council to convene, Major Joel Elliott of the Seventh Cavalry, present to protect the whites at the council, went to hunt buffalo for sport with several of his men. The unnecessary slaughter offended the Indians and, as a result, several soldiers were arrested. Although the whites were accommodating in that incident, they were not nearly so cooperative with the treaty, which was designed to assimilate the Indians into the "civilized," white way of life.

Chief Satanta of the Kiowa expressed the Indians' desire and necessity to main-

Lithographs depicting scenes from the 1867 council at Medicine Lodge that resulted in the Treaty of Medicine Lodge, aimed at negotiating peace between whites and Indians and assimilating the Cheyenne, Arapaho, Kiowa, Apache, and Comanche. *Library of Congress.*

tain their nomadic way of life. He stated that settling down represented death to him and his people. Despite Satanta's impassioned speech, the commissioners still designed the treaty to assimilate the Indians within the confines of reservations, making provisions for churches, schools, housing, and farming.

Although the treaty was signed, many Indians continued to fight to maintain their way of life.

IN THEIR OWN Words

At the mouth of Horse Creek, in 1852, the Great Father made a treaty with us. We agreed to let him pass through our territory unharmed for fifty-five years. We kept our word. We committed no murders, no depredations, until the troops came there. When the troops were sent there trouble and disturbance arose. Since that time there have been various goods sent from time to time to us, but only once did they reach us. Will you help us? In 1868 men came out and brought papers. We could not read them, and they did not tell us what was in them. We thought the treaty was to remove the forts. . . . We do not want riches but we do want to train our children right. Riches would do us no good. We could not take them with us to the other world. We do not want riches, we want peace and love. . . . then I wish to know why commissioners are sent out to us who do nothing but rob us and get the riches of this world away from us? . . . But, by and by, the great Father sent out different kind of men; men who cheated and drank whiskey; men who were so bad that the Great Father could not keep them at home.

—RED CLOUD (MAHPIUA LUTA, MAKHPIA-SHA, MAKHPIYA-LUTA, MAKHPYIA-LUTA [SCARLET CLOUD]), OGLALA LAKOTA CHIEF (C. 1820–1909), SPEECH AT COOPER UNION, NEW YORK CITY, 1870.

---

tribal police

Before the establishment of the reservation system, most tribes followed their own set of tribal codes and had traditional and cultural forms of implementing those codes and customs. Distinguished warriors, appointed by tribal leaders, usually upheld the enforcement of those customs and codes. Tribes like the *Cherokee [III]* had long been in contact with white men and had developed a justice system very similar to the European tradition.

With the establishment of *reservations* in the 1860s, reservation agents determined the need for tribal police and courts. The newly developed laws and codes strongly reflected the white tradition of law. Most Indians who became officers had already experienced law enforcement within the Plains tribes or with the Office of High Sheriff for tribes in Indian Territory.

However, there was opposition to bringing the white man's form of justice and government to tribes with long-established traditions embedded in their individual, unique cultures. In addition, the act of policing one's own people was not looked upon favorably by Indians, nor was there much motivation for an Indian to seek the post, since pay was five dollars a month. Government funding was not granted to the tribal policing system until 1879.

Ultimately, the government installment of the tribal police led to the demise of many Indian traditions. The federal government only provided nominal funding for a policing system they insisted on having. In 1945, the police force was reduced due to lack of funding. Not until 1969, when a review of the 22-page Statistics of Crime was compared to the reservation crime rate, did Congress grant $1 million of a requested $2.1 million to improve tribal police and judicial agencies. The money was used to start the Indian Police Academy, the Indian Offender Rehabilitation Program, and the Reservation Rehabilitation Centers.

Although the money helped the tribal justice system, crime rates in Indian country continued to rise as nationwide crime rates fell. In August 1997, President Bill Clinton assigned the attorney general and the secretary of the Interior to consult with the tribal governments on methods to improve law enforcement in Indian country. The outcome of that council was the Tribal Resources Grant Program. That program gives tribal law enforcement agencies resources and funds to "improve and consolidate the delivery of law enforcement."

Tuscarora conflict

Initially, the *Tuscarora [III]* were friendly to the early colonists. However, by 1710, the colonists were cheating the Indians in trade, squatting on their lands, and kidnapping and selling the Indians into slavery. The Tuscarora, wanting to leave North Carolina and relocate to Pennsylvania, petitioned the North Carolina state government for a note attesting to their good behavior so they could move, as required by the Pennsylvania state government. However, North Carolina refused to grant any such certificate in order to keep their supply of Indian slaves.

In 1710, Swiss colonists, led by Baron Cristoph von Graffennried, settled on land already containing the Tuscarora village. North Carolina's surveyor general maintained that the Swiss held legal title to the land. The Swiss then drove the Indians from their own lands. As a result, on September 22, 1711, the Tuscarora attacked New Bern (the Swiss settlement) and other settlements in the area, killing 200 whites. Graffennried was captured, but negotiated for his release and the Indians' pledge not to attack New Bern again. Some whites, who wanted revenge, captured and killed a local chief which caused another conflict.

With the Indian situation getting out of hand, North Carolina officials asked for help from South Carolina. The South Carolinians amassed 30 militiamen and 500 Indian allies (mostly Yamasee). The ensuing battles took a heavy toll on the Tuscarora and other local tribal settlements.

North Carolina Colonel John Barnwell went to attack Tuscarora Chief Hancock, but withdrew to obtain the release of his men, eventually signing a peace treaty. He then captured a band of Tuscarora and sold them into slavery.

The war began again in the summer of 1712, with South Carolina helping North Carolina again, killing hundreds of Tuscarora and selling approximately 400 Indians into slavery. The Tuscarora who escaped fled to New York and sought asylum with the *Iroquois [III]*. They were admitted into the *Iroquois League* six years later. A small group of Tuscarora who remained in North Carolina signed a peace treaty on February 11, 1715.

United States Civil Rights Commission

From August 28 to 30, 1974, the United States Civil Rights Commission held hearings in Farmington, New Mexico after the beating deaths of three Navajo men by white teens. Tribal leaders testified to other abuses that occurred in border towns near their reservations in Colorado, Utah, and New Mexico.

A study documenting Navajo discrimination, "The Farmington Report: A Conflict of Cultures," was issued a year later. The study also found that Indian Health Services were underfunded, and the doctors who worked for Indian Health Services were not committed to the care of Indians.

On June 11, 1981, the United States Civil Rights Commission issued another major report on the treatment of American Indians. That report recommended that Congress use federal funds to give block grants to tribes to improve their living conditions and health care facilities.

Ute Conflict

In the 1870s, silver was found on the *Ute [III]* Reservation. Many land cessions were made for mining and private interests, including possession of Ute reservation lands in Colorado. The military was dispatched after an Indian agent called for military backup. The Ute believed they were in danger of attack, and violence erupted when a lieutenant waved his hat, as soldiers mistook that as a signal to fire. A weeklong skirmish ensued, followed by peace negotiations. A commission of inquiry later determined that the Ute were not responsible for the violence. However, some Ute who fought were punished, and money for the Ute Reservation was withheld from the tribe.

Walla Walla Council

The Walla Walla Council took on place May 21, 1855, between Governor Stevens and tribes of the Pacific Northwest. The United States' goal for the meeting was to gain control over tribal lands in the area. Tribes participating in the council included the *Nez Perce [III]*, *Cayuse [III]*, *Yakama [III]*, *Spokan [III]*, and Walla Walla.

Stevens promised that a treaty would allow tribes to choose the land for their *reservations*, adding that the government would provide schools, housing, and health care. The tribes were guaranteed the retention of their hunting and fishing rights in exchange for ceding more than 6.4 million acres of lands to the government. The various Indian tribes agreed to the treaty, although many historians believe Stevens used the threat of military force against them.

War for the Bozeman Trail

The Bozeman Trail, a shortcut into new settlements in Montana, was built on Indian land around 1863 by speculator John Bozeman. Conflicts occurred over white immigrant use of the trail for several years. Traffic along the trail increased, along with an accompanying military presence. Three more forts were established on Indian lands, which led to sporadic conflicts. The Fort Laramie Treaty, signed November 7, 1868, established the boundaries of the Great Sioux Reservation and kept a measure of peace until *gold* was discovered, once again, on Indian lands, this time in the Black Hills of South Dakota.

water rights

Riparian water rights are agreements stating that each person who owns land bordering or encompassing a water source will maintain the natural conditions of those waters (i.e., no diverting or damming), and that they will share the water in equal amounts with everyone who owns property containing the water source. Use of the water does not determine who does or does not receive water, nor does ceasing to use the water forfeit the owner's share of the water, a common practice in most eastern states.

However, that method of right allocation was not feasible in western states where arid land conditions required irrigation, nor was it practical during the California *gold* rush. Therefore, "prior appropriation" rights were inaugurated, based on the first-come, first-served concept. Rights to water (including the amount) were determined by the date a permit for water rights was submitted or by first use. Consequently, people having the earliest dates of water use had priority to water use and could claim as much water as they wanted. Those with permits dated later had less priority and had their water supply shorted during droughts. In addition, since priority was determined by use, the cessation of use would forfeit one's priority.

In general, the United States sought to obtain as much land as possible for non-Indian use and to concentrate the tribes in areas not reserved for United States development. Undesirable lands, usually in arid or semiarid regions of the West and Midwest, required intensive irrigation for farming. But because of the "prior appropriation" rule, Indians often found themselves deprived of water, as they did not have enough to irrigate their new farmlands. Such was the basis for *Winters v. United States*, a case that the United States brought to the Supreme Court on behalf the Gros Ventre and *Assiniboine [III]* tribes at Fort Belknap Indian Reservation in Montana in 1908.

The two tribes had agreed in a treaty to surrender a large parcel of land to the United States for settlement and to move their tribes to the Fort Belknap Reservation along the Milk River, where they would attempt to farm. When the government finished an irrigation system for the reservation, Indians still had insufficient water flow to irrigate their fields. The settlers upstream from the reservation diverted the waters to irrigate their own lands by the right of prior appropriation.

The Supreme Court ultimately decided that because the land for the reservation had been selected along the Milk River, and because the agreement was that the Indians would become agrarian people, therefore, the reservation's right to the water was implied and intended especially for them, since their land required irrigation.

The non-Indians argued that they had legal rights to the water under the premise of prior appropriation, and they believed they should be protected from any attempts to appropriate the water. They also pointed out that when the Indians gave up their lands for the reservation in the treaty, they forfeited their priority rights to the water.

The Supreme Court disagreed. The *Winters* opinion rejected the rules of prior appropriation that water rights are determined by water use. The non-Indians did have previous rights, but their claim went against government priority and the Indian intention to turn the reservation into a permanent place to live and farm. Without water, their livelihood would be impossible.

The struggle for water rights continues to this day. Some nations identify water as their most important resource, since without water their very existence is threatened by lack of food. The *Navajo [III]* and other tribes in the Southwest, in particular, continue to struggle for this fundamental right that will allow people and animals to remain on the land.

Wheeler-Howard Act (Indian Reorganization Act)

In 1934, Indian Commissioner John Collier decided to stop the process of Indian assimilation, Indian land allotment, and the paternalism of the United States government. Collier also wanted to ensure Indian freedom of religion and culture. With those goals in mind, he drafted the Indian Reorganization Act, sponsored by House of Representatives member John Howard of Nebraska and Senator Burton Wheeler of Montana. Collier toured reservations and, after consulting with tribes, incorporated some changes into the new legislation. It was passed in 1934, although Congress excluded Oklahoma tribes, who comprised one-third of American Indians in the United States at that time.

Women of All Red Nations

Women of All Red Nations (WARN) was formed in 1974 as an offshoot of the *American Indian Movement* (AIM), partially in response to the sexism women confronted on some Indian organizations. Among the issues on which they focused were reproductive rights and land treaties. WARN was effective in its early campaign on reproductive rights, an issue also adopted by mainstream feminist organizations. They have a membership of a few hundred today who remain active on local land issues. Many members are *Lakota [III]*, who remain involved on the issue of attempting to

Secretary of the Interior Harold Ickes handing the first constitution issued under the Indian Reorganization Act to delegates of the Confederated Tribes of the Flathead Indian Reservation in 1935. *Library of Congress.*

regain possession of the Black Hills for their people. Primarily through efforts such as educational campaigns and speaking, they hope to inform others of injustices connected to land issues and support legal strategies of organizations like the Native American Rights fund, which presses cases through the courts.

Wounded Knee Massacre

For many, the Wounded Knee Massacre of 1890 has become an emblem of the history of white cruelty and oppression. It was also the last Indian uprising against American authority in the late 19th century, and in many ways it marked the end of an era. A history of abuses preceded Wounded Knee: the federal government had usurped *Lakota [III]* lands, including the sacred Black Hills when *gold* was discovered there by Custer in 1874. Lakota and others were forced onto reservations and given limited rations. The prisonlike conditions led to widespread disease, starvation, and death.

In 1889, *Paiute [III]* spiritual leader Wovoka revived the *Ghost Dance [I]* religion, giving some Indians hope for a return to the lives they led before contact with whites. The religion focused on performing prayers and dances in order to attain visions of the new world. In Wovoka's version, not only would the Ghost Dance restore lands and dead ancestors to the Indians, but it would cause whites to die. At the request of a fearful Indian agent at Pine Ridge Reservation, President Benjamin Harrison ordered a military suppression of Ghost Dancers among the Lakota. More than half of the entire United States Army was sent there.

> **IN THEIR OWN Words**
>
> *The men were separated . . . from the women, and they were surrounded by the soldiers. When the firing began . . . the people who were standing immediately around the young man who fired the first shot were killed right together, and then they turned their guns, Hotchkiss guns, upon the women who were in the lodge, standing there under a flag of truce, and of course as soon as they were fired upon they fled, the men fleeing in one direction and the women running in two different directions. So that there were three general directions in which they took flight. . . . There was a woman with an infant in her arms who was killed as she almost touched the flag of truce.*
>
> —AMERICAN HORSE (AMERICAN HORSE [YOUNGER]; WASECHUN-TASHUNKA), OGLALA LAKOTA (1840–1908). STATED TO COMMISSIONER OF INDIAN AFFAIRS SIX WEEKS AFTER THE WOUNDED KNEE MASSACRE.

Having heard of the death of *Sitting Bull [II]*, a Lakota chief named Big Foot led a group of 350 Ghost Dancers to seek safety on the Pine Ridge Reservation. They were intercepted by the U.S. troops and, in an atmosphere of tension, they camped near the banks of Wounded Knee Creek. On December 29, 1890, as soldiers began searching the Lakotas' tipis for weapons, a gun went off. In the highly charged situation, shooting erupted quickly. Surrounded by the troops' cannons and machine guns, approximately 250 Indians were gunned down by the military. The dead Lakota, left in a blizzard for three days, had souvenir body parts removed before being buried in a mass grave at the Wounded Knee site. The Medal of Honor was awarded to three officers and fifteen enlisted men, the most ever awarded for a single engagement in United States history, although some historians have called for a revocation of those medals.

Wounded Knee Occupation

In 1973, Oglala *Lakota [III]* traditionalists from Pine Ridge Reservation went to the *Bureau of Indian Affairs* (BIA) to protest the cancellation of hearings regarding their interests. The Indians, met by armed guards, found all open meetings banned and felt unsafe in the land they called their own. They called the members of the *American Indian Movement* (AIM) to come and support them. On February 27, 600 people crowded into a community meeting. The women spoke up, and it was decided that AIM and the people of Pine Ridge would go to Wounded Knee and make a stand. That night, 300 Indians drove to Wounded Knee. Soon, police arrived, followed by the FBI, BIA police, private armies, and United States marshals. They surrounded Wounded Knee and barricaded all roads leading in and out of the area. Three hundred Indian men, women, and children held out to press their demands for officials to evaluate complaints of tribal police abuse, investigate the BIA, and reexamine their rights under the Treaty of 1868. Some South Dakota Lakota leaders declared an independent Oglala Nation on Pine Ridge. AIM was labeled a communist conspiracy led by renegade terrorists.

The standoff lasted until May 8, 1973, although the leaders had thought it would take only a few days to prove their points. However, Indians arrived from everywhere in the country, and the incident made national headlines. Finally, the government agreed to send a delegate from

Washington, D.C., to discuss the Treaty of 1868. The standoff lasted 71 days, cost $7 million, and was the longest armed conflict in the United States since the *Civil War*. Two Indians died, and one federal marshal was partially paralyzed.

Yamasee Conflict

The Yamasee War followed the *Tuscarora [III]* peace treaty of 1715. Initially friendly with the whites, the Yamasee even aided South Carolina during the *Tuscarora conflict*. Nevertheless, the whites followed a pattern similar to their earlier episode with the Tuscarora, cheating the Indians in trade and kidnapping Yamasee women and children to sell into slavery.

On April 15, 1715, the Yamasee, *Catawba [III]*, and other smaller tribes attacked settlements in what is now Georgia, killing 100 whites. Militia action led by South Carolina Governor Charles Craven soon followed. The tribe was driven almost to extinction. The surviving Yamasee fled to Florida to seek protection from Spanish missionaries.

Bibliography

Acoose, Janice. *Iskwewak-Kah' Ki Yaw Ni Wahkokanak: Neither Indian Princesses Nor Easy Squaws*. Toronto: Woman's Press, 1995.

Albers, Patricia, and Beatrice Medicine. *The Hidden Half: Studies of Plains Indian Women*. Washington, DC: University Press of America, 1983.

Allen, Paula Gunn. *Sacred Hoop*. Boston: Beacon Press, 1986.

_____. *Voice of the Turtle*. New York: Ballantine, 1994.

Axtell, James, ed. *The Indian People of Eastern America: A Documentary History of the Sexes*. New York: Oxford University Press, 1981.

Basso, Keith H. *The Western Apache Language and Culture: Essays in Linguistic Anthropology*. Tucson: University of Arizona Press, 1990.

_____. *Wisdom Sits in Places: Landscape and Language Among the Western Apache*. Albuquerque: University of New Mexico Press, 1987.

Batallie, Gretchen, and Kathleen Sands, eds. *American Indian Women: A Guide to Research*. New York: Garland, 1991.

_____, eds. *American Indian Women Telling Their Lives*. Lincoln: University of Nebraska Press, 1984.

Beck, Peggy, and Anna Lee Walters, eds. *The Sacred*. 1977. Reprint, Tsaile, AZ: Navajo Community College Press, 1991.

Big Crow, and Moses Nelson. *A Legend from Crazy Horse Clan*. Chamberlain, SD: Tipi Press, 1991.

Bingham, Sam, and Janet Bingham, eds. *Between Sacred Mountains: Navajo Stories and Lesson from the Land*. Tucson: University of Arizona Press, 1982.

Black Elk, and John G. Niehardt. *Black Elk Speaks*. 1932. Reprint, Lincoln: University of Nebraska Press, 1979.

Bowker, A. *Sisters in the Blood: The Education of Women in Native America*. Newton, MA: WEEA Publishing Center, 1993.

Biolsi, Thomas, and Larry Zimmerman, eds. *Indians and Anthropologists: Vine Deloria, Jr., and the Critique of Anthropology*. Tucson: University of Arizona Press, 1997.

Bordewich, Fergus. *Killing the White Man's Indian: Reinventing Native Americans at the End of the Twentieth Century*. New York: Doubleday, 1996.

Brant, Beth, ed. *A Gathering of Spirit: A Collection by North American Indian Women*. Ithaca, NY: Firebrand Books, 1988.

Brave Bird, Mary. *Ohitika Woman*. New York: HarperCollins Publishers, 1994.

Brown, Jennifer, and Elizabeth Vibert. *Reading Beyond Words: Contexts for Native History*. Peterborough, Ontario: Broadview Press, 1996.

Bruchac, Joseph, ed. *Survival This Way*. Tucson: University of Arizona Press, 1987.

Bullchild, Percy. *The Sun Came Down: The History of the World as My Blackfeet Elders Told It*. San Francisco: Harper, 1985.

Cajete, G. *Look to the Mountain: An Ecology of Indigenous Education*. Durango, CO: Kivaki Press, 1994.

Calloway, Colin G. *New Directions in American Indian History*. Norman: University of Oklahoma Press, 1991.

Campbell, Maria. *Halfbreed*. Lincoln: University of Nebraska Press, 1982.

Cash, Joseph, and Herbert Hoover, eds. *To Be an Indian: An Oral History*. St. Paul, MN: Minnesota Historical Society Press, 1995.

Castile, George, and Robert Bee, eds. *State and Reservation*. Tucson: University of Arizona Press, 1992.

Castro, Michael. *Interpreting the Indian: Twentieth-Century Poets and the Native American*. Norman: University of Oklahoma Press, 1991.

Cohen, Fay G. *Treaties on Trial: The Continuing Controversy Over Northwest Indian Fishing Rights*. Seattle: University of Washington Press, 1986.

Coleman, M. C. *American Indian Children at School, 1850–1930*. Jackson: University of Mississippi Press, 1993.

Coltelli, Laura. *Winged Words: American Indian Writers Speak*. Lincoln: University of Nebraska Press, 1990.

Cornell, Stephen. *The Return of the Native: American Indian Political Resurgence*. New York: Oxford University Press, 1988.

Crow Dog, Mary. *Lakota Woman*. New York: HarperCollins Publishers, 1990.

Dauenhauer, Nora Marks, and Richard Dauenhauer. *Haa Shuka, Our Ancestors: Tlingit Oral Narratives*. Seattle: University of Washington Press, 1987.

Davidson, Florence Edenshaw, and Margaret Blackman. *During My Time: A Haida Woman*. Seattle: University of Washington Press, 1992.

Debo, Angie. *And Still the Waters Run*. Princeton, NJ: Princeton University Press, 1973.

DeJong, David H. *Promises of the Past, A History of Indian Education in the United States.* Golden, CO: North American Press, 1993.

Deloria, Ella. *Dakota Texts.* New York: G.E. Stechert, 1932. Reprint, Vermillion: University of South Dakota Press, 1978.

_____. *Speaking of Indians.* New York: Friendship Press, 1944; Pierre, SD: State Publishing Co., 1983.

_____. *Waterlily.* Lincoln: University of Nebraska Press, 1990.

Deloria, Philip J. *Playing Indian.* New Haven, CT: Yale University Press, 1998.

Deloria, Vine, Jr., ed. *American Indian Policy in the Twentieth Century.* Norman: University of Oklahoma Press, 1985.

_____. *Custer Died for Your Sins: An Indian Manifesto.* 1969. Reprint, Norman: University of Oklahoma Press, 1988.

_____. *For This Land: Writings on Religion in America.* New York: Routledge, 1999.

_____. *God Is Red.* New York: Grosset and Dunlap, 1994.

_____. *The Nations Within: The Past and Future of American Indian Sovereignty.* New York: Pantheon Books, 1984.

_____. *Red Earth, White Lies: Native Americans and the Myth of Scientific Fact.* New York: Scribner, 1995.

_____, and Raymond J. Demallie. *Documents of American Indian Diplomacy: Treaties, Agreements, and Conventions, 1775–1979.* Norman: University of Oklahoma Press, 1999.

DeMallie, Raymond J., ed. *The Sixth Grandfather: Black Elk's Teachings Given to John G. Neihardt.* Lincoln: University of Nebraska Press, 1984.

Disney, Anthony R. *Columbus and the Consequences of 1492.* Melbourne, Australia: La Trobe University Press, 1994.

Dudley, Joseph Iron Eye. *Choteau Creek: A Sioux Reminiscence.* Lincoln: University of Nebraska Press, 1992.

Eastman, Charles A. *From the Deep Woods to Civilization.* Lincoln: University of Nebraska Press, 1977.

_____. *Indian Boyhood.* New York: Dover, 1971.

Erdrich, Louise. *Love Medicine.* New York: Holt, 1984.

_____. *Tracks.* New York: Holt, 1988.

Evers, Larry, and Ofelia Zepeda. *Home Places: Contemporary Native American Writing from Sun Tracks.* Tucson: University of Arizona Press, 1995.

Evers, Larry, and Felipe S. Molina. *Yaqui Deer Songs/Maso Bwikam.* Tucson: University of Arizona Press, 1987.

Farley, Ronnie. *Women of the Native Struggle: Portraits and Testimony of Native American Women*. New York: Orion Books, 1993.

Fixico, Donald L. *Rethinking American Indian History*. Albuquerque: University of New Mexico Press, 1997.

_____. *Termination and Relocation: Federal Indian Policy, 1945–1960*. Albuquerque: University of New Mexico Press, 1986.

Fox, Richard. *Archaeology, History, and Custer's Last Battle: The Little Big Horn Reexamined*. Norman: University of Oklahoma Press, 1993.

Goldberg-Ambrose, Carole. *Planting Tailfeathers: Tribal Survival and Public Law 280*. Los Angeles: University of California Los Angeles American Indian Studies Center, 1997.

Gonzalez, Mario, and Elizabeth Cook-Lynn. *The Politics of Hallowed Ground: Wounded Knee and the Struggle for Indian Sovereignty*. Urbana: University of Illinois Press, 1999.

Green, Rayna, ed. *That's What She Said: Contemporary Poetry and Fiction by Native American Women*. Bloomington: Indiana University Press, 1984.

_____, ed. *Women in American Indian Society*. New York: Chelsea House Publishers, 1992.

Grinde, Donald, Jr., and Bruce Johansen, eds. *Exemplar of Liberty: Native Americans and the Evolution of Democracy*. Los Angeles: University of California Los Angeles American Indian Studies Center, 1991.

Guillemin, Jeanne. *Urban Renegades: The Cultural Strategy of American Indians*. Norman: University of Oklahoma Press, 1994.

Haig-Brown, Celia. *Resistance and Renewal: Surviving the Indian Residential School*. Vancouver, British Columbia: Tillicum Library, 1988.

Hale, Janet Campbell. *Bloodlines: Odyssey of a Native Daughter*. New York: Random House, 1993.

Harjo, Joy. *In Mad Love and War*. Middletown, CT: Wesleyan University Press, 1990.

Harring, Sidney L. *Crow Dog's Case: American Indian Sovereignty, Tribal Law, and United States Law in the Nineteenth Century*. New York: Cambridge University Press, 1994.

Harrod, Howard. *Renewing the Word: Plains Indian Religion and Morality*. Tucson: University of Arizona, 1987.

Hinton, Leanne. *Flutes of Fire*. Berkeley, CA: Heyday Books, 1994.

_____, and Lucille Watahomigie. *Spirit Mountain: A Yuman Story and Song*. Tucson: University of Arizona Press, 1984.

Hobson, Geary, ed. *The Remembered Earth*. 1979. Reprint, Albuquerque: University of New Mexico Press, 1981.

Hogan, Linda. *Mean Spirit*. New York: Atheneum, 1990.

Holm, Tom. *Strong Hearts, Wounded Souls: Native American Veterans of the Vietnam War*. Austin: University of Texas Press, 1996.

Hopkins, Sarah Winnemucca. *Life Among the Paiutes: Their Wrongs and Claims*. Reno: University of Nevada Press, 1994.

Hoxie, F. *A Final Promise: The Campaign to Assimilate the Indians, 1880–1920*. Lincoln: University of Nebraska Press, 1984.

Hultgren, Mary Lou, and Paulette F. Molin. *To Lead and to Serve: American Indian Education at Hampton Institute, 1878–1923*. Virginia Beach, VA: Virginian Foundation for the Humanities and Public Policy, 1989.

Hurtado, Albert. *Indian Survival on the California Frontier*. New Haven, CT: Yale University Press, 1988.

———, and Peter Iverson, eds. *Major Problems in American Indian History: Documents and Essays*. Lexington, MA: D.C. Heath and Co., 1994.

Hyer, Sally. *One House, One Voice, One Heart: Native American Education at the Santa Fe Indian School*. Santa Fe: Museum of New Mexico Press, 1990.

Iverson, Peter, ed. *The Plains Indians of the 20th Century*. Norman: University of Oklahoma Press, 1986.

Jackson, Helen. *A Century of Dishonor: A Sketch of the United States Government's Dealings with Some of the Indian Tribes*. New York: Indian Head Books, 1993.

Jacobs, Wilbur R. *Dispossessing the American Indian*. Norman: University of Oklahoma Press, 1985.

Johnston, Basil. *Indian School Days*. Norman: University of Oklahoma Press, 1989.

Jones, David. *Sanapia: Comanche Medicine Woman*. Prospect Heights, IL: Waveland Press, 1984.

Josephy, Alvin M., Jr. *America in 1492*. New York: Alfred A. Knopf, 1992.

Kan, Sergei. *The Ghost Dancer: Ethnohistory and Revitalization*. New York: Holt, Rinehart, and Winston, 1989.

_____. *Symbolic Immortality: The Tlingit Potlatch of the 19th Century*. Washington, DC: Smithsonian Institute, 1989.

Katz, Jane, ed. *Messengers of the Wind: Native American Women Tell Their Life Stories*. New York: Ballantine Books, 1995.

Kelly, Lawrence C. *The Assault of Assimilation: John Collier and the Origins of Indian Policy Reform.* Albuquerque: University of New Mexico Press, 1983.

King, Thomas. *Medicine River.* Toronto: Penguin, 1990.

Kickingbird, Kirke, and Karen Ducheneaux. *One Hundred Million Acres.* New York: Macmillan, 1973.

Kiple, Kenneth F., and Stephen V. Beck, eds. *Biological Consequences of the European Expansion, 1450–1800.* Brookfield, VT: Ashgatge/Variorum, 1997.

Klein, Laura, and Lillian Ackerman, eds. *Woman and Power in Native North America.* Norman: University of Oklahoma Press, 1995.

Krupat, Arnold. *For Those Who Come After: A Study of Native American Autobiography.* Berkeley: University of California Press, 1985.

_____. *The Voice in the Margin: Native American Literature and the Canon.* Berkeley: University of California Press, 1989.

Kupferer, Harriet. *Ancient Drums, Other Moccasins: Native American Cultural Adaptation.* Englewood Cliffs, N.J.: Prentice Hall, 1988.

King, A. R. *The School at Mopass: A Problem of Identity.* New York: Holt, Rinehart, and Winston, 1967.

LaFlesche, Francis. *The Middle Five: Indian Schoolboys of the Omaha Tribe.* 1900. Reprint, Lincoln: University of Nebraska Press, 1963.

Lincoln, Kenneth. *Native American Renaissance.* Berkeley: University of California Press, 1983.

Linderman, Frank Bird. *Pretty-Shield: Medicine Woman of the Crows.* Lincoln: University of Nebraska Press, 1974.

Lomawaima, K. Tsianina. *They Called It Prairie Light: The Story of Chilocco Indian School.* Albuquerque: University of New Mexico Press, 1994.

Louis, Adrian. *Among the Dog Eaters.* Albuquerque: West End Press, 1992.

Lurie, Nancy Oestreich, ed. *Mountain Wolf Woman, Sister of Crashing Thunder: The Autobiography of a Winnebago Indian.* Ann Arbor: University of Michigan Press, 1966.

Lyons, Oren, et al. *Exiled in the Land of the Free: Democracy, Indian Nations, and the U.S. Constitution.* Santa Fe, NM: Clear Light Publishers, 1992.

Mankiller, Wilma, and Michael Wallis. *Mankiller: A Chief and Her People.* New York: St. Martin's Press, 1993.

Matthiessen, Peter. *In the Spirit of Crazy Horse.* New York: Viking Press, 1983.

McBride, Bunny. *Molly Spotted Elk: A Penobscot in Paris*. Norman: University of Oklahoma Press, 1995.

McCarthy, James. *A Papago Traveler*. Edited by John G. Westover. Tucson: University of Arizona Press, 1985.

McDonnell, Janet. *The Dispossession of the American Indians: 1887–1934*. Bloomington: Indiana University Press, 1991.

McLaughlin, D. *When Literacy Empowers: Navajo Language in Print*. Albuquerque: University of New Mexico Press, 1985.

McNickle, D'Arcy. *The Surrounded*. 1936. Reprint, Albuquerque: University of New Mexico Press, 1978.

_____. *Earth Power Coming*. Tsaile, AZ: Navajo Community College, 1983.

Mihesuah, Devon. *American Indians: Stereotypes and Realities*. Atlanta: Clarity Press, 1996.

Mishkin, Bernard. *Rank and Warfare Among the Plains Indians*. Lincoln: University of Nebraska Press, 1992.

Momaday, N. Scott. *House Made of Dawn*. New York: Harper, 1968.

_____. *The Way to Rainy Mountain*. Albuquerque: University of New Mexico Press, 1969.

Moore, John H., ed. *The Political Economy of North American Indians*. Norman: University of Oklahoma Press, 1993.

Morris, Irvin. *From the Glittering World: A Navajo Story*. Norman: University of Oklahoma Press, 1997.

Mourning Dove (Christin Quintasket). *Cogewa*. Lincoln: University of Nebraska Press, 1981.

Nagel, Joane. *American Indian Ethnic Renewal: Red Power and the Resurgence of Identity and Culture*. New York: Oxford University Press, 1996.

Niethammer, Carolyn. *Daughters of the Earth: The Lives and Legends of American Indian Women*. New York: Collier Books, 1977.

O'Brien, Sharon. *American Indian Tribal Governments*. Norman: University of Oklahoma Press, 1989.

Ortiz, Simon J. *Woven Stone*. Tucson: The University of Arizona Press, 1992.

Owens, Louis. *Mixed Blood Messages: Literature, Film, Family, Place*. Norman, OK: University of Oklahoma Press, 1998.

_____. *Other Destinies: Understanding the American Indian Novel*. Norman: University of Oklahoma Press, 1992.

Pearce, Roy H. *Savagism and Civilization: A Study of the Indian and the American Mind*. Berkeley: University of California Press, 1988.

Peters, Virginia Bergman. *Women of the Earth Lodges: Tribal Life on the Plains*. New Haven, CT: Archon Books, 1995.

Petrone, Penney, ed. *Northern Voices: Inuit Writing in English*. Toronto: University of Toronto Press, 1988.

Peyer, Bernard, ed. *The Singing Spirit: Early Short Stories by North American Indians*. Tucson: University of Arizona Press, 1989.

Philip, Kenneth R., ed. *Indian Self-Rule: First Hand Accounts of Indian-White Relations from Roosevelt to Reagan*. Salt Lake City: Howe Brothers, 1986.

Philips, S. U. *The Invisible Culture: Communication in Classroom and Community of the Warm Springs Indian Reservation*. Prospect Heights, IL: Wareland Press, 1993.

Prucha, Francis P. *American Indian Treaties: The History of a Political Anomaly*. Berkeley: University of California Press, 1994.

_____. *The Churches and the Indian Schools*. Lincoln: University of Nebraska Press, 1979.

Qoyawayma, Polingaysi [Elizabeth White]. *No Turning Back*. Albuquerque: University of New Mexico Press, 1964.

Reyhner, J. ed. *Teaching American Indian Students*. Norman: University of Oklahoma Press, 1992.

_____. *Teaching Indigenous Languages*. Flagstaff, AZ: Center for Excellence in Education, 1997.

Roessel, R. A., Jr. *Navajo Education in Action: The Rough Rock Demonstration School*. Chinle, AZ: Navajo Curriculum Center Press, 1977.

Rountree, Helen C. *Pocahontas's People: The Powhatan Indians of Virginia*. Norman: University of Oklahoma Press, 1990.

Sarris, Greg. *Grand Avenue*. New York: Hyperion, 1994.

_____. *Keeping Slug Woman Alive: A Holistic Approach to American Indian Literature*. Berkeley: University of California Press, 1992.

Shattuck, Petra, and Jill Norgren. *Partial Justice: Federal Indian Law in a Lineal Constitutional System*. Oxford: Berg Publishers, 1991.

Shoemaker, Nancy, ed. *Negotiators of Change: Historical Perspectives on Native American Women*. New York: Routledge, 1995.

Silko, Leslie M. *Ceremony*. New York: Viking, 1977.

_____. *Storyteller*. New York: Arcade, 1989.

Silver, Shirley, and Wick Miller, eds. *American Indian Languages: Culture and Social Contexts*. Tucson: University of Arizona Press, 1997.

Smith, David. *Folklore of the Winnebago Tribe*. Norman: University of Oklahoma Press, 1997.

Sneve, Virginia Driving Hawk. *Completing the Circle*. Lincoln: University of Nebraska Press, 1995.

_____. *The Trickster and the Troll*. Lincoln: University of Nebraska Press, 1997.

Snipp, C. Matthew. *American Indians: The First of This Land*. New York: Russell Sage Foundation, 1989.

St. Pierre, Mark, and Tilda Long Soldier. *Walking in the Sacred Manner: Healers, Dreamers, and Pipe Carriers—Medicine Women of the Plains Indians*. New York: Simon and Schuster, 1995.

Stein, Wayne J. *Tribally Controlled Colleges: Making Good Medicine*. New York: Peter Lang, 1992.

Stockel, H. Henrietta. *Women of the Apache Nation: Voices of Truth*. Reno: University of Nevada Press, 1991.

Sullivan, Lawrence E., ed. *Native American Religion*. New York: Macmillan, 1989.

Swan, Brian, ed. *Smoothing the Ground: Essays on Native American Oral Literature*. Berkeley: University of California Press, 1983.

_____, and Arnold Krupat, eds. *Recovering the Word: Essays on Native American Literature*. Berkeley: University of California Press, 1987.

Swisher, K., M. Hoisch, and D. Pavel. *American Indian/Alaska Native Dropout Study, 1991*. Washington, D.C.: National Education Association, 1991.

Tapahanso, Luci. *Blue Horses Rush In: Poems and Stories*. Tucson: University of Arizona Press, 1997.

_____. *Saanii Dahataal, The Women Are Singing: Poems and Stories*. Tucson: University of Arizona Press, 1993.

_____. *A Breeze Swept Through*. Albuquerque, NM: West End Press, 1987.

Thornton, Russell. *American Indian Holocaust and Survival: A Population History Since 1492*. Norman: University of Oklahoma Press, 1987.

_____, ed. *Studying Native America: Problems and Prospects*. Madison: University of Wisconsin Press, 1997.

Tierney, William G. *Official Encouragement, Institutional Discouragement: Minorities in Academe—The Native American Experience*. Norwood, NJ: Abex Publishing , 1992.

Underhill, Ruth. *Chona: Autobiography of a Papago Woman*. 1936. Reprint, New York: Holt, 1979.

Verano, John, and D. Ubelaker, eds. *Disease and Demography in the Americas*. Washington, DC: Smithsonian Institute, 1992.

Vizenor, Gerald. *Narrative Chance: Postmodern Discourse on Native American Indian Literature*. Albuquerque: University of New Mexico Press, 1989.

Wade, Edwin. *The Arts of the North American Indian: Native Traditions in Evolution*. New York: Hudson Hills Press, 1986.

Walkout, H. *A Kwakiutl Village and School*. New York: Holt, Rinehart, and Winston, 1967.

Wall, Steve, and Harvey Arden. *Wisdomkeepers: Meetings with Native American Spiritual Elders*. Hillsboro, OR: Beyond Words Publishing, 1990.

Warrior, Robert. *Tribal Secrets: Recovering American Indian Intellectual Traditions*. Minneapolis: University of Minnesota Press, 1995.

Welch, James. *Fools Crow*. New York: Penguin Books, 1986.

_____. *Winter in the Blood*. 1974. Reprint, New York: Penguin Books, 1986.

Wheeler, Sylvia. *This Fool History: An Oral History of Dakota Territory*. Vermillion: University of South Dakota Press, 1991.

White, Richard. *Roots of Dependency: Subsistence, Environment and Social Change Among the Choctaws, Pawnees, and Navajos*. Lincoln: University of Nebraska Press, 1988.

_____. *The Middle Ground: Indians, Empires, and Republics in the Great Lakes Region 1650–1815*. Cambridge, MA: Cambridge University Press, 1991.

Wiget, Andrew. *Native American Literature*. Boston: G. K. Hall, 1985.

_____. *Critical Essays on Native American Literature*. Boston: G. K. Hall, 1985.

Wilkins, David E. *American Indian Sovereignty and the U. S. Supreme Court: The Making of Justice*. Austin: University of Texas Press, 1997.

Wilkinson, Charles F. *American Indians, Time, and the Law: Native Societies in a Modern Constitutional Democracy*. New Haven, CT: Yale University Press, 1987.

Williams, Robert A., Jr. *The American Indian in Western Legal Thought*. New York: Oxford University Press, 1990.

_____. *Linking Arms Together: American Indian Treaty Visions of Law and Peace, 1600–1800*. Oxford, England: Oxford University Press, 1997.

Witherspoon, Gary. *Language and Art in the Navajo Universe*. Ann Arbor: University of Michigan Press, 1977.

Woody, Elizabeth. *Luminaries of the Humble*. Tucson: University of Arizona Press, 1992.

Young Bear, Ray A. *Black Eagle Child*. Iowa City: University of Iowa Press, 1992.

Zepeda, Ofelia. *Ocean Power: Poems from the Desert*. Tucson: University of Arizona Press, 1995.

_____, ed. *Mat Hekid o Ju: O'odham Ha'Cegitoday/ When It Rains: Papago and Pima Poetry*. Tucson: University of Arizona Press, 1982.